SUSAN JULIUS, Ph.D.

THE PARENTS BOOK ABOUT DIVORCE

Of all the uncertainties faced by divorcing parents, the most overwhelming is the fear of what will happen to their children. Now Richard Gardner helps parents negotiate the difficulties of separation in ways most likely to protect their children from emotional distress: how to deal with the guilt and shame both parents and children experience, how to settle custody and visitation problems with the children's welfare in mind. And he describes typical reactions of kids—anger, fear of loss, sexual hang-ups—and explains how with understanding and love these too can be prevented and helped.

THE PARENTS BOOK ABOUT DIVORCE "is far superior, far more comprehensive and constructive than other books . . . A lifeline to parents."

—*The New York Times Book Review*

"Superb suggestions by a sensible and sensitive psychiatrist . . . The best book I know of on the subject."

—Louise Bates Ames, Gesell Institute

D0051784

THE PARENTS BOOK ABOUT DIVORCE

RICHARD A. GARDNER, M.D.

Clinical Professor of Child Psychiatry,
Columbia University College of Physicians
and Surgeons

BANTAM BOOKS

NEW YORK · TORONTO · LONDON · SYDNEY · AUCKLAND

To
my wife Lee
and
our three children
Andrew, Nancy, and Julie

*This low-priced Bantam Book
has been completely reset in a type face
designed for easy reading, and was printed
from new plates. It contains the complete
text of the original hard-cover edition.*
NOT ONE WORD HAS BEEN OMITTED.

THE PARENTS BOOK ABOUT DIVORCE
*A Bantam Book / published by arrangement with
Doubleday & Company, Inc.*

PRINTING HISTORY
Doubleday edition published April 1977
1st printing .. December 1976
2nd printing .. February 1977
Excerpts appeared in WOMEN TODAY, *and* WOMEN'S RIGHTS
MAGAZINE.

Bantam edition / July 1979
2nd printing . November 1980   4th printing ...... June 1983
3rd printing ...... July 1982   5th printing ...... July 1984
6th printing .. November 1985

Bantam Books are published by Bantam Books, Inc. Its trademark, consisting of the words "Bantam Books" and the por-
trayal of a rooster, is Registered in U.S. Patent and Trademark
Office and in other countries. Marca Registrada. Bantam
Books, Inc., 666 Fifth Avenue, New York, New York 10103.

PRINTED IN THE UNITED STATES OF AMERICA

H   14 13 12 11 10 9

ACKNOWLEDGMENTS

First, I wish to express my gratitude to Ms. Barbara Wyden, author and editor, who quite early in my second career as an author expressed her appreciation for my work by publishing it in the New York *Times*. And it was she who recommended this book, while it was still only an idea, to Ms. Betty Prashker of Doubleday, who agreed that it was worthy of publication. I am indebted also to Ms. Prashker for her personal interest in the various phases of its editing and publication.

I appreciate the permission granted me by Dr. Jason Aronson to incorporate herein material from my *Psychotherapy with Children of Divorce* (Jason Aronson, 1976). I am indebted to my secretary, Ms. Linda Gould, who cheerfully typed the manuscript and patiently tolerated my scribbles, messy inserts, and seemingly endless modifications. I deeply appreciate the dedicated efforts of Ms. Frances Dubner, who devoted herself to the editing of the original manuscript and provided me with numerous thoughtful and useful suggestions.

I appreciate the advice of friends and colleagues in the legal profession who have saved me much embarrassment by reviewing those sections related to their discipline. Specifically, I am grateful to Mr. John Finnerty, my brother Mr. Ronald Gardner, Mr. Arthur Kronenberg, and Dean Michael Sovern of the Columbia University School of Law. In order to protect themselves from embarrassment they have requested that I point out that the placement of their names here does not constitute an endorsement of everything I have to say about lawyers and the legal profession.

Lastly, I wish to express my deepest gratitude to the children of divorce and their parents who have taught me most of what is contained herein. Although their names have been changed to preserve their anonymity, their stories nevertheless have enriched this book and will hopefully serve to help others profit from their experiences.

Contents

feels guilty about the separation 52/Reducing guilt over separation 53/Returning to the home of the children's grandparents 54/Encouraging therapy to reduce guilt 58/Using money to reduce guilt 58/Getting the children's permission to separate 59/Shame over telling the children about the reasons for the separation, e.g., an affair or alcoholism 59

Be appropriately truthful 71/The effects of deceit on children 72/Telling about affairs and other touchy subjects 76/Withholding the identity of the initiator 85/Creating an atmosphere of open communication 87/When it is appropriate not to reveal certain information 89/When a parent suffers with significant psychiatric disturbance 90/Some comments on love 90/The marriage as a mistake 91/Reassuring the children that the separation was not their fault 92/Reassuring the children that they will not be deprived of basic necessities 92/Encouraging emotional expression 93

First, parents must come to terms with their own sense of shame 94/The reactions of the children's peers 96/Dealing with the child who tries to hide the separation 98/Fear of the child's divulging personal family information to friends and neighbors 99

Not too many changes at once 103/Visiting the departed parent's new living arrangements 103/Tolerating the children's hostility in the post-separation period 104/The child's assuming the role of the absent parent 105/The perpetuation of parental hostilities 106

wish to live with 304/Parental sexual behavior as a determinant of custody 306/Custody and the homosexual parent 307/Real vs. phony demands for custody 314/Choosing expert witnesses in custody litigation 316

6   The Children's Involvements with Others   341

7   Concluding Comments   388

Introduction

The deeply gratifying success of my *The Boys and Girls Book About Divorce* (Jason Aronson, 1970; Bantam Books, 1971) has prompted me to write this book as a companion volume. Although there is a plethora of books advising the divorcing and divorced (not surprising in this time of ever rising divorce rates), I was not able to find one—specifically devoted to advising parents on how to deal with the problems that could arise in their children— that I could strongly recommend. Either such guidance was confined to one chapter of a book covering an assortment of issues related to divorce or the subject was dealt with in ways that I considered somewhat superficial and/or incomplete. This book is an attempt to fill this gap.

I believe that it provides an in-depth coverage of the most common problems that parents are confronted with when dealing with their children's reactions to separation and divorce. It does not provide any simple answers. The problems dealt with here are complex. Those who would give simple answers to these complicated problems may initially attract a wide audience; however, their solutions are doomed to failure and those who rely on them are bound to become disappointed and disillusioned. This book, therefore, is for those who are suspicious of or fed up with simple solutions and are willing to expend the effort of dealing with these problems more realistically. It describes in detail the ways in which the most common problems arise and are perpetuated. It provides as well guidelines and advice for preventing problems before they arise and dealing with them when they do. In spite of its complexity it is, nevertheless, oriented toward giving practical advice and attempts to be quite specific regarding how one may implement the recommendations provided. My experience has been that those who are willing to take the trouble to understand and apply these more difficult solutions will often find them valuable in producing both immediate and long-standing benefit for themselves and their children.

I do not believe that separation and divorce necessarily cause children to develop psychological problems. However, the situation is one that increases the risk for the development of such difficulties. Most often parents are aware of this danger and do everything possible to prevent such problems from arising. Sometimes one or both parents may be suffering with significant psychiatric disturbance. In such cases the children may develop difficulties as well. It is not the purpose of this book to deal with these situations; rather, such problems generally require counseling or treatment by a mental health professional. Commonly, parents are relatively free of psychological disturbance but may be handling the children in a misguided fashion and in this way contribute to their developing psychological troubles. It is for this group of parents that this book is devoted. (Often, of course, there is overlap between the two groups, that is, parents with psychiatric difficulties may utilize misguided approaches to dealing with their children.) It is my hope that the guidance contained herein will help prevent and alleviate some of the psychological problems that result from parental inexperience, naïveté, and misguidance. Although my advice here may serve to lessen and prevent some of the problems caused in children by parental psychiatric difficulties, I am fully aware that it can play only a limited role in this regard, because such disturbances, as mentioned, usually require much more intensive approaches than mere information and guidance.

1

Contemplating Divorce

This chapter is written primarily for those parents who
have not yet made a final decision regarding whether they
will divorce. My hope is that the information provided
here will prove useful in assisting such parents to make
their decision. Its purpose is neither to help them reconcile
nor to help them separate. This is a decision that must be
made by parents themselves. It is grandiose on the part
of anyone—therapists included—to think that he or she
knows whether a particular couple is better off divorced
or married. Rather, the counselor's role should be to help
the couple gain a clearer picture of their situation and to
provide information that may be useful to them in making
their decision. And this is my purpose in this chapter. Those
parents who have already made their decision to separate,
or who are separated or divorced, may also find much in
this chapter of value to them. I hope it will prove useful
in any present involvements such parents may have with
lawyers and mental health professionals, and that it will
provide guidelines of use in future relationships, especially when troubled, and lessen the likelihood that these
will be dealt with inappropriately if separation becomes a
consideration.

Counseling with a Mental Health Professional

It is important for parents to appreciate that the field of
psychotherapy is still very much in its infancy. As is so
often true of young sciences, there is much that is uncer-

tain—so much so that no two therapists agree on every point. I express here my own opinions and recognize that they may at times be at variance with those held by counselors whom the reader may be seeing. I do not claim to have final answers, nor is it likely that all the views that I express here will be applicable to everyone. The reader does well therefore to read what I say here with receptivity, but not gullibility. He does well to accept and utilize what seems reasonable to him and reject that which does not. An author should not ask more of a reader; nor should a reader ask more than this of himself.

The crucial neutrality of the therapist. I begin with a point, already mentioned, that is so important it warrants further elaboration: the importance of the marriage counselor's strict neutrality regarding whether a given couple is better off remaining married or separating. No one can predict whether a couple contemplating separation will be better off married or divorced. The therapist does well, therefore, to direct his efforts toward providing the parents with a clarification of the issues involved and alleviating inappropriate or disturbed behavior. If he is successful in this regard the parents will then be able to make a healthier and wiser decision. It is most important that, whatever they do decide to do, they have the feeling it was truly a decision made by one or both of them. If the decision turns out to be an unfortunate one, they must feel that they have only themselves to blame. And if their choice proves to have been a judicious one, they should have no one but themselves to thank. Blaming the therapist for an unwise decision is as inappropriate as thanking him for a wise one. If the counselor indeed took a strictly neutral position, and the parents see him as having done so, they are not likely to react with either gratitude or denunciation of him for their decision. Thanking him for his help and dedication is certainly appropriate; thanking him for leading one down a particular path regarding separation reflects a deficient counseling situation.

A therapist who boasts of never having had a divorce in his or her practice is probably (either consciously or unconsciously) pressuring some patients into remaining married when they might have been better off divorced. On the other hand, the therapist with a high frequency of divorces might very well be encouraging divorce (again, either consciously or unconsciously) when attempts at working through the marital difficulties might have been preferable. Sometimes the therapist's own marital history may contribute to his or her applying such inappropriate pressures. If the therapist has been divorced and there was a resultant improvement in his or her life situation, he or she may tend to exaggerate the value of separation. If the therapist's own marriage is gratifying, he or she may encourage patients to maintain their marriages when separation might be more advisable. Lastly, the therapist who has never been married, his or her therapeutic assets notwithstanding, is in a poor position to appreciate fully the problems and conflicts of marriage and does well, in my opinion, to involve him- or herself in therapeutic areas other than marital counseling.

Joint counseling—the best type for the couple considering separation. I believe that the ideal marital counseling situation is the one in which the partners are seen together by a therapist who has had no previous experience with either. In this way the therapist is more likely to be impartial from the outset. When a therapist sees only one of the spouses he hears only one side of the story; in joint counseling he can hear both sides (and the differences may be dramatic). Seeing the partners together also provides the counselor with the opportunity to observe the couple's interaction. Even were the therapist to see each partner separately, he or she would not get as much information about each as the joint sessions can provide. I am not suggesting that the partners only be seen together; in many situations seeing each separately as well can also be helpful. Another advantage of joint counseling is that if it results in a maintenance of the marital relationship, the partners have had a healthy experience in mutual inquiry that should serve them well in their future relationship. If, however, it results in their divorcing, they should have at least become clear about the reasons for their decision. Hopefully, what they have learned in their counseling will help them avoid another injudicious marriage.

In doing such counseling I do not hesitate to express my opinions regarding the appropriateness or inappropriateness of either party's thoughts, feelings, and behavior. Although this may appear as if I am taking sides, it is not the side of the person so much that I am joining, but the side of health. In other words, I support psychologically healthy behavior, regardless of who exhibits it, and discourage unhealthy behavior, regardless of who manifests it. If the therapist is genuinely well meaning, and has the parents' welfare of primary interest, painful confrontations and interpretations will most often be accepted. In such an atmosphere it is not likely that either party will consider the counselor to be favoring the other even though in any particular session one parent may receive more criticism than the other.

In such counseling each partner may try to use the therapist as a tool to serve his or her own ends. The competent therapist is generally aware of such tendencies and will refuse to become involved in such manipulations. For example, a wife may try to enlist the therapist's aid in pressuring her husband into spending more time at home when he has little motivation to do so. Or a husband may try to enlist the therapist's assistance in getting his wife to remain in the marriage when she is strongly inclined to separate.

Even when the therapist is successful in maintaining a strictly neutral role, the partners may attribute to him or her motives that are genuinely not his or hers. Usually such notions reflect their wishes that the therapist exhibit a particular attitude or behavioral pattern. For example, a husband may conclude that the therapist's failure to condemn his wife for an affair served to sanction it. And she too may consider this to be the case. The therapist, however, was only serving in his or her proper role, namely, that of facilitator of understanding—not condemner, imposer of his or her own values, or manipulator of people. A wife may interpret the therapist's neutrality as support for her decision to separate. Such a conclusion may arise from her need for support and encouragement to take such an anxiety-provoking step.

The competent therapist appreciates that both parents are usually quite ambivalent regarding the separation and that they may waver between periods when one or both are quite sure that they will divorce to times when they may feel that they will be able to work things out. Such a therapist appreciates that even when things are going badly in the marriage it behooves him or her to refrain from encouraging either party to make the break. He or she recognizes that each of the parents generally needs a period of getting adjusted to the idea of divorcing and that this takes time. The good therapist shows the greatest respect, therefore, for the parents' ambivalence, procrastination, and indecisiveness. The therapist who does not respect this process, who pushes it along, is doing his or her patients a disservice. Certain things cannot and should not be rushed by others, and the decision to divorce is one of them.

There are therapists who tell parents that their "sitting on the fence" with regard to the question of whether they will divorce is a disservice to their children. They point out that the state of indecision is detrimental to both themselves and the children. Accordingly, they may advise the parents that the longer it takes them to "get off the fence" and decide one way or the other, the longer will both they and their children suffer. I believe that such advice, although well meaning, is misguided. Sitting on the fence is no more or less a position than being on either side of it. Accordingly, there are three positions—marriage, divorce, and indecision—each of which has its advantages and disadvantages for all concerned. To pressure the parents into selecting one of only two of the possibilities is presumptuous on the part of the counselor. He or she may be depriving the parents and children of that situation which, its drawbacks notwithstanding, may be the best of the three options open to them. The therapist who works with the children of such parents should be as receptive to helping them adjust to parental indecision as to helping them adapt to marital difficulties or divorce.

The term counseling (and more so the term therapy)

implies that personality defects or even psychiatric illness is present. Seeking the services of mental health professionals often requires one to admit to oneself that one is sick. I do not believe that all ill-conceived marriages result from psychological illness on the part of one or both partners. (Many, without question, are entered into for such reasons.) Parents who seek marital counseling do themselves a disservice if they automatically assume that they must be suffering with significant psychological disturbance. All individuals suffer various traumas and stresses in life, without psychiatric disturbance necessarily being present or playing a role. In some marriages the primary neurotic thing that the partners may be doing is remaining married; in others the only neurosis may be their wish to separate. Parents who do not avail themselves of such counseling because they fear that it means they are psychiatrically disturbed may be depriving themselves of valuable assistance at a crucial point in their lives—assistance that may prove invaluable to both themselves and their children. In such counseling they can best learn about what sickness, if any, exists. If not present to a significant degree, the knowledge can be reassuring. If present, acceptance of it can be the first step toward its alleviation.

The dangers of individual therapy when separation is being considered. When separation impends, individual therapy with only one presents special problems. If the therapeutic work with the spouse is successful, the changes may cause anxiety in the untreated partner. The therapy of one partner tends to unbalance and disrupt unhealthy balances and interactions that may have served to keep the marriage intact. Sometimes the partner adapts and involves him- or herself in healthier forms of interaction. The marriage then is maintained on a new and more secure foundation. On occasion, however, the untreated partner may be unable to make such adjustments. He or she may then seek others to form unhealthy involvements and gain neurotic gratifications. Therapy, in such cases, may then contribute to the separation. There is no question that this is one of the dangers of therapy and married people who enter into treatment should be told (at the appropriate time) of this possibility.

When a marital partner is in therapy the intimacy he or she shares with the therapist generally causes some feelings of alienation and jealousy in the other partner—and this can be devisive for a marital relationship and intensify marital difficulties. Whatever benefits the untreated marital partner may hope to derive from the spouse's therapy, he or she suffers a certain amount of invasion of privacy that generally results in some resentment toward the spouse and the therapist. If the therapist advises a patient not to discuss what goes on in the session with anyone, including the spouse, further feelings of alienation between the partners may result. To avoid this potentially disruptive effect of therapy, I generally advise my married patients to discuss as openly and as freely as they wish any aspect of their therapy with anyone, spouse or nonspouse. I still respect their right to privacy, but believe that the more open communication there is between people, the less the likelihood of interpersonal and even internal psychiatric difficulties.

Many therapists believe that the ideal therapeutic program for a couple with marital problems is one in which each partner sees his or her own therapist. They hold that the best way of resolving the internal psychological conflicts that are contributing to a marital conflict is for each partner to work out his or her problems alone with a separate therapist. In addition, they believe that the therapist–patient relationship is automatically compromised if the patient sees another therapist for counseling or even if the patient's spouse were to come in for one or more joint interviews. I am in sharp disagreement with this position. A patient's relationship with his or her therapist is not necessarily diluted by seeing a second therapist for counseling. There are therapists who will refuse to see a spouse along with a patient (or alone separately) even for one session, lest the closeness of the therapist's relationship with the patient be diluted. It does not speak well for such a relationship, in my opinion, if it can be jeopardized by a single, or few, or even many meetings with a spouse. This is similar to a parent's saying that he or she only wants to have one child because with two the amount of affection that can be provided for each child will have to be reduced.

It is difficult, if not impossible, for a therapist to avoid siding with his or her patient in a marital conflict. I do not believe that a therapist can be so objective that he doesn't tend to be sympathetic with his patient's view. Hearing only one side of a story deprives the therapist of the opportunity to get the kind of balanced and clear picture of the marital conflict that is necessary if he or she is to come to meaningful conclusions about it. Any therapist who has done marital counseling quickly sees how differently the two partners can see the same situation. Furthermore, the very nature of the therapeutic situation seduces the therapist into losing some objectivity regarding his or her patient and increases the tendency to side with one's patient in a marital conflict. After all, the therapist cannot but be flattered that the patient has chosen him or her—over all the other people in the whole world—to confide in and reveal one's innermost secrets. The therapist cannot but admire a person who shows such good judgment. And after the relationship has been established, and if the patient starts to consider the therapist the most sympathetic, empathetic, understanding, benevolent, brilliant, etc., person he or she has ever had the good fortune to meet, the therapist's admiration and affection for the patient increases even further. We love most those who have the good sense to appreciate our assets. And we love even more those who enumerate these to us at length. Such affection on the therapist's part cannot but blind him or her to some, if not many, of the patient's defects—defects that are contributing to his or her marital difficulties. Often this results in the therapist's developing antagonisms to the spouse that are totally unwarranted.

Frank and Ruth's situation demonstrates well how a therapist's siding with a patient against a spouse had disastrous effects on a marriage. Ruth's father died when she was three, leaving her mother with three children: Bob, age seventeen; Jill, age six; and Ruth. Soon after his father's death Bob left school in order to help support the household. Although Bob rose to this obligation admirably, he also tended to be somewhat condescending to Ruth and frequently put her down. With Bob as the only father figure she could remember, Ruth grew up tending to view all men as critical of her. This contributed to her difficulties with her husband, Frank, whom she often saw as condescending to her when he wasn't. Accordingly, she became excessively critical of Frank, and often had rage outbursts against him over minor and often nonexistent provocations. Frank was a social worker who took a very loose attitude about his obligations. He was sloppy around the house, expected Ruth to pick up after him, and had not advanced in his profession to a degree commensurate with his basic intelligence and experience. This was for the most part due to his low drive and self-assertion. Ruth was a more striving person, had worked her way through college in order to become a schoolteacher, but had interrupted that career in order to raise her and Frank's children. Frank's lackadaisical attitude was particularly painful to Ruth and she was constantly on his back to be more assertive and reliable. In spite of these difficulties, both were extremely devoted to their children, and shared many common interests.

After ten years of marriage, Ruth decided that her marriage was falling apart and suggested that both she and Frank go into treatment. Frank was unreceptive to the idea but agreed that Ruth needed it and he was glad to pay for her treatment. Frank, however, became upset when he learned that Ruth was considering seeing a psychologist who had a reputation for being a very aggressive woman who was generally hostile to men. Frank communicated his reservations to Ruth, even before her first telephone call to this therapist. Ruth insisted that she was drawn to this woman (she had heard her speak at a PTA meeting) and wanted very much to be treated by her.

And so Ruth proceeded with her treatment. Much of her session time was spent complaining about Frank: his sloppiness around the house, his lack of self-assertion, his provocative condescension, and the numerous other ways in which he was constantly irritating Ruth. Ruth would often come home and relate to Frank how her therapist agreed with her that she had "quite a cross to bear" being married to someone like Frank. Frank admitted that he was a low-drive person and that some of Ruth's complaints were justified, but he also felt that Ruth's distortions about his being condescending toward her were not being appreciated and dealt with by Ruth's therapist. He felt that the therapist was being taken in, especially since she had not seen Frank at all and heard his views regarding what was going on between Ruth and himself. Frank requested a joint interview with Ruth and her therapist.

From the earliest minutes of the interview Frank felt that he was on "enemy territory." He felt that the therapist's attitude toward him was unsympathetic and hostile. Such feelings were verified when in the course of the discussion the therapist angrily called him a "male chauvinist pig." Frank became very upset by the therapist's attitude toward him and felt that although there might be some justification for her view of him as taking advantage of Ruth, her angry epithet was unprofessional and unwarranted. He discussed this with friends, who urged him to request another joint session in order to discuss directly with Ruth's therapist his reservations about her. This was arranged and Frank expressed to the therapist his feeling that she was biased against him and inappropriately hostile. The therapist told him that she was justified in being angry at him for the way he treated Ruth. Then Frank responded that *Ruth* might have a right to feel angry; but that he was not doing anything to hurt or provoke the therapist and that it was therefore inappropriate for *her* to be angry at him. The therapist denied that Frank's criticism made any justification and pointed out that this was just the kind of irrational criticism he was capable of that Ruth had spoken so much about. Frank responded that he was now convinced that the therapist was sharing his wife's distortions that he was excessively critical of her, and that his wife saw condescension when there was none. The therapist replied that this was a second unwarranted criticism of her and it confirmed what Ruth, and now she, knew to be true.

Frank felt helpless. He strongly felt that his wife's thera-

pist was inappropriately antagonistic to him and was not
being objective. He felt that the therapist's failure to have
seen Frank for a year, during which time she heard only
Ruth's views, had contributed to this situation. In addition,
he felt that the therapist harbored biases against men that
were also contributing to the difficulties between him and
Ruth, and now among the three of them. He discussed the
problem with friends, some of whom knew the therapist, and they agreed that Frank's view of the situation
appeared to be accurate. Frank urged Ruth to quit treatment, but she refused. Frank (exhibiting now more self-
assertion than he had in the past) once again asked for a
joint interview. During this session he complained to the
therapist about his wife's lack of sexual responsivity, to
which the therapist replied: "If you don't like it, why don't
you go and jerk off!" Frank tried to point out how unsympathetic, unprofessional, and even cruel was this response. But both the therapist and Ruth insisted that this
comment had no hostile implications and was entirely
justified by the situation. Frank could not convince them
otherwise. Accordingly, he informed Ruth that he was no
longer paying for treatment. Ruth, he concluded, had developed an attachment to this therapist that defied logic
and blinded her to the therapist's obvious defects. Ruth
then got a part-time job and combined these earnings with
a small inheritance in order to continue paying for her
treatment. About two years later, by which time Frank saw
his wife's situation ever deteriorating, when her hostility
reached unbearable proportions, Frank initiated divorce
proceedings. Ruth remained with the therapist a number of
years and became ever more deeply entrenched in her
hatred of and disdain for men.

Although Ruth and Frank's situation may appear to be
unique to the reader, my experience has been that it is
more common than is generally realized. Not only does
individual therapy for marital difficulties present the problem of the therapist's being biased by not having close
contact with the spouse, but the therapist's pre-existing
biases can also have a detrimental effect on the marital relationship of his or her patients. Therapists are not near-

ly so free of psychiatric problems as they and many lay-
men would like to believe. But even without the contributing element of the therapist's psychiatric problems, seeing
only one spouse when there are marital problems has
caused, in my opinion, many divorces that should never
have taken place. These are marriages that would have
been saved, to the mutual benefit of parents and children,
if the therapists had seen both partners—not necessarily
in joint counseling and not necessarily with both parties
seeing the same therapist. Just having the opportunity to
see the spouse on occasion might have been enough to
correct the therapist's distortions that contributed to the
marital difficulties. Accordingly, I believe that a therapist
who refuses to meet with the spouse of a patient involved
in a marital conflict is doing his or her patient a terribly
disservice. Although many such therapists are certainly
well meaning, I believe they are misguided in their rigidly
subscribing to a theoretical principle that not only has not
been conclusively validated, but has strong and convincing
arguments against it. Accordingly, if a husband, for
example, is paying for his wife's treatment and if her
therapist absolutely refuses to see him at all when a
marital conflict is a primary problem, I advise him to refuse to pay the therapist and insist that his wife choose a
person with another view. Otherwise, he may be paying a
person to contribute to the deterioration of his relationship even further.

The way in which a therapist's refusal to see the spouse
of a patient having marital difficulties can contribute to a
deterioration of a marriage is demonstrated by Nat and
Barbara's situation. Nat, a mathematics professor, was a
self-absorbed and taciturn man. He was attracted to Barbara's lively and outgoing personality and openly admitted
that one of the main reasons he married Barbara was that
he could rely on her to enliven a conversation when he
could think of nothing to say. Nat was quite dependent on
Barbara. In the early years of their marriage she enjoyed
making decisions for a man she considered her intellectual
superior, but over the years she gradually became ever
more resentful of having to take over the major burdens
of running the household, taking care of the children,

and assuming alone many other responsibilities that are usually shared with or done by a husband, e.g., house repairs, car maintenance, and financial planning. Barbara tended to be controlling of Nat at times—a trait that contributed to her willingness to take over these extra household responsibilities in spite of her complaints. Barbara was seductive with men. Although she had had no affairs, she liked to titillate men and would seduce them into propositioning her—only to reject them immediately upon their making sexual overtures.

During their twelfth year of marriage Nat became more withdrawn and depressed. He became fearful of driving, yet he was still able to drive to the university to teach. At this point he went into treatment with a psychoanalyst who was on the faculty of the same university where Nat taught. The analyst rigidly adhered to the classical Freudian approach, and saw Nat on the couch five times a week. During the sessions the psychoanalyst had very little to say to Nat, and there were even sessions when he made absolutely no response at all to Nat's associations. During Nat's third week of treatment Barbara asked Nat if he had discussed with his analyst the fight they had had over Nat's refusing to take his car to the garage for repairs, thereby leaving Barbara in the position of having to take it herself or else Nat would not have been able to go to work. Nat replied that his psychoanalyst suggested they focus on the infantile roots of such problems as this and strictly refrained from providing specific advice and recommendations. In addition, Nat told Barbara that his analyst had told him that it was against the interests of the treatment for him to discuss what had gone on in the sessions with anyone, even Barbara.

During the ensuing weeks Barbara began to suspect that Nat was not discussing at all many of their problems. Sexual difficulties were becoming greater (Nat had lost interest completely and Barbara was considering an affair). Nat was becoming extremely irritable with Barbara, had rage outbursts, and had even hit her on a few occasions. When Barbara asked Nat if he had discussed these new developments with his analyst, Nat replied that he had not, had no intention of doing so at that time, and that it was none of her business what he spoke about with his analyst. He then added that he wasn't even supposed to have said what he just had; that telling Barbara he hadn't spoken of the things she wanted him to was, in itself, a revelation of what had gone on in his sessions and was therefore breaking his analyst's rules. Nat told her that he had concluded that she was a very controlling person, that her questions about what went on in his sessions were proof of this, and that she was an important source of his difficulties. Barbara admitted that she had a problem in this area, but also felt that a joint session with Nat's analyst might be useful so that he could gain some picture of what was going on at home. Nat reported back that he had discussed Barbara's request with his analyst and was told that such an interview would be impossible because it would be an intrusion on the privacy of Nat's treatment. Ever more frustrated, Barbara asked Nat if the two of them could go to another psychiatrist for counseling. Again Nat returned with a refusal—this time he was told that such counseling would "dilute" Nat's relationship with his psychoanalyst and thereby compromise, if not completely destroy, his treatment.

The situation deteriorated rapidly after that. Barbara pleaded with her husband to seek treatment from another man, but Nat refused. He quoted his analyst's high credentials, and began speaking of him as if he were all-wise. Barbara pointed out to him that the classical Freudian theory was still very much a *theory* and that a majority of psychiatrists and psychologists do not strictly subscribe to it in every way, and that there are many Freudian analysts who would see a spouse. Her pleas were to no avail. There was no feedback from Nat's analyst, no way of Barbara's communicating with him (a letter she wrote the analyst requesting to see him, either alone or with Nat, was unanswered), and no way of budging Nat from his rigidly defending the kind of treatment he was receiving. When asked how he expected to work out their marital problems if his analyst might never even hear her views of their mutual difficulties, she was told that it wasn't necessary for Nat's analyst to have that information to help Nat with his marital problems, that when Nat got better their marital troubles would be reduced. In addition, she was told that if she got her own analyst then there would be an even better chance that their marital problems would be solved. Barbara agreed that she might profit from treatment, and that there were problems within her—problems having nothing to do with Nat—that might be helped by individual therapy for herself. However, she could not see how their marital problems could be significantly helped by such treatment. She could not see how her complaining to a therapist about Nat, a therapist who might never see Nat (because of Nat's therapist's convincing Nat that such a visit would jeopardize his therapy), could help their marital problems, and so she did not enter treatment herself.

Within two years of Nat's entering treatment, Barbara asked for a divorce because the marital situation had deteriorated to the point where she felt it was hopeless. And she saw no reason to believe that Nat's treatment was ever going to make things better; in fact, she had every reason to believe that it was making things worse for them.

There are probably readers who consider this story a caricature, who will find it hard to believe that such things actually happen. Those of us in the field, however, know such occurrences to be commonplace. Fortunately, however, fewer therapists are so strictly adhering to the classical Freudian theory of treatment and so such experiences are occurring with less frequency.

I believe that the ideal therapeutic program for a couple with marital problems is one in which both parties can be seen by the same therapist, in both individual and joint sessions. When, however, there is a significant amount of material that each does not wish revealed to the other (whether appropriately or not), then it is probably best for the two to be seen by separate therapists. A patient's therapy is compromised when the therapist has relevant information that cannot be divulged. When the spouses have separate therapists there should be joint sessions as well. These are best conducted, in my opinion, by the two therapists alternating in accordance with which therapist would be preferable for focusing on a particular issue. The therapists should be free to communicate with one another and to reveal to one another, at their discretion, what they consider to be indicated and constructive. Each should appreciate that he or she should not burden the other therapist with information that cannot be revealed to the patient. Counseling by a third party, although a reasonable alternative, is not as advisable as one of the two therapists doing the counseling. There are enough potential contaminants with two therapists involved (distortions, communication errors, rivalries); a third can often compound these complications.

Family interviews can sometimes be helpful in counseling couples contemplating separation. Younger children are not generally valuable sources of direct information; however, observing the parents with them can often provide useful data. Adolescents, however, if they are comfortable enough to reveal their opinions and observations, can be a valuable source of information. On occasion, I have seen one or more of the parents of the couple anticipating separation. At times they are playing an important role in the decision. We never outgrow completely the influence of our parents and even after they die their wishes and thoughts enter our minds and influence our behavior. I believe that parents of couples anticipating separation are not utilized frequently enough in the counseling process. I believe that if this were to become more common practice, the efficiency of the counseling experience would be enhanced. Of course, one should not go overboard with regard to family interviews and bringing in spouses' parents. There are many issues that are justifiably discussed alone—intimate issues that are of no direct concern to other parties.

Another type of counseling experience that I have found useful as an adjunct to the individual work and as an alternative to seeing the couple alone, is couples' group therapy. I have found three or four couples to be the optimum number for such a group. Two couples do not provide enough variety of opinion and richness of interaction, and when one or more people are absent the group gets too small for efficient work. More than four couples makes the group too large for each couple to get optimum opportunity for airing their difficulties. The couples meet with me for an hour and a half, once a week, and then alternate after-group meetings at one another's homes, where they have the opportunity to observe one another in their natural surroundings. The post-group discussions are kept on the same therapeutic level and generally last two to four hours. In addition, the five or so hours of exposure increases the chances that people will relax and reveal themselves.

Some important suggestions for the couple contemplating separation. It has been my experience that many couples divorce because they naïvely believe that their situation will be immeasurably improved in another marriage. They believe that the euphoria or romantic love should exist continuously and the failure of such intense feelings to persist is evidence of a deep deficiency in the relationship. Such a view has enjoyed its widest popularity as a result of the mass media. I believe that a certain amount of romantic euphoria can enrich a relationship and counterbalance some of the pains and frustrations that are an inevitable part of marriage. However, the individual who feels that it is possible to maintain such feelings practically uninterruptedly throughout the course of a lifetime is doomed to disappointment. He will inevitably be disillusioned, no matter how many times he gets married. As with the narcotic that romantic love resembles, the individual will ultimately develop tolerance, will require more and more to get the same effect, and will ultimately find that it fails to provide euphoria at all.

Accordingly, I generally advise couples who are planning divorce to look carefully at those around them—especially those whom they consider to be enjoying "happy marriages." I suggest that they give special attention to those who have been divorced and remarried to see whether such couples have found the happiness that the separating couple anticipates in a remarriage. I recommend that they talk as intimately as possible with close friends and relatives who are willing to discuss their marriages and see if they can find anyone *in the real world* who even approaches the kind of happy marriage they are seeking.

It is indeed amazing how few people do this and how many blindly believe they will be able to accomplish what no one off the movie screen has been able to achieve.

In addition, I try to help such parents appreciate that marriage invariably involves significant frustration and restriction—its gratifications notwithstanding. I ask them to try to weigh the disadvantages of the marriage against the misery they may suffer when separated and divorced. I suggest they talk carefully with friends and relatives who have been separated and divorced, and think seriously about whether they wish to suffer such pains and discomforts and whether their present pain is greater. It is important for the therapist to direct the parents' attention to these considerations as part of the process of helping them weigh the pros and cons of the separation and divorce. It should not be part of an attempt to keep them together. To do so would be a terrible disservice and might contribute to their perpetuating a sick and extremely painful situation.

On occasion, an individual may seek treatment because a spouse threatens separation unless he or she goes into therapy. Because such a person's motivation for therapy comes from without, rather than from within, there is little likelihood that meaningful changes will occur. Unless a person is motivated to change things within, because of inner pain experienced over the problems, the individual is not likely to derive much benefit from a therapeutic experience. Such a person may come with the hope of altering those behavioral patterns that are alienating the spouse or may wish to learn a way to manipulate the partner into remaining in the marriage. Again, with such intentions the therapy is most likely to fail.

I wish to emphasize that I believe that therapy can be a very valuable experience for couples with marital difficulties. It may save many marriages and put them on a more secure foundation. It can help others, who are better off getting divorced, do so in the least traumatic and most sane manner—and it can help those so separated make more judicious relationships in the future, both in and out of marriage. As described, however, there are certain therapeutic practices that can be detrimental to a marriage. If one is aware of these and avoids implementing them, then one can gain the advantages of the psychotherapeutic approach and need not expose oneself to these potentially harmful and divisive experiences.

Counseling with a Lawyer

When one marries, one enters into a contract. Certain obligations are then assumed which are enforceable by law. In order to dissolve a marriage one usually signs a new contract. Again, the new obligations are enforceable by law. Most people do not engage lawyers when they marry, because the customary commitments of marriage are understood and expected. However, when the parties wish to add special stipulations to the marriage contract, then lawyers are usually engaged. For example, one of the parties may have significant assets that he or she would not want to be available to the other, either within the marriage or if divorce ensues. If the other party accepts this stipulation of the marriage, then such an agreement might be finalized in a prenuptial agreement that would be part of the marriage contract. Although the services of a lawyer are rarely engaged when people get married, the overwhelming majority of people use lawyers when they get divorced. Although it is possible to dissolve a marriage without a lawyer, most recognize that to do so would be a risky business. The divorce contract commonly stipulates lifelong obligations. To agree to such binding commitments without the advice of someone experienced in such matters may be foolhardy. Even when the parties part in the most friendly fashion, without any desire to wreak vengeance on the other or to extract as much as one can, it can be dangerous to dissolve the marriage without the contract being drawn by a lawyer. As every divorcing person should well appreciate, human beings' feelings toward one another have a way of changing over a period of time: benevolence changes to malevolence, love turns to hate. Only by a firm contract can even the most kindly and well-meaning separating spouses protect themselves from the consequences of an ex-spouse's change of heart. There is an old saying in the medical profession: "A doctor who treats himself has a fool for a patient." Similarly there is an old legal adage: "A lawyer who represents himself has a fool for a client." I would add to such wisdom: "Divorcing spouses who legally represent themselves have fools for clients."

Lawyers and obstetricians: You may think you can get along without them, but they're nice to have around when there's trouble. Engaging the services of a lawyer when contemplating divorce can be compared to enlisting the aid of an obstetrician for childbirth. In both cases there is usually pain involved, and in both cases the goal is most often ultimately reached. The baby gets born; the divorce decree is granted. The overwhelming majority of babies are delivered without complications; and the vast majority of pre-divorce disagreements are resolved without a courtroom conflict (although a short court appearance usually is required). It is when the complications arise that the professional's expertise is vital. It is then that the obstetrician's skills are so crucial in determining the outcome. Similarly, it is when the separating parties cannot agree on the terms on the divorce that the lawyer's skills become so crucial. And to carry the analogy one step further. Just as the pediatrician may be of value to the infant who has sustained childbirth complications, the mental health professional may be of service to parents (and children) who have sustained divorce complications. It is not within the scope of this book, nor is it within my area of competence, to discuss the broad subject of the client's involvement with the lawyer. Rather, I will focus on certain aspects of divorcing parents' encounters with legal professionals that have relevance to their and their children's psychological well-being.

Therapists who recommend lawyers—a dangerous practice. I consider it unwise for people in psychotherapy who are contemplating separation to ask their therapists to recommend a divorce lawyer. Similarly I consider it injudicious for therapists to comply with such requests. Even when the patient's spouse is not being seen by the therapist, such a referral can compromise the treatment. A divorce is one of the most serious decisions that a person makes in his or her life. As mentioned, it is the therapist's job to help clarify issues, not to fight a cause. The lawyer is being hired specifically to side with his or her client in a conflict. By recommending a particular lawyer the therapist becomes a party (admittedly in a minor way) to the conflict. The therapist's recommending a lawyer carries with it the implicit message that he or she supports the divorce decision. One cannot claim neutrality in a conflict in which one is supplying one side with ammunition.

If things do not go well between the patient and the lawyer, or if the lawyer was not successful in getting the patient all he or she desired, the patient may feel that he might have done better with another lawyer. He is likely then to resent or be disappointed with the therapist for having suggested the particular lawyer. Since no lawyer is perfect, or can be all things to all people, or can satisfy everyone, it is likely that some patients are going to be dissatisfied with the lawyer recommended by the therapist and that such dissatisfaction will be warranted. Because there is this definite and predictable risk that the patient will be justified in being resentful of the therapist, he or she does well to advise patients to use their own resources when seeking a lawyer in a marital conflict. And when both parties are being seen by a therapist, recommending two lawyers is an even riskier business. Even though the therapist may believe that the lawyers are equally qualified, and even if he or she suggests that the patients themselves choose which one they will consult, the chances of dissatisfaction are even greater, and the feeling that one lawyer isn't as good as the other, even more likely. The therapist does well strictly to refrain from such recommendations; and separating spouses do well to avoid the risk of contaminating their treatment by asking their therapists for such referrals.

Therapists often do not appreciate their power over their patients. A recommendation made by a friend or neighbor will generally not carry as much weight as one made by one's therapist. The patient may fear refusing the referral lest the therapist be displeased with him or her. Such a patient may then passively tolerate qualities or

activities of the lawyer that he or she considers objectionable because of the fear that the therapist's affection will
be diminished if the referred lawyer is criticized or dis-
charged. Or the patient may transfer onto the lawyer the
admiration and respect (either justified or not) that he
may feel toward the therapist. He or she may then deny
deficiencies within the lawyer, the accurate observation of
which would have been useful, if not crucial, in the patient's litigation.

There are therapists who would argue that those who
follow my advice here might be deprived of a good lawyer. Just because some of these referrals do not work out
is not a good reason, they would hold, for depriving all
patients of such referrals. Besides, they might argue, if
the therapist were recommending a lawyer with the full
conviction that he or she was performing a valuable service, then there is no justification for a patient's being
critical. If the patient reacts inappropriately to the lawyer,
just because he or she was referred by the therapist, that
is the patient's problem—not the therapist's. The therapist
had the best intentions, and resentment toward him or
her in such a situation would be a sign of the patient's
psychological disturbance. In fact, some would hold that
the patient's inappropriate reactions to the lawyer and/or
resentment toward the therapist for a referral that did
not work out are useful issues for the patient to work on
in treatment. Although this view is not without merit, I
believe that the potential benefits to be derived by the
patient from focusing on such problems are more than
counterbalanced by the damage that might be done by
the therapist's poor choice of a lawyer.

Although I think it unwise for a therapist to recommend a lawyer to a patient, I do not consider it inappropriate for a therapist to point out to a patient defects
in the lawyer that may become apparent in the course of
the treatment. The therapist must be cautious, of course,
regarding making such criticisms. After all, a therapist is
not a lawyer and legal issues are beyond his or her expertise. In addition, patients may distort the problems with
the lawyer that are being described to the therapist. In

spite of these dangers, there are times when the therapist is fairly certain that the lawyer is not handling things appropriately. In such situations it behooves the therapist to impart this opinion to the patient. In doing so he or she is providing information and clarification. The patient will then be in a better position to make decisions regarding his or her dealings with the lawyer.

There are easier ways for a lawyer to make a living than handling divorce cases. It is important for separating spouses to appreciate that most lawyers do not generally relish the idea of involving themselves in divorce litigation. Especially when the clients are miles apart from resolution of their differences, when there is a likelihood that the case will become prolonged and "sticky," do lawyers become hesitant to involve themselves. Lawyers whose financial situation is such that they can refer the case on to someone who specializes in matrimonial law, or to someone whose financial position does not warrant his or her being so selective, will often do so. The messy divorce case can consume a vast amount of time and most clients are not wealthy enough to pay a lawyer an amount that would make his or her deep involvement worthwhile financially. Accordingly, what frequently occurs is that many lawyers do a reasonable job in the simple and straightforward cases; but when complications arise they generally do not devote themselves to the degree that is warranted and in the best interests of their clients. With the recognition that their clients are in no position to pay them for extensive involvement, they work at a level substandard for the case and hope that somehow things will work out. Their clients then find them inaccessible. They seem always to be in conference or in court when the client calls. And telephone calls are not returned. When the client finally does have the opportunity to speak with the lawyer he or she is unfamiliar with important facts. Letters that have been sent to the lawyer, bringing him up to date on recent developments, are still stacked up, unread. The problem is compounded by the fact that the client has generally given the lawyer a sizable advance fee, a retainer, some or all of which might be lost if the lawyer's services were dispensed with. Furthermore, starting all over again with another lawyer, and having to acquaint him or her with all the details, is a task that the client does not welcome. Accordingly, the client feels trapped. Such experiences can exact a terrible psychological toll and add unnecessarily to divorcing individuals' burden at this unfortunate period in their lives.

In order to help my patients avoid adding to their troubles by involving themselves with such a lawyer, I generally suggest that when seeking one they should inquire beforehand regarding his or her accessibility to clients and whether he or she can be relied upon to return telephone calls. (For obvious reasons such inquiries are best made of previous clients than of the lawyer.) In addition, I suggest that they discuss at the outset the financial arrangements in great detail. The client should be willing to pay the lawyer for his time (including time spent reading letters and affidavits and time spent on the telephone); and the lawyer should be willing to devote such time to the client. Some attorneys will quote one total fee for handling the case; others have an hourly rate. Many will quote one fee if the case is not contested (that is, differences are resolved without resorting to court litigation); and a higher fee if it is contested. If the client wants, and is willing to pay for, the kind of lawyer who will respond to requests for frequent conversations, he or she should state so at the outset. The attorney may agree to this or may prefer not to get involved in a case where such great availability is demanded. In the latter case he or she does well to refer the client to another lawyer or suggest that the client seek one who will satisfy this request. The important thing is that both clarify and agree to, at the outset, the kind of arrangement they are going to have. In this way disappointments are reduced and conflicts avoided. Most attorneys do not charge for the initial consultation in which such arrangements are discussed. Following the verbal agreement many lawyers formalize the attorney–client relationships in a retainer letter that sets forth the terms and objectives of their representation and the various factors which will determine the final bill. If the lawyer does not routinely provide such a letter, the client does well to request it.

The lawyer who discourages his clients from divorcing: well meaning, but misguided. When a person seeks a lawyer's assistance in getting a divorce, it is a common practice for lawyers to encourage the client to try first to work things out. Ostensibly, this is a rational and humane approach. The lawyer's benevolent and non-self-serving motivation in making this recommendation is confirmed by the fact that its implementation by the client will result in the lawyer's being deprived of the fees that would accrue to him if the client were to proceed with divorce litigation. Many lawyers pride themselves on their strict adherence to this principle, consider it proof of their commitment to high ethical standards, and may boast of the number of marriages they have thereby "saved." The recommendation to "try and work things out" is based on the assumption that marriage is necessarily better than divorce. As many who have been divorced will testify, this assumption is often invalid. Accordingly, such advice may be a disservice to a client. It may have taken the client many years to reach the point where he or she has gained enough courage to institute the divorce proceedings and it may be a healthy step. The lawyer's discouraging the divorce, under the assumption that maintaining the marriage is in the client's best interests, may be squelching this healthy move and may drive the individual back to many further years of pain and psychiatric trauma.

On the other hand, the lawyer owes it to the client at least to inquire into the reasons why divorce is being sought and to consider the possibility that the decision is being requested for frivolous or inappropriate reasons. If the lawyer senses that there is not a justifiable reason for proceeding, he or she should recommend the consultation of a mental health professional. At times it may even be obvious that the lawyer's suggestion to try to work things out (with or without professional counseling) is the appropriate course. What I am criticizing is the blanket suggestion to all clients that they try to maintain the marriage. The lawyer should be far more discriminating in making such a recommendation and should appreciate that at times it may be harmful.

The bombastic lawyer: he may do you more harm than good. I often suggest to my patients that they avoid engaging the lawyer who is prone to be bombastic. Many patients gravitate toward such lawyers because they believe that such loudmouths will accomplish the most for them. When one fights a war, they hold, one does better with huge cannons than with rifles. Sometimes such lawyers believe this as well; other times they appreciate that such is not the case (that well-aimed rifles are usually preferable to aimless cannon barrages) but put on their act because they sense that this will attract the client. I try to help my patients appreciate that the most effective way to fight a battle is through calm deliberation and that bombast is often resorted to when one's position is weak. The lawyer who subscribes to the adage "Speak softly and carry a big stick" will generally do a far better job for his client than the one who rants. This is especially true in court. Most judges have greater confidence in the lawyer who calmly and firmly presses his points than in the one who is given to shouting, clowning, and dramatics. In fact, the judge may be so turned off by such antics that the client's case may be seriously weakened.

The lawyer as therapist and the lawyer as lover. The relationship between a lawyer and client can often be a highly charged one—and this is especially true in divorce cases. The stakes are high; the decisions can affect the whole future course of one's life. Accordingly, the reliance on the lawyer can be formidable and the need to deny any deficiencies in him or her may be great. Just as the very sick patient may have to believe that his or her doctor is all-knowing, the client going through a painful and difficult divorce may gain strength from believing the lawyer to be more powerful and knowledgeable than he or she actually is. The more helpless and weak the client feels, the more dependent he or she may become on the lawyer. And the lawyer may enjoy the position of power he or she is then placed in, may play the role convincingly (both to him- or herself and the client), and may thereby increase the idolization. The situation does not well lend itself to calm deliberation of the problems at hand and working toward their alleviation in the most effective manner. A client in such a setting may attempt to use the lawyer as a therapist. And the lawyer may be grandiose enough to assume the role. In such situations the client is not only getting poor therapy (lawyers are not trained for such work) but probably inferior legal representation as well (the lawyer who does not recognize the boundaries of his expertise is likely to be deficient within the confines of his calling).

A related problem in the lawyer–client relationship is more common among women. A woman, for example, whose husband has left her, may attempt to relate to her male lawyer as if he were a substitute husband. He lends himself well to this role because he is sympathetic to her position, fights for her cause, and may provide solace. The vast majority of lawyers recognize this tendency on the part of many such women, keep their distance, and do not let the client gratify too intensely such cravings. However, there are lawyers (admittedly a small minority) who enjoy the situation, and reciprocate their client's wishes for a deeper involvement. And such reciprocity runs the gamut of possible involvements from the purely psychological, to the affair, to actually marrying the client. Although the gratifications that both may derive from such relationships may be deep and lasting (they may also be superficial and short-lived), the situation will generally compromise the lawyer's objectivity and thereby make him less useful to his client. (The situation is similar to the one in which a patient becomes socially involved with his or her therapist. Although what may be going on may be a source of deep satisfaction to both, the therapist's loss of objectivity in such situations compromises him or her significantly at a therapist.) Accordingly, don't use lawyers or therapists as the nucleus of a new social life.

The Lawyer vs. the Mental Health Professional

I can best begin my comments on this conflict with a vignette that epitomizes quite well the kinds of problems

with which the therapist is often faced when invited to be
of service in divorce litigation. On many occasions I have
received telephone calls from lawyers that go like this:
The lawyer first introduces him- or herself, may mention a referral source, and then will ask me if I would be
interested in testifying in custody litigation. The attorney
is often quick to tell me that he or she wants me to know
first and foremost that the welfare of the children is up-
permost and that this consideration supersedes all others.
And then he or she asks me if I would be willing to testify
(or sometimes to consider testifying) on behalf of his or
her client. Most appear to see nothing inappropriate in
their asking me to testify on behalf of a client without my
even having had the opportunity to see the client—the
father or the mother whom the lawyer is representing—
and decide whether or not I can support with conviction
that party's position. My usual reply at this point: "Sup-
pose, as the result of my evaluation, I conclude that your
client should not get the children. Will you still use my testimony in court?" After some pause the lawyer will usually
hesitantly respond: "I'm sure you appreciate, Doctor, that
my first obligation is to my client; so I couldn't possibly
use your testimony." To which I respond: "I thought you
said before that your first obligation was to the children."
The lawyer will usually mumble and fumble at that point
and apologetically (and sometimes angrily) agree with
me that the children's welfare may be a less important
consideration than the obligation to support the client's
position.

The adversary system from the therapist's point of view.
The interchange typifies the difficulties that lawyers and
psychotherapists have in their relationship with one another. The lawyer is deeply committed to the principle
that one should do everything legally possible to support
one's client's position. In the service of this goal the attorney is obliged to present to the court all information
that will strengthen the client's case and to withhold (to
the degree that it is legal and ethical) all data that may
be harmful to the client's cause. This is an aspect of what
lawyers refer to as the adversary system. This system is

based on the assumption that an official body is more likely to learn the "truth" about a dispute between two parties by having each side present its case as strongly as it can, rather than having an official, with all of his or her biases, conduct the inquiry. It is important that we respect the fact that this system has developed over centuries and that it has a deep tradition which evolved after countless legal proceedings. Other systems have also been tried; but the adversary system has generally been considered the most just—its deficiencies notwithstanding.

Because of its ancient heritage, as well as the deep inculcation of its technical application central to most law school curricula, lawyers, in my opinion, tend to be somewhat blind to some of the defects of the adversary system. They make the assumption that because it may be a workable arrangement in a criminal proceeding it will prove useful in other situations in which there are conflicting opinions. Even when the "grounds" for divorce were considered criminal acts by most, the system was ill suited to divorce conflicts because divorce laws required that one party be designated "guilty" and the other "innocent," when both generally contributed to the difficulties. If both parties were guilty, or if neither one could be "proved" so, the divorce was not granted. More recently, when the traditional grounds for divorce are no longer being considered crimes, the adversary structure is even less applicable.

The whole procedure of selective revelation of information from a client is totally antagonistic to the psychotherapist's approach to a problem. The therapist works on the principle that one must be free to get as much information as possible from one's patient and that nothing should restrain the therapist from gaining any data that he or she may consider relevant. Although attorneys, as well, profess that they do best when their clients are completely honest with them—and may decry the fact that their efforts are hampered in many cases by a client's dishonesty with them—there are certain factors intrinsic to the practice of law that tempt the attorney not to adhere so strictly to this principle. Some lawyers, for example, will suspect strongly that their client is indeed guilty and will in subtle ways encourage the client's lying to them. They will not ask those questions that may place the client in the position of revealing information that may be harmful to his or her legal position. Or the attorney may overtly or covertly encourage the client not to disclose any information to the lawyer that might compromise the client's position—lest the lawyer be placed in an ethically conflictive situation. A kind of tacit agreement is made between the attorney and client that certain things will not be revealed. Such a conspiracy of silence may be necessary to the maintenance of the lawyer–client relationship. In this way the lawyer can rationalize that he or she is being ethical, avoids lying to the court, and cannot be considered to be encouraging perjury on the client's part or otherwise permitting a fraud to be perpetrated on the court. And not incidentally, such a conspiracy of silence may be necessary if the lawyer is to keep the client and the attendant fee. If a therapist, however, suspects that the patient is withholding information, it behooves him or her to inquire into the particular matter and to help the patient appreciate that the therapist is ill equipped to help if he or she is being deprived of any information relevant to the patient's difficulties. Although, strictly speaking, it is unethical for an attorney to engage in such a conspiracy of silence with a client, the temptation to do so is often present, and so the practice is common. Therapists, having no such temptation, can more easily adhere to the principle that they do best for their patients when the whole truth is known to them.

In certain respects therapists tend to be more naïve than lawyers with regard to believing a patient's statements. Generally, therapists expect their patients to be truthful with them. They may at times be doubtful about the validity of a patient's statements; their antennae may be out sensing for deceptions; but usually these are the patients' self-deceptions—things that they are trying to hide from themselves. Most often, patients in treatment do not consciously try to deceive the therapist. The lawyer, however, more frequently expects his clients to be untruthful and routinely assumes that his adversaries' clients will be even more so. Having more experience with this type of deception, the attorney may often be more astute than the therapist in detecting it. Accordingly, therapists such as myself are poorly equipped to evaluate patients involved in legal proceedings. For example, when we evaluate a parent in a custody determination in which it behooves the parent to withhold (either consciously or unconsciously) information that might be detrimental to his or her cause, our expectation of honesty and inexperience with conscious deliberate deceit may compromise significantly our efficacy.

The therapist generally works in accordance with the principle that if one has no conviction for what he or she is doing with the patient the chances of success in the treatment are likely to be reduced. So if, for example, the therapist's feelings for a patient are not strong, if he or she does not have basic sympathy for the patient's situation, if the relationship is not a good one, or if he or she is not convinced that the patient's goals in therapy are valid, the likelihood of the patient's being helped is small. Without such conviction the therapy becomes boring and sterile—with little chance of anything constructive coming out of it. The lawyer, on the other hand, generally believes that one can be as successful in helping a client whose cause the lawyer may not be particularly in sympathy with, as one can be with a client whose position one strongly identifies with. From law school days the lawyer is deeply imbued with the notion that the obligation of a lawyer is to serve the client and to do the best possible job, even though not in basic sympathy with the client's position and even though one might prefer to be on the opponent's side. Most law schools require their students to have what they call "moot court" experiences. They are similar to college debating societies in that one is assigned to take a side without regard to whether one is basically convinced of that position. In fact, it is often considered preferable for educational purposes for the student to take the side that he or she is not in sympathy with. I agree that such experiences can be educationally beneficial. We can all learn from and become more flexible by being required to see a situation from the opposite vantage point. However, I believe that lawyers are somewhat naïve in believing that one's lack of conviction can be so squelched and hidden that it will not affect the kind of job one does. A person works less efficiently when there is little enthusiasm for the purpose of the work. A lover pleads his or her case less ardently when feelings are not strong; and the recipient of the lover's affections generally senses the weakness of the loving professions. And lawyers cannot but plead less convincingly and fight less ardently for the client whose position they do not basically believe has merit. Although a lawyer may try to dissuade a client from pursuing a particular issue that he or she is not in sympathy with, many if not most will still argue that cause if the client insists. And it is a rare lawyer who will refuse to accept a client because he or she has too little conviction for the client's position.

The lawyer and the therapist both deal with human problems and with disputes between people. The orientation of the therapist, however, is generally that of trying to help the individual change the personality patterns and the behavioral manifestations that contribute to such disputes. Although the lawyer, at times, may be respectful of and sympathetic to these underlying processes, his or her orientation is much more toward resolving disputes through structured verbal *conflict*. The dispute is solved when one party *wins* and the other *loses*. Attorneys very easily get so swept up in their desire to win, that they may lose sight of how much is *lost* in the process of trying to *win*. Accordingly, practitioners of the two professions, because of their differing goals and orientations, view divorce litigants very differently and have great difficulty communicating and working with one another in this area.

Lawyers are often criticized for inflaming their clients, adding to their hostility, and thereby worsening the divorcing spouses' difficulties. A common response to this criticism is: "We are only doing what our clients ask us to do." Such lawyers claim that they are just the innocent tools of their clients and that their obligation is to respond to their clients' requests—even though they may appreciate that a client's course may be detrimental to him or her, the spouse, and the children. I suspect that the lawyer has greater freedom to disengage him- or herself from a client's destructive behavior than he or she claims, and that financial considerations often contribute to the lawyer's going along with the client in such situations because of the appreciation that if he or she does not, the client and the attendant fee will be lost. (Unfortunately there are physicians, as well, who recommend unnecessary medical treatment. For both professions the practice is unconscionable.) Many lawyers discourage litigation out of awareness of its psychological destructiveness and the appreciation that they may reduce their income per hour if they go to court—because only the wealthiest clients can afford the formidable expense of protracted court litigation. For the wealthy client, the latter consideration does not serve as a deterrent for the lawyer and the psychological considerations are often then ignored.

Of course, the overwhelming majority of divorces are uncontested, and do not involve the vicious litigation that I have been describing. It may very well be that over 90 per cent of divorces are worked out between the attorneys—with a minimum of strife. More often in the past than at present, this was possible only after one or both parties agreed to certain deceits at the time of the court appearance. In such situations one party may have agreed to be the adulteress or the adulterer, or the one who had inflicted mental cruelty on the other. "Witnesses" were brought in (usually friends or private detectives who were willing to lie in court) to testify in support of the various allegations, and everyone agreed to go through the little theatrical performance. Even the judge knew that the play was necessary to perform if there were to be grounds for granting the divorce. All appreciated the co-operation of the witnesses and there was practically no danger of their being prosecuted for their perjury. Since the passage of no-fault divorce legislation such spectacles have become less common.

The therapist may not see those people whose divorces run "smoothly." He or she gets involved with those who have not been able to work out their differences. The therapist sees those individuals whose problems interfere with their agreeing to the compromises necessary to successful resolution of a divorce conflict. They are the people who do not seem to recognize that compromises will ultimately have to be made and that they are best made by the individuals themselves—with the help of lawyers as advisers, not as battle leaders. The therapist sees those people who do not seem to appreciate that a court decision may be the worst one for them. It cannot easily be reversed and one may have to live with it for many years, if not throughout life. A judge may have spent only a few minutes or a few hours before deciding the case. Anyone else who seriously considered the issues at hand would have found them mind-boggling and would have wanted many days and even weeks to study the problems before coming to any conclusions. I tell my patients that they know their situation best and that they have it within their power to settle their differences themselves. The more they involve themselves with litigation, the more they are placing their fate in the hands of others, the more helpless they will feel with regard to what is happening to them, and the more psychological suffering they are likely to bring to themselves and their children. Sometimes my advice is heeded; often not. The power to wreak vengeance is strong, the need not to "let him (or her) get away with it" is deep, the receptivity of the lawyers to get swept up in the fray is ever present, and the resulting psychological devastation of the family becomes commonplace.

The "no-fault divorce." With increased recognition of the inappropriateness of the adversary system to divorce proceedings and the psychological toll of divorce litigation, there has been a rapidly growing trend in recent years for state legislatures to adopt what is referred to as the *no-fault divorce laws*. Until recently divorce laws in most states were based on concepts of guilt and innocence, that is, within the context of punishment and restitution. The divorce was granted only when the complainant, or petitioner, proved that he or she had been wronged or injured by the defendant, or respondent. In most states the acceptable grounds for divorce were very narrowly defined and, depending upon the state, included such behavior as mental cruelty, adultery, abandonment, habitual drunkenness, non-support, and drug addiction. The law would punish the offending party by granting the divorce to the successful complainant. If the court found that both the husband and wife were guilty of marital wrongs, a divorce might not be granted. In such cases some courts would grant the divorce to both parties—each being considered to have proved him- or herself wronged by the other. However, as I have described, the parties usually agreed to alter the truth in a way that would result in their obtaining a divorce. Often this would require one party to take public blame—court proceedings in such cases are usually open to the public. Although such proceedings rarely make headlines in the newspapers, they are potentially available (through newspaper accounts) for public scrutiny and distribution. The knowledge of this possibility became an additional burden to the person who, because of the greater desire for the divorce, would be willing to be considered guilty and the spouse innocent. In addition, there were possible untoward psychological consequences resulting from the acceptance of the blame and this could contribute to residual problems following the divorce.

In recent years there has been greater appreciation by state legislatures of the fact that the traditional grounds for divorce were not applicable to most marital conflicts. There has been increasing recognition of the fact that marital breakdown is caused not simply by wrongs and injustices perpetrated by one party against the other, but that both parties have usually contributed to the marital difficulties. With such realization came the appreciation that adversary proceedings (in which one party is found guilty and the other innocent) are not well suited to deal with marital conflicts. Accordingly, an ever-growing number of states have changed their laws regarding the grounds for divorce and the ways in which people can dissolve their marriages. These new statutes do not require designation of guilty and innocent parties, i.e., no one must be considered to be *at fault*. Such statutes provide much more liberal criteria for the granting of a divorce. For example, living apart for a prescribed period of time is a commonly acceptable criterion. In most states this period is a year, eighteen months, or two years, but sometimes the prescribed period will be shorter if no children are involved. One does not have the problem of designating a guilty and an innocent party. Some states will grant a divorce on the basis of "incompatibility" or "irreconcilable differences." The terms may not be defined any further and it may be quite easy for the couple to demonstrate that they are incompatible or irreconcilable.

The passage of no-fault divorce laws is, without question, a significant step forward. Divorce, by being removed from adversary proceedings, is more readily, less traumatically, and usually less expensively obtained. However, many no-fault laws require the agreement of *both* parties to satisfy the new liberal criteria. Divorce can rarely be obtained unilaterally. If one party does not agree, then adversary proceedings are necessary if the person desiring the divorce is to have any hope of getting it. In addition, the new laws have not altered the necessity of resorting to adversary proceedings when there is conflict over such issues as splitting of property, visitation, support, alimony, and custody. Also, in most states, traditional "fault" grounds for divorce still coexist with the "no-fault" laws. Spouses and lawyers may attempt to interject these fault grounds to gain leverage when negotiating over property allocation, alimony, or support. A spouse, for example, at the suggestion of or reinforced by a lawyer, may threaten to sue for divorce on a fault ground unless his or her proposal for property distribution and support is accepted. The hope is that the party who is guilty of a marital transgression (such as adultery) will give in rather than face the ugliness of a courtroom battle and public disclosure.

One of the unfortunate drawbacks of these new laws has been the dissolution of marriages that still might have been viable and workable if the parties had been required to stick it out a little longer. With a little more maturity and realization of the fact that every marriage has its necessary adjustments and frustrations, the individuals might have remained together—with benefit to both themselves and their children—and avoided all the hardship that resulted from the divorce. The disadvantages of the new liberal laws notwithstanding, I am still strongly in favor of the principle. Just because a few might be adversely affected by them is no reason to deprive the overwhelming majority of the opportunity to extract themselves easily from an arrangement that could prove psychologically devastating to themselves and their children.

Litigation and counseling: a very poor, if not impossible, combination. Because of the differing orientations of the lawyer and the therapist, counseling a couple contemplating divorce becomes a difficult, if not impossible, situation if either party is consulting a lawyer. Effective counseling requires a basic degree of honesty among the participants. If either party is being advised by a lawyer to withhold certain information from the counseling, lest his or her legal position be weakened, the counseling becomes so compromised that it could be worthless. I generally advise couples in such a situation that they will be seriously hindering our work if they are simultaneously being advised by lawyers about what they should and should not say. I tell them that I recognize that by being completely honest in the counseling they may be jeopardizing their future legal positions, but they must decide themselves if the counseling is important enough for them to take their chances regarding this. Again, I do not tell people what to do, I do not tell them not to get legal advice. I only inform them about potential consequences and respect their freedom to make their own decisions.

It is inappropriate for the lawyer to play the role of therapist, Similarly, a therapist has no business providing legal and financial advice. These are the roles of the lawyer and the accountant. Patients in counseling and therapy should be wary of any therapist who is grandiose enough to consider himself capable of providing such advice. Although many of the issues pertaining to divorce have both legal and psychological implications, it is generally not difficult to draw the lines where each adviser's expertise ends. Just as it is dangerous for the lawyers to provide psychotherapy because they have not been trained to provide such, it is dangerous for therapists to give legal advice. By doing so they are likely to add to the patients' burdens and to contribute to an entrenchment and even intensification of their psychological problems.

Mandatory Conciliation Counseling

Many states require mandatory conciliation counseling before a divorce can be granted. Each of the three words —*mandatory, conciliation,* and *counseling*—warrants discussion.

Meaningful counseling cannot be mandated. I believe that meaningful psychological counseling cannot be *mandatory.* The likelihood of an individual's gaining anything from a counseling situation in which he or she is compelled to participate is very small. If psychological counseling is to be meaningful, the individual must (1) be suffering with psychological pain and (2) believe that by revealing him- or herself completely to the counselor some alleviation of the pain might ultimately be brought about. The person who satisfies these two criteria will often seek counseling. If he or she does not satisfy them, it is unlikely that counseling will be sought, and if mandated it is unlikely that he or she will profit from the experience. Generally, if a couple doesn't wish to avail themselves of the counselor's services, doesn't wish to be there, but is required to attend the session, they will sit out their time and when the prescribed number of counseling sessions has been satisfied, will breathe a sigh of relief that it's over with, and leave without having been in any way affected by the experience. During such sessions the counselor will usually appreciate the clients' lack of motivation and this cannot but compromise significantly his or her own commitment to the process. The time-wasting sham cannot but be a cause of irritation and shame to all the parties engaged in it. Some therapists claim that a small percentage of those who are forced to submit to such counseling do become meaningfully involved and profit from the experience. Although I believe that this can occur on occasion, I also hold that it still does not justify subjecting the majority to this wasteful and expensive enterprise.

I believe, therefore, that it is naïve on the part of the law to require individuals to participate in this farcical experience. I suspect that more sensitive and sophisticated lawmakers are well aware of the futility of trying to mandate counseling but have agreed to require such counseling as a concession to those who rigidly subscribe to the view that all marriages should be preserved regardless of the circumstances—a concession often necessary for the passage of more liberal divorce laws. Such traditionals have such a deep commitment to the marital relationship that they have to blind themselves to the psychological toll that enforced maintenance of a marriage can have on parents and children.

It should not be the purpose of counseling necessarily to conciliate. I also find the word *conciliation* objectionable as used in the context of mandatory counseling. It indicates that the purpose of the counseling is to bring back together couples who are contemplating separation. Furthermore, the word carries with it the implication that people having marital difficulties would be better off remaining together than separated. This, in the opinion of most competent mental health professionals, should not be the purpose of counseling or therapy. The therapist's position should be one of trying to help the couple with marital difficulties clarify the problems that have brought about their troubles. His or her hope should be that the information so gained may be useful to them in making their decision—whether to separate and divorce or to try to make a go of it again. In addition, if they decide to separate, what they have learned in the counseling will, it is hoped, help them avoid making similar mistakes in their interpersonal relationships—both within and out of the marital situation. In short, the counselor's purpose should not be reconciliation, but clarification and possibly mediation of problems attendant to the divorce. Even if not mandated, his or her aim should not be to conciliate. To do so is to risk causing those who should otherwise have gotten divorced to remain in a psychologically traumatic situation.

Who's going to do all this counseling? With regard to the term *counseling*, those who would mandate it often make the assumption that counselors are going to be available. In the United States alone hundreds of thousands are divorcing every year. One would indeed have to have an army of counselors if such laws were to become more widespread and their provisions implemented. What has happened in those states where counseling is mandated is that there are so few people available for such counseling that, in order to comply with the law, their services have had to be spread so thin that their counseling is practically worthless. In addition, the standards and requirements as to who shall qualify for such positions are often so ill defined that many unqualified and poorly trained individuals are used. Furthermore, the salaries offered generally do not attract the more competent people—further worsening the situation. Such "counseling" often ends up with an incompetent "counselor" advising counselees who have absolutely no desire to be counseled, let alone conciliated. Obviously this is a disgraceful situation—a terrible waste of time, money, and human resources. In addition, the counselees are often asked to fill out questionnaires in which they are asked to describe intimate details of their personal lives. These are often written to an as yet unknown counselor and placed in files of an unknown degree of privacy. It is naïve on the part of those who devise such programs to think that accurate and meaningful data are going to be provided under such circumstances. The practice contributes to the defeat of the process from the outset. Furthermore the invasion of privacy that such a procedure entails raises questions about the basic constitutionality of the process. Recognizing these drawbacks to such counseling some states are now rescinding the requirement.

I myself would recommend that *voluntary* counseling be provided for those who seek it. I would not call it conciliation counseling, because that would not be its purpose—although for some it might produce this result. With such voluntary counseling available to couples considering divorce—with no one being *required* to use such services—there would be fewer people seeking them; but those who sought them would be more highly motivated and more likely to profit from them. Since fewer counselors would be needed, a higher percentage of highly qualified counselors would be available and competitive salaries could more readily be offered. Those who avail themselves of such counseling will have done so voluntarily—it will not have been coerced—and so their chances of learning something beneficial will be enhanced.

The Psychological Effects of Divorce on Children

Does divorce cause a child to develop psychological disorders? I do not believe that divorce necessarily produces harmful psychological reactions in the child. However, the child of divorce is more likely to develop such reactions than the child who grows up in an intact, relatively secure home. This book is based on this assumption.

It is almost impossible to differentiate the effects on the children of the divorce itself from the effects of the various traumas they may have suffered before, during, and after the parental separation. It is the exposure to a detrimental environment over a period of time—rather than the acute trauma of the separation—that causes the child to develop unhealthy psychological reactions. Of course, years of separation from a parent could be a chronic psychological trauma; however, it need not be. If the parent who lives away from the home maintains a good, consistent relationship with the child *and* relates reasonably to his former spouse, the child may be spared the development of unhealthy reactions to the divorce.

Factors in the divorce situation that may contribute to children's developing psychological disorders. There are certain aspects of the divorce situation that increase the risk that a child will develop psychological difficulties.

Obviously, two parents can provide children with far more guidance, sustenance, and protection than one, and are more likely to prevent the kinds of psychological disturbance that may result from deprivations of these necessities. I often compare the need of the child for two parents with the need of the human being for two eyes or two kidneys. Nature seems to have provided us with a "spare" for each of these organs. If a person loses one, he or she may still get by with the other. However, the individual with one eye does suffer the inability to perceive in depth and there may be some compromise of kidney function for the person with only one kidney. The loss of both organs, however, like the loss of both parents, can be devastating. When one parent is temporarily absent from the intact home, it is likely that the other will be available to gratify the child's needs in a loving way. This is not so readily the situation in the divorced home. Most will agree that children need an intimate relationship with both a male and female adult if they are to learn how to function adequately with others, both as children and subsequently as adults. A boy needs a father as a model for identification and a girl needs a mother for the same purpose. The child of each sex has to learn to relate to adults of both sexes if he or she is to get along optimally in life, and growing up in a home with a mother and a father is probably the most effective way to accomplish this. Then one can have living experiences in a natural setting that serve to accomplish this goal. Accordingly, children who are significantly deprived of one parent are more likely than those who have good relationships with two parents to exhibit impairments in their psychological development and interpersonal relations. In addition, no parent can provide sustained affection. Children are inevitably frustrating and a source of resentment to a parent. Having a second parent available in the home lessens the chances that the child will suffer during the periods when he or she is rejected by the first parent. Deprivation of parental affection is one of the most common and predictable causes of childhood psychiatric disturbance. And children of divorce, having only one parent available in the home, are more likely to experience such deprivation. Lastly, it is not hard to see how children of divorce will come to view human relationships as basically unstable. From their vantage point the significant individuals in one's life may suddenly abandon one forever. With such distrust of human relationships, it is likely that their involvements will tend to be weak and their psychological development unstable.

It is not surprising then that many psychological studies find a greater incidence of psychiatric disorder in children from broken homes than in those from intact, stable homes. If these findings of a greater incidence of psychological disorder in children of divorce were not valid, if such children were not found to be a greater risk for the development of psychiatric disturbance, then one would have to re-evaluate the assumption that a child's living with two parents is preferable to his living with one. The studies, therefore, indicate that such re-evaluation is not warranted and that my assumption regarding the importance of a child's having two, opposite-sexed individuals with whom to relate is supported.

There does not appear to be any specific kind of disorder produced by marital discord. Similarly, there is no typical psychological disturbance exhibited by children of divorce; rather, there is a whole range of possible reactions.

Staying Together "For the Sake of the Children"

Parents contemplating divorce generally will give consideration to staying together "for the sake of the children." They will generally recognize that their unhappy relationship may very well be detrimental to the children, but they fear that the alternative of divorce will even be more devastating. Accordingly, they may decide to remain together, even though unhappy, in order to protect the children from the harmful effects of a separation.

A number of studies have been conducted by mental health professionals that attempt to determine whether children are better off living in a home in which the parents are unhappy or one in which the parents have separated. Such studies are difficult to conduct and few claim that their results constitute anything like proof. However, then one studies large groups of children, it does appear that *on the whole* children living in an intact but unhappy home suffer more psychological disorder than children living in a home with only one parent. It would be a serious error to conclude then that unhappily married parents do best for their children by splitting up. Even though these studies indicate that *more* children do better in single parent homes than intact but unhappy homes, there were still some children who probably did better in the intact unhappy home than they would have had their parents divorced. Accordingly, one cannot predict which of the two situations would be preferable for any given child. Although the statistics may support the decision to separate, there are still children in separated and divorced homes who are worse off than they would have been had the parents remained together.

There are mental health professionals who recommend that parents not consider the divorce's effects on the children when making their decision. They suggest that the parents make the decision as if the children were not being affected (although they agree that they might be harmed). They consider concern for the children's welfare to be a contaminant to such decision making and advise the parents to make that choice which is best for them and to hope that what will be in their best interests will be in the children's as well. My own belief is that the effects on the children should be one of the considerations in making such a decision, but it should not be the major one. The major determinants should be whether or not the parents feel that there is enough pain in their relationship to warrant its being broken. However, in addition to considering the frustrations each will suffer following the separation and divorce, they should also take into account the effects of their decision on their children. Obviously, such deliberations are difficult, especially because one cannot predict the future with accuracy. Although such considerations may be inaccurate and speculative, parents still do well to take them into account. They should not just assume that their children will be better off if they divorce, or that whatever will be best for them will be best for the children as well.

Sometimes parents will claim that they are staying together for the sake of the children when in reality the relationship is being maintained for other reasons such as: fear of the unknown, fear of criticism of relatives and friends, reluctance to suffer the financial pressures that the divorce will entail, fear of being alone, fear of the increased responsibilities that will result from the divorce, and so on. Professions of concern for the children may often only be rationalizations to buttress various neurotic interactions. For example, the couple may have a sadomasochistic relationship in which one partner gets neurotic gratification from suffering pain and the other has a neurotic need to inflict it. Or one may need a marital partner who serves as a parental figure and the other enjoys infantilizing the spouse. Or both may be basically fearful of sexual encounters and would be made anxious by a more sexually assertive partner. In such cases, the couple may complain bitterly about their frustrations with one another and vow that if not for the children they would have split long ago. Actually, the children may be serving as a convenient excuse for their staying together and maintaining the neurotic gratifications that they provide one another without their having to admit that this is the case.

James and Carol's situation provides an example of how a neurotic involvement between parents was the actual basis for the marital relationship, but they justified staying together "for the sake of the children." Carol had always been a shy girl, who dated infrequently. She met James when she was in nursing school and he was a medical student. From as early as the first grade James had always been an obsessive student, invariably being among the highest in his class. He had never had many friends, so devoted was he to his studies. James and Carol married when James graduated from medical school and she worked in nursing to help supplement his small salary as an intern and resident in surgical training. Throughout this period they saw little of one another because of the long hours of work that James's training required. And when James was home he was absorbed in studying his medical books and journals.

When James opened his practice, Carol quit her job and started having children. Again, building up a practice kept James away from the home. He gradually gained the reputation of being one of the most dedicated doctors on the hospital staff. No patient's problem was too small for him to give his complete attention. He was not only devoted to caring for his patients' surgical needs but spent much time with them, as well, reassuring and counseling them, and discussing in detail other matters which they would confide to him. Nurses and patients alike commented admiringly how he was one of the first doctors to arrive in the morning and one of the last to leave. Meanwhile, back at the ranch house, Carol completely devoted herself to the upbringing of their children. She and James had little social life because one never knew when James would have an emergency. Since they were living in a town distant from both of their families, there was little contact with relatives as well.

My first contact with the family came when Linda, the oldest of their three children, developed severe facial tics and was obsessed with fears that harm might befall her parents, especially her father. Her fears for her father's welfare became especially prominent when his work load was particularly heavy—when, for example, he had to work all day Sunday, rather than his usual half day. I considered Linda's symptoms to be related to the anger she felt toward her father for essentially abandoning her and toward her mother, who, although attentive and caring, was not a very warm or affectionate person. The anger could not be directly expressed and as it built up she became tense—and such tension caused her facial tics. In addition, I considered her obsessive fears that harm would befall her father to be related to the repression of her anger toward him. Such fears often reflect unconscious hostile wishes. Although consciously Linda very much wanted her father to be safe and in good health, another part of her was deeply angry at him. Such anger was repressed and then expressed with visual images of his being harmed. Experiencing the wishes as fears lessened the guilt she would have felt if she accepted such thoughts as desires.

In my interviews with James, it became apparent that he had little interest in Carol. He found her dull and boring. Their sex life was practically nonexistent, but he had had affairs from time to time that provided him with adequate sexual outlet. However, all these relationships were transient and he denied any meaningful involvement with any of these other women, or the desire for such. Yes, he had thought of separation from time to time, but felt that it would be bad for the children, even though he admitted that they might see more of a stepfather than they were seeing of him.

Carol denied any discomfort over her marriage. She denied any resentment over James's long absences from the home, stating that she knew when she married him that she would be leading this kind of life. She had no strong sexual urges—never had—and so was quite content that James didn't "bother her" about sex. She considered the possibility that he might be involved with other women, especially when he could come home at two or three in the morning after "emergency operations," but denied any jealousy over such possible involvements. She felt that they could give James sexual release and thereby relieve her of the obligation to provide such gratification for him. She did not fear that he might get more involved with another woman, and possibly leave her, because she did not see him as the kind of man who gets emotionally involved with women in that way. Yes, James had talked to her on occasion about separation but she could not see why he would want to, considering that this might be upsetting to the children.

It was clear that James and Carol were two people who were essentially remote from others and from one another. Psychologically they had never really been married. They were not only incapable of involving themselves deeply with one another, but with their children as well—and this was especially true of James. When I asked James if he could see his way clear to spending more time with the children, he made feeble attempts to do so. However, his medical obligations always seemed to be pulling at him and he was soon back to his original schedule. Carol too was unable to relax enough to coddle, play with, and involve herself more meaningfully with her children. I finally recommended that the parents hire a very warm housekeeper, as well as a teen-ager to come and play with the children a few times a week. In addition, I worked with Linda and attempted to help her recognize and accept her parents' emotional deficiencies, to get what affection could come from them when it was available, and to seek compensatory gratifications elsewhere from both peers and adults. Under this program these goals were accomplished to some degree and there was a diminution of her anger and the symptoms that were caused by it.

It was clear that, for James and Carol, staying together for the children's sake served as an excuse to remain in a marital situation that each was essentially comfortable with. Both being quite distant people, they would have been made anxious by partners who were capable of deeper involvements.

Effects of Separation on Children at Different Ages

Some mental health professionals consider there to be certain periods in a child's life when a divorce can be particularly harmful. Accordingly, they suggest that parents contemplating divorce wait until a child has passed the particular period in his or her development before separating. There are mental health professionals who consider the period which psychoanalysts refer to as the oedipal phase to be a time when children are particularly vulnerable to the effects of separation. This is the period, usually between ages three and five, when a child develops a strong possessive attachment to the opposite-sexed parent and a concomitant desire to take over the role of the same-sexed parent. At times the attraction can take on mildly sexual overtones toward the opposite-sexed parent and the child may demonstrate rivalrous hostility toward the parent of the same sex. The sexual desires are generally not for intercourse, the child being too young to appreciate that act. Rather they are for more generalized physical-sexual gratification. For example, a boy may become very affectionate with his mother, be-become hostile toward his father, and even entertain wishes that the latter leave the home so that he will have his mother all to himself. And a girl may entertain similar possessive fantasies toward her father and jealous resentment toward her mother. Generally, the healthy child passes through this phase without incident and grows up to direct his attentions toward more appropriate and available love objects. If, however, a parent leaves the home during this period, the child may develop what some psychoanalysts call oedipal problems. The little boy, for example, may believe that his father's leaving was the direct result of the boy's wishing that he do so. Accordingly, he may develop unrealistic ideas about the power of his wishes and guilt over the fact that he has brought about such a catastrophe in his home. He may develop feelings of inferiority over his awareness that he is not capable of assuming all the responsibilities he believes are his, now that he has won possession of his mother over his rival. And the daughter of such a father may develop difficulties in her relationships with males, both present and future, because her basic model for males is not so readily available. Males become to her strange creatures with whom she cannot relate in a comfortable manner. Or she may come to expect rejection from males when there is no evidence for such. Similarly, when it is the mother who leaves the household, her daughters may develop the kinds of problems related to the fantasy that one has won the oedipal rivalry, and her sons may develop the kinds of difficulties that may result when a female figure is not available to them. An extension of this theory holds that there is a reactivation of the oedipal conflict in the early- to mid-adolescent period. Accordingly, this period is also considered to be one in which the youngster is especially vulnerable to the psychological effects of parental separation and the aforementioned problems especially are likely to appear.

Some claim that the couple should wait until the youngest child has started school. In this way, the mother will not be left with the burden of having to take care of many young children at home and will have greater opportunity to earn money and to avail herself of various activities that may enrich her life and compensate her for the pains and frustrations she may suffer in association with the divorce. Others advise parents not to separate at the time school starts because then the child is exposed to two separations simultaneously.

On the basis of my own experiences as a therapist I am not convinced that there are particular periods during which the child is especially vulnerable to the effects of parental separation. Rather, I believe, that from the day of birth the child needs both parents and that the removal of either is likely to have harmful effects on his or her psychological development. Although a boy may not need his father as a model for identification during the first few months of life, he does so after that (possibly even until the time that the father dies). I do not see the three-to-five-year period or adolescence to be particularly crucial with regard to such identification; rather I view the identification as a continuing process which tapers off in late adolescence and early adulthood. However, the process may continue to a lesser degree, throughout a person's life. With regard to the little boy's interest in his mother, I believe that her role as the model woman begins at his birth and continues throughout life. Because she is the model upon which all other women are built and compared, her loss can result in significant difficulties in the boy's relationship with females. The earlier the boy is deprived of his father and/or his mother, the longer he will suffer the aforementioned privations and the greater the likelihood that psychological disorder will result.

With regard to the girl, I believe the same considerations hold. The earlier a girl is deprived of her father, the greater the chances she will have difficulties relating to men. Similarly, the earlier she is deprived of her mother, the greater the likelihood she will not only suffer problems in identification with females, but with other difficulties as well—difficulties associated with the generalized emotional deprivation resulting from the mother's loss. For both the boy and the girl I am in agreement that parental loss during the oedipal and adolescent period can be very detrimental; but I am not convinced that parental loss during these periods is more harmful than loss during other phases.

The only generalization with regard to this matter that I do believe to be true is that the younger the child is when the loss occurs and the longer he is exposed to the loss, the greater will be the harmful effects. However, I do not suggest that parents wait until the children get older so that they may be less affected by the separation. I tell them that I believe that the older the children are at the time of separation the more opportunity they will have had for the beneficial effects of living with two parents. However, I quickly add that they must take into consideration the harmful effects on the children of an unhappy home, as well as the many other factors of importance in making their decision. I do not recommend that they consider the ages of the children to be the most critical issue.

Even if there were such critical periods, it is not likely that such advice would be useful or practical for most families. If there is only one child in the family, then it might be possible for the parents to wait until that child has grown beyond the point when the divorce would be particularly traumatic. However, most families have two or more children. Accordingly, it is likely that after one child has passed the critical period, a younger child will probably be entering it. It is possible that parents who took such advice very seriously, and decided to stay together until all the children had passed beyond the various critical phases, might have to wait ten to fifteen years before getting a divorce.

Another reason why such advice is misguided is that it fails to take into account other considerations that are important at the time when a couple is contemplating divorce. It may have taken the parents many years to have reached the point where they have finally decided to separate—the point where the pain of their remaining together outweighs its advantages. To suggest that such parents maintain their relationship for months and even years, to allow the child to grow past a critical phase, gives priority to a theoretical and unproven need of the child over an actual need of the parents. Heeding the advice may result in their suffering years of further hardship and misery. And parents who do not follow the experts' advice on this issue may add an additional burden of guilt to that which they already suffer over the effects the divorce may have on their children. Believing that their children are suffering more than they had expected, because of the particular timing of the separation, cannot but make them feel even worse about what they are doing. In addition, it is quite common that one or both parties has already become deeply involved with a third person. By following such advice to wait, the parties concerned may be caused additional and unnecessary suffering. They may be deprived of the opportunity for freer involvement in a new relationship that may well serve to lessen some of the pains associated with the divorce. There is probably no better way to reduce the pains, frustrations, and humiliations associated with a divorce than to find oneself another person who considers one loving and worthwhile. Those who follow such advice may be depriving themselves of this important compensatory experience.

Parental Pre-separation Guilt and Shame

Shame over counseling. Even in this so-called enlightened time, some parents are quite ashamed to seek pre-divorce counseling. Those who are considering counseling would do well to appreciate that the benefits that they can potentially derive more than outweigh any embarrassment or other discomfort they may experience as a result of the experience. In addition, such parents should appreciate that it is often more courageous to admit that one has psychological difficulties and needs the assistance of a trained impartial person than to deny one's difficulties.

The healthy, concerned parent feels guilty about the separation. Most parents are significantly guilty about a divorce. They generally appreciate that no matter how much they and their children may benefit from the divorce, the children are still likely to suffer. Perhaps they will suffer less than they would have had the marriage remained intact, but the children will still experience certain deprivations. There is guilt not only over what has gone before, i.e., the detrimental effects of the pre-separation parental conflict on the children, but over what is to come, i.e., the harmful effects of living in a home without one of the parents. One has to expect some feelings of guilt. In fact, if a parent does not feel guilty over the divorce (all promises of a better life notwithstanding), I would consider there to be a deficiency in that parent's affection for the children and/or an unrealistic understanding of the potentially harmful effects of the divorce on the children.

Reducing guilt over separation. In counseling such guilty parents I attempt to help them differentiate between two kinds of guilt. I compare them with the man who buys an automobile and because of a manufacturing defect has an accident in which someone is hurt. This driver is treated quite differently by the courts from the one who purposely injures someone with his car. The first man is not considered a criminal, whereas the second is. Although the victim's pains and injuries may be identical, and it may make little difference to him or her whether the injuries were accidentally or purposely caused, the drivers are very different regarding the appropriateness of their guilt. I try to help separating parents appreciate that their marriage was an error and that the suffering their mistake has brought to both themselves and their children was the result of their well-meaning, but ill-advised union. In some situations the marriage may not initially have been a mistake, but the partners have just grown apart. They may have been quite compatible at first, but either one has matured more than the other, or both may have developed in different directions. Again, I try to help such partners appreciate that this is another kind of mistake that might not have been anticipated or prevented. I try to reassure them that to the best of my knowledge they have both tried very hard to do what they considered best for their children. I attempt to impress upon the parents that I view them as being similar to the man driving the car with the factory defect. Although it may be true that the victim would not have been injured had the man not been driving the car at that time, it is also true that the driver was in no way at fault. Neither the driver nor the separating couple inflicted pain through malicious intent.

I do not stop at that point, however. I try to impress upon the parents that what I have said will do far less to reduce their guilt than their taking constructive action to interrupt any perpetuation of an unhealthy atmosphere to which they may have been exposing their children. By doing everything possible to help their children "pick up the pieces" and make the best of a difficult situation, they can most effectively lessen their guilt. To the degree that they can actively contribute to the improvement of their children's situation, to that degree will their guilt be reduced. If the parents continue to embroil the children in their problems (if that has been the case), then they can expect them to continue suffering and they can thereby anticipate a continuation of their own guilt. Many parents are so swept up in their antagonisms that they lose sight of the effects of the continuing conflict on their children. For most, however, the fighting finally dies down and then the parents may first see how harmful the unnecessary perpetuation of the hostilities has been. One could argue that I am providing such parents with unnecessary additional guilt with such warnings. I am in agreement that I am producing guilt; but I am not in agreement that it is unjustified. There are many individuals whose psychological difficulties involve a deficiency in guilt-producing mechanisms—with the result that many around them suffer needlessly. Fostering some guilt in many parents of divorce may not only be helpful to them in reducing their incessant conflicts, but can have a healthy effect on their children as well.

Returning to the home of the children's grandparents. The parent who returns to his or her parents (usually the mother) is often doing so for very practical reasons:

there is a financial savings and grandparents may be well suited to help take care of the children. However, immaturity on the mother's part may contribute to such a decision. A mother who is still quite dependent on her own parents is more likely to resort to this alternative than one who is more mature. In addition, overprotective grandparents, who still want their daughter to relate to them as a child, are more likely to encourage such return. The mature woman will generally find a return to her own home humiliating and infantilizing, and will be willing to suffer the frustrations and deprivations of an independent existence rather than subject herself to the shame of "returning to the womb." And grandparents who do not have the need to overprotect and infantilize their daughter will not be receptive to her returning to their home. Of course, there are situations where the economic hardships that such a mother might suffer outside the home would be so severe that returning to the home of her parents is the most reasonable alternative—and such return would not indicate that psychological problems were present in either her or her parents.

Martha married Bill when she was seventeen and he, twenty. During the first three years of their marriage they lived in the home of Martha's parents, while Bill studied accounting at a nearby college. Martha worked as a secretary during the first year of marriage, then became pregnant, and stayed at home with her new baby. Even during this early period, Martha sensed that things were not going well between Bill and herself. He often liked to stay out late with his boyfriends, whom he described as still single and "free." Martha felt that Bill still had some growing up to do and had to get youthful escapades "out of his system." From the outset, as well, there were frequent fights over what Bill felt was intrusiveness by his in-laws into his and Martha's marriage. Particularly, he felt that his mother-in-law was forever telling his wife what to do and she was always complying. He felt his wife didn't "have a mind of her own."

Soon after graduation Bill got a job and the couple decided to find their own apartment. Martha was pregnant again and decided it would be a good idea to find a place near the home of her parents, so that Martha's mother would be available to help her with the children. Although Bill preferred a place at a greater distance, in order to be less accessible to his in-laws, he reluctantly agreed to Martha's request. Martha's mother spent hours at the house, and, in addition, there were three or four telephone calls each day to Martha's parents' home.

During the next few years Bill spent less and less time at the apartment. Ostensibly this was related to long working hours. Actually, he felt excluded from the continuing close relationship between Martha and her parents and came to feel ever more uncomfortable at home. Not surprisingly, he met another woman, began to have an affair, and finally told Martha that he wanted a divorce. Not surprisingly, also, Martha and her two children moved back into the home of her parents.

My first contact with Martha occurred when Tom, her oldest child, was nine years old. Tom was doing poorly in school in spite of high intelligence, only concentrated on his schoolwork in a one-to-one relationship with his teacher, and had few friends. He was very passive with peers, was easily taken advantage of, and would go home crying to his mother when teased. He was frequently called "Momma's baby" and "Sissy." It was clear that Tom was a very immature child who was overprotected by his mother and grandmother. Accordingly, he had become quite dependent on others and this interfered with his applying himself independently to his schoolwork. In addition, he had never had the "toughening up" that enables most youngsters to tolerate the usual taunting that just about all children are exposed to. Beside the overprotection of his mother and grandmother, Tom got little if any guidance or protection from his father, who rarely visited. Although Martha dated, she had not remarried because "Mr. Right" had not yet come along. On further inquiry, Mr. Right would have to have been someone who appreciated the value and beauty of the close relationship Martha had with her mother.

In his first session Tom drew a picture of a tree, on which a bird came to land on its branches. Each time the bird alighted the branch broke, and so it tried another branch. And each subsequent branch broke as well, even though the bird was very light. The bird then went on to a second tree and suffered the same experience. Finally, he found a big tall tree, on the top of a high mountain, whose branches held him. I considered the first tree to represent Tom's father, who had proved himself unwilling to provide Tom with emotional support. The second tree, I believe, symbolized Tom's mother, who, because of her dependency on her own mother, was not viewed by Tom as someone who could support him either. And the tree on the top of the mountain stood for his grandmother, the one who really had the power in the family. This interpretation of Tom's picture and story was confirmed in a dream which Tom related during his second session. It was a short dream but it nevertheless stated well Tom's situation. In it Tom walks past his mother and goes up to his grandmother and asks her for some money to buy ice cream. His grandmother gives him the money and he happily skips off to the store. I considered the dream to reflect Tom's feelings that his grandmother was the source of power (as symbolized by the fact that she, not his mother, is the dispenser of money). In addition, the ice cream, as the most delicious and desirable food known to children, well symbolizes all the material things and affection that a loving person can provide. And it is the grandmother, not the mother, who is seen as the provider of such goodies.

In Tom's case I felt that work with Martha as well was important if I was to help Tom. It would have been extremely difficult to help Tom with his overdependency problem if the only parent he had to identify with was an overdependent person herself and if, in addition, she was continuing to overprotect him. In this case, things went well in treatment. Martha came to see how much a child she still was in her relationships with her parents and as she matured in treatment, Tom became more respectful of her and identified more with her maturity. In addition, Tom was helped himself to become more independent. After about fifteen months of treatment Martha got a job and moved out of her parents' house. Although it was rough going at times, Martha managed to function on her own. About a year after leaving her parents she met a man whom she ultimately married—this time forming a relationship that was much more mature and egalitarian than that which she had with Bill.

Encouraging therapy to reduce guilt. Some husbands (often previously unreceptive to their wives' going into treatment) will encourage such a step around the time of the separation. Generally, such a husband's change of heart is not particularly motivated by the desire to pay for his wife's gaining increased insight into her underlying psychological processes; rather it is a manifestation of his desire to lessen his guilt over leaving her. The husband may fear that his wife will "fall apart" and he hopes that by putting his wife "into good hands" the therapist will prevent the impending calamity, to which he may consider himself a contributor. Others may hope that the therapist will substitute for them and thereby help fill the void for their wives. Wives themselves, either consciously or unconsciously, will often seek therapy for this reason. If this is the primary motive for such a wife's being in treatment, the likelihood that anything therapeutically beneficial will come out of the arrangement is quite small. A therapist's primary role is to provide therapy. If, incidental to that function, he or she provides some solace from the pains of loneliness, fine. If the latter, however, is the therapist's primary function, the patient is paying a heavy price for something that she might get equally well and at no cost from a friend. Although less common, a woman who initiates the separation may encourage her husband's involvement in treatment for the same reasons.

Using money to reduce guilt. Although divorce imposes formidable economic hardships on the overwhelming majority of parents, there are some who will use money in an attempt to assuage the guilt they feel over what they consider to have been an abandonment of their families. Of course, such a guilt-alleviation is most readily utilized by the wealthy. Alimony laws in most states are particularly well suited to assist such individuals. We are all familiar with the astronomical settlements, common among the rich, that enable the woman to "live in the life-style to which she was previously accustomed." The wives of such men can generally be relied upon to help their husbands reduce their guilt in this way. But even poorer individuals may offer (or allow to be taken) more money than they can reasonably afford in order to lessen their guilt. Again, alimony laws can be useful to help implement, and wives can generally be counted upon to comply with, the neurotic offering.

Getting the children's permission to separate. There are occasional parents who will actually consult their children regarding *their* opinion as to whether the parents should get divorced. The reason sometimes given to justify enlisting the children's opinion is that it is a sign of democracy in the family. Since the children will be directly affected by the divorce, such parents argue, they should have a say in it. I am not a believer in such a democratic system, believing as I do that the judgment of children is not as good as that of most adults. Often, such parents are essentially asking for the children's permission. The inquiry is approached with the hope that the children will provide it and, thereby, lessen the parents' guilt over the breakup of the home. Others may be quite frightened of anyone's expressing anger to them—regardless of the age of the angry person and the appropriateness of his or her anger. Consulting the children about the divorce and asking permission is done in the hope that the children will not be angry. Such children may have long since learned of the parents' ultrasensitivity to angry responses on their parts and so they may comply with the parental wish that no anger be expressed. Accordingly, they may provide the "permission" and squelch their real disapproval, lest they hurt their parents even more. The healthy parents recognize the inevitability of the children's angry responses to the divorce and have enough personality strength to tolerate such hostility.

Shame over telling the children about the reasons for the separation, e.g., an affair or alcoholism. A parent may not wish to tell the children about the reason for a divorce because of shame. Most commonly an extramarital affair as the cause of divorce is the reason which the parent is ashamed to disclose. However, other problems such as alcoholism, obsessive gambling, and drug addition are common causes of divorce that may be a source of great shame to the afflicted parent. In the latter cases the children are usually aware of the problem anyway. When an affair is the cause they may or may not have become aware. Because I believe (as I will discuss in Chapter 2) that children should be given information about the *major issues* that brought about the separation (and I would consider infidelity to be in that category), the parent does the child a disservice when withholding such vital information.

Parents should understand the importance or providing the children with this kind of information. Although enumerating the reasons for disclosure may make the parent more receptive to divulging the affair, it does not reduce the shame. To lessen this I generally try to help the parent appreciate that the word infidelity in itself is disparaging. Strictly speaking it refers to one's being unfaithful or disloyal. If the infidelity was the result of significant difficulties in the marital relationship and was an attempt to gain some solace and affection when there was little, if any, at home, then I try to help the parent appreciate that the affair was human and almost predictable. If the faithful spouse exhibits condemning intolerance for the infidelity (especially when it was an infrequent occurrence and/or unassociated with deep involvement) and if that spouse is unreceptive to attempting to work out any problems that may have contributed to such infidelity, then I try to impress upon the unfaithful spouse the inappropriateness of the partner's attitudes. I describe to the parents what I consider to be the unfortunate social, moral, and religious condemnation that is unfortunately the lot of the unfaithful. And I try to impress upon both parties the fact that the human being's desire for variety is deep-seated and that marriage demands a greater degree of tolerance for frustration of one's desires for variety than practically any other situation. I try to impress upon the parents that some people are willing to accept the frustrations associated with the inhibition of their desires for sexual variety because they are not willing to tolerate the repercussions of infidelity. Others choose to gratify these desires, either openly or secretly, to greater or lesser degrees. In short, I try to lessen shame to the point where the parent is willing to divulge the fact of infidelity as a reason for the divorce. This is not to say that I suggest divulging necessarily the identity of the individual or individuals involved, or details of the parents' sexual life—either with the spouse or the third party(ies). There may still be some shame left, and appropriately so, because, whatever the circumstances, a trust has been broken. My aim is to lessen exaggerated and inappropriate shame to the point where the parent can, with minimal discomfort under the circumstances, provide the children with a proper degree of information concerning the reasons for the separation.

2

Telling the Children

How Old the Children Should Be Before Being Told

The question of whether there is a certain age below which children are too young and/or psychologically fragile to tolerate the news of parental separation reminds me of a question asked an ear, nose, and throat specialist who was an instructor of mine in medical school. A student asked him: "How old should a baby be before one would provide him with a hearing aid?" The instructor's response: "If it were a breech delivery, I would wait until the head comes out." Although I would certainly not spend time giving a newborn infant, or one a few months old, a talk about a parent's forthcoming separation from the home, I would allow the toddler access to such conversations with older children. Certainly by eight to nine months of age most babies differentiate their parents from strangers and, I believe, are significantly affected by a parent's departure from the home. If the child is old enough to recognize the existence of a parent, he is old enough to be told (at whatever level of communication that may have to be utilized) that that parent will no longer be living in the home. The fact that he may not be able to comprehend fully the import of what is being told to him is no justification for the information not being given. He is entitled to the message in the hope that it will be appreciated at some level, no matter how primitive.

The situation is analogous to providing children with

information about sex. Most mental health professionals agree that if a child is old enough to ask a question about sex, he is old enough to get an answer commensurate with his developmental level and his capacity to understand the response. A three-to-four-year-old who asks about how babies are born might be told about the growth of the baby in the mother's "belly" and its birth through the vagina. One would not, of course, attempt full explanations of anatomy, menstrual cycles, etc. More important than the child's understanding is the child's experience that the question has been answered honestly. The child thereby comes to view the parents as people who can be relied upon to provide direct and honest answers to his or her questions. The child will have plenty of time to question the parents again in the future and correct any distortions that may have resulted from the inability to comprehend fully what has been explained. What cannot be easily rectified are the detrimental psychological effects of parents' not responding openly and honestly to sexual questions. It is in such an atmosphere that guilt and inhibition are created—attitudes that are at the foundation of many types of sexual problems. Similarly, for the child whose parents are separating, if he or she is old enough to appreciate that one of the parents is no longer going to live in the household, or is old enough to ask about the absent parent's whereabouts, the child is old enough to be given an honest explanation.

There are parents who do not tell preschoolers (and occasionally even older children) about an impending separation with the explanation that "they're too young to understand." Such an attitude is often an excuse for avoiding the embarrassment or guilt the parents would feel upon revealing to the children their plans to separate. By convincing themselves that the children are too young to understand what is happening, they do not have to face the children's tears and pleas to the parents that they reconsider their decision. Some parents justify their withholding the information with the excuse that young children would be so pained by the disclosure that psychological damage might result. Again, such a view might serve as an excuse to enable the parents to avoid the psychological discomforts they might have to suffer by revealing the separation. Parents who use such excuses should appreciate that they do their children more harm by withholding the information than revealing it. Children are far less fragile regarding such matters than many parents appreciate. The immediate pain of learning of the separation is far less traumatic psychologically than the anxieties associated with an atmosphere of secretiveness. The child senses that things are not right, but since he is not given any information about what has gone wrong, he generally views the situation as worse than it really is. Furthermore, his trust in his parents is reduced at a time when he can least afford it.

When They Should Be Told

As with many of the other issues dealt with in this book, there are no simple answers to this question. On the one hand, telling children long in advance may provide them with the opportunity to adjust to and work through their reactions in a setting where the departing parent is still available to help the children work them out. It is a generally accepted psychological principle that it is preferable to work out a problem one may have with another individual in a setting in which one has direct access to that person. For example, it is extremely difficult, if not impossible, to resolve completely problems one may have had with a parent who has died. Since there is no opportunity for feedback, compromise, and experiences that might have corrected distortions, the likelihood of successfully dealing with such interpersonal difficulties is small. Similarly, children have the best opportunity to work out their reactions to a parent's forthcoming departure while that parent is still in the home and available to them. In such a situation, they not only have greater opportunity for discussing their questions and reactions to the forthcoming separation, but can have living experiences that convince far better than words. For example, the parent who is preparing to leave may tell the children that he or she still loves them and will continue to love them after moving to the new home. Such a statement is far more convincing when the children have had the living experience that the parent is still relating in a loving way—and this is best accomplished while he or she is still living with the children. They will be left then with greater confidence that such affection will be maintained after the departure.

A further analogy with the death of a loved one is also applicable here. If one has advance notice, one has the opportunity for anticipatory mourning and this increases the likelihood that one will adjust adequately and in a reasonable period after the person dies. When there has been no expectation—when one has been shocked by the news—the mourning period becomes more difficult. Because it is the purpose of mourning to help the survivor adjust to the death, anything that hinders its progress interferes with the bereaved person's ability to become accustomed to the loss.

However, long periods of time between the announcement and the actual departure may serve to deepen and fix the child's denial mechanisms. Observing the departure makes it harder for the child to deny its occurrence. When a long period elapses after the announcement of the separation, it is easy for the child to conclude that the departure will not take place. In addition, younger children are not appreciative of time passage with the accuracy of adults and so significant advance notice is of little value. To a two- or three-year-old there is little difference between five weeks and five years. It is similar to the adult's trying to appreciate the difference between a star five trillion miles away and one fifty trillion miles from us. Furthermore, the long waiting period may prolong the children's agony and thereby increase their chances of developing psychological disturbances.

Giving the children short notice does have the advantage of reducing the painful waiting period. However, it may deprive the children of the opportunity to work through their reactions and to adjust adequately to the trauma. There are some parents who tell the children at the last possible moment, ostensibly to shorten the children's agony as much as possible. My experience has been that in such cases it is more likely the parental agony that is of concern. With bags packed, the departing parent informs the children that he or she is leaving—and then rushes out of the house. Concern for the welfare of the children and "getting it over quickly" for their benefit is used as an excuse for covering up parental cowardice, shame, and lack of concern for the children's need to work through the separation. This misguided approach to the problem only increases the children's difficulties. Any advantages there may have been to "getting it over with quickly" are more than counterbalanced by the disadvantages of their having been deprived of the opportunity to work out their reactions in advance.

Usually the most appropriate time to tell the children is when a *definite* decision for separation has been made. I emphasize the word definite because it is cruel and psychologically detrimental to subject children to the numerous tentative decisions for separation that often precede the final one. And most couples go through many such cycles before making their final decision. Such cycles of dashed and then raised hopes cannot but be psychologically harmful to them. It is as if a ticking time bomb were placed in the house and the children never knew if and when it would explode. Of course there may be times when the parents have made a definite decision to separate, tell the children about it, and then decide to try again to make a go of it in the marriage. The children must be told about the changed plans and will probably not suffer from one such cycle. The more frequent they become, however, the greater the likelihood that new traumas will be added to those to which the children have already been exposed. If the parents have decided upon a trial separation, the child should be told about this. Although this presents the danger of the back-and-forth situation, their not being told many result in new problems arising—problems which relate to loss of trust and other effects of parental secretiveness and dishonesty.

If the time between the decision to separate and the actual time of separation is long (many weeks, or even months) then one might wish to withhold the information until a few weeks prior to the separation. This is a justifiable plan in that it protects the children from prolongation of their pain and yet provides them with an adequate opportunity for working through their reactions. Because of the range and variations in the capacity for humans to adjust to a trauma, one cannot have any hard-and-fast rules regarding the optimum time between disclosure and departure. Practically no advance warning is clearly damaging as is the subjugation of children to every ambivalent decision. There is less danger, in my opinion, in the child's being told in advance and much to argue for it. And a few weeks in advance appears to be the optimum time for this disclosure in most families.

Who Should Tell Them

I have found that it is preferable for the parents to tell the children together. Such an approach lessens the likelihood that one parent will try to make the other solely responsible. Although there certainly are divorces in which one of the parents is more responsible than the other for the deterioration of the marriage, the more common situation, in my experience, is that both partners have contributed. The children's erroneously viewing the separation to have been caused by only one of the parents can contribute to the formation of some psychological difficulties. Both parents' telling can serve to lessen the inevitable insecurities that befall children at such a time. Implicit in the fact that both parents are providing the painful information is the notion that, although soon to be separated, they will both be available to discuss further the separation and divorce issues. Having two parents available for consultation, support, and discussion is certainly better than one and may lessen the chances that the children will feel abandoned. In addition, when both parents conduct such a discussion, the stage is set for similar such talks with each one of them alone in the future. Each one of them at that point is establishing a reputation for himself as being receptive to and available for such conversations.

Sometimes a parent may not wish to be the one to tell the children and prefers that the other do so. At times the reluctant parent is ashamed of what may be revealed in such a conversation. Such a parent may be fearful of the children's probable angry response and may not be able to tolerate their hostility. Others may be so guilt-ridden over the impending separation that they cannot face their children's pained responses. Such a parent may request, and even try to coerce, the other parent into withholding vital information from the children. Generally, this is done in the service of withholding information that might be harmful to the uncommunicative parent's image— both to him- or herself and to the children. I generally advise the parent who wishes to communicate such information seriously to consider doing so. I recommend that he or she respect the partner's request to withhold information that should appropriately be withheld from the children but not to respect the withholding of data that is important for the children to have if they are to adjust optimally to the separation. The main issues of the separation should be divulged to the children. One need not provide every specific detail; rather, only those general issues that give the children a meaningful explanation of the cause(s) of the separation. The parent who withholds damaging information (real or presumed to be so) from the children (information that they should know if they are to deal optimally with the separation) in order to protect the image of the spouse is doing the children and the spouse a disservice. Such "protection" causes the children to lose trust in the parent who is withholding the vital information (because they generally sense that the parent is holding back) and confuses them about the parent whose liabilities are being covered up.

Sometimes a parent who wishes to provide more information complies with the withholding parent's demands from passive dependency on the spouse. Although recognizing the value of the disclosure, the parent is too fearful of invoking the anger of the partner to do what would be in the best interests of the children.

How Should They Be Told

The best arrangement is one in which both parents sit down with all the children together and tell them about the impending separation. There are some who believe that the children are best told separately because their different age levels require explanations of varying sophistication. Although I agree that separate explanations may very well be necessary, I see no reason why these cannot be provided in the presence of the other children. Although time may be lost in having to repeat the explanation in order to make it commensurate with the children's various levels of appreciation, there is much to be gained by the children's hearing the news together. They can gain a sense of closeness with one another that is not possible when they are told separately. And this sense of closeness is even more important at the time of impending parental separation. Being told separately invariably involves their "comparing notes" and the likelihood thereby of errors being introduced.

Separate discussions create an atmosphere of secretiveness and a distrusting attitude toward the parents. The child who is waiting outside is not likely to accept the explanation that he or she is not old enough to understand what is being told an older sibling behind locked doors. The child is more likely to conclude that things are being withheld that he or she would like to know—and has a right to know. Or the child may conclude that he or she is being talked about—not an unreasonable conclusion when one is prevented from being party to a conversation. The whole atmosphere then becomes one of secretiveness and from this develops distrust of the parents and even the siblings. At this time the children can ill afford further compromises in their relationships with their parents. Telling them together avoids this drawback of the separate discussions. If, in the attempt to avoid these consequences of separate discussions, the parents decide to tell each child at such time when the others are not around, difficult logistics may be required. Even if this difficulty is overcome, the chances of A saying something to B before the parents do is great. (Children, like adults, are not famous for their abilities to keep secrets or withhold burning information.) This system, then, contains the risk of the child's being told by a sibling, rather than by a parent—a situation that is bound to undermine the child's confidence in the parents.

Many parents will hesitate to involve themselves in such discussions for fear that they will "break down" in front of their children. A parent may exclaim, "I just don't want them to see me crying; it will just make them even more upset." There are even professionals who advise parents to make sure that when they do tell the children they do so at a time when they are so composed that they will not show how upset they are—lest the children become upset as well. I believe that such a position is naïve and misguided. Dealing with the divorce (for both parents and children) is an experience analogous to the mourning period following death. During this time the individuals accustom themselves to the trauma, desensitize themselves to its pains, and work through their reactions to it. Vital to such accommodation is the expression of the various feelings that inevitably arise in such a situation. The parents must serve as models for the children in fostering the expression of such emotional reactions. If the parents hold back their feelings, the children are likely to as well, with the result that various psychological problems may arise. Bottled-up thoughts and feelings are among the most common causes of psychological problems. Parents do well then to express, in moderation, the emotional reactions they have to the separation. I am not suggesting that the parents begin telling the children about the forthcoming separation at a time when they are overwhelmed with their feelings. It is preferable that they wait somewhat until their feelings are at a relatively low level and they can discuss the situation with some degree of objectivity. However, they should be accepting of the appearance of stronger reactions and, although painful, appreciate that their expression *in front of their children* can be a healthy experience for all concerned. It is healthy for the parents because they are expressing their emotions and thereby lessening the chances that they will develop psychological problems in reaction to the separation. And it is healthy for the children because their observations of their parents' freedom to release their feelings will enhance the likelihood of the children's doing so as well. Of course hysterical outbursts are not in order. This would be substituting one form of inappropriate handling of emotions with another.

Some parents hesitate to discuss the reasons for the divorce with the children lest their bitter angry feelings toward the spouse be revealed. They fear that such expression will undermine the child's respect for and relationship with the partner. It has been my experience that the children are usually very much aware of the angry feelings that exist between the parents. It is rare that the separation comes as an absolute surprise. Furthermore, if no angry feelings are exhibited, then the child might wonder why the parents are getting separated. Such suppression can only serve as a model for the children to suppress their own anger and such inhibition of expression is a common cause of psychological trouble. Finally, the child who grows up in an atmosphere in which he has been protected from criticisms of a parent may develop unrealistic views about that parent and this will interfere with his identification process, as well as his ability to relate healthily to others.

What Should They Be Told

Be appropriately truthful. Parents do best when they describe to their children the *basic reasons* for the divorce. It is surprising how frequently parents do not provide their children with this important information. I believe that some of the disturbances that children of divorced parents suffer result from the fact that their parents, often with the best intentions and even supported by professional authority, are not *appropriately* truthful about the divorce to their children. I use the word *appropriately* because parents' lives should not be an open book to their children. Still, many parents hide from their children things that they have a right to know, things that, if disclosed, would help them deal more effectively with the separation. Such information is usually withheld because the parents consider its divulgence to be psychologically harmful to their children.

The effects of deceit on children. Children are far less fragile than most parents realize, and they are much more capable of accepting painful realities than is generally appreciated. What is more difficult for them to handle (and this is true for adults as well) are the anxieties associated with ignorance and parental furtiveness, because then fantasy runs free and their worst anticipations can neither be confirmed nor refuted. Half-truths produce confusion and distrust, whereas truth, even though painful, produces trust and gives children the security of knowing exactly what is happening to them. There are then in a better position to handle situations effectively.

If the parents are being deceptive to the children regarding the primary reasons for the separation—even though well meaning—the children will sense the parental dishonesty. This will undermine their trust in the parents at a time when they are most in need of a trusting and secure relationship with them. An unnecessary burden is thereby added to those they already must bear. In addition, such deception creates a new burden for the parents. Generally, one lie must be built upon another in order to keep the system secure and to prevent the reasons for the divorce from being divulged. If, for example, the children are told that Father is away on a business trip, new lies must be created to explain the failure of the father to return and as time goes on, these become even less credible. When the children learn the truth (and they ultimately do) they cannot but become disillusioned with those who have lied to them about such an important issue. Again, this occurs at a time when the children can ill afford such a compromise in an already deteriorated relationship with their parents. A child's basic trusting relationship with the parents is at the foundation of healthy personality development. Parental dishonesty can predictably shake this foundation.

In the situation in which parents provide little, if any, information about the separation the children become curious about the causes. They may question each parent alone and gradually extract information about the reasons for their parents' decision. They may compare notes with one another regarding what they have learned. Whatever excitement they may be to such an investigation, the process of having to gain information in this way cannot but be humiliating to the children. It is as if they have become spies on their parents. Furthermore, the likelihood of their accurately determining what has been going on is small, and with false and distorted data they will be less likely to cope adequately with the situation.

The way in which deceiving a child about parental separation can have devastating psychological effects on a child is well demonstrated in a case reported by a colleague of mine. Rather than tell her three-year-old daughter that her parents were separated, the mother informed the child that her father had gone to work in another city and would not be returning to the home. The child's first assumption was that she and her mother would soon join the father. She repeatedly asked the mother, "When are we going to Daddy?" As time passed, and such a visit did not materialize, the child began to assume that her father was dead, and entered into a mourning period. She stopped asking questions and began repeating to her dolls, "My daddy's dead. I'll never see him any more." Although the mother appreciated that there would inevitably be some contact with the father, she did not correct the child's false assumption that the father had died.

Suddenly, one day, the father appeared. The little girl went into a state of shock. She became apathetic, listless, and demonstrated no affection for him. Whereas previously she had been gay and outgoing, she became withdrawn. The experience was totally incomprehensible to the child— it was as if the dead could come back to life. She protected herself from the anxieties of her incomprehensible world by withdrawing into a state of apathy. It was only through psychiatric treatment that the child was able to come out of this state.

An experience from my own practice well demonstrates the possible harmful effects of a parent's withholding vital information about a family catastrophe from a child. Although in this case it involved the death of a teen-age brother, the child's reactions were similar to those that could occur if a child were misled regarding the reasons for a parent's sudden disappearance. In addition, the therapeutic approaches were similar to those that I would use if a separation were similarly handled by a child's parents.

Ruth, a four-year-old girl, was referred because of phobic symptoms of six months' duration. When Ruth was two, her brother, Scott (then sixteen), was stricken with leukemia. Scott survived for a year and a half, during which time the mother's involvement with the boy left her little time for Ruth. The child was not told that her brother's illness would be fatal, and at the time of his death she was told that he had gone to heaven, where he was very happy. The family was South American, and the father had been temporarily assigned to his firm's New York office. The family returned to their native country for the burial. Unknown to the patient, her brother's body was in the cargo compartment of the airplane. Ruth did not attend the funeral. She was told that she and her parents had returned to South America to visit friends.

Upon returning to the United States, Ruth began exhibiting the symptoms which ultimately brought her to me. Whereas she had previously attended nursery school without hesitation, she now refused. When the doorbell rang, she became panicky and hid under the bed. She refused to visit the homes of friends, something she had previously done without fear. She seemed comfortable when close to both parents and would scream hysterically if they left. Upon their return to the United States, Ruth repeatedly asked questions about her brother, and was told that he was happy in heaven with God. All of Scott's personal effects were destroyed with the exception of a few of his treasured possessions, which were stored away lest the patient be upset by them. Within a week of their return, Ruth stopped asking questions.

I considered the phobic symptoms to be directly related to the way the parents had handled Scott's death with Ruth. From her vantage point, people, without explanation, could suddenly disappear from the face of the earth. It is as if Ruth were saying: "Every place is really dangerous because one knows nothing about the way in which such disappearances occur. It might be that people come to the door and take you away; or perhaps it happens at nursery school; or maybe neighbors do it. No place is really safe. Also, there's no point in trying to get a reasonable explanation from my parents as to how it happens. They too cannot be trusted to be truthful." Ruth, without doubt, sensed her parents' duplicity.

I asked the parents what their genuine beliefs were concerning the dead brother's whereabouts. Both believed that there was no type of existence in the hereafter and although born Catholics, they had no particular religious convictions. They felt that divulging their true feelings about their dead son would be psychologically harmful to their daughter. I explained to them what I considered to be the source of their child's problems. I told them that I knew that they had always done what they considered to be in the child's best interests, but that they had, in my opinion, made some errors regarding their handling of their son's death with Ruth. I suggested that they go home and tell Ruth exactly what had happened to their son—as simply and as accurately as possible. I advised them to tell her, as best they could, what their true beliefs were regarding his present state. I suggested also that they give her one of the brother's mementos and tell her that it would always be hers. They were most reluctant at first, but they finally gained some conviction that my suggestions might be valid.

I then explained to them the psychological significance of mourning and how Ruth had been deprived of this important experience. I told them that it was most likely that Ruth would ask the same questions over and over, and that it was important that they patiently repeat their answers, because this was a part of the mourning and adjustment process. In addition, I suggested that they urge her to face once again the phobic situations; and each time reassure her that she, unlike Scott, would not be taken away.

The parents were seen again one week later. They reported that my suggestions had been followed, and the child had responded well. She cried bitterly when told the details of the brother's death. As I had foretold, Ruth's questions during the next few days were practically incessant. She was given a picture of her brother, which she carried around at all times. She showed it to everyone she could and explained to them that it was her dead brother. She then told how he had died and said that he was in the ground in her native country.

There was a concomitant lessening of all her fears. By the time of the second visit she was again attending nursery school without difficulty; she no longer cowered at the ring of the doorbell; she was visiting friends; and she exhibited only mild anxiety when her parents went out at night. No further sessions were scheduled and the parents were advised to call me if they felt the need for such, which they did not.

Telling about affairs and other touchy subjects. One can provide children with the basic facts regarding the reasons for the separation without necessarily divulging personal intimacies that are not their business. For example, if the parents are getting divorced because the mother is having an affair with another man and no longer wishes to remain married to her husband, the children can be told, "Mommy doesn't love Daddy any more. She loves another man and wants to spend her time with him." If a frigidity problem is an important contributing cause of the breakdown of the marriage, the child can be told, "Mommy doesn't like to hug and cuddle with Daddy very much and this makes Daddy feel very bad. For a long time we have tried to solve the problem, but we can't. So we are getting divorced." A similar explanation will generally suffice for a husband's impotency problem. A child, especially when older and more sophisticated about such matters, may ask questions about such intimacies that the parents might justifiably not wish to answer. In such situations I generally suggest that the parents respond in this vein: "There are certain things that Mommy and Daddy consider personal and we do not consider it proper for us to discuss these things with you. As you grow older you'll have more and more personal things that you will not consider proper to talk about with us. We want you to still ask all the questions that come to your mind. We will answer most of them. However, if there is a question that we do not wish to answer, we will tell you so. We will not make believe we are answering it when we really aren't." If the parent does not state directly that he or she is not answering a question, but responds evasively or with a non-answer, the children's further questioning will be discouraged and this will deprive them of the benefits to be derived from gaining accurate information.

Many problems may arise for parents with regard to the question of what to reveal to the children when an extramarital sexual involvement has been the precipitating cause of the separation. This is a complex issue and I do not claim to have any final answer. There are those who claim that jealousy over a marital partner's sexual involvement with a third party is immature—a residuum of childhood needs for exclusive possession of loved ones. When both spouses fully subscribe to this view they may be able to accept each other's extramarital sexual activities without resentment. They do not look upon these affairs as signs of infidelity, because no trust has been broken, and would not consider such invovements reasons for divorce. Such couples (sexual revolution notwithstanding) are still in the minority. In most marriages at least one of the partners (and more often both) does not tolerate well the spouse's extramarital sexual involvement and becomes deeply pained when such a liaison is revealed. It is viewed as infidelity because the partner has been unfaithful to upholding one of the vows made (either explicitly or implicitly) at the time of the marriage. Most couples today do not quickly separate when such an affair becomes divulged. They often try to determine if there have been difficulties in the marriage (even on the part of the partner who has not been so involved) that contributed to the infidelity. If such problems cannot be resolved, then divorce may result. In some cases the partner who has been involved in the affair does not believe it to have been caused by any major deficiencies on the part of the spouse and may consider the latter's inability to tolerate the infidelity as his or her only defect. If such individuals cannot resolve their conflict, or come to tolerate their differences, then divorce may ensue.

When such involvements have been a central cause of

the separation the children do best if they are told. (I am not suggesting that the identity of the third party need necessarily be revealed.) In the situation where both partners consider the infidelity to be a symptom of more basic difficulties in their relationship, difficulties that they have been unable to resolve, they do well to present to the children the fundamental contributions of each and describe the affair as a common outcome of such problems. Affairs still carry with them some degree of social stigma and so the parent who has been so involved may be embarrassed over revealing it to the children. Such a parent does well to appreciate that his or her shame will probably be temporary and that it is a small price to pay for the benefits to be gained by the divulgence. To withhold the information may make the parent more comfortable, but the children will be impeded in their abilities to deal optimally with the trauma of the separation. The distrust of the parent(s) produced by the children's appreciation that they are not being honestly dealt with will compromise the parent–child relationship. Knowing the exact causes of the separation helps the children learn about the kinds of things that can bring about marital discord and may make it less likely that they will make similar mistakes themselves in the future. Learning about parental deficiency makes it more likely that the children will tolerate deficiencies within themselves and others. Not living up to excessive and unreasonably high standards in oneself is a common factor in producing insecurity and self-esteem problems. And having unrealistically high expectations from others can result in lifelong disillusionment in one's interpersonal relationships, as each person fails to live up to one's expectations.

In the situation in which one parent is quite comfortable with extramarital sexual involvements (both for him- or herself and the partner) and the other finds such liaisons intolerable, the children do best when told about their parents' differing philosophies on this matter. When the affair results from the spouse's inability or refusal to engage in sexual relationships, every detail need not be revealed. I believe that the children have the right to know the basic problems that contributed to the separation (and affairs are an example); the parents, however, still have the right to certain privacies. (The suggestions regarding what to tell the children when an unresolved impotency or frigidity problem has contributed to the decision to separate serve well as an example of how to discuss this type of infidelity problem with the children.) I do not claim to have covered all possible types of conflict over extramarital liaisons that may contribute to divorce. I have only focused on a few of the more common situations. Whatever the exact nature of the problem, however, the parents do well to consider seriously divulging it in accordance with the guidelines and qualifications presented.

In the last few years many homosexuals have "come out of the closet" and openly revealed their homosexuality. Some have been married, have led a "double life," and now proclaim that they refuse to live in this way any longer. And they divorce in order to lead more freely the homosexual life with which they basically feel more comfortable. More homosexual men than women have taken this course in recent years and so I will discuss this issue from the man's point of view, but the principles that I suggest are, I believe, equally applicable to the female homosexual.

Before such a man and his wife can decide how to deal with the question of whether the children should be told about this reason for the separation and, if so, exactly what they should be told, the homosexual man must first decide whether he is going to divulge his homosexuality to others besides his wife. I believe that the healthiest choice that such a man can make is to reveal the homosexuality to friends and relatives under the same circumstances that he tells of the divorce and in a manner similar to that which one would use when describing other reasons for divorce such as infidelity, alcoholism, and continuous personality conflicts. Considering the terrible stigma that homosexuals are still subjected to, this course is also the more courageous. Although the alternative of hiding the homosexuality may protect the man from the criticism and even scorn of many, such withholding is not without its drawbacks. Living with the fear of disclosure is anxiety-provoking, degrading, and cannot but lower the homosexual man's feelings of self-worth. If the homosexual man decides he would rather tolerate the discomforts associated with concealment, he must rely on his wife to comply with his request for secrecy. If she is willing to do this, then the parents might tend to give the children an explanation that is false or evasive. The parents who choose this course should be aware of the already described harmful effects on children of such explanations for the separation and take this into consideration when attempting to conceal the homosexuality from them. I say *attempt* to conceal because such withholding is very difficult to accomplish. Even when the man is not overtly effeminate, his way of life is often sensed as being homosexual by others. And when others learn of or even suspect the father's homosexuality, the children ultimately learn about the father's homosexuality from others or come to appreciate it themselves. It is far preferable that children learn directly about a father's homosexuality than to have it revealed by others or by their figuring it out themselves. When they learn of it via these indirect routes they lose trust in the parent(s) who have withheld this vital information from them and may lose respect for the parent who has not been courageous enough to reveal it. I recognize that there are men whose very livelihood may depend upon their concealing their homosexuality and to reveal it might cause them and their children more psychological damage than would result if the information were withheld. I agree that their concealing the information may be the most judicious choice, but the advantages they gain from such concealment are somewhat counterbalanced by the potential psychological complications of concealment—both for the fathers themselves, their wives, and their children.

If the joint decision is made not to reveal the homosexuality to the children, then the parents do best to tell the children about those causes of the divorce that are not specifically related to the homosexuality, and communicate as well that there are other reasons that are personal and private that they do not wish to divulge at that time. Although such an explanation produces curiosity, it is preferable to evasions, providing alibis, or giving reasons that have no validity. When this is done the children will sense that they are being deceived and the aforementioned problems that can arise from such dishonesty are likely to occur.

If the father requests that his wife not reveal the homosexuality to others and she refuses to respect this request, then such a wife has a choice regarding whether she is going to disclose the information to her children or just to others. If the children are younger than four or five, then informing them of their father's homosexuality is likely to be confusing and they would probably not suffer from such withholding at that time. However, such a mother does well to tell the children when they get older. To choose the course of telling others but not the children runs the risk of their learning it from others or their sensing it themselves, and the consequences of their learning it in this way have already been described. Before telling the children, such a wife does well to try first to decide whether she believes her husband's homosexuality to be a normal human variant or a psychological disorder. This will not be an easy decision for her to make, because mental health experts themselves are sharply divided on this subject. In spite of the difficulties such a wife may have in coming to some conclusion on this matter she does well to try to form some opinion.

A mother who believes that her husband's homosexuality is a manifestation of psychiatric disorder might say: "Most men love women and want to be married to a woman. Daddy really likes men more than women and doesn't want to live with Mommy any more. And he doesn't want to live with any other woman either. I think that this is a sickness. Although I am very sad and angry about this, I also feel very sorry for Daddy that he has this illness." Older children, especially adolescents, should be given a more specific explanation and provided, if necessary, more information regarding exactly what homosexuality involves. (This does not warrant, however, their being given more specific information about the father's private sex life.) The mother does well to impart to the children her belief that homosexuality is a psychological disorder so that they will be more likely to have some compassion for their father and not just resentment over his leaving the household. If the mother does not believe that homosexuality is a psychological disorder, but a normal sexual variation, she might say: "Some men like to be with women and others like to be with men. Daddy has decided that he no longer wants to live with Mommy. Rather, he wants to spend more time with his men friends. I feel very sad that Daddy is this way, because he will no longer be living in the house." Again, older children can be provided a more specific and sophisticated explanation. Such a mother cannot introduce the compassion element that would be appropriate if she were to view homosexuality as a disease. If the mother has no firm conviction about the nature of homosexuality, she would probably do well to try to communicate to the children that there are two opinions on the subject, try to explain as best she can what they are (at the children's level of comprehension), and explain to them that as they get older they will be in a better position to decide with explanation seems most reasonable to them. If the two parents disagree on this issue, they do well to explain to the children that even Mother and Father have different opinions regarding the cause(s) of homosexuality and that as the children get older they will be better able to try to come to some conclusion themselves. If both parents are in agreement that the children be told about the homosexuality, they do well to use the kinds of comments described above.

Although I personally believe that most, if not all, homosexuals are suffering with a psychiatric disorder, I believe that the social stigmatization they have suffered because of their disorder has been cruel, inhumane, and has caused them needless psychological trauma and grief. It is understandable that in such a world a homosexual might not wish to have his sexual orientation generally known. Such a father might want the children to be among the intimate few who are told. Obviously, this course would most likely to be taken after the children are old enough to understand the significance of the divulgence and can be trusted to respect their father's wish not to reveal his homosexuality to others.

As the reader can well appreciate, the question of whether to tell children about a parent's homosexuality is a complex one and whatever course one takes there are likely to be problems. I have discussed the more common issues that must be considered when a parent separates because of homosexuality and have tried to provide some general guidelines regarding the question of whether and what to tell the children. I hope these will be of use, as well, to those whose situations do not exactly coincide with the examples I have provided.

Sally's experiences provide an example of the way in which divulging the cause of a separation can be psychologically valuable to a child. Sally was referred to me at age seven because of disruptive behavior in the classroom and refusal to co-operate with her teacher. She was then in the second grade, extremely bright, and could easily have accomplished her academic tasks. However, because of her failure to concentrate and apply herself, she was functioning at first-grade level.

Her parents had separated about one year prior to Sally's first visit with me. Her mother had initiated the separation because of her husband's alcoholism. He, however, totally denied that he had a drinking problem. He agreed with his wife that he did indeed consume large volumes of alcohol, but considered himself to "have a wooden leg," so that the alcohol had absolutely no effect on him. Sally's mother claimed that her husband's hostile outbursts and sadistic behavior toward her occurred primarily when he was drinking; her father either denied the outbursts and justified them as warranted by his wife's nagging behavior and other provocations which he could not well specify.

When the parents separated, the mother decided that it would not be in Sally's best interest to tell her that her father had a drinking problem. Rather, she said nothing about the causes of the separation and when Sally asked about them she was responded to with evasive answers like "Your father and I just don't get along" and "We just don't love one another any more." On a few occasions Sally pointedly asked her mother about her father's drinking and whether it was the reason for the separation. (She had overheard many arguments over the father's alcoholism.) Sally was emphatically told by her mother that her father did not have a drinking problem. Her father, of course, denied the problem as well, claimed either that there was no such difficulty at all, or told Sally that it was all her "mother's imagination."

With such contradictory explanations it was no surprise that Sally became confused about the reasons for her parents' separation and distrustful of them because of their evasiveness and dishonesty. In my early work with Sally it became apparent that these were important contributing factors to her problems.

In conference with Sally's parents, her father denied that there was any drinking problem and her mother insisted that there was. From what I could learn from a detailed inquiry, I concluded that the father did indeed have a significant drinking problem and that it was not merely his wife's "imagination." I then explained to Sally's father that it was my opinion that it would not only be in his best interests to admit the drinking problem, but in Sally's as well. He angrily responded that my advice proved to him that I was incompetent. He told me that he would no longer pay for treatment, but that if his wife wanted to waste her money on me, he could not stop her. He left the room.

Sally's mother told me that she thought it would cause Sally to lose respect for her father if she were told about his drinking problem. I explained to her that it would reduce somewhat her image of him, but that this would be less harmful to her than the atmosphere of confusion and deceit that had been created by her husband and herself. After further discussion she agreed to tell Sally the truth —which she did the same day. Within the next three weeks Sally asked her mother many questions about her father and not only became clear regarding his drinking problem, but his denial difficulties as well. At my suggestion, the mother tried to convey a sense of compassion for the father, which she was able to do in spite of her anger toward him. I too worked on these issues in my sessions with Sally. Over this period there was a marked improvement in Sally's classroom behavior. Although other problems were still present that had to be worked on, telling Sally the truth about her father's difficulties played a significant role in reducing her own psychological problems. She became less confused and more secure in her relationships with both parents. She now knew she could rely on her mother to provide honest answers to her questions. And with her father she became more knowledgeable about what kind of person he was—areas where she could count on him and those in which she could not.

Withholding the identity of the initiator. It is common for the person who initiates the separation to request that his or her identity not be revealed to the children. The initiator fears that the children will place all the blame on him or her no matter how justifiable the decision was and no matter how much the reluctant spouse contributed to the marital difficulties. Such an anticipation is realistic because it is quite common for children to blame the parent who takes the initiative in the separation and to view the other parent as the innocent party. This notion is further intensified when the spouse who does not wish to separate tells the children that he or she has no desire to divorce and portrays him- or herself as the faultless sufferer who is being unjustifiably rejected.

While the initiator's reluctance is understandable, he or she must accept the fact that his or her identity is not easily hidden from the children. It is far better for them to be directly told rather than their being placed in the situation where they sense things are being withheld from them. It is far better for this information to be revealed by the parents themselves in order to reduce the distrust and distortions that result from concealment. The initiator must also accept the fact that he or she is going to be viewed as the "bad guy"—no matter how justifiable the decision—and that the reluctant spouse is going to be seen as "Mr. Innocent." If the parent who takes the first step apprises the children of his or her identity and, in addition, informs them of the reasons for the decision, there may be some lessening of their tendency to put full blame on the initiator. Being provided with information about the deficiencies in the rejected spouse (real or considered to be real by the initiator) that led to the decision can help the children gain a more balanced view of the causes of the separation. Even if the initiator's views of the repudiated spouse are distorted, they are still believed by the initiator and contributed to the decision. Hearing as well the opinions of the rejected spouse can help the children correct any distortions that may have arisen. Also, as the children grow older they will become more competent themselves to make decisions regarding each parent's role in the marital conflict.

Even with such discussions, in which the children hear both sides, it is likely that the parent who initiates the separation decision will be considered to be more at fault than the hesitant spouse. Such an eventuality should not be a reason for a parent's remaining in a marriage which he or she considers to be miserable. Nor does it justify withholding this important information from the children. Nor does it warrant the initiator's requesting that the rejected parent conceal the initiator's identity from the children. The initiator should be willing to suffer a little mar on his or her repuation for the advantages that will accrue to the children from being given accurate information. To withhold this information may make the initiator a little more comfortable but is a disservice to the children. The parent who takes the first step should have the strength to rely on his or her own assets as the ultimate determinants of how he or she will be viewed by the children. Each parent is likely to be judged by the children on the basis of personality characteristics (both desirable and undesirable) exhibited to the children over years of involvement and experience; not on the basis of whether he or she was the initiator of the divorce decision.

The repudiated spouse does well, then, not to comply with a spouse's request to withhold information regarding who first decided to separate. He or she does well to try to convince the initiator of the problems that can result from attempting such concealment and to encourage divulgence. If, after such discussion, the initiator still refuses to reveal his or her identity, the rejected spouse does well to reveal it. However, to the degree that the reluctant spouse portrays him- or herself as "Mr. Innocent," to that degree he or she does him- or herself, the spouse, and the children a disservice. Although both parents are bound to have somewhat distorted views of one another during this period, they still do well to convey their opinions of one another to the children and hope that with time all parties concerned will gain more accurate views of one another. Simple, straightforward statements of a spouse's deficiencies may result in some loss of respect of the children for the criticized parent. But, as mentioned, there are many benefits to be derived from such awareness. The undesirable psychological effects on the children caused by exposure to and appreciation of such parental deficiencies are generally far less than those resulting from campaigns of vilification and endless hostilities between the parents. This is what should be avoided; not accurate communication of parental assets and liabilities.

Creating an atmosphere of open communication. More important than the information that the children gain from their questioning is the open atmosphere of communication that such interchanges foster. The children cannot generally fully comprehend all at once what is being told them. They will need to repeat their questions over a period of time in order to comprehend what is happening. They must be given the feeling that their questions will be welcomed at any reasonable time and that every attempt will be more to answer them directly and honestly. They will then gain the trust and security that comes when such accurate information is provided. And there is nothing that will more predictably squelch this important experience than parental dishonesty and evasiveness.

Having repeated opportunities to question the parents about the separation enables the children to adjust better to the trauma of the separation. It is not the gaining of information here that makes such repetitious questioning so beneficial, but the *process* of repeating the questions. It is as if each time the children discuss the separation, it becomes a little more bearable. And this desensitization to the pain of the separation is central to the children's adjusting to it. The children's repetitious questioning may serve yet another purpose. It can provide them with reassurances about the parents' interest and availability. The questions then are not asked so much for the information they may furnish but for the opportunity the process of posing them affords the children for involvement with the parents. Parents who appreciate that these factors may be operating when their children repeat the same questions over and over are more likely to be tolerant of the children. Parents who are too quickly put off by such repetitious inquiries will deprive their children of important opportunities to work through in a healthy way their reactions to the separation. Parents do well to appreciate that such questioning by the children may extend over a period of months, and even years. As the children mature they become ever more appreciative of the many factors that may have operated in bringing about the separation. When younger they were not sophisticated enough to ask certain questions, and they should not be deprived of answers just because the inquiries take place long after the event. Regardless of when a child asks a question, the very fact that it has been asked indicates that some issue has not yet been fully resolved.

In providing the children information about the forthcoming separation it is important for the parents to communicate *concrete* information, rather than vague statements. For example, the children should be told exactly when (to the degree possible) the departing parent will leave and exactly where he or she is going to live. As early as possible, the children should have the opportunity to visit the new home of the departing parent. Optimally this should be done prior to that parent's departure. Having a mental image of exactly where he or she will be going lessens anxieties—especially abandonment anxieties. Detailed information should also be provided (if possible) regarding the planned frequency of visitation and the settings in which the visits will occur. Such information can also help the children feel more secure about a continuing relationship with the parent who is leaving the home. If the custodial parent and the children are planning to move (to a smaller apartment or to the home of grandparents, for example) the children should be given as much detailed information as possible (when, where, etc.).

In providing information, however, it is important for parents to appreciate that it is unwise to confront the children with too many facts at once. There are parents who will, in their desire to follow the above advice, dump a barrage of facts on the children and hope that they will be able to sort things out themselves. The children then become overwhelmed and confused and more may be lost than gained by the disclosures. It is for this reason that I generally suggest that the setting where such discussions take place be one in which there is ample opportunity for open discussion in a relaxed fashion. Information can then be provided in piecemeal fashion in accordance with the children's ability to comprehend and absorb it. In addition, parents then have the opportunity to use the child as a guide to determine how much should be given and at what pace.

When it is appropriate not to reveal certain information. There are times when it may be appropriate that the parents not provide a child with information regarding the reason(s) for the divorce. For example, if a father has been involved in criminal behavior and if legal proceedings are under way, it may be detrimental to the father's position if the children were to learn the information and divulge it to others. Such children might then justifiably be given only partial information. For example, they might be told, "Mommy doesn't love Daddy and any more and no longer wishes to live with him." The statement is true, as far as it goes, and so the children have not been lied to. However, vital information has been omitted and so the truth has been compromised. As the children grow older and the disclosure no longer jeopardizes the father's legal position (most legal proceedings ultimately end) then the children can safely be given further information. There are times when identifying a third party involved in the divorce proceedings may be inappropriate and undesirable. For example, if the divorce is the result of a father's having an affair with a married woman and her husband is not aware that she is implicated, it is inappropriate to divulge this information to the children. The parents will probably have to respond differently to the children's questions regarding the identity of the third party in accordance with each one's age and level of sophistication. The younger child may have to be told: "We have answered all of your questions so far and were happy to do so. However, there are certain questions that we will not answer because they are too personal, and this is one of them. Right now we cannot tell you who this person is, but we may be able to do so in the future." An older child might be given more of the reasons that would justify the third party's identity not being revealed.

When a parent suffers with significant psychiatric disturbance. When the divorce is the result of one of the parents suffering with a significant psychiatric disturbance, it is important for the nonafflicted parent to try to communicate to the children a sense of sympathy for the disturbed parent. For example, if a mother has decided that she can no longer tolerate her husband's alcoholism, in addition to telling the children about some of the indignities that she may have suffered because of the father's drinking, she should try to communicate to them the notion that the drinking is a psychiatric illness and cannot simply be cured by willpower. She would do well to tell the children (if they don't know already) about how tolerant she has been and about how much she has tried to be helpful. Although she should express the resentment that she feels, she should also try to engender an attitude of "he's more to be pitied than scorned." A similar approach can be useful when the divorce is the result of a parent's compulsive gambling, drug addiction, or criminal behavior.

Some comments on love. When telling the children about the forthcoming separation, I generally advise parents to mention that they *did* love one another at the time of their marriage (if this was the case, and it generally is). This can provide the children with some security at a time when they are most likely to become quite insecure. Appreciating that they were the products of love—that they were born at a time when their parents wanted them and anticipated that they would be living together—can serve to enhance their feelings of self-worth at a time when their self-esteem is most likely to be damaged. In the same context I also suggest that the parents try to impart to the children the notion that although they do not love one another any more, this does not preclude each of them loving the children. The children must be helped to appreciate that in any triangle consisting of three individuals A, B, and C, that A and B may not love one another, but A and B can each love C. Conversely, C can love both A and B even though A and B do not love one another. Although this may seem like an obvious statement, it may not be obvious to the children and they, more often than not, will conclude that if the parents don't love one another that they too may become unloved. This is not a totally irrational supposition. If Father, for example, can stop loving Mother, what is to stop him from discontinuing his love for his children? The child in a stable home may not consider the possibility that anyone is going to stop loving anybody. For the child in a broken home, such an eventuality is very much in his scheme of things.

The marriage as a mistake. I also advise the parents to communicate to the children that they realize now that their marriage had been a *mistake*. All too often children look upon their parents as perfect. Unfortunately, there are parents who try to perpetuate this myth by withholding any information that would reveal their deficiencies. Although such a practice generally stems from parental insecurity, it is usually justified as being in the best interests of the children to have a perfect image of their parents. Nothing could be further from the truth. Children do best in an atmosphere where they come to see their parents as having both assets and liabilities. Furthermore, they do well to learn which of the parental characteristics are in each of these categories. In this way they will grow up with realistic expectations from others and will be less likely to become disillusioned as each individual ultimately reveals defects. The parental deficiencies should be revealed in natural situations, that is, situations in which the revelation of the defect is warranted and appropriate. Admitting the marriage to have been a mistake is one way in which the parents can provide their children with a healthy sense of their imperfection. Such disclosures can also lessen the likelihood of the children's becoming perfectionistic.

When the "mistake" relates to the fact that the parents have grown apart—without any particular parental defect being the cause of the marital failure—the children should be helping to understand what has happened. Learning firsthand about this cause of marital dissolution may make it less likely that they will make the same mistake in their own marriages in the future.

Reassuring the children that the separation was not their fault. I generally recommend that the parents impress upon the children that the divorce was not the children's fault. Children commonly develop the notion that the divorce was due to their own misbehavior. Although such reassurances may not play a significant role in reducing their delusion of guilt, it may contribute somewhat to its alleviation and so this reassurance should be communicated. When I discuss in detail the guilt reactions of children of divorce (Chapter 4), I will elaborate on the more definitive approaches to the alleviation of this form of guilt, which is extremely common among children of divorce.

Reassuring the children that they will not be deprived of basic necessities. Many children fear that following the separation they will suffer deprivations of vital necessities such as food, clothing, and shelter. Often the children will have overheard parental concerns and conflicts over their forthcoming financial arrangements that will add to their insecurities in this area. It is important, therefore, for separating parents to reassure their children that although things may be tighter, they will all still have enough to eat, a reasonable supply of clothing, and a place to live.

Encouraging emotional expression. When children become very upset and cry on being informed of the forthcoming separation, it is common for parents to make such comments as "See how brave you can be," and "Big boys and girls don't cry." Such comments serve to inhibit the children's natural emotional reactions, can interfere with their adjusting adequately to the separation, and can contribute to the formation of some of the symptoms to be described subsequently. Parents during this period should be encouraging their children's expression of feeling, not squelching it.

I have attempted in this section to cover the common issues that are focused upon when parents discuss separation with their children. It is important for parents to go beyond what I have discussed here and invite their children to raise whatever questions may be on their minds. I have covered here the more common problems. A child may have special concerns of his or her own that are not predictable. These must be given serious consideration. The open discussion of these problems can contribute significantly to the alleviation of difficulties that might have ensued had the issues not been raised or had they been squelched. The mutual inquiry and co-operative discussion that can ensue often serve to reduce the disruption of parent–child relationships that divorce so often brings about.

3

Early Post-separation Adjustment

Telling Friends and Neighbors

There was a time, in the not too distant past, when divorce was generally looked upon as a disgraceful thing. Although social attitudes toward the divorced person have improved significantly in recent years, there are still remnants of this unfortunate attitude on the part of society. For example, a divorced person is generally at a disadvantage when running for public office or when being considered for promotion to a position in which one is very much in the public eye. Rather than being looked upon as someone who has suffered an unfortunate experience, the divorced person is still viewed by many as being somewhat less righteous, psychologically healthy, or moral than those who have never been divorced.

First, parents must come to terms with their own sense of shame. Because of the mar on his or her reputation that the divorced person anticipates, he or she may try to hide the fact as much as possible. This is an unfortunate attitude and can only add to the divorced person's burden. The individual who tries to conceal it reveals that he or she is basically in agreement with those who are prejudiced toward divorced people—that there is indeed something to be ashamed of. Accepting as valid for oneself the social intolerance causes one to feel less worthy at a time when one's self-esteem is already suffering as a result of the failure of the marriage. Worrying about

94

whether the secret will be disclosed cannot but provide the divorced person with another, entirely unnecessary burden. The healthiest attitude that a divorced person can take is that there is nothing to be ashamed about in being divorced and that those who would think less of a divorced individual have some problem of their own. Therefore, the divorce should be disclosed and discussed at appropriate times and in appropriate places, in as matter-of-fact a manner as possible.

If divorced parents deal with the divorce in this way, it is likely that their children will do so as well. If, however, they basically feel shame over what has happened, it is likely that the children will feel it as well. I would go further and say that the most important determinant as to whether the children will be ashamed of the divorce is parental shame. Even if the parents do not directly tell the children how ashamed they are, the children are bound to pick up the parental feelings and react similarly. The first thing that divorced parents must do to prevent their children from becoming ashamed of the divorce is to get it clear in their own minds that there is absolutely nothing shameful about the breakup of a marriage. It is a sad and sometimes tragic event, but in no way is it justifiable to consider it to be a blot on one's reputation. When the parents can genuinely and with conviction believe this, then the children are likely to do so as well. Once having worked this out in their own minds, the parents will not only have created an atmosphere that will make it less likely that the children will not react with shame, but the parents will be in the best position to deal with such shame if the children do exhibit it. The parents who are still basically ashamed of the divorce are not likely to be very effective in helping their children reduce their shame. As with the cigarette-smoking parent who warns his or her youngster about the dangers of the habit, the child is not likely to take the warning seriously. And even when the shameful parent tries to hide the feelings of disgrace, the child will generally sense the parent's underlying attitude, will appreciate the parent's basic lack of conviction for what he or she is saying, and will not profit from the advice.

The reactions of the children's peers.   Once the parents have straightened things out in their own minds regarding the inappropriateness of shame over the divorce, they should advise their children to tell their friends about what has happened. The parents do well not to attempt to discuss in advance with the children any inappropriate reactions that their playmates may have, in order to be prepared to deal with them. To do so is to cause the children to anticipate problems that may never materialize and may add to their fears at this already difficult period in their lives. None of the unhealthy reactions that children may encounter outside the home will generally be that harmful to them that advanced preparation is crucial. Parents do well also to appreciate that their children's friends will generally be threatened by the news and that many of their reactions will be manifestations of their attempts to deal with such threat. For the friends, divorce may have been something that they read about in books and heard takes place elsewhere. However, when it occurs to one's own neighbor, in one's own back yard, so to speak, it gets too close to home and the friends may fear that the same calamity may befall them. One way of dealing with such fears is to become oversolicitous of the child whose parents are separating. A boy, for example, may reveal a surprising degree of sympathy for a little girl whose parents are divorcing, much to the amazement of observers who may never have realized how much sensitivity the youngster had. Actually, what is going on in such a situation is that the boy has identified himself with the girl, sees himself in her, and by consoling her he is really consoling himself. It is as if each time he ministers to her, he is ministering to the projected image of himself that he sees in her. The boy's unanticipated benevolence then takes on new meaning. It is less altruistic than it appears to be and serves more the needs of the consoler than the child who is being consoled—although basic concern for the suffering child's situation may still be present. In addition, in the course of providing comfort the consoler may gain information that may be useful should such a calamity befall him or her.

The problem that may arise from such consolations,

especially if the child is the recipient of such attentions from a number of children, is that the child whose parents are divorcing may become more fearful than he or she was before. Each consoler may tell the child not to worry, and may even enumerate all the things that he or she need not worry about. Accordingly, the child may be introduced to concerns that never entered his or her mind before. When this occurs the parents can only attempt to reassure the child that the particular concern is not valid (if, of course, such is the case). If it is a reasonable concern, then the parent does well to discuss the matter and try to help the child deal with it as effectively as possible. (Most, if not all, of the problems described in this book would serve as examples of the kinds of difficulties that the child may learn about during such periods of consolation by friends.)

Taunting is another reaction from friends that may derive from the sense of threat that the child of divorce produces in his peers. A girl, for example, may respond first with a "there but for the grace of God go I" attitude after learning of the breakup of a little boy's home. Such awareness may be too anxiety provoking and she may then deny her fears with "it can never happen to me" deliberations. This form of self-reassurance can be further strengthend by emphasizing the differences between herself and the boy. "His parents are getting divorced and mine are not" quickly becomes "Ha, ha, your parents are getting divorced and mine are not." The more she mocks the boy, the more superior she can convince herself she is to him, and the more she hopes to reassure herself that his plight will not be hers. It is difficult for a parent to explain to a child what is really going on when he or she is exposed to teasing that serves this purpose. The best that one can do is to try to help the taunted children appreciate that there is something wrong with someone who would laugh at a person who has had a sad experience. Furthermore, children who are so teased have to be helped to appreciate that they are not necessarily what others claim them to be. Another reassurance that can sometimes be helpful is the traditional "sticks and stones may break my bones, but names will never harm me" response. At times, the mocking child is expressing the intolerant attitudes of his or her own parents. In such cases the divorcing parents do well to point out the distortions of thinking that exist in the minds of the adults concerned.

On occasion, the divorce will have occurred because of parental behavior that is socially alienating, e.g., chronic alcoholism, drug addiction, or prostitution. When such problems become known to the community (as they often do) the children may be subjected to terrible ridicule and mockery. It is very difficult to help children rise above such derision and appreciate that there is something significantly deficient in someone who would ridicule a child for the behavior of a parent. Such children have to be helped to see that guilt by association is unjust and that such a defect in a parent does not warrant a child's being scorned similarly. They have to be helped to recognize that the law does not punish children for the crimes of their parents and those who taunt them exhibit their ignorance of this ancient and humane principle. Such children have to be helped to appreciate that if they are friendly and fun to be with, they will be accepted by most for what *they are* and not rejected because of what their *parents are or were.*

Dealing with the child who tries to hide the separation. There are children who may try to hide the divorce from their friends even when there has been no parental contribution to such attempts at concealment. The child may compare himself unfavorably with those who have an intact home and feel different from them. Obviously, such a reaction is more common in situations where the child encounter few, if any, children from divorced homes. Many children equate *difference* with *inferiority* (many adults do so as well) and will therefore feel inferior to peers whose parents are married. Such a child might decide to keep the divorce a secret and go to great lengths to ensure that his disgraceful situation is not revealed to the world. A boy, for example, may tell friends that his father takes numerous lengthy business trips and that is why they never see him in the home. Or he may refrain from inviting friends to his home, lest they become aware of his father's absence. Children who deal with the divorce in this manner add to their burden because they live under the constant threat of disclosure of their secret. A parent should suspect that the child may be resorting to this method of dealing with the separation when there is a sudden reduction in visitors to the home and/or when the child is observed to be finding all kinds of flimsy excuses for not having friends over. Such children have to be helped to appreciate that because one may be different does not mean that one is inferior. That they are no better or worse than a child whose parents are living together—just perhaps a little less lucky. I say *perhaps* because such children also have to be helped to recognize that all parents who stay together are not living in wedded bliss and that many children living in intact homes are far worse off than they. Many children in intact homes are exposed to continual strife and chaos whereas for children of divorce the conflict has most often ended. Lastly, such children must be helped to appreciate that they will ultimately be judged by their friends on the basis of the kinds of people *they* are, not what their *parents* are or were. If they are friendly and fun to be with, they will have friends—even if their parents are divorced. And if they are not, then they will have no friends—even if their parents are married.

Fear of the child's divulging personal family information to friends and neighbors. Parents who follow my advice that they be open and honest to their children regarding the basic reasons for the divorce may be confronted with the problem of what their children will then transmit to their friends and neighbors. This is a difficult problem to which there are no simple answers. First, I believe that one's first obligation with regard to the question of what to tell the children should be to do that which is in the children's best interests. The problems that may arise for parents from possible transmission or leakage of information about the divorce to others are generally not that great that they should refrain from telling the children the basic reasons for the separation. As previously mentioned, I do not suggest that the children be given *all* information, especially that which, if divulged, would cause significant harm to other parties. For example, if revealing the name of a partner in an affair might result in grave consequences to the parties concerned, then such a revelation to the children would not be appropriate. Children should be given the basic facts and they should *not* be given information which, if spread, might cause harm to others. They might be encouraged, however, not to discuss with others some of the things that they have been told, because certain family matters are private. The younger the child, the less likely he or she will be able to be trusted to respect such a request. All children have to learn to appreciate that there are private family matters that are not appropriately discussed with outsiders, and the reasons for a divorce come under this category. Parents should recognize, however, that their children may still divulge some or all of what has been told to them. They should refrain from telling the children those things which, if revealed, would cause significant and unnecessary harm or embarrassment to others; but they should be willing to risk suffering some embarrassment if some of their own personal matters are revealed—because withholding these will contribute to their children's difficulties.

Telling the Teacher

Some parents argue against the teacher's being told about parental separation because they believe that such divulgence is likely to add to the child's difficulties. They fear that the teacher will treat the child differently and make a "special case" out of him or her. And being made a "privileged character" by special attention and indulgence will invite the ridicule and alienation of classmates. Or the parents may anticipate such spectacles as the child's being brought up in front of the class and asked to tell everyone how it feels when one's parents separate. Or they may fear that the teacher will be prejudiced against the child because his or her parents are divorcing, that is, he or she will exhibit the yet common intolerance that many still have toward divorced individuals and their children. Although such reactions by a teacher may certainly occur, I believe that they are rare. Their possible occurrence, however, does not warrant the child's being deprived of the benefits of the teacher's being told.

Some believe that the teacher should not be told unless the children's reactions to the separation draw attention to them in the classroom and disrupt their work there. Only then, they hold, should the teacher be informed so that his or her aid can be enlisted in dealing with the children's difficulties. I find it hard to imagine a child's not reacting strongly to parental separation—even when the separation provides a respite from continual bickering and domestic unhappiness. A parent is still leaving the home —and this cannot but be traumatic. To wait until the child exhibits symptoms may deprive him of valuable early intervention—intervention that might reduce and even prevent the development of more serious reactions. When the teacher has been told in advance about the separation, he or she, possibly more than anyone else, can serve as a substitute for the departed person. Even if the teacher is of opposite sex to the parent who has left, he or she can still serve as a second adult to compensate for the loss the child has suffered. The teacher is with the child six or seven hours a day, five days a week, and is in an excellent position to provide support, reassurance, advice, etc. Furthermore, involving the child in classroom activities (especially pleasurable ones) can serve as an antidote to the child's suffering.

Those who would withhold the information from the teacher are not only depriving the child of important substitutive gratifications but, in addition, are being naïve. It is practically impossible to keep such an event from a child's teacher for a long time. Even if the child does not tell anyone about it, the word invariably gets around. Neighborhood children learn of the event and it soon spreads to classmates. Parental separation creates anxiety among peers. The other children cannot but become frightened that the same calamity may befall them if it can happen so close to home. And a common way of reducing such fear is to discuss the matter at length—among themselves, with their parents, and with individuals such as their teachers. Accordingly, the teacher is bound to learn of the separation. It is far better, therefore, for the parents to tell the teacher themselves so that he or she will have the most accurate information and thereby be in the best position to be of assistance. On the other hand, when a teacher is not told about parental separation he or she is not likely to be as tolerant of the child's abnormal behavior as would be the case when the teacher is forewarned. When not informed, the teacher is more likely to react with disciplinary and punitive measures to such behavior and thereby worsen the child's plight.

Because there may be some teachers who may handle the situation inappropriately does not justify, as a blanket policy, never telling the teacher. A teacher whom the parents suspect might deal inappropriately with the situation might be discouraged from doing so by the parents discussing their concerns with him or her beforehand. My experience has been that most teachers are sympathetic and understanding, and even those who might tend to handle the situation inappropriately can be reasoned with in regard to such tendencies.

Adjusting to Two Households

Children whose parents separate not only must adjust to the fact that one parent will be absent from the home but must also become accustomed to the departed parent's new living arrangement. Immediately following the separation the departed parent's absence becomes very acute. Little things that were taken for granted now loom large, with a kind of deafening silence. Father is no longer shaving in the bathroom and there's no commotion regarding when he'll be finished. The child wishes he were in there and would welcome the traditional battle for priorities. Or Mother is no longer in the kitchen making breakfast and somehow Father just doesn't know how to cook things right. Father's new home looks so small. The new place where Mother is living is all right, but the bed isn't very comfortable. These adjustments make formidable demands upon the child and even with the most sensitive and judicious advance warnings and discussions they still come as a shock. Hearing about something that is going to happen and experiencing the actual occurrence are two very different things, especially for a child.

Not too many changes at once. Separating parents do well not to complicate matters further by making other changes in the child's life at the same time (if they can possibly be avoided). For example, if Father leaves the house and Mother plans to move, she does well to wait a few months at least so that this additional adjustment is not required of the children at the same time as those already mentioned. Parents must appreciate that such a move does not simply involve a change in home atmosphere; it generally involves a change in school, and a loss of friends. It should not be taken lightly and the child does best when he or she has had some chance to recover from the trauma of the separation before being required to adjust to these additional stresses. When a new home has been chosen, the custodial parent does well to show the child the new dwelling at the earliest possible time (even though it may be weeks, and even months, before moving). Having a visual image of exactly where he or she will be living lessens the child's anxiety about the move. Similarly, visiting the new school, seeing the new neighborhood, and if possible meeting the new neighbors, can also reduce the child's fears. The more knowledge one has about an anxiety-provoking situation the less anxiety one generally has about it. And after the move has been made, the parent does well to invite old-neighborhood friends (if practical) as soon as possible in order to smoothen the transition.

Visiting the departed parent's new living arrangements. Prior to the separation the children would have done well to have visited the new living quarters of the departing parent. Such a concrete image of where the parent will be lessens fears of abandonment. After the parent leaves, the children's actually seeing the parent in the new home can reduce further their fears of never seeing that parent again. And the sooner such a visit can be arranged the sooner will this aspect of the children's anxieties be lessened. The children should be provided with the telephone number of the departed parent's new home and encouraged to call with reasonable frequency. Although the content of such calls may appear trivial, they generally serve the more important purpose of the children's gaining reassurance that the absent parent will still be available to them. In addition, such calls can provide the children with opportunities to ask questions and discuss other aspects of the separation which, as described, are important for the children if they are to adjust optimally to the divorce.

Following the departure the parent with whom the children live also does well to keep open the lines of communication. Hopefully the children will continue asking questions and discussing what has been going on. The custodial parent, as well as the absent parent, has the obligation to be available to the children for such interchanges, because they are among the most effective ways of preventing the children's developing psychological problems in reaction to the separation.

Tolerating the children's hostility in the post-separation period.   Both parents should appreciate that considerable hostility on the children's part is a common reaction during this early period. Parents do well not to react to such anger in such a way that their children will become inordinately guilty over their resentment. Parents' tolerance for their children's anger must be increased during this period and they must allow for more disruptive and rambunctious behavior (within limits) than normally would have been permitted in the past. Not to do so fosters the development of excessive guilt over and suppression of anger and this sets the stage for the formation of various unhealthy psychological reactions to the separation. In addition, the children must be helped to direct their anger into appropriate and constructive channels. For example, a girl who is angry because her absent father does not consistently return her telephone calls, should be encouraged to speak with her father about this rather than have temper tantrums as she awaits the call.

The child's assuming the role of the absent parent. Soon after the separation, children of the same sex as that of the departed parent may attempt to assume the role of the parent who has left. This may occur in association with the oedipal impulses that I have previously described. The child with unresolved oedipal problems is more likely to do this than the one who has successfully worked through the oedipal phase. Accordingly, boys may try to take over the role of their father and girls of their mother. Generally, it is only when the parents comply with these tendencies (because of their own problems in this area) that difficulties may arise. If, after a father has left, a boy tries to assume his father's role in the family, the mother does well to permit only a reasonable degree of such identification. In the divorce situation he will have to assume some of his father's obligations and to encourage the assumption of such responsibilities is appropriate. However, is it important for the mother not to encourage such identifications to an unreasonable degree. Comments such as "Now that your father has left, you're going to be the man of the house" and "From now on you're going to be like my husband" are inappropriate for a mother to make and reveal excessive encouragement of the boy to assume the father's position. It is reasonable to allow the boy some cuddling and short periods of resting together in his mother's bed (as is appropriate, in my opinion, when the father is present). However, if a boy begins sleeping in Mother's bed throughout the night, on a continual basis, the likelihood that oedipal problems will arise is great. Both mother and son are entitled in such a situation to some compensatory affection, physical contact, and solace with one another. However, when such contact and involvement become intensified and prolonged, and when seductive elements are introduced, then the likelihood is great that psychological problems will result. And what I have said about the relationship between a mother and son holds equally for a father and

daughter when they are the ones who remain together
following the separation. Of course, the same problems
can arise when a child visits an opposite-sexed departed
parent and the same warnings hold.

The perpetuation of parental hostilities. Immediately
following the separation there is likely to be a continuation of the same hostilities that brought about the separation in the first place. It is important for parents to
appreciate that the longer these are perpetuated, the
greater the likelihood the children will suffer harmful reactions to the divorce. During this period, frequent contact
between the parents is necessary in order for them to
work out the innumerable arrangements associated with
the separation. Generally, their hurt feelings and resentments color practically every negotiation and transation.
I cannot emphasize strongly enough the importance of
parents attempting to resolve their difficulties as soon as
possible: the longer the hostilities continue, the greater
the likelihood their children will become disturbed. I am
not simply suggesting that parents suppress their resentments or argue outside of the children's presence (both
of which have a place in reducing the child's exposure to
their hostilities). Rather, the parents must do everything
possible genuinely to resolve their remaining difficulties
in the most civilized fashion. The failure to do so is one of
the most predictable ways of producing psychological
disturbances in the children.

Time Alone Together

The most potent preventive of psychological disturbance
and one of the most effective antidotes to such disorder is
the parent's spending varied periods of time alone together with each child. I usually recommend to all parents, regardless of whether their child is in therapy, and
regardless of whether the parents are divorced, that they
set aside a time every day when they can be alone with
each child without distraction or interruption. Each sibling should have his own time, from which the others
are firmly excluded unless others are invited by mutual

agreement. And this time alone together should be canceled only under unusual circumstances. It should have the highest priority for both parents and child.

These periods are most effective when both parent and child are genuinely enjoying themselves. If the parent only *pretends* enjoyment in a game or activity, the child will sense the inevitable resentment stemming from the parent's reluctant involvement, and the time spent together will thereby become a detrimental experience for the child. This time can also be profitably used for talking about one's feelings and for sharing the day's experiences —for finding solace, commiseration, and understanding, and for relating anecdotes, achievements, and disappointments. Or the parent and child might spend the time reading together, playing games, or listening to music. It is during these moments of shared feeling and empathy that loving feelings flourish, and both the child and the parent become enriched by them. Such experiences deepen the relationship between the parent and child and thereby serve to protect the child from developing the various kinds of difficulties that arise from impairments in the parent–child relationship. Such periods of time along together can be most effective in assuaging the pain and frustration of children whose parents have just separated. These shared times together are even more vital during the post-separation period than at other times and can be extremely valuable in warding off and preventing post-separation psychological disorders. For the custodial parent such times alone together should take place every day. And for the parent who lives away, every day of visitation. I cannot recommend them strongly enough.

4

Dealing with Children's
Post-separation Problems

Denial of the Separation and Its Implications

Denial is one of the most primitive of the psychological mechanisms that one can use to protect oneself from feeling mental pain. What easier way is there to avoid suffering the painful psychological reactions to a trauma than to deny its existence? The person protects himself from such pain by blotting from conscious awareness the fact that the trauma exists. Generally, an individual does not consciously decide to do this; it is an unconscious process. The person is unaware of the painful situation and does not recognize that the blindness to it has been self-induced. The ease with which one can utilize this protective mechanism is often dependent on how frequently it is resorted to by people around one, especially family members. Accordingly, the family pattern plays a significant role in determining whether the child of divorce will utilize this mechanism.

Parental contribution to children's denial. There are certain parental personality characteristics and ways of dealing with children that may contribute to their developing the denial mechanism as a way of handling the separation trauma. There are parents, for example, who believe that fighting in front of their children will necessarily be detrimental to them. Although they may have had serious disagreements between them, throughout their marriage they have strictly refrained from arguing with one another in front of the children. Continual squabbling in front of the children is certainly harmful to them. On the other hand, witnessing occasional arguments between their parents, arguments that are neither violent nor sadistic, can be a useful experience for them. It helps them appreciate that no one is perfect and that in every marriage there are times of conflict and friction. Such exposure makes it less likely that they will have unrealistic views of what constitutes a reasonably stable marriage. Accordingly, it is less likely that they will become disillusioned in real relationships and possibly even divorce because of such disappointment. Parents who never fight in front of their children provide them with a continuous lesson in inappropriate suppression of angry feelings. Although a fight may represent a failure in the parents' ability to settle their differences in a more civilized manner and to have dealt with the conflict at earlier stages of irritation, it should inevitably occur, at times, in the healthy marriage, because no one can handle all conflicts in an ideal and judicious way. This is the normal and expected environment in the relatively intact home. The parents who strictly enforce the rule of never fighting in front of their children may contribute to their becoming inhibited in expressing anger. Accordingly, they may contribute to their children's repressing their angry reactions to the divorce (reactions that are inevitable) and contribute thereby to their denying their angry feelings.

There are parents who are basically silent and non-communicative people. The general atmosphere in the home is a quiet one and people may only communicate about matters that are essential to the proper functioning of the household. Such parents may be especially inhibited in expressing feelings. Accordingly, they will serve as models for such suppression in their children. When a separation takes place they are not likely to communicate very much regarding details of what is going on, especially their emotional reactions. In such an atmosphere it is hard to imagine their children's not developing similar denial patterns themselves.

As previously described, there are parents who will

justify their not giving their children information about the separation with excuses such as "They're too young to understand," and "They're too young to have it affect them." For example, a father may leave the home with absolutely nothing said to the children. If the youngsters do ask questions no explanations for the departure are given, again with the rationalization that they are too young to understand. Such parents, of course, usually have other reasons for not communicating the separation to the children—for example, guilt and shame. And such withholding of vital information is likely to contribute to the children's denying their own thoughts and feelings about the separation.

The denial mechanism is an extremely powerful one. The human being's ability to blind him- or herself to the obvious is at times astounding. There are people who will take a few days to accept the fact that a loved one has indeed died. Many soldiers will enter combat with the delusion that others around them may be killed but that they somehow are immune. Similarly, there are parents who will actually separate and, amazingly, act then as if the separation had not taken place. Although living in separate domiciles, they will act as if nothing new has happened. Each goes about his or her business as if life will continue just as before. Father's empty chair is ignored and supper is served without any reference to the fact that an important family member is missing. Such parents will usually admit, if asked, that they are living separately but deny that there are any other effects of the separation, either on themselves or the children. The children of such parents are likely to follow the parental pattern and deny themselves that they have any untoward reactions. They, too, may continue living as if there were no changes.

Parents who actively encourage their children to suppress their emotional reactions to the divorce may also contribute to the development of the denial mechanism. Comments such as "Be brave" and "Boys don't cry" foster suppression of emotions and contribute thereby to the development of the denial adaptation. When the child complies with such parental advice he or she is considered to have "taken it well" and is praised for his or her "maturity" and forebearance. Reacting stoically to a traumatic experience is a highly sanctioned quality in our culture. The woman who doesn't cry when her husband dies is said to have "taken it well." At the time of President Kennedy's assassination hardly a television announcer did not compliment the President's wife, Jacqueline, on her forbearance, and people in high places serve as models for the rest.

There are parents who, following the separation, will act as if the party who is no longer living in the home has never existed. When the absent parent has totally abandoned the family, he or she still exists in memory and to deny this deprives the children of the opportunity to express their reactions and work them out. In addition, it contributes to the development of their denying the event. However, in the usual situation, where the absent parent is very much involved, the utilization of this reaction by the remaining parent requires an even greater degree of denial of reality; yet it may be utilized and the children encouraged to react similarly. The remaining parent may strictly avoid any mention of the absent parent and act not only as if he or she doesn't now exist but also as if he or she had never existed. And the children, in order to remain in the good graces of the parent with whom they live, may react similarly.

Common ways in which children deny the separation. There are children who will deny the separation without significant parental model, encouragement, or active contribution. Because it is such a primitive mechanism and so easily utilized, it is not surprising that children may resort to it with facility. A child may react to the announcement of the separation with such calm that the departing parent may question the child's involvement and affection. Generally, such a reaction is not related to the absence of a feeling of loss. Rather, it may be a manifestation of the child's failure to appreciate time lapses. To the average preschooler, there is little if any appreciation of differences among waiting periods of three days, three weeks, or three months. Or it may relate to the child's inability to appreciate fully an occurrence until he or she actually observes it ("If I don't *see* it happening, then it's *not* happening"). Or it may be a manifestation of the child's wish to deny that the separation will take place. Even after a parent has left and the remaining parent repeatedly invites the child to express his or her reactions, there may be none forthcoming. Even though the child may be told that the departed parent is no longer going to be living in the home, he or she may repeatedly ask when the parent is going to return. Each time the child questions as if he or she had never before been told the answer.

On occasion children will hide their anxieties by viewing the separation as a newsworthy event. They will excitedly tell their friends about their "calamity" but do so in such a way that the observer readily senses that the pleasure they are getting from the attention they are receiving while reporting the news seems to far outweigh any grief they may be suffering. Such a denial mechanism is most frequently seen before the actual separation. Once the child has the living experience that the parent is no longer in the home this "laughing on the outside crying on the inside" mode of adjustment generally breaks down and the tears may burst forth.

There are children who are told specifically the facts of the separation and who yet will speak and fantasize about the absent parent's returning. They make such statements as: "Daddy comes home very late, after I fall asleep. He leaves very early in the morning, before I wake up." "Mommy's living at Grandma's house. Grandma told me." "Daddy's working late." "Mommy's coming home very soon." And "Daddy's on a business trip."

A child may deny any concerns over the separation but may become very concerned over the welfare of another person or a pet. Such a child is displacing his or her worries over the well-being of the departed parent onto a substitute. The result is that the child, while obsessively concerned with the welfare of a pet, appears to be oblivious to the fact that a parent has just left the household forever. This type of denial mechanism is often seen in patients suffering fatal diseases. When visited in the hospital they talk little about themselves but become excessively concerned over the most minor illnesses of their friends and relatives. In a related type of denial the child takes an attitude of "It's their problem, not mine." In this attitude of "I couldn't care less" the child denies his own concerns and sees the problem to be entirely that of his parents. But rather than show sympathy for them he or she exhibits disdain and scorn—a reflection of the anger that is felt toward the parents.

Sometimes a child's denial may relate to fear of and guilt over expressing anger. What appears to be denial is more a manifestation of inhibition in expressing the inevitable angry feelings that the separation has produced. The child fears saying anything about the separation lest his or her angry feelings become revealed in the process. Often, such inhibitions are the result of parental attitudes toward the child's expressing hostile feelings.

Some children involve themselves in play and fantasy that serves the function of restoring the absent parent. A boy, for example, may fantasize that he is involved in various activities with his father, e.g., driving in the car or sailing. Or the child may play the role of the absent father in such games as "house." Although this is to a certain degree normal, the child of divorce may become obsessed with such a role. By identifying with the absent parent the child hopes to regain him or her. On occasion, this mechanism may operate following the death of a parent. A child (and even adults exhibit this) may suddenly (it seems to appear overnight) take on many of the qualities of the absent parent: vocal intonations, gestures, personality characteristics, and even opinions. At times the transformation is almost uncanny.

At times a child will fantasize that he or she is actually with the departed parent. This usually occurs at the age of from two to four years, the time when children most commonly develop imaginary friends. The child will talk to the invisible parent as if he or she were still there and becomes involved in prolonged games with the fantasized parent. In addition, the child may exhibit many of the other behavioral patterns that typified his or her involvement with the fantasized parent. The child may express resentment when someone sits down in the chair often occupied by the departed parent and loudly exclaim to someone who is seated in that chair: "Get out of that chair. You're sitting on my mother." When leaving home the child may cry out to the mother: "We forgot to take Daddy. He's still inside." The child may then return to the home and bring along the fantasized father.

Idealization of the absent parent, with an associated denial of any deficiencies, is a common reaction. Parents' strictly refraining from criticizing one another can foster such idealization. Related to such idealization is the denial that an absent parent is disinterested. In the extreme, a child may still insist that the departed parent still loves him or her even though the parent has neither been seen nor heard from in many years. The notion is obviously related to the child's wish to avoid the painful realization that the absent parent no longer loves him or her. An abandoned mother, whose husband has not been heard from in years, may foster such denial in her son with comments such as "Your father still loves you, he just can't show it." Although such a comment may be well meaning on the part of the mother, it is misguided. The parent in such a situation is obviously trying to protect the child from the traumatic effects associated with the realization that his father has abandoned the family and does not love him. Such a mother does better to confront the child with the painful reality and impress upon him that the deficiency lies in the abandoning father, rather than in the boy. She should help the child appreciate that there is something seriously wrong with a parent who cannot love his own child. In addition, she should also encourage the child to involve himself with others, both peers and adults, who will demonstrate that he is still lovable. The child must be helped to realize that although his own natural parent may not love him, it does not follow that no one else in the whole world can either.

Commonly, children will react as if they were denying having any reactions to the announcement, because it has not come as a surprise. For months, and even years, they may have been seeing and hearing their parents fighting and talking of divorce. (Parents are often amazingly oblivious to their children's witnessing their altercations.) Accordingly, when the announcement is finally made they do not exhibit strong reactions because they have been accommodating themselves to the event for a long time.

Dealing with children's denial. It is important for parents to appreciate that the denial mechanism, although most often maladaptive, is created to produce a certain degree of psychological stability. We all must utilize a certain amount of denial if we are to remain sane. Were we clearly to see every danger and emotionally react to all traumas—past, present, and potential—it is unlikely that we could preserve our sanity. All of us must build a psychological cement wall around ourselves if we are to gain protection from the multiple painful stimuli that bombard us.

There are times when it is a disservice to a child for a parent to attempt actively to remove the denial mechanism. The most obvious example of this is the way we deal with a person who is dying. The woman with a fatal disease who displaces fears of her own well-being onto others should not be told that her real concerns have have nothing to do with her friends and relatives but are merely displacements of her concerns about herself. I am not suggesting that one routinely support denial mechanisms exhibited by a person who is dying; rather, I am suggesting that they be respected. Sometimes denial may deprive the person of lifesaving treatment. At such times denial mechanisms should not be respected. At other times, no purpose is served by attempting to get the person to see reality clearly. Some dying people may wish to discuss their real feelings; others may not. Although the attempt to remove the denial mechanism in a dying person may be inhumane, it is generally not cruel to attempt to do so in a child of divorce. The repercussions from such removal are not generally so detrimental.

Most often, the utilization of the denial mechanism by children of divorce is maladaptive. Although they may be protecting themselves from some psychological pain, the use of the mechanism most often is ill advised. Its maintenance interferes with the development of healthier adjustments to the separation. Direct discussion of the child's utilization of this mechanism is generally anxiety provoking. Parents who try the direct head-on approach, by repeatedly confronting such children with their distortions, may find that the children respond with even more adamant adherence to their denial mechanisms. In such cases I recommend pulling back and allowing time and experience slowly to have their opportunity to help the child see more clearly the reality of the situation.

Parents whose children exhibit the kinds of denial I have described do well to examine their own behavior and determine whether they have been contributing to their children's denial in the ways I have discussed. Parents who try to reduce their children's denial of the separation and its implications while utilizing denial themselves are not likely to be effective in helping their children give up the denial form of adjustment.

Child therapists well appreciate that children will discuss their difficulties much more readily when talking about third parties, animals, and other symbols of themselves. Children's self-created stories and verbalized fantasies can be a valuable source of information about underlying problems that they are dealing with. Often, the particular concerns that the child may be denying, both to himself and others, may be thinly disguised by such stories. Although it may be obvious to adults that children are really talking about themselves in such stories, it is generally not apparent to the younger children—especially those under the age of seven or eight. By discussing with such children the events in the lives of the symbolic figures one can impart important communications to them without their experiencing the anxiety they would have if they knew they were talking about themselves.

Although mental health professionals are often trained to understand such stories, some are so obvious that many parents without such training can readily interpret them.

With the increased understanding of what is going on in the child that such stories may provide, the parent may be in a better position to help the child. For example, a boy who appears unperturbed by his father's departure may tell a story in which a dog's father runs away and the dog is left starving and can only get food by hunting for it in garbage cans. The dog in this story obviously represents the little boy, who sees himself as having to resort to scrounging for food from garbage cans after the departure of his father. I will respond to such a story with one in which the same dog fears that collecting food from garbage will be his fate after his father departs, and he even spends restless nights dreaming of himself searching for food in garbage cans. However, he is reassured by his older-brother dog that they still have their mother, who then proves herself to be an adequate provider. In this way, I affirm that the absence of his father does not mean that the child is totally abandoned. He still has his mother. I do not deal directly with the denial mechanism but rather with the underlying factors that have contributed to its formation and perpetuation. Hopefully, when such a child is reassured that his mother will still take care of him *and when she proves to do so,* he will more readily accept the separation. In working with such a child I may or may not try to help him understand the true underlying meaning of his story. If I sense that he will be made anxious by such direct confrontations, I will confine my discussions to the symbolic representations. We talk about the dog, for example, and how *he* can best deal with *his* father's departure. If the child can tolerate discussions of the real issues being dealt with then, of course, I am happy to engage him in such conversations. Although dealing with such stories and fantasies is best done by a trained therapist, many of the stories are so transparent that many parents should be able to make use of them for the benefit of their children. The basic principle to follow is that if one can alleviate some of the fears that underlie and contribute to the child's denial, the child is less likely to deny. And when the denial is reduced the child is in a far better position to deal effectively with the separation.

Grief

Similarities between grief following divorce and grief following death. Although there are definite differences between the reactions children may experience following a divorce and those they may suffer after the death of a parent, there are certain similarities as well. One such similarity is the occurrence of a grief reaction. A discussion of the grief reaction following the death of a loved one can be helpful in understanding the grief that children may feel at the time of separation. Generally, after the death of a loved one the mourners become preoccupied with thoughts of the departed person. This preoccupation provides for a piece-by-piece desensitization to the trauma. Each time one thinks about the dead person the pain associated with his or her loss becomes a little more bearable. The phenomenon is similar to the kind of reaction soldiers may suffer in response to extremely traumatic combat conditions. In "shell shock" or the "combat neurosis" the individual relives in fantasy and dreams the battlefield traumas and may even hallucinate the shells falling around him. Most are familiar with war movies in which such a soldier, while in a military hospital, wakes up at night in panic and dives under the bed to protect himself from the shells that only he hears. Although each repetition may be associated with terrible states of terror, there is a gradual reduction in the intensity and frequency of the panic states. Such repetition appears to be part of the natural process of accommodating to a trauma. Although such a soldier appears to be "sick," the sickness in this case is actually the curative process. The doctors can do little in such situations but to protect the man from hurting himself and causing undue alarm to others, while awaiting the desensitization to run its course. Even though tranquilizers might reduce somewhat the soldier's anxiety, one would not want to remove totally the preoccupation. If one could do so, one would be depriving the man of the opportunity to desensitize himself and thereby to adjust optimally to the traumas he has suffered. Similarly, following a death the mourners may not only talk at length about the loves one, but may utilize various possessions of the departed person as a focus for such discussions. Objects that may have previously been of little significance now become treasured mementos. They not only provide a symbolic link with the departed person, but can serve as a focus for desensitizing preoccupations and discussions. For the purpose of this discussion, I will use the term grief to refer to this desensitizing process, the purpose of which is to enable the individual to adjust optimally to a loss. Once this is accomplished the individual is then free to involve himself in a substitutive relationship. If grieving does not occur, the person may not adjust adequately to the loss and various kinds of psychological abnormalities may also result.

Helping children grieve.   Although children of divorce do not actually lose a parent, they may never again live with the departed parent and are likely to react grievously to the separation. In fact, considering the healthy purposes of the grief reaction, I would consider it unhealthy if a child who is old enough to appreciate what is occurring did not react with grief. However, in those rare situations where the child actually welcomes the separation because it promises a cessation of the misery he or she has been suffering, then the failure to have a grief reaction would of course not be a sign of a psychological problem. Parents who inhibit their children in expressing their feelings by such comments as "Be brave" and "Big boys and girls don't cry" will generally squelch their natural expression of grief. Parents who will not cry and express other emotions of remorse and regret in front of the children—in the misguided belief that it is best to protect them from such displays—serve as poor models for their children's expressing their grief. Parents who show little tolerance for their children's repetitious questioning may be depriving them of the repeated discussion and preoccupation that are crucial if the grief reaction is to provide desensitization and release of the emotions caused by the loss. Only by such release can the children achieve the psychological relief necessary to their avoiding the problems due to pent-up feelings. And, of course, parents who provide little or no information about separation further impede their children's profiting from a grievous response. Such information provides issues for preoccupation and stimulates emotional release. It gives the children specific things to think about and particular concerns over which they can have emotional reactions. Without such data there is less chance children will grieve. In addition to the value of the specific information gained, the *process of acquiring and receiving the information* in itself enables the children to reassure themselves of parental interest and involvement.

Although children of divorce may not need mementos of the departed parent (the real person is usually still available), they should have the opportunity for frequent contact with the person who has left the home, either personally or via telephone. Parents should recognize as well that withdrawal into fantasy during this period need not represent an impending psychiatric deterioration; rather, it can serve as part of the grieving process and enable the child to work through his reactions to the separation. Play fantasy may serve similar purposes. For example, a little girl may re-enact with her dolls the various events concerning the separation. Each time she does this the pain becomes a little more bearable. Or she may play that she is visiting her father in his new home and thereby lessen the pain of her separation. Or a child may become preoccupied with a storybook that depicts either directly or symbolically events related to the separation. Stories in which a parent leaves or is removed from the home lend themselves well to such utilization by the child. Often a story with a happy ending is selected, one in which the parent returns. Obviously, such selection relates to the story's wish-fulfillment potential for the child. Parents must appreciate what is going on in such preoccupations and not discourage children from indulging themselves in them to some degree. Only when children become so preoccupied that they neglect significantly important areas of functioning (such as school and peer play) should such withdrawal be discouraged. When such fantasies have served their purpose, and if the child has generally adjusted well to the separation, the time devoted to such fantasies will gradually diminish.

Differences between grief following divorce and grief following death. Following divorce an identifiable mourning reaction is less frequently seen than following the death of a parent. This is partly due to the fact that there is less of a loss. A parent's living elsewhere (even at a great distance) is a very different thing from a parent's being dead. Secondly, death is a sudden event—no matter how long anticipated. Separation, on the other hand, is the next step in a series of events that have slowly led up to it. It is rarely as shocking as death, therefore more easily accommodated to, and so less mourning is required to deal with it. When one adds to these factors the child's tendency to deny, as well as parental grief-suppressing influences, it is not surprising that so few children mourn overtly at the time of the separation. In spite of its infrequency, it does occur and I believe that it is preferable that it should. It behooves parents to encourage its development and expression, because failure to do so may result in the child's developing disturbed responses to the separation. There is no single type of unhealthy reaction exhibited by the child who has not had a grief reaction to the separation. Rather there are a host of problems that can result from such suppression. Many of the symptoms described in the remainder of this chapter result from the failure of children to have expressed their thoughts and feelings about the separation.

Sadness and Depression

Unless the children react with relief to the separation because it brings about a cessation of parental strife in the home (the rare situation) the children are bound to be sad over the departure of one of their parents. I will use the term *sadness* to refer to the milder state of unhappiness with which children may respond to the separation and the term *depression* to the deeper and more painful state of sorrow that may result from the parental departure. Sadness is the more common and predictable state.

Depression is usually an outgrowth of the sadness and generally suggests that psychological problems are present in the child, in the parent(s), and in their relationships with one another. Because normal sadness may evolve into depression there may be times when one may have difficulty making the differentiation. Nevertheless, the distinction may be useful. Sadness usually subsides with time and is generally of short duration. Depression may last for a considerable period of time and since psychological problems are usually contributing, additional symptoms are present and treatment (for the child and/or the parent) may be necessary if it is to be alleviated.

Sadness.   Probably the main manifestation of sadness in children whose parents have separated is diminished capacity for pleasure. The things that had previously produced enjoyment in such children no longer seem to have the capacity to do so. Accordingly, these children may no longer be able to derive pleasure from play or from watching their favorite television programs. When they do play they may become preoccupied with themes involving a search for a lost loved one, or the magic reappearance of someone who has disappeared. Or they may not be able to enjoy spending time with peers and may withdraw from them. They may walk around in a forlorn state and resort to their daydreams as their primary source of gratification. Sometimes such children may try to escape from their feelings of sadness by compulsive involvement in physical activities or their academic pursuits. Some do all right in school, where they can become distracted from their unhappiness; but when home alone they become absorbed in their unhappy preoccupations. Some try to deny their sadness with comments such as "It doesn't bother me" and "I'm happy all the time." Most observers, however, recognize that these children are "laughing on the outside and crying on the inside." The stiff-upper-lip front usually doesn't hold up too long and they may burst out in tears at times, only to resume again the facade. The sadness of many such children may be deepened by their feelings that they have ben abandoned because they are not worthy of affection and that no one can possibly ever like them.

For most children there is gradual improvement in the unhappy state. Similar to what happens after the death of a parent, they somehow adjust to the loss, involve themselves once again in their previous activities and sources of pleasure, and give up their unhappy preoccupations. The most important determinant as to whether such sadness will be short-lived is the rapidity with which they become reassured that the absent parent is still involved. In addition, if the parents are able to avoid involving themselves in significant power struggles, then it is likely that the sadness will go away even more rapidly. If, however, these sad children do not have these healthy experiences, it is possible that the sadness will continue and turn into depression.

Depression.   A state of depression in children is usually characterized by: loss of appetite; diminished interest in and concentration on studies; general apathy; loss of enjoyment from play and peer relationships; helplessness; hopelessness; irritability; obsessive self-criticism; and withdrawal. In addition, some children exhibit feelings of impotence and vulnerability, extreme boredom, inability to complete projects and assignments, poor motivation, low frustration tolerance, and inability to use play to work out their reactions to the separation. In severe cases depressed children may become preoccupied with self-destructive fantasies, become accident-prone and unconcerned for their personal safety, and may exhibit suicidal gestures and even attempts. The full-blown picture, of course, does not have to exist to justify using the term—there are varying intensities of depression that would warrant the label. Because of their natural lightheartedness (as well as the ease with which they can utilize primitive denial mechanisms) children tend not to become as readily depressed as adults in response to traumatic events. However, parental separation is a depressing event and children do become depressed in response. In part, the depression of such children is a reaction to the separation. The loss of a parent from the home *is* something to be depressed about. Accordingly, it is one of the expected reactions to the separation. If few or none of the additional factors to be mentioned contribute to or entrench the depression, it should lift within a few weeks (or months, at the most). The healthy human being is quite resilient—and children are especially so. If the depression persists, it is likely that other factors are contributing to its perpetuation—factors within both the children and parents.

In children who have not exhibited a healthy mourning experience, the pent-up feelings may contribute to a general feeling of discontent. Emotional expression is followed by feelings of psychological cleansing and even elation; whereas suppressed feelings continually press for release. The internal psychological conflict produced between the feelings that press for release and the forces that repress them is emotionally draining and anxiety-provoking. Such states rob one of the capacity for enjoyment and contribute to depression. Accordingly, parents of children who have not had a grief reaction do well to attempt to help them have a mourning experience—even though belated. They do well to encourage such children to talk about their reactions to the separation, point out the value of crying and releasing one's feelings, and should serve as models for such release themselves.

Another factor that may contribute to children's being depressed is parental depression, especially in the parent with whom the child lives. If the custodial parent welcomes the separation and sees it as an opportunity for a better life, it is likely that the children will take a more positive attitude toward it as well. If, however, the custodial parent becomes distraught and depressed and views it as the end of his or her life, then the children are likely to react similarly.

The loss of a loved one is one of the most important factors that can cause an individual to become depressed. And children of divorce have certainly sustained such a loss. Healthy children are usually able to tolerate this loss, because they generally have another parent who can help to make the deprivation more tolerable. In addition, they have the capacity to find substitute gratifications with other adults. Accordingly, the depression of such children is usually short-lived. If, however, the child has been overdependent on the absent parent, the loss is felt much more sharply and the depression may become more severe. The feelings of helplessness may become profound as the child comes to fear that he or she cannot survive. Sometimes, such a child has been overprotected by the departed parent and made to feel that his or her very existence depends upon the maintenance of a close tie with the parent. Such children must be helped to understand *and* experience that they have the capacity to function without the absent parent and that survival does not depend upon his or her continuous presence. In addition, if overprotective parents can reduce their pampering and indulging their children, this too can contribute to the alleviation of the children's depression.

Another factor that may contribute to depression in children whose parents have separated is interpreting the parent's leaving as a rejection and abandonment of themselves, rather than of the remaining parent. Such children may not only consider the parent's leaving as a statement that they are not loved, but, in addition, that they are not lovable. A girl whose father has left the home (however benevolently) may reason: "If he loved me, he would stay. His leaving means that he doesn't love me. If he doesn't love me no one can love me. I am unlovable!" The resultant feelings of self-loathing contribute to the child's depressive reaction. In working with such a child I would try to help her appreciate that in any triangle of three people, A, B, and C, A and B can dislike one another, but each can love C. I try to help her recognize that her father still loves her, even though he no longer loves her mother; and that her mother still loves her, even though she no longer loves her father. In situations where there is indeed some deficiency in the absent parent's affection, I try to help children appreciate that this does not mean that they are unlovable. I try to help them understand that the deficiency lies more in the unloving parent than in themselves—that the parent who has little, if any, love for his own children is a defective person. If I can get such children successfully to gain affection from substitutes, this message is more likely to be incorporated as the child has living experiences that verify it.

Anger is one of the inevitable feelings children experience at the time of parental separation. This is not surprising considering the fact that such children are losing one of their most treasured possessions—a parent. Some children are very inhibited in expressing their anger. Often they grow up in households where they were made to feel guilty about their angry feelings—especially those felt toward their parents. Even without a family environment that induced inhibition in anger expression, children of divorce are in a particularly difficult position regarding the expression of their anger. They may fear expressing anger toward the departed parent, lest they see even less of him or her; and they may fear directing it toward the custodial parent, lest he or she too will abandon them. Many psychological symptoms are caused by such pent-up anger. The guilt such children feel over releasing their anger and/or the punishments they anticipate for such expression prevent them from revealing it. They may, however, direct it against themselves—thereby accomplishing its release without guilt or fear of retribution. The target is a safe one and can be relied upon not to retaliate. The most common manifestations of such self-directed anger are the self-critical comments with which some of these children become obsessed. They may berate themselves mercilessly with comments such as "I'm no good," "I'm terrible," "I can't do anything right," and "I'm worthless." And such self-criticism contributes to the child's depression. An observer may find such self-berating confusing because there doesn't seem to be anything the child is doing or saying to warrant such severe self-loathing. The comments become readily understandable when one replaces in such statements the name of the child with the name of the actual person at whom the child is angry (generally one or both of the parents). "I'm no good" then becomes "He (or she) is no good." "I'm terrible" becomes "He (or she) is terrible," and so on. When such children can be helped to express more guiltlessly the anger they feel toward the primary target they will have less need to direct their anger against themselves and hence will be less depressed.

Some children exhibit their depressive tendencies via self-destructive preoccupations, accident proneness, and even suicidal tendencies. Although suicide is rare among children below the age of twelve, it certainly does occur. It is often difficult to differentiate in this young age group bona fida suicides from death resulting from feigned attempts in which the child's poor judgment resulted in his accidentally killing himself. A significant percentage of the bona fide suicide attempts by children in this age group occur among those from broken homes. Despair and loneliness associated with feelings of being unloved and unwanted may be too much for such children to bear and they may take their lives. A revenge element is often present. A boy, for example, may have the fantasy that his parents, whom he sees as rejecting, will be painfully guilty over the way they have maltreated him. He may fantasize being buried while his guilty parents cry out remorsefully how bad they feel about their neglect of him and how they wish that they could once again have the chance to show their affection. But it is too late; they must live with their guilt. Sometimes the suicidal attempt is associated with a desire for death and rebirth into a happier life with truly loving parents—parents who never divorce. Some children feel so insecure and inadequate that they do not feel that they can survive without the loving care of both parents and so they kill themselves rather than suffer a slow, torturous death.

George, a nine-year-old boy who was referred to me for treatment, demonstrated well the relationship between denial, repressed hostility, and depression. George's father was a heavy drinker who could not keep a job because of his alcoholism. His mother, a masochistic woman, not only supported her husband but meekly submitted to his verbal and physical abuse as well. George too was beaten frequently by his father, even as early as the age of nine months. Finally, when George was three, his mother left her husband and returned to the home of her mother. During the following year George saw his father on two occasions. Once the father took him to the movies and once he was taken along while the father visited with drinking friends. After the age of three George never saw his father again and at the time of referral the father's whereabouts were unknown.

George came to treatment because of depression. Few activities gave him pleasure. Although a good student, he got little enjoyment from his academic accomplishments. He had little interest in being with friends became he got so little pleasure from playing with them. He criticized himself mercilessly over the most minor mistakes and indiscretions. When asked about his father he spoke of him in the most glowing terms. He described three or four years of frequent visits during which they enjoyed together only the most pleasurable activities. When confronted with his mother's version of what had happened between George and his father, he claimed that his mother's memory was at fault. About his stepfather, who was also cruel to George at times (but nowhere nearly as much as his father had been), George stated: "He's almost as good as my father was to me." It was quite clear that George had to deny his father's rejection as well as the anger he felt over it. Such repressed anger was contributing to his depression and self-depreciation. Even the anger he felt toward his stepfather could not be expressed and was contributing as well to the depressed feelings that brought about his referral to me.

In closing, I wish to emphasize that I have only touched upon some of the factors that may contribute to depression in children whose parents are separating. The suggestions I have given may be of limited value in lessening such children's depressed feelings. A child who is moderately to severely depressed generally has significant psychiatric difficulties—difficulties the complex origins of which are beyond the scope of this book to discuss and beyond the capacity of parents themselves to alleviate. Accordingly, I cannot recommend strongly enough that parents whose children are depressed seek psychiatric treatment for them, even though there may be no evidence for suicidal tendencies. The treatment of such children is vital because depressed children are likely to become depressed adults, and suicidal children (if they survive) are likely to become suicidal adults. And the broken home, in which children have been exposed to significant strife and deprivation, appears to be a most important contributing factor to the development of adult depression and suicide when the children grow older.

Fear of Abandonment

Children of divorce will often consider the departing parent to be abandoning them. Although continually reassured that this is not the case—that they are still loved very much—they tend to hold on to this concept of what is going on. Their world, then, becomes a shaky place indeed. If one parent can leave the home, what is to prevent the remaining parent from doing so as well? Children living in an intact, relatively stable home are not concerned to a significant degree with a breakup of the home. For children of divorce such an event is part of their scheme of things. They tend to generalize from their experiences in the home and may come to view all human relationships as potentially unstable. It is almost as if no one can be trusted. If the custodial parents was the one who was instrumental in causing the departed parent to leave, what is to prevent the children from being similarly ejected from the household? The resulting insecurity and instability can indeed be frightening.

The parents' preoccupation with their conflicts prior to the separation and with the various legal and other details associated with the separation may give them little time for emotional investment in their children. Although both parents may still be in the house, the children already feel abandoned. And when a parent then leaves the home, further feelings of rejection are produced. Furthermore, the new obligations that the custodial parent usually then has to assume may result in the children's having even less time with the remaining parent than they had before.

A mother may have initiated the divorce proceedings because of certain activities of the father that she found objectionable. From the children's point of view, the father has been forced to leave the house because he has been "bad." What is to stop their mother then from similarly forcing them to leave the house when they are bad. They may come to feel that no matter how much love their mother may have for them, they have now become an added burden for her. Were she not to have had them, her life would indeed be much easier. The pressures of time, work, and money she must now suffer on their behalf are often formidable. Her awareness that having children lessens her chances for remarriage must, at times, be painful. Thoughts about how much easier her life would be without the children are inevitable. These may even be verbalized by the mother; but even if not, the children sense them and react with fears that their mother may abandon them in order to lessen her burden. Commonly, such a mother displaces the resentment she feels over her situation onto the children, and this further intensifies their fears of rejection and abandonment.

Some children may react with panic states in which there may be sweating, palpitations, trembling, agitation, and an assortment of fears such as fear of their getting sick with no one to care for them, and there may be associated fears of dying. Other children may not exhibit these panic states but rather become generally tense over their fears of abandonment. Such tension may reveal itself by generalized irritability, low frustration tolerance, difficulty in falling asleep, trouble concentrating in school, and tics (especially of the face). Difficulty concentrating on television is a very sensitive indicator of tension in the child. Although the abandonment fear may contribute to such states of tension, other factors often contribute. A boy, for example, may harbor intense hostility toward one or both of his parents and he may feel very guilty over his anger. He may become anxious then when his rage builds up to the point where it can no longer be contained. In order to protect himself from the terrible consequences he anticipates from the expression of his anger, he may continue to squelch his hostility. And his fears that his anger will be exposed can contribute to his tension. Such a child not only needs the reassurances and the living experience that his fears of abandonment are unwarranted, but he has to be helped to feel less guilty over his hostility.

Following the separation, the child may wander around

the house looking for the departed parent even though re-peatedly told that he or she will no longer be living in the home. The child may search the closets and under the beds, or pathetically stand at the door awaiting his or her return. Some children will express fears that the departed parent will find substitutes for themselves elsewhere. One little girl roamed around the house crying, "I'll need a new father." Many children in response to their abandonment fears will reach out to strangers, pathetically craving for affection. Often children's play will serve to lessen abandonment fears. For example, they may create stories in which all the homes are intact and the children receive an abun-dance of love and care. Or, more symbolically, the play fantasies may include animals whose caretakers provide them with dedicated protection and affection. The ani-mals, of course, represent the children themselves. It is as if each time the child bestows favors on the animal he provides himself with similar gratifications. Some chil-dren will deal with their abandonment fears by endless conversations with the departed parent on a toy telephone.

A child may become overly dependent upon and cling excessively to the custodial parent. Separation anxieties may develop, and the child may refuse to visit friends or go to school. When the school becomes the special focus of such fears, the term "school phobia" is often used. The la-bel is a poor one because it implies that the child is afraid of the school; actually the child is afraid to part with the parent at home and if that parent were permitted to stay with the child in the classroom, there would generally be no fear. Many factors contribute to such separation anxieties, not simply the departure of a parent at the time of separation. For example, the custodial parent may be-come overprotective in order to compensate the child for the loss of the spouse, or to lessen guilt over the sep-aration. And such overprotection entrenches the child's overdependency and fear of separation. In a more com-plex way, the child may be very angry at the parent (for having instigated the separation, for example) and fear that his or her hostile wishes will be realized by harm be-falling the parent or by the parent's dying. By clinging to the parent and keeping him or her ever in sight the child reassures him- or herself that the hostile wishes have not caused the parent any harm.

Some children will try to lessen their feelings of abandonment by provoking punishment from one or both parents. They are willing to suffer the pain that such punishment entails for the reassurance that the parent is still very much there. What better way is there to confirm a parent's existence than to be struck or maltreated by him or her? Other factors, of course, may be contributing to such behavior. For example, the provocative behavior may serve as an outlet for the hostility the child feels over the separation. The child may feel guilty over the anger felt toward the parents for their having separated and the punishment received for such provocations may serve to reduce this guilt. All children want controls and will often test parents with various provocations in order to learn from experience what is acceptable behavior and what is not. The child living with only one parent will have to use that parent more frequently for this purpose and so will appear, from that parent's vantage point, to be more provocative than previously.

Some children, in an attempt to lessen abandonment fears, will involve themselves in various maneuvers designed to increase the affection for them of each of their parents. For example, a boy, in order to enhance the affection of his parents for him, will say to each that which he suspects will ingratiate that parent. Accordingly, when with his father he will side with him against the mother, refrain from saying positive things about her, and confine himself to those criticisms that he knows his father wishes to hear. And he will involve himself similarly with his mother. In this way the child attempts to ensure that he is in the good graces of both parents and he may thereby avoid further rejection and abandonment. When parents appreciate that they are being so used, they do well to communicate to the child that such "games" cause him to lose, not gain, affection. The child should be helped to appreciate that his parents cannot but be resentful over being so taken in and that this detracts from rather than adds to their affection for him. He therefore will suffer more rejection than he might have otherwise. In addition, he should be helped to see that he cannot feel good about himself lying in this way, and that the feelings of unworthiness so produced are adding unnecessarily to his difficulties. In short, he must be helped to appreciate that no one likes a liar: neither the people he lies to nor the liar himself.

When a mother moves back with her own parents following the separation the children are less likely to suffer with abandonment fears. Although they no longer live with their father, their two grandparents may make them feel that the trade wasn't really so bad. However, the situation usually isn't so simple. The grandparents often resent their new obligations. It is easy being doting grandparents when one visits the home of one's grandchildren. It is another story entirely having the children living in one's home. Mother may be out working and the responsibilities of child care may be something the grandparents were glad to have had behind them. Accordingly, the grandparents' resentment over their new obligations may cause the children to suffer further feelings of rejection and fears of abandonment. The mother who returns to the home of her parents may be a very dependent person. (I believe that a more mature mother would not choose this alternative, the obvious financial and other benefits of the arrangement notwithstanding.) Moving back with her parents only entrenches her dependency. Her children's observing her immature relationship with her parents cannot but weaken their respect for and feelings of security with their mother. The situation may produce even greater feelings of insecurity in the children.

Many abandonment fears diminish with time. As the children have the living experience that their fears are unwarranted, that they still have good relationships with both parents, that the parents are still available to them in spite of the separation, their abandonment worries will generally lessen. Distortions of and misconceptions about reality often contribute to many children's abandonment fears. And it behooves parents to help their children correct such distortions. They must be helped, for example, to see that Father has indeed abandoned *Mother,* but not *them,* and that although Father no longer wishes to have contact with Mother, he very much wishes to see his children. They must be helped to appreciate that they still have *two* parents, and that if something happens to the custodial parent they can still live with the non-custodial. In addition, the parents should discuss with the children exactly which friends and relatives would be available to take care of them in the event that both parents could not. (All children, in my opinion, should be told who will be caring for them if their parents die or become so incapacitated that they cannot care for them. For the children of divorce such information is even more important to impart.) In addition, in situations in which there are few, if any, friends or relatives who would be available to care for the children if something were to happen to both parents, then boarding schools and foster homes should be discussed. The children's gaining the feeling that no matter what happens, there will be someone to take care of them is crucial to the alleviation of abandonment fears. It can also be useful to impress upon children with such fears the fact that as they get older they will become more and more independent and less at the mercy of adults who might reject them. The older the children the more appreciative they will be of the importance of their applying themselves to their educational and career pursuits so that they will be less beholden to others and less impotent to deal with rejections.

Actual Abandonment

As mentioned, most children consider themselves abandoned by the parent who leaves the home when separation takes place. In most cases this view of what has occurred is false and the departing parent maintains an active interest in the children. However, there are situations in which the term abandonment is appropriate. Either the parents cuts him- or herself off from the children entirely, or the contacts are so infrequent and/or made with so little conviction that the children are essentially deprived of a meaningful relationship with the absent parent. It is to this problem of truly abandoned children (either abandoned in fact or psychologically so) that I direct my comments here.

Total abandonment. A parent who totally rejects his or her children is suffering from a psychological disturbance. I believe that maternal and paternal instincts are inborn and strong in the psychologically healthy individual. As with all other human functions, there is probably a wide range among individuals regarding the strength of the parental instinct. But all, I believe, are born with it and those in whom it is either very weak or nonexistent have psychological inhibitions that interfere with the expression of this function. A parent with little or no overt expression of parental feeling will often try to convince him- or herself and others that there is no deficiency. Some believe that they just weren't born to be parents and having had children was or would be a mistake. Others take the position that it's best for the children that they have no contact at all with them following the separation. "It's best that I make a clean break of it," such a parent may proclaim, or, "Rather than see them once in a while, and raise their hopes and then disappoint them, it'll be better for them if I never see them at all." An extreme form of rationalization for rejecting children goes like this: "When one divorces, it's best for the departed parent and children to consider one another *dead*. Each must pick up the pieces and start life anew, without in any way impeding one another." Although it is obvious how the children can be seen as interfering with the adult's remaking his or her life, no explanation is given as to how the children's continuing contact with the adult hinders *their* growth and healthy development.

There are times when a parent, who was somewhat rejecting of the child prior to the separation, becomes so much more so afterwards that he or she can justifiably be placed in the category of parents discussed here. A father may suddenly become so swept up in his "freedom" that dating, traveling, and self-indulgence may result in his neglecting his children. A mother may become so burdened by her new responsibilities that she will have little time and conviction for affectionate involvement with her children; or the new resentments she now harbors may compromise significantly her maternal expression.

"Always reassure the children that the absent parent still loves them." When abandonment occurs, it is common for the remaining parent to protect the children from what he or she considers to be the harmful effects of revealing to the children the truth about the abandoning parent. Statements that are frequently utilized in the service of this goal include: "He loves you inside; he just can't show it." "He doesn't want to be mean; he can't help it." "I guess he forgot. His memory was never very good." Parents who protect their children in this way are generally well meaning. Often they are supported in this approach by professional authorities who espouse the view that the child's learning that a parent doesn't love him or her will cause psychological trauma. "Always reassure the children," they advise, "that the absent parent still loves them." Unfortunately, both the parents and professionals here are, in my opinion, misguided. The explanations provided the child cannot but confuse him. "What can this thing called love be all about," the child can only wonder, "if someone can love you and never (or rarely ever) show it?" I do not claim to have a firm definition of the word love; but the word does not, I believe, apply to a situation in which the so-called lover has practically no interest at all in being with the alleged loved one. Love is not love without reciprocity. Such communications are likely to contribute to the children's growing up with distortions about love that will interfere with their forming successful relations with others in the future. In addition, they are likely to be somewhat incredulous of a parent who provides them with such rationalizations. They will often sense, at some level, the parent's lack of conviction when he or she tells them. Accordingly, such cover-ups breed distrust of the remaining parent. The child has had enough distrust produced in him already with the departure of one parent; he certainly doesn't need to develop distrust of the remaining parent—and such comments are likely to cause this to happen.

Children in such a situation should be told exactly what the situation is with regard to the absent parent's depth of involvement. If the parent's interest amounts to an average of one visit or greeting card a year, then the children should be told that the parent has little love for them but does think enough of them to extend him- or herself to that degree. If there is no contact at all, then the children should be told, in as sympathetic a manner as possible, that the parent does not love them. However, I would not simply stop with such an explanation. It would be cruel to tell such abandoned children that the absent parent doesn't love them and leave it at that. I would try to instill the notion that something is seriously wrong with a person who cannot love his or her own children. In a sense, such a parent is more to be pitied than scorned. To be angry at the abandoning parent is reasonable; but to pity him or her as well is also appropriate. Regarding the anger, the children have to be helped to become comfortable with their angry reactions to the abandonment and not feel guilty over their resentful feelings. They have to be helped to appreciate that angry thoughts and feelings (including profanities and death wishes) are natural and inevitable in such situations. However, mere expression of the anger accomplishes little more than providing temporary release. It will build up again if not used constructively. The children should be helped to use their anger in the service of effecting a more meaningful relationship with the absent or deficient parent. If these efforts do not prove effective (and they most often fail with such parents), the children should be helped to appreciate that the angry feelings will best be dispelled by their gaining substitute satisfactions from others. Regarding the pity, the child should be helped to gain a sense of pity for the parent because the latter is missing out on one of the most enriching experiences of life, namely, loving and rearing one's child. In addition, I would try to help the children appreciate that just because their own parent does not love them does not mean that they are unlovable. Others, both peer and adult, can love them both in the present and in the future. It behooves them, however, to seek such relationships in compensation for the deprivation they may be suffering over the loss of the parent. Such children, however, will only believe that they can indeed gain affection from others when they have *living experiences* that this is true. Mere words and reassurances will generally not work. Only after the children have enjoyed such substitute relationships will they really be convinced that the defect does not lie within themselves. If the children show signs of trying to gain the affection of a parent who has proved him- or herself incapable of providing love, they should be discouraged from such a futile pursuit. And telling the children that an unloving parent really loves them can contribute to these futile endeavors and is thereby another reason for not providing the children with such "protective" explanations. I not only recommend these approaches to parents in such a situation, but utilize them as well in my treatment of such children.

Partial abandonment. There are many degrees of parental rejection and abandonment and only in extreme cases is there total separation between the child and the parent. The more common situation is the one in which the rejecting parent has varying degrees of contact with and interest in the children. It behooves the custodial parent to help the children gain as clear a picture as possible of the degree of involvement that the rejecting parent has. Such children must be helped to resign themselves to the reality of their situation and discouraged from trying to extract more affection than the absent parent is capable of or willing to provide; e.g., two postcards a year, one visit a year, one Christmas present a year, etc. They should be helped to recognize that some degree of rejection is not the same as total abandonment. The children of such a deficient, but nevertheless partially or minimally involved parent, do well to try first to gain more affection from the parent by expressing their grievances. Also, they should try to determine if they may be contributing to the parent's alienation and attempt to alter those behavior patterns that may be causing some of the parent's withdrawal. When all these efforts have produced maximum benefit (such contributions by the children usually play a minor role in parental withdrawal) the children do well to accept from the parent what there is to be gained (however limited) and not strive to acquire that which is impossible to obtain.

Children who decide to have nothing to do with a parent because he or she has so little to offer (and this decision is more common among adolescents than younger children) may be depriving themselves of some valuable gratifications from the relationship. And custodial parents who actively try to prevent minimal and unpredictable contact with the argument that the rejecting parent's unreliability and infrequency of contact are not in the children's best interests, are doing their children a disservice. (Sometimes such parents may even try to prevent legally the deficient parent's infrequent and unpredictable involvements.) They may justify their intervention with the argument that such sporadic involvement and its attendant frustration for the children does them more harm than good. I believe that unpredictable involvement, even with its associated frustrations for the children, is generally better for children than no contact at all. The children of such a parent have to be helped not to place themselves in positions where their hopes are going to be unnecessarily raised and then dashed. They have to be helped to resign themselves to what they can realistically expect to gain from the deficient parent. We all have to learn how to make such compromises in life in our relationships with others, and accomplishing this in childhood can be useful in preparing children for similar experiences in later life. If both the deficient parent and the children still wish to have contact with one another, in spite of the parent's defects, this should be respected by the custodial parent (except, of course, in situations where the children are exposed to physical brutality, severe sadism, or other obviously damaging behavior on the rejecting parent's part). To sever artificially the relationship because of the absent parent's deficiency may cause the children unnecessary deprivation. Often the custodial parent who tries to enforce such a cessation of the relationship with the deficient parent does so not much from what is considered to be the child's best interests but from a desire to wreak vengeance. In such cases the parents's deficiencies serve as the excuse for such action. By depriving the absent parent of any contact with the children the custodial parent believes he or she is gaining the maximum in retribution. Of course, the children's needs here are being ignored in the service of such vengeful gratification.

Criteria by which children can determine the degree of parental affection. Most children of divorce are quite confused about the extent of the absent parent's affection for them. Whether the parent is deeply loving, moderately affectionate, partially abandoning, or totally abandoning, the children are generally confused about the departed parent's degree of love for them. Often these children have similar questions about the custodial parent's affection as well. In helping such children gain a clearer idea of how much affection a parent has, they can be encouraged to look for certain behavioral patterns in the parents that can provide useful information about a parent's degree of affection. I appreciate that the criteria for parental affection that I will present cannot be measured precisely and there is the distinct possibility that children (especially younger ones) will have difficulty utilizing them accurately. For example, a five-year-old girl may consider her father's three visits per week to be deficient and conclude that he has little affection for her. It behooves both parents to help children correct such inaccurate interpretations of parental behavior, lest the misapplication of these guidelines cause children unnecessary worry and feelings of deprivation. Because there is some danger of misinterpretation is no reason to deprive children of these criteria. Most parents, I believe, will agree that there are valid ways to judge parental affection. Children should not be deprived of their benefits because of their occasional misapplication.

One measure of parental affection is the frequency with which the parent wishes to be with the children. Children have to be helped to appreciate that parents have other duties and obligations than spending time with them; however, in spite of these, a loving parent will want to spend a significant amount of time with his children and will somehow manage to do so. The parent who frequently finds excuses for not having such contacts (visitation limitations notwithstanding) may very well be somewhat defective in the depth of his or her feelings for the children.

Another criterion children can utilize to evaluate a parent's degree of affection is the willingness of the parent to go out of his or her way in order to be of help to the children—especially when the children are sick, injured, or suffering with other difficulties. I also encourage the children to observe how much pride the parent appears to have in their accomplishments. And I also suggest that children try to determine how often the parent speaks favorably about them to others. If the children never, or hardly ever, observe such conversations, it is likely that there is parental deficiency.

I try to help children determine how much involvement the parent has in the things that interest them. If they observe the parent to be bored or involving him- or herself in a forced manner, then it is likely that there is some deficiency in the parent's affection. Children should also be encouraged to see how often the parents enjoys *doing* mutually pleasurable things with them. If this rarely occurs it suggests some deficiency in the parent.

Children should be encouraged to ascertain the amount of physical contact the parent desires to have with them. Parents who are somewhat compromised in their affection for their children have little desire to have such contact. The younger the children the greater the likelihood that such physical contact will involve lying down in bed with them from time to time, cuddling, tucking them in, wrestling, and allowing the children to come into the parent's bed on holidays and weekend mornings.

Children should be helped to appreciate that it is normal and expected that a parent will get angry at them from time to time and even a few times a day is within the normal range. However, if a parent is consistently grumpy and irritable with them, then some deprivation is probably occurring.

Although these criteria for parental affection may be difficult to apply, I have found them extremely useful in my therapeutic work with children of divorce. As mentioned, one does these children a disservice by depriving them of their benefits just because they may occasionally be misinterpreted. When properly utilized by parents who are willing to discuss them openly and honestly with their children they can provide valuable information that may be useful for the children in averting, as well as dealing with, many of the psychological disturbances that may result when parents divorce. They are particularly useful for children who feel that they have been abandoned. If this indeed has been the case (either actually or psychologically) then their suspicions will be confirmed and they will be in a better position to resign themselves to their misfortune and take those steps necessary to deal with the situation more effectively. And if the criteria demonstrate that the children's fears of abandonment were not warranted, they can provide invaluable reassurance and lessen an unnecessary burden that such children may have been taking on.

Running Away from Home

Although not common, running away from home is one of the ways some children react to parental separation. As with most, if not all, behavior, many factors may contribute. Accordingly, parents do well to appreciate that there is generally no one single reason for a given child's flight from the home and that one or more of the factors described below may contribute in varying combinations.

Common reasons for children's fleeing the home. First, a child's disappearing from the home is an act that is predictably going to attract the attention and involvement of his or her parents. In fact, of all the things children could do to attract attention to and concern for themselves it is one of the most powerful. Such parental concern may reassure runaway children that they are still wanted —that they have not been totally rejected and abandoned. Fears of their being abandoned are thereby reduced. These reassurances are especially enjoyed at the time when runaway children finally return home. The parents may have spent hours, days, weeks, and even longer—distraught with guilt and grief and obsessed with thoughts about their children's welfare and whereabouts. The aid of police may have been enlisted, and sometimes the public media. When they finally make their grand entrance or are dramatically discovered (often with the child's conscious or unconscious assistance) the parental sighs of relief, thanking God that they are all right, etc., reassure them that they are loved and wanted. Even if they are punished after this initial period of parental elation and joyful reunion, the attention-getting purpose has been served. With the punishment comes the reassurance that their absence has caused pain and they truly have been missed.

Running away from home can lessen rejection and abandonment fears in another way. By running away the children may fantasize themselves the rejectors rather than the ones who were rejected. It is as if the children were saying to themselves: "It is not we who have been abandoned. We are the abandoners. We decide if separation of parents from children is to take place. We decide how and when it will occur." A face-saving element is also present here. The reasoning is similar to that of the jilted boy who claims that it was he who rejected his girl friend and not vice versa. By considering himself to have initiated the rejection he gains a sense of power and control over the event and protects himself from the humiliation of having been the one who was rejected.

Fleeing from the home may serve as a cry for help from outside sources. In the inevitable discussions that take place after these children return, the assistance of people such as ministers, relatives, and therapists may be enlisted. As a result of the involvement of these parties the child may gain help for himself. Sometimes the children will invoke the counselor's aid in encouraging the parents to reconcile. In accordance with what I have said previously, it would be unwise, if not intrusive, of such a counselor to comply with the children's wishes that he or she intervene on their behalf and encourage the parents to stay together. To do so is to allow oneself to be used as a tool in the children's manipulations and only encourages them repeatedly to run away again for this purpose or to utilize similar forms of manipulative behavior.

A common fantasy among most children (and probably many adults) is that of grief and regret being suffered by those who have maltreated one during one's lifetime. In the typical fantasy the contrite parties weep at the funeral of the maltreated one, regretting the neglect, cruelty, insensitivity, etc., that they exhibited in their relations with the departed. The fantasy provides attention, affection, and vengeful gratification. So powerful is this fantasy that there are some in whom it plays a significant role in their suicidal acts. Of course, the suicidal person appears to lose sight of the fact that even though the suicide might indeed provoke such displays, he or she will not be there like a hovering angel to observe it and gloat. Runaway children often entertain similar images of their families' response to their disappearance. Accordingly, they not only gain the aforementioned attention and affection, but vengeful gratifications as well. Such children may derive immense satisfaction from envisioning the pain and grief their families suffer during their absence. Such a child might even verbalize during his or her ruminations while away: "My father has hurt me by leaving the home; I'll hurt him in the same way. Just as I was sad when he left, now he'll be sad that I'm gone."

There is a more complex way in which running away relates to children's anger. Anger over which an individual feels guilt may be projected onto someone else. It is as if the person denies that he or she harbors any anger, and assumes that it resides in others. Children who are guilty over their angry feelings may project them onto their parents and then expect that their parents will act out such anger toward them by various forms of punishment. And they may flee from their homes in the hope of avoiding the cruel treatment they anticipate.

Other factors, as well, may contribute to children's fleeing the home. Some children consider the separation to have been the result of their having been "bad," and they may run away in order to avoid causing even worse trouble in the home. Some children may believe that the guilt that their running away will produce in their parents will be so great that they will change their minds and stay together in order to avoid further flights from the home. Such flights then are best viewed as guilt-provoking devices, designed to manipulate the parents into staying together. Fleeing the home can serve the forces of denial. If the child is not home to observe a parent's absence, he or she can more easily believe that the parent is still there. Some children may flee the general atmosphere of loneliness and depression that has prevailed in the home since the separation. Some run away from home in search of a departed parent who has truly abandoned the family and whose exact whereabouts are unknown. They hope to find the parent, live with him or her, or convince the parent to return. Sometimes the more complex mechanism of identification with the departed parent may be contributing to the child's flight. When a parent dies some children (sometimes almost overnight) take on personality qualities of the deceased parent. Children of a parent who has left the home may act similarly. Such identification is an attempt to reunite with the absent parent by taking on his or her personality qualities oneself. And running away from home, just as the mother or father did, can serve through identification to lessen the child's sense of loss. By imitating the absent parent's behavior (in this case, departing from the home) such children act as if they have a piece of that parent within themselves and so gain a sense of closeness that they might not otherwise have.

Dealing with children who run away from home. In handling children who run away from home parents do well to try to surmise exactly which factors may be operating. In this way they will be in the best position to deal with the child on his or her return. When a child announces beforehand that he or she is going to leave, the parent generally does well to discourage the child and take reasonable precautions and impose practical restraints. The parent who responds to a runaway threat by packing the child's belongings and accompanying him or her to the door is only deepening the child's problems.

A child who makes such a threat is often asking for more attention and affection; by inviting the child to leave, he or she cannot but feel even more rejected. Parents who pack the bags may do so because they recognize the threat as manipulative and do not wish to allow themselves to be coerced. One need not go so far to avoid manipulation. One can still refuse to comply with such children's inappropriate demands *within the house*. Accompanying them outside, rising to the dare, only increases their sense of rejection and adds further humiliation when the plan is defeated. Telling the children that running away is not allowed, that under no circumstances will they be permitted to do so, that they are still loved and that their absence would cause terrible pain for the parents, will provide the reassurance that they are wanted and prevent them from doing what they really don't want to do anyway. Letting them go so that they will have the living experience of how terrible it can be outside the home also causes children to feel rejected and thereby compounds their problems.

Most children who leave the home usually go to a place where they will easily be found. Their fear of the unknown and their appreciation of the fact that they do not have the wherewithal to fend successfully for themselves causes them to stay close to home. Often they will hide in a nearby park or in the basement of a friend's house—long enough to accomplish some of the aforementioned goals. When they feel that they have gotten enough mileage from their absence they will allow themselves to be discovered. Or they may return home with some feeble excuse, the implication of which is that they really wanted to stay away but had to return home because, for example, they weren't sure the cat would be fed, or because they had forgotten to take a toothbrush.

On occasion, a child will stay at the homes of friends whose parents are not appreciative of what is going on. When the friend's parents do find out what is occurring they generally insist that the youngster return home and usually inform the child's parent of his or her whereabouts. However, there are neighbors who take pride in protecting children from the indignities they describe themselves to be suffering at the hands of their parents. Such neighbors may basically feel insecure about their parental capacities and therefore revel in the praises bestowed upon them by the runaway. They may be rivalrous with and antagonistic to the runaway youngster's parents and gain hostile gratification from haboring the child. Such "good Samaritans" do runaway children a disservice. Instead of encouraging the youngster to go back and try to work out the problems with his or her parents, they only widen the gap between them. Parents whose child is so harbored do well to inform such neighbors that they wish their child home immediately. If, after simple explanation, there is some resistance, they should not hesitate to include in their ensuing comments such words as "illegal," "police," and "kidnapping." Generally, this will reduce the "benevolence" of the protectors and usually result in their reconsidering their position. Even on those rare occasions when the youngster is fleeing from real abuses, parents should not take it upon themselves to provide protection. Rather, there are social agencies that serve to intervene in such cases.

I believe that the best attitude for parents to take when runaway children do come home is to express one's gratitude that they are safe, but to express as well the rage that has been felt toward them for having caused the parents such grief and torture. In response to the parents' grateful feelings that the children are home and safe they should be embraced. In response to the cruelty of their act —for having caused the parents to go through such an ordeal—they should be severely punished. One wants to let such children know that they are still loved and missed; but one also wants to help them appreciate how much pain they have inflicted upon their parents. And a reasonably harsh punishment may deter them from ever running away again.

Immaturity

In response to a trauma, or to any situation in which a child's usual satisfactions are not adequately provided, it is common for him or her to <u>regress</u> or go back to earlier developmental levels in the hope of regaining gratifications enjoyed previously. Or the child may remain fixed, and not advance beyond the level he or she has reached in order to avoid taking on the newer demands attendant to higher levels of maturation. And parental separation is the kind of trauma that may result in such regression or fixation.

Regressive manifestations. Following the separation some children may start sucking their thumbs again, using baby talk, and becoming in general more infantile and demanding. They may ask to be fed or to resume using the bottle. Fully toilet-trained children may start soiling again or may ask the parent to wipe them when they go to the bathroom. Bed-wetting may be resumed. The child may feign illness (stomachaches, headaches, nausea, etc.) in order to have an excuse to avoid the demands of school and to remain home and be put to bed and be pampered. Temper tantrums, irritability, and low frustration tolerance may be exhibited more frequently. Some children may respond to the new responsibilities of living in a one-parent home by whining and complaining that they just cannot do the things asked of them. They may become clinging and refuse to go out and play or visit friends, when they had previously done so without difficulty. Clinging behavior (to the mother and/or teacher), rocking, or resumption of the need for a security blanket (or toy, doll, etc., that serves the same purpose) may also appear. The child may take longer to go to sleep and resume the earlier practice of providing endless excuses to get the parent to return to the bedroom ("I want a glass of water"; "I have to go to the bathroom"; etc.). Or the child may want to sleep in the parent's bed. Maturbatory play may appear or, if previously present, may increase. Some children exhibit fears of separation (after having reached the point where such fears were no longer present) and may ask the parents to help them perform tasks they have previously proved themselves competent of accomplishing on their own. An older sibling may become parentified to provide dependency gratifications beyond what the parent(s) can offer. In school such children may only work well with individual attention by the teacher, whereas previously they could work well independently. In their fantasy play they may become preoccupied with such themes as feeding, cuddling, and protecting. Such regressive behavior is generally more common in younger children (they are closer to the infantile state and are less likely than older children to have "forgotten" immature patterns). Lastly, the presence of younger children in the household will often provide a model for such regressive manifestations and makes their appearance more likely.

Parental contributions to children's immaturity. Generally, such fixations and regressions are transient and clear up within a few weeks or months following the separation. When they persist, other factors are usually contributing, the most common of which is parental overprotection and other forms of encouragement of the immature behavior. And the divorced parent is very likely to provide such encouragement as a result of the guilt he or she may feel over the split in the family. Overindulging a child is one of the most common ways to reduce such guilt. Visiting fathers, especially, are prone to do this. They, as the "abandoners," almost routinely feel guilty and are most likely to attempt to alleviate such guilt by providing their children with continual fun, games, and freedom from discipline during their limited visitation time. Because noncustodial fathers generally see the child when they are not working, they have the time for these indulgences. The custodial mother, however, cannot so readily provide such gratifications for her children if she is most effectively to run her household. Yet she may do so as well, her time limitations notwithstanding.

A mother left with the children may try to lessen her feelings of abandonment and loneliness by keeping them in a more dependent state than is warranted. She may have had past insecurities in relating to adults and the failure of her marriage may intensify these. Fearing further failures and rejections from adults (especially men), she may become excessively involved with her children—captive companions who have already proved their deep affection for her. Such a mother may find excuses for the children's not playing in the street, visiting friends, and taking other steps toward independence. Under the guise of concern for their welfare she provides herself with companionship and makes herself feel more useful. In the extreme, such children may develop neurotic inhibitions in school and social relationships because such involvements and successes, as steps toward independence, create feelings of disloyalty toward their mother. They may even remain in their homes when adults, never leaving the mother who "needs them so much."

Either parent may see the separation as a threat to feelings of adequacy as a parent. The parent may therefore overindulge the child, thereby hoping to prove his or her competence. Or the parents may compete with one another over who can be the better parent, and the degree to which one can keep the children happy may be used as the measure of competence. Each parent may overindulge the children in order to win their affection away from the other or to gain an ally in the parental conflict. Such children are being used as vehicles to express parental hostility and are being bribed to serve as pawns in the parents' battle.

A woman may feel that she has failed as a wife, but may try to compensate by proving herself successful as a mother. She may need to overdo this and become overindulgent. Or she may try to use a male child as a substitute for her lost husband. (It is less common for a husband to do this with a daughter, because his opportunities to find another woman are greater than his wife's to find another man—especially when she has custody of the children.) Such a mother may become seductive with the child, make comments about how he is now to be "the man of the house," make the boy her adviser and counselor, and reveal confidences to him. (The oedipal problems that may result in such a boy will be discussed subsequently in this chapter.)

A parent may overindulge children as a reaction against basic feelings of hostility toward them. Such a parent may resent the obligations, frustrations, and restrictions of parenthood and be too guilty over such feelings to allow them to come into conscious awareness. The overprotection serves to deny and repress these hostilities. This mechanism reveals itself most clearly in the parent who frequently anticipates harm befalling the children even when the situation does not warrant such concern and when other parents do not envision danger in the same situation. Of course, the separated parent may have additional hostilities toward the child to deal with. For both parents, the children cannot but place restrictions on their lives that they could very well do without. The children's very existence requires both parents to maintain a relationship with one another that they most often would have liked to sever completely, and they make each parent somewhat less attractive as a potential mate to others. These additional sources of potential resentment are likely to intensify the parental overprotectiveness that is used to deny hostility.

Overindulgence of children can be used in the service of vicariously gratifying parental dependencies. The parent, by projecting himself onto the child, can satisfy his or her own desire to be indulged. It is as if each time the child is ministered to, the parent is ministering to himself. And the more gratification the child derives from such indulgence, the greater the parent's. A divorced parent may experience an intensification of such dependencies after the separation. This is especially true of a parent who has been abandoned.

Masochistic parents—who get morbid gratification from pain (more commonly psychological than physical) —may find opportunities for suffering by making painful sacrifices for the child. And they may use overindulgence as a way of making such sacrifices. Another aspect of masochism pertinent to this discussion is the feeling among masochists that they are not basically of much use or value to others and that if they ask anything of others they will be rejected and abandoned. They believe that they will only be accepted by others if they relate on their terms. More specifically, they see themselves as capable of attracting only sadistic people—those who measure the affection of others by how much pain they are willing to suffer for them. Accordingly, masochists operate on the principle "The more pain I suffer on behalf of the one I love, the more I prove my affection." Therefore, they allow themselves to be maltreated—to be used as scapegoats, as targets for the release of others' hostility and maltreatment. Allowing oneself to be taken advantage of can also provide masochistic gratifications, as can "giving until it hurts." And sacrificially giving to a child can provide just such gratification. Ever satisfying the overdemanding regressed child can provide a masochistic parent with continued opportunities for feeling put upon and exploited. The masochistically inclined parent who gets divorced may react to the separation by an intensification of the need for masochistic gratification. The wife, for example, married to a sadistic husband, may have to find a new person to torture her after he leaves. And a child may be the most convenient person to serve as a substitute. And sacrificial giving (and its attendant overprotection) may be selected as the mode of gratifying this need.

A parent may try to compensate for feelings of inadequacy by trying to produce and rear a perfect child. Oversolicitous attitudes may develop in the service of this cause. Working on the premise that a perfect child is one who is always happy, the child's requests are rarely refused. The divorced parent may have even more reason to feel inadequate: the failure of a marriage cannot but lower one's self-esteem. Such overprotection, as a method of compensating for lowered feelings of self-worth, is likely to be utilized by divorced parents and may contribute to their children's regression.

A parent may overindulge a child in order to obtain vicarious gratifications that compensate for his or her own frustrations in life. Parents who raise their children in accordance with the principle "I want to give them everything I didn't have" can gain through the children some compensation for the disillusions and disappointments of their own lives. Overprotection can enable such parents to live through the children and compensate for their own privations. And such parents need not use the children to gratify past deprivations—present and even anticipated privations can be lessened via this mechanism. Making the child into everything the parent *wished to be but wasn't and will never be* can provide such a parent with solace for disappointments with his or her own life. We all do this to some extent and it is healthy to a degree because it serves to provide children with parental encouragement in their life's pursuits. However, when a parent's view of the ideal existence for children is that they always get what they want, when they want it, then parental over-indulgence occurs and the children are likely to become overdependent. The divorced parent, having another reason for feeling deprived, may have an even greater need than the parent in a relatively stable marriage to utilize this compensatory mechanism.

There are parents who overindulge a child because they cannot tolerate anger—regardless of the age of the person who exhibits it and regardless of its appropriateness. Such a parent may live by the principle "I must never do anything that will get another person angry at me." The best way to avoid the hostility of others is to avoid their being frustrated, that is, to do everything they want. When this principle is applied to such a person's child, the latter becomes overindulged and pampered. Since the children of divorce are likely to be angry and even more demanding than usual (at least around the time of separation), the likelihood of their being over-indulged by such a parent becomes greater.

Parents may keep a child at an immature level in order to protect themselves against the lowered feelings of self-worth that would result if the child became their equal. Such insecure parents are essentially in competition with their children. They keep them down in order to maintain a false sense of superiority. They frequently communicate to their children such messages as "You're not old enough to do this" and "You're not mature enough to handle that" in areas where the parents of their children's peers see no difficulties. The divorced parent is even more prone to feel insecure and may therefore be more likely to use this form of overprotection.

Helping the immature child. Parents should appreciate that children's regressive behavior following separation is common and normal. Parents do well to allow intermittent gratification of such regressive cravings, especially in the period immediately following the separation. However, these indulgences should be gradually reduced, lest they become entrenched. The failure to allow limited gratification of regressive tendencies during this period may result in inordinate craving for regressive gratification and such frustrations can contribute to the formation of various kinds of psychological disturbance. Although some indulgence of immature behavior is warranted, parents do well to refrain from providing regressive gratifications for behavior that is suggestive of a specific psychological disorder. To do so may result in the child's developing the particular disturbance when it could have been prevented by withholding regressive gratification in the early stages of the disorder's appearance. For example, parents should not comply with a child's request to stay home from school because of minor physical symptoms. Rather they should keep a child home from school only when there is bona fide evidence of physical disease. It is better to err on the side of sending a sick child to school than to risk the development of a psychological disorder in which the child uses the most minor, and often imagined, physical complaints as an excuse to avoid separation from parents or the minor discomforts and frustrations that he or she may experience in school and elsewhere. Parents of such children do well to appreciate that the risk to their children's physical health in being sent home from school because they are ill is so negligible that for all practical purposes it is nonexistent. Only in extremely rare diseases will a child's health be jeopardized by such an experience.

The child who starts to wet should be asked to assist in the changing (and even cleaning) of the sheets. And children who soil should also assist (to the degree appropriate to their age) in cleaning themselves and their underwear. Beyond the early post-separation period infantile demands should not be complied with more than one would have had the separation not occurred. The child should not be allowed to manipulate his parents with temper tantrums. Baby talk should be discouraged by the parents' refusal to respond to communications made with infantile intonation. Children who had previously eaten on their own and persist in wanting to be fed should not be, even at the risk of their not eating. Some parents become so fearful of the child's developing severe nutritional deficiencies in such a situation that they readily comply with such children's demands. The likelihood of this happening in the overwhelming majority of children is practically nonexistent. Practically all will begin to eat on their own when they become hungry enough. The child's request to have his or her bottle again might be complied with to a limited degree (in accordance with my previous statement about allowing for some indulgence in the regressive pattern). And appropriate disciplinary measures should be imposed on the child who shirks from his usual (and now new) responsibilities.

Some of the forms of parental overindulgence that contribute to children's regression are related to parental misguidance. In such cases the parents may be able to give up easily their pampering and indulgence and alleviate thereby their children's aggressive manifestations. In other parents, however, the overprotectiveness may be deepseated and provide many neurotic gratifications. But even in such cases, a certain amount of conscious control is usually still possible—so that the parental contributing factors may still be reduced.

An appreciation of the socially alienating effects of a form of behavior can contribute to a child's trying to gain conscious control over exhibiting a symptom. Although such suppression does not get to the underlying causes of a problem, it does, in my opinion, play a role in its alleviation. Such confrontations must be made benevolently, however, if they are to have any chance of being effective. For example, one can say to the child who sucks his thumb: "If you knew how you looked when you put your thumb in your mouth, I don't think you'd do that in front of others." The primary approach to the alleviation of regressive symptoms should be on reducing the underlying contributing factors, not merely trying to suppress and discourage the symptom. In each child different underlying factors are operating and one must try to determine what these are if one is to reduce optimally the regression. For example, a common cause of children's regressing is the belief that the separation will deprive them entirely of the absent parent. Such children have to be reassured that this will not be the case (except, of course, in the rare situation when it is). However, such children must also have *living experiences* demonstrating that such predictions are true. Only then will the reassurances contribute to a reduction of their need to regress. These children must be helped to acquire substitute gratifications and to appreciate that separation need not result in the terrible deprivations they may anticipate. To this end, more meaningful relationships with peers and other adults should be encouraged. Again, it is only when these are actually accomplished that the children will be able to lessen their needs for the regressive adjustment to the separation.

Hypermaturity

When parents separate, their children are generally required to assume additional responsibilities and obligations. Some regress in response to the new demands and others rise to the occasion and attain a new and healthy maturity. There are others, however, whose new maturity looks good on the surface but is actually a form of poor adjustment to the separation. It has an exaggerated, misguided, or inappropriate quality that suggests that it is not basically a stable and healthy form of maturity. It is to this unhealthy form of maturity, this hypermaturity, that I direct my attention here.

Some children may manifest hypermaturity by becoming caricatures of adults. They may take on adult mannerisms, speech intonations, and affectations. Large words and adult terminology may be utilized at every opportunity. They may try to relate to other children as if they were parents and treat them in a condescending manner (much to the latter's alienation). Scolding, reprimanding, disciplining, and lecturing younger children may become quite common. At school such children may become teacher's helper (sometimes invited, sometimes not). The naïve teacher may welcome the help and be delighted with such a child; the classmates, however, may refer to the child as a "goody-goody" or "teacher's pet."

A number of factors may operate both singly and in combination to produce such behavior. At times there is parental encouragement for the exaggerated maturity. The parents may be impressed with the child's adultlike behavior and even show him or her off to friends—thereby providing significant reinforcement to the pattern. A parent may use the child as a confidant, thereby encouraging premature acquisition of adult behavioral patterns. Seductive behavior and utilization of the child as a substitute for the absent parent can also contribute to the child's developing the hypermaturity adaptation. The dependent parent may try to get the child to replace the absent parent, who served as a protector and adviser, and may pressure the child into assuming the parental role.

Even without parental encouragement, some children appear to become hypermature on their own. At times, by becoming hypermature the child can symbolically regain the lost parent. By identifying with the lost parent, and becoming like him or her, the child retains the parental image within him- or herself and thereby can vaguely believe that there really wasn't a loss. Such an adjustment is seen most frequently following the death of a parent, but is also utilized by children after parental separation. The adaptation may be a way of compensating for the sense of helplessness that many children may feel over the separation. Children are weak and helpless; they have no choice but to bear the rejections, abandonments, and other forms of maltreatment they may suffer at the hands of adults. By assuming adult status the child gains a delusional protection from such indignities. The child may view the separation as proof of the unreliability of adults; by becoming an adult himself—and self-reliant —he reduces such anxieties. Boys, especially, may acquire a new toughness in order to defend themselves against the sense of impotence that the separation causes in them.

In another way, as well, the hypermaturity may be an an attempt to regain the parent who has left the home. A girl may have learned that Father left Mother because she wasn't a good wife. Accordingly, she may try to surpass Mother as a wife in order to attract Father back to the household. Similarly a boy, learning that Father was asked to leave the house because he wasn't a good husband, may use this as an excuse to become hypermature in the attempt to attract his mother. The children may understand that the separation took place because one, or both, of the parents was "bad." Accordingly, they may try to be very "good" in order to protect themselves from being similarly ejected from the household. And assuming an adult role, in which the child behaves in an exemplary fashion, can provide protection against this eventuality.

Blame

Long before the parents' decision to separate is made, their children are exposed to the concept of *blame*. In their fighting the parents usually blame each other for the difficulties between them and so it is only natural that when the separation does take place the child tends to think along the lines of who was at fault. The problem is further compounded by the traditional legal system, which would only grant a divorce if one of the parties could demonstrate that he or she had been wronged by the other (who was considered to have exhibited such reprehensible behavior as adultery, mental cruelty, alcoholism, or drug addiction). Although no-fault divorce laws have evolved from the recognition that both parties have usually contributed (often through psychological difficulties) to the deterioration of the marital relationship, the spouses themselves usually are quite strong in their opinions as to who was at fault. And when the couple needs to resort to adversary proceedings (whether to get divorced or to settle other conflicts such as those over alimony, support, and custody) the lawyers can be relied upon to intensify the problem of faultfinding. Lastly, the children are likely to consider the parent who has initiated the separation proceedings to be the one who was at fault. They often do not fully appreciate that both parents usually contribute to some degree to the parental difficulties and that the party who first decides on separation may have done so only after years of tolerating terrible humiliations and indignities and may be, in reality, the less culpable of the two partners.

The idea that there is one party who is to blame is the most likely conclusion that children will come to, even apart from parental influence. Children tend to think in the most simplistic terms and the younger they are, the less likely they can appreciate the subtleties of joint contribution to the parental difficulties. In addition, in their own conflicts, those below seven or eight tend to consider one person (usually the other guy) to be at fault. It is rare for a young child to say, "I started it." Children's understanding of their own personal conflicts in terms of there being one guilty and one innocent party contributes to their considering their parents' altercations to be similarly derived.

Parents of children who tend to blame one of them entirely for the marital difficulties do well to impress upon them the concept of joint contribution to many, if not most, conflicts between people. To make the discussions more meaningful, they do well to describe specific examples from their own conflicts. Such discussions, of course, are much more meaningful if the parents have provided the children with the basic reasons for the separation. Parents do well to try to help their children appreciate that there are varying degrees of control a parent may have over his or her own alienating behavior. Differentiation should be made between those acts that a parent can control (such as striking another person) and those that cannot be controlled or can only be controlled with great difficulty (such as alcoholism). In addition, the children should be helped to differentiate between parental behavior that causes children pain as the result of parental misguidance and mistakes (such as marrying the wrong person) and parental behavior that purposely causes children pain (such as cruel punishments). Hopefully such discussions will result in the children's becoming more sympathetic to their parents' difficulties and less prone to blame either one of them.

If the children's need to see one of their parents as perfect contributes to the problem, they must be helped to recognize the universality of human imperfection. And parents who may be presenting themselves as free of imperfection (or mostly so) do well to appreciate that they do their children a disservice. Growing up with such an unrealistic view of a parent will not only contribute to the children's becoming perfectionistic themselves but intolerant of all others who inevitably reveal deficiencies (which includes just about everyone). Of course, there are situations in which one of the parents has indeed been the one primarily responsible for the deterioration of the marriage. In such cases, the children should be apprised of his or her responsibility. Lastly, children must be helped to appreciate that blame preoccupations are generally nonproductive and that their time and energies are better spent directed into more constructive ways of handling their reactions to the separation.

Guilt

I use the word guilt to refer to the feelings an individual experiences in association with ideas (whether valid or not) that he or she has done something wrong. Whereas in blame one accuses another of wrongdoing, in guilt one accuses oneself. When an individual harbors thoughts or desires that are considered reprehensible by the significant figures in one's life, or or she is likely to feel guilty over them. And if the person acts them out he or she is likely to feel more guilty. In fact, the failure to experience such guilt would be a manifestation of malfunctioning within that environment. Producing guilt within individuals is necessary for the survival of a civilized society. If each individual were allowed to indulge him- or herself in every act, no matter how much harm it caused others, we would live in a world of fear and chaos. By producing guilt in children during their formative years society can relax somewhat its vigil and most (but certainly not all) adults can be relied upon not to indulge themselves in those acts that are against the best interests of the majority.

Associated with the ideas of wrongdoing that are central to guilt are feelings of worthlessness. It is as if the individual were saying to himself: "How terrible a person I am for what I have done." Generally, there is also an anticipation of punishment in the guilt reaction, but this may not be clearly realized. There is a vague feeling that something unpleasant or painful is going to happen because of the transgression; but the individual may not be able to pinpoint exactly what. In some situations, of course, the particular consequences are well known. The guilt reaction is inappropriate when it is exaggerated, when the consensus of the group within which the individual lives is that the act is not blameworthy, and when the individual fancies himself responsible for an event for which he was in no way responsible. Guilt reactions, especially those of the inappropriate type, are common among children of divorce.

Children to whom guilt is communicated. There are situations in which the child, in a sense, has played a role in the parental conflict. If a child learns that his or her conception was planned in an attempt to improve a faltering marriage and the "marital therapy" didn't work, he or she is likely to consider the separation to be his or her fault and believe that another child might have been more successful in keeping the parents together. If the child learns that his or her birth was unplanned and that the burden of its upbringing was a contribution to the marital discord, he or she is also likely to feel guilty about the separation. If the parents separate soon after the child is born because of the unwillingness on the part of a parent to assume parental responsibility, the child when older is likely to surmise that his or her birth contributed to the breakup.

A parent may be unable to tolerate the demands and burdens of raising a handicapped child and wish to get out of the marriage in order to avoid such responsibilities. The parent may state this overtly or may provide other reasons for the withdrawal—excuses that serve to cover up the true motives. The healthy parent of a handicapped child inevitably has such thoughts at times, but is willing to assume the burdens of his or her upbringing because of love for the child and does not act out flight fantasies. The immature or irresponsible parent may do so.

The child of such a parent is likely to appreciate (even if not directly told) that his or her handicap was a major contributing factor in the parent's abandonment (a word that has more applicability to this situation than other types of parental departure from the home). Accordingly, the child will feel guilty and is likely to say: "If I wasn't so sick, my father (mother) wouldn't have left." Such a child must be helped to appreciate that the real fault lies within the rejecting parent rather than within him- or herself, and that the healthy parent recognizes the fact that a child may be born ill or become so, is willing to accept the responsibilities of care, and does not abandon the child. Such children inevitably feel angry over their parents' rejection of them; yet they may become inhibited regarding expression of their anger lest they suffer even further abandonment. Venting of such children's anger reactions must also be encouraged; however, they must be helped, as well, to resign themselves to the rejection and obtain substitute gratifications so that there will be less anger generated. Also, encouraging in them a "he's more to be pitied than scorned" attitude toward the rejecting parent can reduce anger and lessen their loss of self-esteem.

There are people who are not ready for parenthood or who may never be capable of such a role, and yet they have children. Such a parent may have a perfectly healthy child and yet may not be willing or capable of taking care of it. Such a parent's leaving is, in a sense, the child's fault—because had the child not been born, the marriage might have remained intact. And the child of such a parent is bound to recognize this and feel guilty. Such a child is best approached in a manner similar to that described above for the handicapped child.

There are situations in which parental differences over the raising of the children are a significant factor in the marital discord and this can result in their children's feeling that the separation was their fault. When a father complains bitterly that he is overwhelmed by the financial burdens of the household, then leaves, and does not fulfill his financial commitments to the family, the child is also likely to feel guilty.

In all these situations the separation has indeed taken place because of the parent's view that the child is in some way responsible for the marital breakup. Most often this is communicated to the child, either overtly or covertly. Sometimes such parents attempt to lessen such children's guilty reactions by trying to convince them that the separation was not their fault. But it is their fault in the sense that had they not been born the marriage might still be intact. In such cases, therefore, the children must be helped to appreciate that such parental reassurances, although well meaning, are presented in the attempt to reduce parental guilt over their awareness of the fact that they are indeed rejecting their children for attributes over which the children have no power. Such children must be helped to appreciate that the real fault lies with deficiencies not in themselves but in the parent. In addition, concomitant anger and self-esteem problems should be dealt with as described in previous sections.

Guilt as a way of gaining control over the uncontrollable. One of the most common reactions of children of divorce, especially around the time of separation, is the feeling that they were somehow the cause of their parents' difficulties—when there is absolutely no evidence that this was the case. Some children consider their having been "bad" to be the cause of the separation and they may promise their parents repeatedly that they will forever be "good." Any indiscretion or transgression, no matter how slight, may be seized upon as the cause, and the preoccupation may reach obsessive proportions. They may even quote comments made by the parents to justify their conclusion that the separation was their fault. For example, a boy may interpret a father's saying to his mother, "I can't stand being in this house any longer," to mean that *he* is the objectionable one, rather than his mother. Some children may repeat the act(s) they consider to have caused the separation in order to strengthen their notion that it caused the parents' separation. Such children may even *start* doing bad things in order to maintain this notion. On occasion a child may begin to exhibit antisocial behavior after the separation and then claim that the parents separated because of his or her bad behavior.

Although many factors may operate in the development of this delusion of guilt, the one that is most significant and frequent in my experience is the need to control the uncontrollable. Implicit in the statement "It's my fault" is the notion of control. Such children feel helpless to change their parents' minds regarding the divorce decision. If, however, they can convince themselves that they were the cause—that something *they* did brought about the decision to separate—it follows that there is something they can do to bring about a reversal of the decision. If they can delude themselves into believing that their being bad caused the parents to separate, then all they need do is to be good and the parents will reconcile. A typical plea of such a child to a departing parent usually goes like this: "Please, Daddy, don't leave. I know you're going because I've been bad. I promise I'll never be bad again. I promise I'll never fight with my sister again, or do any other bad things. From now on I'm only going to be good. I'll take out the garbage every day, walk the dog. . . ."

Although most often this type of guilt reaction arises without any direct influence from the parents or others, there are times when there may be an active parental contribution. For example, the family atmosphere may be one in which personal responsibility is always invoked to explain any incident, especially an unfortunate one. No matter how capricious the event and no matter how innocent the family members may have been in bringing it about, somehow someone is considered to have caused it. This tradition of finding out who was at fault can contribute to the children's looking to themselves when parental separation occurs.

The parent who consults a child regarding the divorce decision, even to the point of asking the child's permission, may contribute to the child's developing this form of guilt. Sometimes the child's permission is not really being sought; rather, the parent hopes that the child will approve so the parent can feel less guilty. In such cases the parent would generally have gone ahead with the decision, but without the child's approval would feel much more guilty about it. Others, however, may take the child's view into serious consideration and may even stay together because of the child's disapproval—so great is the parental guilt and fear of angering the child. In such cases the child's feelings of control are not delusional; he is *told* he has control and *in some cases may actually have it.* (The child who does indeed have the power to keep his or her parents together may develop a different kind of guilt: guilt over the responsibility for keeping parents together in a state of misery.)

Reassuring such children that the divorce was in no way their fault is usually futile. Parents may become quite frustrated over the fact that their repeated reassurances to such children that the separation was in no way their fault are to no avail. When one appreciates the mechanisms that underlie such guilt, these children's failure to respond to reassurances becomes understandable. Because the guilt in such situations provides the child with the false security of being able to control and even reverse the calamity of parental separation, he or she does not give up the delusion so easily. To do so would result in the child's having to accept his or her impotence—something most people do not willingly do. It is to the impotence-potency issue that one must direct one's attention if this problem is to be reduced. Such children have to be helped to appreciate that there are certain things in life that one *can* control, and others that one *cannot.* Parents do well here to help the child select and discriminate between things people can control and things they cannot. For example, one *can* control whether one throws a ball, does one's homework, eats a piece of candy, hits one's brother, etc. One *cannot* control such things as rain, snow, lightning, the movement of the sun, etc. And in the latter category one must include for the child: parental divorce. Such children must be helped to resign themselves to this reality. However, one should not stop there on that somewhat defeatist and depressing note. One must help such children recognize that they have it within their power to *do* certain things that can help them lessen the pain of separation. They have it within their power to gain substitute gratifications to compensate for the loss of the parent by involving themselves more meaningfully with others, both peer and adult. When they are able to accomplish this goal, a contributing element to the delusion will have been removed. And when they have real experiences in which they learn to differentiate the controllable from the uncontrollable, to change what they can, and not futilely to try changing what they cannot, then another element in this type of guilt reaction will have been reduced.

Guilt over disloyalty. Most children with separated or divorced parents have loyalty conflicts. Most youngsters are brought up with a deep sense of commitment to the members of their family, especially their parents. All children are supposed to love and respect their parents, and may even learn to feign or profess such attitudes if they do not in fact exist. Even when the marriage is faltering, both parents may continue to attempt to foster in their children (often without conviction) these attitudes toward the spouse. At the time, however, the child may nor be required to take sides or express preferences. But when the separation occurs, children may find themselves in a situation where their loyalty is openly tested, where they are required to make decisions and take actions that reveal without question their preferences. At such times children's feelings of guilt may be profound—even to the point of paralyzing them from taking action or making decisions.

Some children take the side of whichever parent they are with at the time in order to avoid alienating that parent; but they will at the same time feel guilty over their disloyalty toward the absent parent. Generally, such children must be helped to avoid taking sides, even to the point of risking the alienation of a parent. The younger the child the more difficult it may be for him or her to avoid getting drawn into taking sides or professing agreement without conviction. Older children become freer to extract themselves and it is common for adolescents in such situations to take the position "I wash my hands of both of them," or "A plague on both of their houses." The parent, of course, whose behavior is significantly alienating and reprehensible (to the spouse and/or the children) spares his or her children guilt over their disloyalty. The children's rejection of such a parent becomes so justifiable that there is little guilt, only relief.

Some children will feel guilty for having a better time with their fathers on visiting days than with their mothers at home. They must be helped to appreciate that many children have better times on visiting days because there are fewer restrictions being placed upon them. Mother has to make them get up early, go to school, do chores and homework. Father, however, may not have to do such "dirty work" and often comes off as the "good guy." Such children should be helped to appreciate the normality of these reactions and preferences. Non-custodial parents can reduce such guilt by providing their children with more realistic visitation experiences. Providing the children with continual fun and games (often to assuage guilt) is not in their best interests. A more balanced experience—one that includes usual routines and occasional, inevitable, but not contrived frustration—provides children with a healthier experience and avoids the development of this type of guilt.

Visitation schedules may be rigidly defined in the separation agreement and divorce decree. Generally, the more specific these are the less flexibility and trust there has been between the parents. The child's needs for a visit of specific length at a particular time may not be consonant with what his or her parents have legally agreed upon. A child may feel guilty and disloyal for not wishing to visit with a parent at a particular time, or for wishing to have a visit shorter than the allotted period. In such situations the parents do well to inquire into whether reasonable visitation experiences are being provided. If not, then attempts should be made to rectify the situation. But even when this may be accomplished, the child may prefer an alternative arrangement, e.g., a shorter visit, bringing along a friend, or even a skipped visit (with advance notice to both parents, of course). And children must be helped to appreciate that such modifications and compromises of the visitations need not be a reflection of disloyalty: a piece of paper drawn up by the parents and their lawyers need not reflect the children's needs and wishes all the time.

The situation that is more likely than any other to produce disloyalty guilt in children of divorce is custody litigation in which the children are asked to state their preferences regarding which parent they wish to live with. Some argue that children should not be placed in such a position and that the judge, lawyers, and parents should be able to make the decision without exposing the children to such a traumatic inquiry and placing them in such a vulnerable position. Siding with a parent in the course of an argument is one thing. Expressing preference for living with a parent until adulthood, is another thing entirely. When making the latter choice the child is likely to fear that he will alienate forever the rejected parent. Recognizing this, the parties involved in custody litigation may hesitate to ask the children to express directly their preferences. However, to refrain from doing so may deprive the decision makers of valuable information. My own way of handling this is to ask such children their preferences after I have developed some kind of relationship with them. If a child hesitates to provide an answer, I do not press him or her. Rather, I try to surmise from the child's comments, play fantasies, dreams, etc., which parent he or she would prefer to live with. And this information is taken into consideration with other data in making my recommendation. Such children will feel less guilty if the judge orders them to live with the parent whom they basically prefer than if they were overtly to make the choice themselves. They can then take the position to the rejected parent: "It was not I who rejected you, the judge has ordered me to live with Mommy (Daddy)." Placing the decision in the judge's hands not only lessens fears of retaliation by the rejected parent but disloyalty guilt as well, as such children can convince themselves that they played no part in making the choice.

Guilt over hostility. A child's self-blame may relate to his or her guilt over expressing the hostility toward one or both parents that is generally produced by the divorce. Except in those relatively uncommon situations in which the child welcomes the parents' separation, the parent who leaves the home is viewed by children as an abandoner and this cannot but make them angry. Children of divorce may fear expressing anger toward the parent who has left the home, lest they see even less of that parent; and they may fear expressing anger toward the parent with whom they live, lest that parent leave also. If parents believe that a child's being angry at them is inappropriate, "wrong," or "bad," then the child is likely to become even more inhibited. Communicating to the child that hostility toward a parent is "wrong" can be accomplished both overtly or covertly. The parents may actively tell a child how terrible he or she is for having hostile thoughts or feelings and that "good" children never entertain such terrible ideas. Or they may be the kinds of people who never (or rarely ever) express their anger and thereby serve as models for the children's not expressing theirs either.

A more subtle way in which parents may inhibit a child's anger is provided by Marc's situation. Marc's parents separated when he was four. His father left the home and much time was spent with his maternal grandparents, who visited him frequently. On one occasion Marc said to his grandfather: "I'm not the kind of boy who would think mean things about his daddy." The grandfather responded: "Of course not. We know that you're not that kind of boy. We know that you'd *never* think anything mean about your own father." The grandfather related the conversation to Marc's mother, who related it to his father. During the ensuing weeks, every time Marc asked his parents or grandparents whether they considered him to be the kind of boy who thought mean things about his father he was reassured that "no one, even for one minute, thought that Marc would ever be that kind of boy and think such terrible things." And the more Marc was reassured, the more reassurance he asked for. This was no surprise to me, because the family members, under the guise of reducing Marc's guilt over his hostility, were actually increasing it. Their "reassurances" were actually confirming to him that a boy who has such thoughts is inceed loathsome. Because Marc was inevitably having such thoughts (as all children of divorce, at some level, must)—and his statement that he was *not* the kind of boy who has such thoughts is proof that he was having them—he could not but conclude that he was loathsome as well. All concerned would have done better to have made comments along these lines: "All boys and girls have mean thoughts about their parents at times. There's nothing wrong with having such thoughts. When a parent does something that a child doesn't like, the child is bound to have mean thoughts and feelings. There's nothing wrong with you for having them. The best thing you can do with such thoughts is let them out—is to talk about them—so we can then best find out what to do about the things that are making you angry." Accordingly, I advised the parents and grandparents to switch their tactic, to tell Marc that they had made a mistake when they had reassured him as they had, and to provide comments along the lines described above. This was done and there was a disappearance of Marc's preoccupations and questions. In addition, the expression of his angry feelings resulted in his father's visiting more often.

Observing the parents' altercations and the destructive effects of their anger on one another can so frighten children that they may become inhibited in expressing their anger. Oedipal hostility may contribute to the child's guilt. A boy, for example, may wish (consciously or unconsciously) that his father leave in order that he be left with full possession of his mother. Such wishes may be associated with fantasies of the boy's forcibly ejecting the father from the household, or wishing him dead. When the father indeed does leave, the boy may believe that he was responsible.

The anticipation of punishment (which may or may not be clearly realized) is intrinsic to the guilt feeling. Punishment (even self-denigration and social alienation) can as a rule reduce guilt. Such children may try to lessen their guilt with punishment. They may overtly or covertly encourage scapegoatism. They may become accident-prone. Or they may become disruptive and do just those "bad things that will predictably get them punished. Clearly, such methods for reducing guilt are self-destructive and only worsen the child's condition. One must help the child become less guilty over his or her hostility (in a manner appropriate to each of the above-mentioned guilt-inducing situations) if one is to reduce the child's need to lessen guilt with self-destructive maneuvers.

Self-blame as a denial of parental blame. Some children will place the blame of the divorce on themselves in order to deny parental participation and fallibility. It makes such children feel more secure to view their parents as perfect. And if the parents have the need to present themselves as such (by never admitting defects, for example), then such tendencies on the children's part may be enhanced. A separation is a clear statement of deficiency in at least one parent (and generally both). Children with an exaggerated need to maintain images of parental perfection may consider the personality defects that led to the separation to have been theirs rather than their parents, and may dredge up a host of deficiencies to confirm this notion. Generally, the fantasized defects are similar in kind to those utilized to gain a sense of control over the uncontrollable ("I was bad"; "My allowance is too big"; "I fight too much with my sister"); however, here they serve to maintain the delusion of parental infallibility.

Parents who need to present themselves as perfect must appreciate that they are doing their children a disservice and that they are lessening rather than enhancing their children's respect for them. They must recognize that maintaining a facade of perfection is a sign of weakness; and that the stronger and more mature person is willing to admit his faults. They should recognize that their children will ultimately realize that they are covering up their deficiencies and will lose even more respect for them because of their dishonesty and weakness. The healthy parent has enough confidence to appreciate that any loss of the children's respect he or she may suffer from the revelation of occasional liabilities will be more than counterbalanced by their appreciation of his or her assets. Whatever loss of respect a parent suffers from revealing deficiencies is generally small compared to the loss incurred by the children's awareness of the parent's lack of courage to reveal occasional defects. Parents do well, therefore, to expose their deficiencies to their children to an appropriate degree—every personal flaw need not be disclosed—in a natural way. To do so in a planned and contrived way is not likely to work. Rather, this should be done as situations arise (and they inevitably do in the course of living) that would warrant such revelations. And the divorce situation is one that can allow for such appropriate disclosures. Parents should recognize as well that children's viewing their parents as perfect will contribute to their developing interpersonal difficulties with others. Such a notion will produce inevitable disappointment and disillusionment with all others they may encounter, who will inevitably reveal their defects. In fact, this very factor might contribute to dissatisfaction in and even dissolution of their own marriages someday. In addition, such an image of their parents may result in their setting perfectionistic standards for themselves. And this may result in continual dissatisfaction, as they can never live up to the impossibly high standards.

Some children's need to see their parents as perfect may also stem from lack of confidence in their own abilities to cope with many situations that they in fact are quite capable of handling. Attempts to enhance self-confidence and competence are important in helping such children give up the delusion of parental perfection. Later in this chapter I will discuss in detail some of the approaches I utilize to help enhance a child's self-esteem.

Reconciliation Preoccupations

The reaction of most children to the announcement of their parents' separation is to plead that they not separate. Except in the rare situation when children have been so traumatized by the departing spouse that the separation is welcomed by them, children would generally prefer to live with the pains, frustrations, and discomforts of their parents' conflict than to be deprived of one of them. Generally, it is the parents who are suffering much more than the children. Children by nature are very narcissistic (they don't differ very much from adults in this regard) and are not generally affected by arguments that Mommy or Daddy cannot stand the pain any more and will be happier living out of the home. Nor can they project themselves too well into the future and believe that they may be better off after the parents have separated.

The children's pleas that the parents not split up can be one of the most guilt-provoking experiences a divorcing parent may have to suffer and there are many who remain together in order to avoid such guilt. Separating parents do well to appreciate that their guilt is healthy and predictable and an inevitable concomitant of their decision. After all, because of the separation the parent has contributed to the children's unhappiness (even though he or she has not wished to do so). Whether the spouses remain together or separate, the children are likely to suffer. And even though the divorce may result in their suffering less, they are still being deprived of the desirable atmosphere of a stable, two-parent home. If the parent(s) wishes to gain the benefits the divorce will bring about, he or she must be willing to suffer some of the discomforts also associated with the decision. And guilt over the separation's effects on the children is one of the most common and painful of such discomforts. The most effective way for parents to reduce this guilt is to do everything to prevent and alleviate unnecessary suffering for the children. Parents should appreciate also that the children's pleas that the parent(s) reconsider the decision are proof of their affection; that were they not preoccupied with a reconciliation it would reflect a deficiency in their relationship with the departing parent.

The reconciliation preoccupations can take many forms, other than simple pleas to the parents that they reunite and fantasies that they will. For example, some children will utilize varying threats to the absent parent that are often pathetic and impotent, e.g., "If you don't come back home I'll tell everyone you're mean," or "If you don't come back, I'll tell Grandma." Some try to bribe: "I'll give you all the money in my piggy bank," "I'll paint a beautiful picture of you and we'll hang it up in the living room," and "I'll never be bad again." Some try to use money as a manipulative tool: "I'll steal all his money, then he'll have to come back home," and "We'll spend so much money that he won't be able to afford to stay divorced." Some may use depressive symptoms ("Look how miserable you've made me") and even suicidal gestures ("Without you life isn't worth living") in order to produce so much guilt in the departed parent that he or she will return. And others attempt to use force: they hope to make the absent parent so miserable by their incessant tantrums, outbursts, and tirades that he or she will finally submit and return.

George, who was eight years old when I first saw him in treatment, serves as a good example of the kinds of pre-occupations exhibited by children with reconciliation obsessions. George's parents had divorced a few years prior to his first visit and his father was living abroad. He frequently wrote letters describing in great detail his intense love for George. Sometimes the letters promised that the father would be visiting the United States very soon and would then spend much time with George. Exact plans were always to be provided in the next letter. However, each succeeding letter only contained further excuses and procrastinations. Other letters would promise airplane tickets so that George could visit his father where he was living. Again, these were always to be sent in the next letter and, needless to say, they were never forthcoming. George felt like a Yo-Yo, his hopes ever being raised and then dashed.

In an early session George drew a picture of a boy on a beach chasing a butterfly. The butterfly was described as very beautiful. However, each time the boy was about to catch the butterfly, it managed to escape—just as he was about to grab it. And the story ended with the boy's never catching the butterfly. A clearer statement of George's predicament could not be asked for.

Normally reconciliation preoccupations diminish with time as the children become used to their new life-style and become resigned to the fact of the divorce. However, there are children who persist for many months, and even years, in trying to get their parents to reconcile even though they have been repeatedly told that there is no chance whatsoever of the parents' remarrying. There are children who will entertain fantasies of their parents' reuniting even after one or both have remarried. When such preoccupations persist beyond the usual time for their disappearance, other factors are usually operative—factors that go beyond the mere fact of divorce and the natural desire to resume what the child considers to have been a happier state of affairs.

Malevolent ties between the parents as a cause of children's reconciliation preoccupations. I believe that the most common reason for the persistence of reconciliation preoccupations in children is the failure of the parents to become *psychologically* divorced. Although they may be *legally* divorced, and even remarried to others, they may still maintain a psychological tie that can be quite strong. The persistence of such ties (even though subtle and disguised) is, in my opinion, the most powerful contributing factor to continuing reconciliation fantasies in children. The most common manifestation of such a parental tie is the maintenance of hostilities. Arguments over alimony, support, visitation, etc., can persist for years. And lawyers and the courts can be relied upon to contribute to this prolongation. Although a hostile relationship may appear to be one that should offer the child little hope for reconciliation, it actually provides much more hope than the parental relationship in which matters have been settled and there is little, if any, residual hostility. Children appreciate, either consciously or unconsciously, that a hostile relationship between their parents is a much deeper one than little if any involvement at all. In the malevolent relationship the ex-spouses expend significant time and energy involved with one another (either directly or through their lawyers). When the separated parents are frequently fighting, mental images of the parents' involvement with one another are frequently produced in the children's minds. And such imagery contributes to the children's reconciliation obsesssions. Whereas when the parents have essentially settled their differences such fantasies of "togetherness" are less likely to occur. The children of the hostile parents appreciate—sometimes clearly, sometimes vaguely—that their parents still need one another—even if the need is for sadomasochistic gratification (and divorce provides one of the best opportunities for such satisfactions for those with the propensity). Sensing their continuing needs for one another cannot but produce hopes in the children that their parents will once again live together.

Some children may actually foment difficulties between the parents and help perpetuate their fighting from the appreciation that any contact between the parents is more likely to bring about a reconciliation than their having no contact at all. And the parents' needs to continue their hostilities may make them easy prey to their children's schemes to bring about such involvements between them. Each may be selectively gullible to the children's critical and provocative comments about the other; whereas on any other topic they would be judiciously cautious regarding their belief in what the children say.

An even more subtle form of interaction may contribute to the perpetuation of the children's reconciliation fantasies. The parents may decide that any type of friendly and civil involvement on their part may produce reconciliation fantasies in the children. Accordingly, they may strictly refrain from any contact in front of them and reduce their other communications to an absolute minimum (even less than would be naturally indicated and desired). In most cases, such an arrangement is only apparently made for the benefit of the children. Usually, it is a rationalization for the parents to protect themselves from acting out on or giving in to their residual attraction for one another. The facade of coolness and aloofness protects them from expressing their strong desire for involvement. As is often the case, malevolence is used as a device to protect the individual from benevolence. In such a situation, the energy utilized in maintaining "distance" is greater than that expended if there were the usual and necessary contacts. And the amount of mental imagery involving the ex-spouse is greater than in those who have more relaxed attitudes toward one another. As is often the case, the mental life of the parent becomes the mental life of the children. They too become involved in the strict adherence to the rules and regulations of the distance-keeping operations and they thereby get involved in this tie, which only looks like a non-tie.

Benevolent ties between the parents as a cause of children's reconciliation preoccupations. The frequency with which separated and divorced people maintain benevolent ties with one another is hard to determine. Not only does embarrassment often lead such individuals to hide their involvements, but legal factors may play a significant role. Many states will not recognize a period of separation to be valid if there has been a resumption of sexual contact during the period. In other words, the individuals may have to start counting the days of separation all over again if they wish to qualify for a divorce. Even among those who definitely plan to divorce, intermittent sexual contact is not uncommon. Although the children are generally not exposed to such sexual involvement, they are generally aware of the continued benevolent involvement out of which such sexual contacts take place. Seeing their parents still getting along well together cannot but stimulate fantasies of reconciliation in them.

With greater receptivity on society's part to varying life-styles, the "on the fence" arrangement is becoming more widespread. People go on for years never making a final decision. The departing spouse comes back and forth, never being able to decide what to do. One father, for example, may spend two or three nights a week at the home; another stays for a few days or weeks, departs, only to return again for another stint. In such situations the children cannot but have persistent reconciliation fantasies. The children may add to the frequency of the visits and contacts by structuring situations that encourage or provide the parents with excuses for such involvements. They may, for example, insist that both parents be present at every possible school function, birthday party, etc. Even the aid of grandparents and other relatives who support a reconciliation may be enlisted by them.

Just as the children may try to find excuses to promote their parents having contact with one another, the parents themselves may use similar tactics. Mother may call Father for advice on inconsequential matters or to tell him about something cute the child did that day. Father too may find justification for contacting Mother about trivial things that pertain to the children. Each parent here is using concern for the children as a rationalization for involvement with the spouse. And such involvements perpetuate reconciliation fantasies in the children.

Just as artificial aloofness may be used to disguise deep attraction, false friendliness may be used to hide hostility. The parents may present facades of friendliness with the rationalization that it is bad for the children for them to show their deep rage. When they do come together one can feel the coolness of the atmosphere but their words and gestures are ever so polite. Generally, the children are not fooled; they appreciate (albeit vaguely at times) that there is still a lot going on between their parents. Again, the situation contributes to the perpetuation of reconciliation fantasies because the basic continuation of the hostilities is present.

A common parental contribution to reconciliation preoccupations in a child is similar fantasies on the part of a parent. A mother, for example, who persists in her hopes that she may ultimately be reunited with her husband makes it extremely difficult, if not impossible, for her children to resign themselves to his departure. Even if she refrains from verbalizing her hopes, the children somehow sense them. Her statements to the children that their father is never returning cannot be made with any convincing degree of conviction. The feeling of longing that is conveyed when she speaks of her husband will also communicate her true feelings. And her taking every opportunity to resume contact will also reveal her genuine feelings. Similarly, a father who persists in trying to convince his rejecting wife to reconsider her decision to separate will strengthen his children's reconciliation fantasies regardless of the firmness of their mother's refusals.

Factors within the child that cause reconciliation obsessions. When the departed parent offers the child much more gratification than does the custodial parent, reconciliation preoccupations are likely to persist. There was a time, not too long ago, when the court was required to give a mother custody unless gross and extreme negligence could be definitely established. Only if the mother were a prostitute, drug addict, or severe alcoholic, or she exhibited other forms of severe neglect, could the father hope to gain custody of the children. (Even then prolonged litigation was often necessary.) The assumption was that the female was innately superior to the male in performing parental functions. Accordingly, many children were forced to remain with mothers who were far less equipped to take care of them than were their fathers. Fortunately, in recent years, the courts have come to appreciate that femininity is not necessarily to be equated with parental capacity; as a result, although the percentage is still quite small, many more fathers are now being granted custody, and this contributing factor to reconciliation preoccupations is therefore becoming less common. Living with the preferred and more suitable parent results in the children's being less obsessed with the return of the absent parent.

Children who are excessively guilty over conscious or unconscious hostility toward the departed parent may become obsessed with his or her returning to the home. They may be preoccupied with the latter's welfare, fear frequently that the parent is sick or injured, and seek the continual reassurance of the parent's well-being that his or her return to the home can provide. As mentioned, such concerns provide reassurance that the hostile wishes have not been realized and that no harm to the parent has resulted from them. There may be associated separation anxieties which make the termination of each visitation especially difficult. And reconciliation obsessions provide hope for the reduction and even cessation of such separation anxieties.

Oedipal problems may contribute to a child's obsession with parental reconciliation. A boy, for example, living with a dating mother may find the seemingly endless flow of men in and out of his mother's life an unbearable burden. He had enough trouble dealing with the jealousy he felt toward his father for the intimacies he shared with his mother. Now it appears that practically every man in the world—with the exception of himself—has such opportunities. Preoccupations with his mother's remarrying his father may be his only way of stemming the tide of these unwanted strangers. Similarly a girl, even though living with her mother, may learn of her father's dating and develop similar reactions. Toward the parents of the same sex as well, the child may develop jealousies over dating and see reconciliation as the only hope for reducing such feelings of rivalry. For example, a girl may be jealous over all the attentions her mother is receiving and long for the time when only one man demonstrated these.

Children whose guilt over their parents' separation is a manifestation of the need to control an uncontrollable situation may also become preoccupied with their parents' reuniting. Typically, they are preoccupied with ideas that the divorce took place because they are "bad," and, conversely, that the parents will reconcile if they are "good." As they view the situation, only by their parents reuniting can they hope to reduce such guilt and feel better about themselves.

Some children live in areas where divorce is either very uncommon (increasingly rare) or where the child of divorce is stigmatized (also becoming rare). Such children may try to hide the fact that their parents are separated and may avoid having friends to their homes, lest the secret be divulged. In the service of avoiding such disclosure they may become preoccupied with reconciliation.

I can best introduce my next point anecdotally. There are well-known psychological experiments in which a hungry rat in a cage is taught to press a bar in order to obtain a pellet of food. Psychologists differentiate between the strength of such learning when the pellets are given *periodically* and when they are given *aperiodically*. In what psychologists refer to as *periodic reinforcement* the rat is rewarded (reinforced) with a pellet in accordance with a fixed relationship between bar presses and pellet release, i.e., the rat receives a pellet with every press, or every second press, or every fifth press, etc.—depending upon the plan of the experiment. When the rat appears to have learned to press the bar in order to obtain pellets, he is said to be *conditioned*. In *aperiodic reinforcement* there is a random and ever varying relationship between bar presses and the release of a pellet, i.e., sometimes the rat may receive a pellet immediately after a bar press, then he may not get one until he has pressed the bar ten, twenty, thirty, or even more times, and then he may get two, three, or more pellets in succession.

Let us now imagine an experiment in which three rats in three separate cages each receive a total of 100 pellets in the conditioning process. The first is given a pellet after *each* press of the bar. Then no further pellets are given. Let us say that after x number of presses the rat returns to the random frequency of bar presses present before reinforcement was instituted. In other words, the rat, no longer gaining pellets, stops pressing the bar more than he normally would in his chance encounters with it as he roams the cage. The conditioning is then said to have been *extinguished*. If the second rat is also conditioned with a total of 100 pellets, but each one of his is given only after *five* bar presses, i.e., on the fifth press after four unrewarded presses, it may take $5x$, $10x$, $15x$, or even more bar presses before the rat returns to his previously random frequency of bar presses. Having expected unrewarded presses, he has become accustomed to them and expects most of his presses to be unrewarded. Accordingly, it takes him a much longer time to become deconditioned. Let us now consider a third rat, who is rewarded aperiodically. Sometimes he may receive two pellets in a row, or three pellets out of five presses, and at other times he may go fifty or a hundred presses before being rewarded. His tolerance for unrewarded presses is far greater than that of the other two rats and the extinction of his conditioning may take significantly longer. In fact, he may require $100x$ or $200x$ or even more presses before returning to his random frequency. He may never give up and may even continue pressing until he drops from exhaustion—so powerful is the aperiodically conditioned response.

I believe that parents who provide their children with little affection, but who still give some in an unpredictable way, are likely to foster the kind of response exhibited by the third rat. Children of such parents may become obsessed with parental reunion in the service of gaining affection from the lost parent. They just never seem to give up trying to extract affection from a parent who appears to have little (but not *no*) capacity to provide it. They may spend their whole lives in this futile quest and others can only wonder why they never give up, never seem to be able to see the obvious.

Another behavioral pattern observed in lower animals that may also exist in humans and play a role in children's reconciliation preoccupations is called *imprinting*. If one takes the fertilized egg of a duck, removes it from the mother, and allows it to hatch in a cage in which there is a moving mechanical toy (not necessarily resembling a duck), the newborn duckling will develop a strong attachment to the toy similar to that it would have developed with its natural mother. More specifically, if during the first thirty-six hours of the duckling's life it has absolutely no contact with any other moving objects (animate or inanimate), and if it has the opportunity for physical contact with the moving toy (especially during the thirteen-to-sixteen-hour period), it will follow the toy wherever it goes in a manner similar to the way it would have with its natural mother. It follows the toy whenever it can and tries to be close to it as much as possible. The following and attachment response is said to have become *imprinted* and the phenomenon is referred to as *imprinting*. So powerful is such imprinting that the duckling will follow the mechanical device even when its natural mother appears and the preference for the toy will persist throughout the duckling's life. It appears that for ducks and many other lower animals (such as chicks, lambs, and monkeys) there is the capacity to form a deep bond with the *first moving object* with which the animal has physical contact. The most important determinant as to whether this bond will form is that the contact take place during the earliest hours after birth, generally referred to as the *critical period*. (For chicks and ducks the critical period is the first thirty-six hours of life. The duration varies with the species of animal.) It is during the critical period that the animal has the greatest capacity to form the attachment and after that time attachments are either weak or impossible to accomplish. If a duckling spends the first thirty-six hours with its natural mother, it will no longer be possible to get the bird to form a following attachment with another adult duck or a mechanical toy. If an animal is totally isolated from moving objects or animals during the critical period it will exhibit significant impairment in forming attachments bonds throughout its life.

So strong is the imprinted bond that the animal forms with the first moving object that it may persist even when the original object becomes a source of pain and even when pleasure-giving substitutes are present. In fact, if the first moving object provides the animal with pain during the critical period (in the form of mild electric shocks, for example), the attachment may become even stronger. In what is referred to as the "law of effort," the bond appears to be strengthened if the animal has to make greater efforts than would normally occur in order to have contact with the first moving object. For example, if the duckling has to walk up an inclined plane each time it wishes to have contact with the object, it forms a stronger attachment bond than if the object were more easily accessible.

Such inborn reaction patterns are more readily demonstrated in lower animals than in human beings and, of course, they are more readily studied in controlled experiments. They have been well demonstrated in animals close to us on the evolutionary scale. There is good reason to believe that humans have similar inborn reaction patterns but we are less beholden to respond to them in an uncontrollable and reflex way. It appears, for example, that the migration of birds to warmer climates in winter is a manifestation of such a pattern. It is likely that the bird has little if any control over such behavior. Humans obviously have much more control over their mobility regarding movement to a more comfortable environment. In lower animals mating behavior becomes fairly ritualized and appears to be reflex. Humans have far more control over their behavior when sexually stimulated. In spite of our greater control over such patterns, it does appear that they do exist in modified form in humans.

It is probable that the attachments that children make

to their mothers and fathers in the earliest months of life may become so deeply embedded in the psychological structure that they are compelled to attach themselves to their parents no matter how rejecting a parent may be. It is even possible that the parent who provides pain or the parent who is hard to reach may be harder to give up than the one who has been more benevolent. Children in residential treatment centers may run away in order to return to parents who have subjected them to the most cruel and inhumane treatment. And the staff members, who have made every attempt to treat the children with love and care, are perplexed as to why such children are so compelled to return. Perhaps these animal experiments are providing us with an explanation. And perhaps they explain, as well, why children may become preoccupied with hopes that an absent parent will return even though that parent has treated them in the most rejecting and cruel manner.

Additional ways of helping children reduce reconciliation preoccupations. As part of the process of adjusting to parental separation the children do well to provide themselves with substitute relationships, both adult and peer. In this way they can partly compensate for the loneliness and deprivations of the parents' separation. The child who fails to do this, whatever the reasons, is more likely to develop preoccupations regarding the departed parent's returning. Of course, reconciliation obsessions per se can interfere with the development of such relationships and a vicious cycle is thereby set up. Accordingly, parents do well to encourage their children to develop such substitute relationships as soon after the separation as possible.

Since the parental factors in children's reconciliation obsessions may be formidable, it is not likely that children's preoccupations with their parents being reconciled will be reduced as long as the parents maintain their contributions. Many parents, when apprised of the kinds of contributing factors that I have described, may be able to alter their behavior and reduce thereby their children's reconciliation preoccupations. Some may require personal counseling before they can accomplish this. In many cases the only hope for the children's giving up this obsession is joint counseling of the parents. Such counseling presents special problems for the therapist for a number of reasons. Firstly, the parents' actual participation may in itself foster the very symptom it is designed to alleviate. The fact that the parents are co-operating in an activity may very well increase the children's hopes for reconciliation. This drawback should not be a reason for their not involving themselves in such joint work, because this disadvantage may be far outweighed by the advantages. In addition, separated and divorced parents generally prefer to have as little to do with one another as possible. Accordingly, they are generally not going to be receptive to joint counseling, even for the benefit of their children. Those who are maintaining their relationship via hostile integration may agree to counseling, but often use it as a platform for expressing grievances or perpetuating their conflict rather than cooperatively trying to reduce the hostilities. And when lawyers are still on the scene such counseling may make a mockery of the therapy as each party withholds that which might compromise his or her legal position. For these reasons I have had little successful experience with joint counseling of separated or divorced parents whose maintenance of hostilities has been the primary factor in their children's reconciliation obsessions or other difficulties. Working with one of the parents is more common, while the other parent may or may not be seeing another therapist. On occasion, I have been able to counsel both parents in a constructive way, but such situations have been rare. When treating such children I have on a number of occasions had the experience that the malevolent interaction between the parents has been so deep and fierce that I have had to inform them that I am working against insurmountable odds, that it is unlikely, if not impossible, for me to help the child as long as the parental hostilities are maintained at such a pitch. And the therapy has failed because they have been unable to extract themselves from their continual conflict.

Children whose social stigmatization contributes to their reconciliation fantasies must be helped to appreciate that the problem lies with those who stigmatize rather than with them. And those who try to hide the fact of divorce must be helped to appreciate that they are adding new and unnecessary burdens to those they already have to bear.

Although true psychological divorce is far more important than legal divorce in reducing reconciliation obsessions, informing the children when the divorce has been finalized can still be of value. At such times I generally suggest that parents actually show the children the divorce decree. Of course, the younger the child, the less significance such a document can have. Older children might be shown significant clauses that clearly state that the marriage has terminated. There is a certain power that printed words have over the spoken, and children are especially subject to their influence. And when remarriage takes place, a further reduction in reconciliation obsessions may occur. However—and I cannot emphasize this point too strongly—even with remarriage on the part of both spouses, if they are still psychologically involved with one another, their children are likely to be given hope for reconciliation, no matter how vigorously the parents deny the possibility.

Sexual and Identification Problems

Growing up in a household with only one parent is likely to deprive the child of the psychological benefits to be derived from the two-parent household. The boy's relationship with his mother and the girl's with her father serve as models for their future relationships with the opposite sex. In addition, the same-sexed parent serves as the most important model for the child's own sex role. Although most single parents are aware of the importance of the children's having a good relationship with the absent parent, even the best efforts to accomplish this do not usually provide the child with the full benefits of the relationship. Living with someone in the same home is very different from visitation—love, interest, proper guidance, etc., notwithstanding. In this section I will focus on two possible sources of difficulty that may arise in the divorce situation, namely, sex identification and oedipal problems. Although children of divorce may develop other kinds of sexual problems, these are not only the two most common, in my experience, but serve as the basis for other types that may, on occasion, arise.

The Freudian theory of the Oedipus complex. Many psychiatrists, psychologists, and other mental health professionals (but by no means all) consider Sigmund Freud's theory of the Oedipus complex to provide a reasonable explanation of many of the sexual problems of both children and, subsequently, adults. Some even hold that many, if not all, neurotic problems (even those without any obvious sexual implication, for example, phobias and compulsions) are best understood as being derived from oedipal difficulties. Although I do not consider myself among the strict subscribers to this theory (I will explain subsequently my views regarding the theory), an understanding of it can be useful in helping children of divorce deal with sexual problems that may arise—either related or unrelated to the divorce situation.

Toward the end of the third year of life, Freud believed that all psychologically healthy children develop sexual interest in the parent of the opposite sex. Associated with the desire for sexual contact with the opposite-sexed parent is the desire to get rid of the same-sexed parent so that the child can enjoy total possession of the loved parent. This phase is said to last until the age of five or six. Freud called such preoccupations and fantasies the Oedipus complex. The term *oedipal* was derived from Oedipus, the hero of the Greek tragedy *Oedipus Rex,* written by Sophocles about 430 B.C. In the play, Oedipus, through a series of fateful events, actually consummates the oedipal act; namely, he kills his father and has sexual intercourse with his mother. The term *complex* refers to a constellation of thoughts and feelings centering on a particular theme. Briefly, then, the child with an Oedipus complex manifests a genital-sexual attraction to the parent of the opposite sex and an associated feeling of jealousy and hostility toward the parent of the same sex. The urges are considered to be genital-sexual, although not necessarily specifically associated with heterosexual intercourse as the primary source of genital gratification.

Oedipal fantasies, according to the classical Freudian school, may include a variety of misconceptions regarding the exact nature of the parents' sexual life: the child may fantasize that the parents get pleasure by looking at one another's genitals; by engaging in oral-genital contact; by rubbing themselves against each other; or by going to the toilet together. Included also are the child's fantasies of marriage to the opposite-sexed parent. Boys crave to father the mother's babies or, for the son who does not appreciate the relationship between sexual activity and pregnancy, to be in some way responsible for the mother's getting babies. And girls similarly become preoccupied with longings to bear the father's children. In each case, the child fantasizes him- or herself in the role of the rival parent. In addition, the boy may fear that his hostility toward his father will result in the latter's retaliation, especially by cutting off the boy's genitals, and this produces what Freud called castration anxiety.

Freud's explanation for the development of the Oedipus complex in the male was far simpler than in the female. The boy's possessive love of his mother and murderous rage toward the father is a natural extension of the loving relationship the mother has always provided him. The term *resolution* is used by psychoanalysts to refer to the passing or the disappearance of the Oedipus complex. The resolution of the Oedipus complex for the boy involves resigning himself to the fact that he cannot totally possess his mother—a resignation made easier by his fear of castration by the father. Observing the female's absence of a penis confirms for him that his own penis can be removed. In addition, through identification with his father, the boy takes in the latter's dictates against incest and murder. Such identification further assists him in repressing his oedipal impulses. He develops a contempt for all who could or would have sex with his mother, be it himself, his father, or anyone else. Lastly, Freud considered normal biological maturation to contribute as well to the resolution. Freud considered such fantasies to be very much in conscious awareness during the oedipal period. On resolution, however, much is said to become relegated to the unconscious and so most men have little, if any, recollection of having had such fantasies during this period of their lives.

For the girl, according to Freud, things are more complicated. When she first observes that the little boy has a penis, she considers herself to have been deprived of a most valuable organ. Her mother, who bore her this way, is blamed, and the little girl turns to her father for love. (Because the mother also lacks this invaluable part, the girl's respect for her markedly diminishes.) The father, as the possessor of a penis, is looked upon as a more likely source of gratifying the little girl's desire to have one herself; and through fantasied sexual intercourse with the father, the female child hopes to obtain a penis. The adult female, by bearing a male child, can satisfy her desire to produce a penis of her own. Even if the baby is a female, it can still symbolically represent the longed-for penis. Other factors that contribute to the girl's transfer from the original mother-love to father-love relate to the girl's anger toward her mother. The mother becomes an object of hostility because she inhibits the little girl's masturbation. In addition, because the mother refuses to give up her affection for the father in order to devote herself totally to the child, she is further resented.

In the female's oedipal resolution, too, the child resigns herself to the fact that her mother's love for her father is such that she can never have him completely to herself. Rebuffed by her father, she renounces and represses her oedipal wishes. Since her father will not provide her with the penis she so desperately wants, getting one symbolically through childbearing is the best she can hope for, and she must turn eventually to other men for this purpose. Like the boy, the little girl represses most, if not all, recollection of these fantasies at the time of oedipal resolution.

The concept of the Oedipus complex that seems most reasonable to me. I do not strictly adhere to the Freudian theory of the Oedipus complex. The view that I present here is based on modifications that have been suggested by others as well as my own understanding of the phenomenon gained from clinical experience with children—both normal and those with psychiatric problems.

First, I believe that there is a biological sexual instinct that attracts every human being to members of the opposite sex. From birth to puberty this drive is not particularly strong, because during this period the child is not capable of fulfilling the drive's primary purpose, namely, reproduction. Although weak and poorly formulated during the period prior to puberty, it nevertheless exhibits itself through behavior that I consider manifestations of *oedipal interest*. The normal child may speak on occasion of marrying the parent of the opposite sex and getting rid of his or her rival. These comments may even have a mildly sexual component, such as "and then we'll sleep in bed together." But I do not believe that psychologically healthy children have the desire in this period for genital-sexual experiences with the parent, nor do I believe that their sexually tinged comments are associated with strong sexual-genital urges. Rather, what the healthy child may on occasion want is a little more affection and attention, undiluted by any rivals.

I believe that in a setting where a child is not receiving the affection, nurture, support, interest, guidance, protection, and generalized physical gratifications (such as stroking, warmth, and rocking) that are his or her due, he or she may, in frustration, become preoccupied with obtaining such satisfactions and develop the kinds of sexual urges, preoccupations, and fantasies that Freud referred to as oedipal. The instinctive sexual urges, which are normally mild prior to puberty, have the *potential* for intensive expression even as early as birth. Getting little gratification from the parents, the child may develop various fantasies in which the frustrated love is returned and the rival is removed. Such fantasies follow the principle that the more one is deprived, the more one craves and the more jealous one becomes of those who have what one desires. Such manifestations can appropriately be called *oedipal problems* in the classical Freudian sense. Thus the foundation for the development of neurosis is formed not, as Freud would say, through the failure to resolve successfully one's sexual frustrations regarding the parent of the opposite sex, but through the failure to come to terms with the more basic deprivations the child is suffering.

Freud considered oedipal preoccupations to arise in the child automatically, but held that parental seduction played a significant role in intensifying the Oedipus complex and made it more difficult for children to resolve their Oedipus complexes. The seduction could be overtly physical or it could arise through verbal provocations or titillating experiences such as a parent's undressing in front of an opposite-sexed child. Deriving some degree of oedipal gratification from such seductivity, the child becomes less likely to give up the attraction to the parent and go on to more appropriate choices. Whereas Freud believed that the Oedipus complex arises spontaneously, and that parental seduction intensifies it, I hold with those who believe that it does not necessarily arise spontaneously, but that environmental factors (such as parental seductivity) may give rise to the kinds of preoccupations Freud termed oedipal. Similarly, parental hostility toward the same-sexed child would be another environmental influence that could predispose a child to oedipal obsessions—in this case hostile rivalrous feelings.

My experience has been that children rarely, if ever, exhibit such clear-cut attraction to the opposite-sexed parent and hostility toward the same-sexed. Rather, they generally harbor ambivalent feelings toward both parents, that is, a mixture of loving and hateful feelings. The boy with a depriving yet seductive mother has good reason to be both attracted to and angry at her. He is deprived of basic affection and provided with seduction as a substitute. The anger may be revealed directly, but more commonly it is handled by a variety of mechanisms that I will describe later in this chapter. A boy may still harbor, in addition to his rivalrous hostility toward his father, deep-seated loving feelings and dependent longings toward him. The hostility may cause anxiety that he may lose the father. And this may result in symptoms similar to those utilized to protect the child from the guilt he would experience if he or she were consciously aware of the anger (again, these mechanisms will be discussed in detail). Anyone who has observed what is sometimes referred to as a childhood "oedipal panic," whether in the boy or in the girl, will readily confirm that intense feelings of love, hate, and fear regarding both parents dominate the clinical picture.

Neuroses, most would agree, are the result of many factors acting in various combinations: cultural, social, familial, psychological, and biological. For Freud, the psychological and sexual factors were crucial and he considered the unresolved Oedipus complex to be at the root of all neuroses. In my opinion, whatever cultural, social, and biological factors may be operative in causing neurotic symptoms, parental—and especially maternal—deprivation is essential to the formation of most, if not all, of them. Neurotic symptoms are in part an attempt to cope with this basic deprivation; and the way in which the child chooses to adapt to such deprivation is determined by biological, cultural, social, and familial influences. Some deprived children become overdependent, an adaptation fostered and perpetuated by their overprotective parents. (An overprotective parent is still depriving because he or she is not providing the child with an environment conducive to his or her growing up into a self-sufficient, independent adult.) Other rejected children react by withdrawing, an adjustment with which their neglectful parents are comfortable. Others discharge in sports the hostility they feel toward their rejectors—sports being, in addition, an activity of premium value in most cultures. Others take drugs or become juvenile delinquents because that's how kids on their block adjust to the deprivation. With drugs they desensitize themselves to the pain of their rejection and their delinquent behavior provides an outlet for the anger they feel over the parental rejection. Others use symptoms such as exaggerated reactions to minor physical illness or feigned physical complaints to gain compensatory attention, to trap parents into giving attention that they might not otherwise obtain. And so it goes. One could cover the wide range of psychological symptoms and find the common element of deprivation in most, if not all, of them. I am fully aware that symptoms are most complex and many factors contribute to their formation, but the adaptation to emotional abandonment is central and ever present. The well-loved child is generally relatively free of psychological disturbance.

I use the term *oedipal* then to refer to those mechanisms by which the child, in the attempt to compensate for early emotional deprivation, obsessively craves for and tries to gain the affection of the opposite-sexed parent. Oedipal problems are likely to arise in a situation of parental seduction or paternal authoritarianism, but they can appear in other family settings as well.

The range of psychological reactions to parental rejection is broad. When the predominant theme appears to involve obsessive attempts to gain the love of the opposite-sexed parent or excessive rivalry with the same-sexed parent, then one can conveniently apply the term *oedipal*. The male homosexual, for example, often comes from a home in which his mother has been seductive, overprotective, and used him as a father substitute, but rarely to the point of overt sexual involvement. In addition, the fathers of male homosexuals are often rejecting and even sadistic. Why then should such men claim that they love men when their experiences suggest that they should grow up hating them? This is readily explained when one appreciates that the obsessive "love" of homosexual males for men is often, among other things, a thinly disguised attempt to deny an underlying hatred of men. They fear women because they too closely resemble their forbidden, seductive mothers. Accordingly, because their difficulties fundamentally reflect the oedipal formulation, they can be considered to have oedipal problems. When a patient's adjustment to the privation involves, for example, compulsive eating, the term *oedipal* is not usually used even though the food may be a symbolic representation of the mother's love. The more remote the overt symptom is from the themes of mother-love and father-hate (or vice versa), the less likely it will be labeled oedipal. However, if the compulsive eater has a dependent, thinly disguised sexual relationship with his or her mother, the problem would more likely be considered oedipal.

Thus the term *oedipal* is misleading because it purports to describe a symptom complex that rarely, if ever, exists in pure form. Most often, if not always, there are elements of problems other than sexual. In addition, to use the term *oedipal* is equivalent to naming pneumonia "cough" or encephalitis "headache." Just as cough and headache are the superficial manifestations of the more general underlying diseases, pneumonia and encephalitis, the Oedipus complex is only one possible symptomatic manifestation of a whole class of symptom complexes resulting from the basic disorder of parental deprivation. Also, the term is restrictive because it tends to focus undue attention on the sexual elements in the adaption while disregarding the more important, non-sexual aspects. It suggests that the primary problem is sexual, which it is not in most cases.

My comments on the Oedipus complex here in no way constitute a total theory. Nor do I wish to suggest that parental deprivation of love can successfully explain all oedipal problems or indeed all neuroses. There is still much in this field that requires re-examination and classification. My intent is merely directed to correcting widespread distortions and making Freud's basic concept more directly applicable to contemporary society.

The resolution of the Oedipus complex. The normal child, according to Freud, resolves his Oedipus complex by the age of five and a half to six. He then supposedly enters a six-year period of low sexual activity—the latency period—which terminates at puberty. There is, indeed, little sexual interest in this period, but not, I believe, because of repression of oedipal drives and resolution of the Oedipus complex, but rather because, as I have described, there is relatively little genital-sexual urge to be repressed in the first place. It is not until puberty, with physiological genital maturation, that sexual urges of adult intensity are normally present. The child has the potential to exhibit such interest and achieve such gratification, but to do so on a frequent basis would be, in my opinion, a sign of psychological difficulty.

In spite of this low level of sexual activity during this period, there is probably more sexual interest and fantasy than in the preceding phases of life, not less, as Freud indicates. Because of the child's greater experiences with those outside his home, he is more likely to have encountered arousing sexual stimuli.

The word *resolution* is generally used to refer to the cure or dissolution of the Oedipus complex, but I prefer to use the term *alleviation*, because oedipal involvements and interests are never completely resolved. At best oedipal problems can be alleviated. And the problems to be alleviated are not usually the result of parental sexual seduction but rather of more generalized emotional deprivation. Therefore, I consider the improvement in the parent–child relationship crucial to the alleviation of oedipal problems in the child. The boy who has obtained little emotional gratification from his mother may become obsessed with obtaining it. His entire life may be devoted to this futile pursuit. It is as though he reasoned that there is no point in moving on to seek satisfaction from others. If his own mother does not provide him with enough affection, how can he expect strangers to offer it? Such gratification in childhood will make him more confident about his ability to obtain similar satisfactions from others in the future. Oedipal problems, or others that stem from this frustration, are best alleviated by an improvement in the youngster's relationship with his mother. The earlier this is accomplished the less the likelihood the problems will become deeply entrenched. Similarly, when a girl develops oedipal problems (such as excessive cravings for male attention and affection) or other symptoms resulting from deprivation of paternal affection, an improvement in the father–daughter relationship in childhood is the best way of alleviating such problems. Of course, when the psychological problems result from deprivation of affection from the same-sexed parent (also common), then improvement of that relationship is necessary if the problems are to be alleviated.

In order to accomplish an improvement in the parent–child relationship that might alleviate oedipal and other problems stemming from parental deprivation of affection, changes must be effected in the parent(s) and the child. It is beyond the scope of this book to deal in depth with the wide range of problems in a parent that might impair affectionate involvement with his or her child. Much of the advice contained in this book is designed to reduce those impairments that can be alleviated by such instructions and recommendations. For parents whose problems are of such depth that the approaches described here are inadequate, counseling or therapy may be necessary. Here I will focus on those things a parent can do to lessen the child's contribution to difficulties in the parent–child relationship—especially those that produce oedipal problems related to the failure to resolve or alleviate the Oedipus complex.

One has a greater chance of helping children reduce their contribution to difficulties in the parent–child relationship if they can be brought to the point of appreciating that they are playing a role in the difficulties. Children are not famous for the readiness with which they admit their own contributions to their problems (adults do not excel in this department either) and so the task to get them to see their participation may be a difficult one. Although such insight is helpful in getting them to change the behavior patterns that are contributing to the difficulties, it is not crucial. The various suggestions presented here may still be utilized without the child's actually consciously realizing that the changes one is attempting to effect have as their goal an alleviation of the child's role in his or her difficulties with the parent(s).

Such children should be helped to gain a more accurate picture of their parents, especially of the areas in which the parents can provide them with meaningful gratifications and those in which they cannot. They must be helped to accept the fact that they cannot completely possess either of their parents and that the affection and attention of each of them must be *shared* with other members of the family. This sharing concept is an important one to impart. Children must be helped to appreciate that no one can possess another person completely: father shares mother with the children; mother shares the father with the children; and they have no choice but to share mother with father and the siblings. In the context of sharing, however, they *must be reassured that, although they may not get as much as they might want, they will still get something.*

Such children should be encouraged to seek satisfactions from their parents in the areas in which they are genuinely capable of providing them, at such times as they can be provided, and to pursue elsewhere those gratifications that the parents are incapable of giving. Deeper involvement with peers is encouraged to help them compensate for parental deficiencies, and they should be consoled with the hope that as they grow older they will be increasingly able and free to enjoy meaningful relationships with others. Identifications with assertive adults should be fostered so that their future chances of obtaining a desirable mate will be enhanced. Although men in our culture still take the more assertive role in dating, courting, mating, and other forms of sexual pursuit (the Women's Liberation Movement has not been too successful in changing this tradition), women still must learn to assert themselves (generally in a more passive-seductive way) if they are to enjoy successful relationships with men. Teachers, camp counselors, scoutmasters, ministers, recreation directors, etc., can serve such functions for these youngsters.

Whereas for Freud the resolution of oedipal conflicts results from fear of castration, resignation, and natural biological processes, in this approach attempts are made to help the children gain compensation for the parental loss or deficiency, thereby making it more likely that they will be able to give up the oedipal obsession. Children with oedipal problems have not pursued these alternatives on their own and must be helped to do so. I cannot imagine true resolution without such substitutes.

Attempts should also be made to diminish the guilt children may feel over their sexual or rivalrous hostile thoughts and feelings toward the parents (especially the same-sexed) and to correct misconceptions that contribute to such guilt. They should be repeatedly told, for example, that their impulses in these areas are shared by most, if not all, children. They should be reassured that hostile thoughts, by themselves, cannot harm and that anger is best used constructively to bring about a reduction in frustration and resentment. One does well to encourage such children's entering situations where they may have the living experience that the expression of anger does not generally result in the dire consequences they may anticipate. Even when the child's symptoms are overtly sexual, emphasis on the relatively non-sexual approaches I have described is generally more effective in alleviating oedipal problems.

Regarding the resolution of oedipal conflicts, one final point should be made. The term *resolution* implies a final working through, a complete solution, a coming to peace with one's Oedipus complex. I think that the more one has been deprived, the less the likelihood that one can fully resolve his or her reactions to early deprivations. No parent is perfect; all parents deprive their children somewhat; no child is ever fully satisfied that all of his or her desires have been gratified by the parents. Children rarely fully appreciate the efforts of their parents and the time and energy involved in their upbringing. They often recall more clearly the frustrations and deprivations. It is common for children to be excessively critical of their parents, because they project their own hostilities onto them and thereby exaggerate parental malevolence. Even when children become parents and they have had the opportunity to view the parent–child relationship from another vantage point, they still tend to maintain their childhood distortions and see parents as more depriving than they really have been. (Of course, there are those who carry into adulthood idealized views of their parents. But distortions in the direction of excessive criticism and feelings of deprivation are more common, in my experience.) Accordingly, the foundations for oedipal and deprivational problems lie within all of us and the likelihood of their being totally resolved is, in my opinion, quite small.

Parental factors that contribute to oedipal problems in children of divorce. As mentioned, many mental health professionals believe that when separation occurs during the oedipal period the child is particularly vulnerable to the development of problems related to the failure to resolve the Oedipus complex. For example, without a father fully available to identify with, the boy is not likely to incorporate parental dictates that contribute to the repression of his sexual desires toward his mother. He may interpret his father's leaving as the fulfillment of his wishes that he do so, i.e., he may consider himself to have been the victor in the oedipal rivalry. The girl is deprived of her model man, and so is likely to develop difficulties in her relationships with men, both present and future.

I believe that every period of childhood presents its own special problems for the child when a separation occurs. Each developmental level has its own needs and is subject to its own particular frustrations. I do not believe that the oedipal period is the one in which the child is *most* sensitive to the loss of a parent. Rather, I believe that the younger children are at the time of separation, and the longer they live without two parents, the more deprivation they will suffer and the greater will be the likelihood of psychological disturbance occurring.

Some parents may deal with the frustrations they experience over the loss of a spouse by attempting to get their child to serve as a substitute. A mother, for example, may tell her son, "You're the man of the house now that Daddy's gone." Although such a boy may find the comment anxiety-provoking because he does not feel equipped to assume the awesome responsibilities that such a position entails, he may also find it gratifying because it suggests that he can satisfy cravings for fuller possession of his mother. Oedipal resolution is thereby made more difficult, especially if the boy has a prolonged experience in which he becomes the mother's confidant and is frequently required to assume many responsibilities that his father ordinarily would have. A girl, similarly, may be encouraged to take her mother's place by her father—with similar repercussions.

When the parent becomes sexually seductive with the child, the chances of oedipal problems arising become even greater. I am not referring necessarily to actual overt sexual experiences with the children—these are rare—but to such common forms of stimulation and subtle seductivity as undressing in front of older children, titillating embracing and stroking, and frequent talk about sex and nudity. The parent may be seductive because it can provide an outlet for sexual cravings. This may be especially true for the mother, who may have few opportunities for sexual gratification. Having failed in a marriage (even though the father's difficulties may have been the most significant in bringing about the separation) will generally make her insecure in her relationships with other men, and this may contribute to her choosing her son—someone who is "captive prey" and has already proved his loyalty and affection. And similar considerations hold for fathers and their daughters.

A good example of the way in which a divorced mother's seductivity can affect a boy is provided by Jim, who was referred to me at age eight because of facial tics and generalized tension. Jim's father had divorced his mother two years previously because he considered his wife to be "neither a good wife nor a good mother." He complained that his wife's interest is nightclubbing, socializing, and vacationing were far greater than in staying home being a wife to him and a mother to Jim and his younger brother. Jim's mother felt that her husband was basically a boring person who never wanted to have fun, and was receptive to his request for a divorce. Although Jim's father felt his wife to be somewhat deficient as a mother, his lawyer discouraged him from trying to win custody of the children, claiming that the court was most unlikely to consider her defects as a mother so severe that it would deprive her of custody. In addition, Jim's father was ambivalent about fighting for custody because he was not ready to assume the extra burdens that his gaining custody would have entailed. Accordingly, following the separation Jim and his brother lived with their mother.

Jim's mother considered herself to be "modern and liberal" with regard to undressing in front of her children, that is, she freely did so, but in a way in which it was clear that she flaunted her nakedness. She never closed her bathroom or bedroom door, often slept in the nude, and claimed that this would help her boys grow up uninhibited. Jim and his brother were discouraged from ever closing their bathroom and bedroom doors. Every night, before going to sleep, the boys gave their mother a back rub and then she would give each boy one in return. She was one of the first to go bra-less when the style came into vogue and often wore low-cut dresses and blouses. She complained that she was always being propositioned by men, even at social gatherings where her husband was present, and claimed not to understand why. (She invariably reported such overtures to her husband.) Similarly, she wondered why wives often seemed to be cool to her, and even antagonistic at times, even though she had had little or no contact with them. In spite of all this seductivity she had had only one short-lived affair during her marriage and got little pleasure from sex.

Jim's main presenting complaints were severe tics of the face, neck, and shoulders, and marked tension. Although present about three years, the tics had increased during the two years since his father had left the home. In my evaluation of Jim it became apparent that, even though eight years old, he was being sexually excited by his mother and his tension resulted from his pent-up sexual urges. In addition, the anger he felt toward his mother for so titillating him was also repressed and contributed to his tension.

I knew from the outset that the chances of my helping Jim were not good. My experiences with reducing the seductivity of such mothers had been poor. The attentions, positive feedback, and other gratifications that such women gain from their seductive behavior are so great that they generally have little or no motivation to reduce it, let alone give it up. In women such as Jim's mother the seductivity has become so deeply ingrained in their personalities that they hardly know how to act any other way. Their gait, gestures, and vocal intonations are ever sexualized. Even when serious, sad, and crying there is still some sexualization of their behavior. If such women enter therapy with complaints unrelated to their sexual exhibitionism and seductivity, the therapist will generally have to wait until a good relationship has been established (and this can take many months, and even longer) before dealing with the sexual problem. And even then his or her chances for success may be small. Since Jim's mother had established no such relationship with me and had anticipated that my treatment would focus on him alone, she was unreceptive to any comments of mine directed toward changing her behavior—whether or not they were related to her seductivity.

Accordingly, it was no surprise when she denied that she was being seductive with Jim. Nudity was just being "modern," back rubs have nothing to do with sex, bralessness is just a style—nothing provocative about it— sleeping naked is healthy, etc. My inquiries only made her suspect that even though I was a psychiatrist I probably had a "dirty mind," like most men. In spite of her resistance to my explanation that Jim's tics were related to her seductivity, she stated that she would be willing to follow some of my advice. She agreed to stop undressing in front of Jim and to cut down on the back rubs. However, she would not promise to give them up completely, because "they felt so good." At the same time I advised Jim to refrain from undressing in front of his mother and to discontinue the nightly back-rubbing ritual.

During the next few weeks Jim's mother reported that she was trying hard to follow my advice but every once in a while she "made a mistake" and would leave a door open when undressing or going to the bathroom. An incident that she described three weeks after I had given my advice convinced me of how futile my attempts were. She had taken a shower and had "forgotten" to bring a towel into the bathroom. "Fortunately" she had not closed the door and so she called out to Jim and asked him to bring her a towel. However, in accordance with my suggestion that he not view her naked, she asked him to cover his eyes with his hand as he came into the bathroom. I asked her what she thought he might be thinking as he inched his way toward her with the towel. As I expected, she denied that he might be visualizing her nakedness. When Jim sheepishly admitted that that was exactly what he was thinking, she expressed surprise and disbelief. At the beginning of a subsequent session I came into the waiting room, where Jim and his mother were sitting together looking at a magazine. As I approached them I heard Jim's mother say, "Do you think they have nude swimming there?" When they came into my office I asked Jim's mother what had prompted her question. She told me that they were looking at an advertisement inviting tourists to New Zealand. The picture in the advertisement depicted a beach scene. Yes, the bathers were all clothed and Jim's mother was just wondering aloud when looking at the picture if they had nude bathing in New Zealand. No, she did not think that her question conjured up visions of naked people in Jim's mind and was again amazed when he hesitantly admitted that it had.

As the reader probably suspects, I made very little progress with Jim. His mother was compelled to be seductive to him, managed to circumvent every suggestion I made to her to reduce her seductivity, and had practically no insight into her behavior. It was no surprise that she discontinued Jim's therapy after a few months and concluded that all my talk about sex was making her son worse.

A parent may be seductive with the opposite-sexed child, not so much for sexual release but as a manifestation of feelings of rivalry with the absent spouse. The seduction, then, is part of a broader campaign to win the child away from the spouse. It becomes a vengeful and hostile maneuver. Feeling insecure as a marital partner, the parent may try to prove him- or herself extremely effective as a parent. And seduction may be utilized to enhance the child's affection—and thereby the parent's self-esteem.

The seductive parent builds up the child's hopes for more intense gratifications—which are generally not forthcoming. The frustrations and resentments so produced may result in attitudes of distrust toward all members of the opposite sex and can contribute not only to difficulties in oedipal resolution but in the child's future relationships with the opposite sex.

The way in which a father's parade of dates can contribute to a child's oedipal problems is well demonstrated by Carol, whose parents divorced when she was thirteen. Her father had had numerous affairs and often made no secret of them to his wife and children. When Carol's mother could no longer tolerate her husband's infidelity and saw no reason to believe it would stop, she divorced him. Subsequent to the separation he was compulsively

"on the make," never being able to involve himself with
one woman for more than a few months. In addition, he
seemed to have a strong need to have Carol meet his
girl friends during her visits with him, no matter how
transient the relationship. Even when he would pick her up
at his former home, he would often have a woman friend
in the car, almost flaunting her to his former wife.

When I first saw Carol at sixteen she could have passed
for twenty-three. Well dressed and well groomed, she had
taken great pains to be attractive. When I spoke with her,
I did not feel that I was with a teen-ager but a sophisticated (albeit pseudo-, at times) young woman. She denied having any problems, but claimed that her mother
wanted her to see a psychiatrist because of Carol's refusal
to date boys her own age or a little older. She insisted
that she found high school and college boys "immature"
and found herself much more comfortable with men in
their thirties. The event that caused Carol's visit to me was
her mother's finding in Carol's drawer a picture of her at
a nightclub with a man who could have been no less than
forty, and probably closer to fifty. Carol discussed how
she found her school work "boring" and was planning to
quit school and become a receptionist in a large New York
City firm. There she felt she would be in the best position
to meet men who were "interesting and mature." She had
been having sexual relations since age fourteen, did not
particularly enjoy it, but found that it prevented many
hassles with men if she submitted, and kept them interested in her for longer periods of time. She did not
concern herself with whether the men she dated were married. "It's none of my business," she said, and besides she
often found married men "exciting." Carol insisted that
she did not need therapy, but was willing to come one
time in order to get her mother "off her back."

During the two years after her parents' separation Carol
had visited her father practically every weekend, and on
most of those occasions some time was spent with one of
his dates. On a few weekends she accompanied her father
and a girl friend to resorts. During the year prior to
Carol's consultation with me visits to her father tapered
off as she became more interested in her own dating. Near

the end of the interview Carol stated: "I know you think that I'm jealous of my father's dating all these women and that I'd really like him to be dating me. I think that's a lot of psychological crap. I know you probably think that I'm going out with all these older men because I want to sleep with my father. I know you think I probably have an Oedipus complex or something. Well, I think that's a lot of crap too."

Carol refused another interview and never returned. About five years later, I learned from the person who had referred her to me that she had indeed quit school and become a receptionist. She was then living with a man in his middle forties, but was firm in her decision that she would not marry him. One need not be a psychiatrist to appreciate that the explanation that Carol attributed to me and then considered "crap" was indeed an accurate statement of what was going on.

Factors in children of divorce that contribute to oedipal problems. In the vast majority of cases of separation it is the father who moves out of the home, leaving the mother with the children. Such a situation is likely to evoke many fantasies, especially in boys, that relate to the Oedipus complex. It is the boy's wish that he win his mother away from his father and gain total possession of her. To achieve this end the boy will fantasize his father's leaving and, at times, even dying. Often the fantasies take the form of fears rather than wishes. A child who is guilty over directly expressing hostile wishes, may unconsciously turn them into fears of the same occurrences. To *fear* that harm will befall a parent does generally not produce guilt; to *wish* that a parent suffer harm is very likely to. In both cases the visual imagery allows for fantasized release and gratification of the hostility. Therefore, whether the fantasies take the form of fears or wishes, they accomplish the same end, namely, removal of the rival for the mother's affection. When the father leaves it is likely that the boy will consider the departure to have been caused by his wishes. Boys whose fathers have separated will also feel guilty over their wishes that Father depart and may anticipate punishment and retaliation from the father. They may entertain fantasies of being punished in order to lessen their guilt or may fantasize the father's returning—removing thereby any reason for their feeling guilt. In the less common situation, when it is the mother who has left the home, the female children may entertain similar fantasies.

It is important to emphasize to such children that thoughts cannot in themselves bring about events. In my therapeutic work with such children, in which I am telling a story about a boy with the idea that his thoughts caused his father to leave the home (children will often more readily accept therapeutic messages when they are told about other parties), I might say: "And the little boy wished very, very hard that his father would leave the house so that he could be all alone with his mother. But no matter how hard he wished, the father still stayed. The thoughts just couldn't make the thing happen." I might, with play dolls, have the child and me both wish that a particular male doll will remove itself from the play house by our wishing that it do so. We both wish very hard and then observe that the doll continues to remain where it is—no matter how hard we wish it to move. The story might then continue: "Then one day the father decided to leave and he said to the boy, 'I'm leaving because your mother and I don't love one another any more. I've decided to leave. It has nothing to do with your thoughts. Your thoughts and wishes can't make me leave. I decided by myself.'" I might play similar games or tell similar stories about a girl who wishes her mother to be hit by a car and in spite of her wishing very hard, no accident occurs. But even when it does I am careful to repeat that the wish and the event are unrelated and cause and effect.

A boy may fantasize that his mother has forced his father out of the house in compliance with his wishes that she do so. Or the child may believe that Mother herself wanted Father out of the house so that she could live all alone with her son. Such fantasies usually stem from the projection onto the mother of the child's own wishes for full possession of her. In other words, he assumes that she too wanted to get rid of his father for the purpose of living alone with her son, and he interprets the father's departure as the result of the mother's desire to reject him in favor of her son.

A girl may believe that her mother knew of her designs on her father and forced him out of the house in order to thwart the liaison. She may fantasize that the mother knew of her desires that father and daughter force mother out of the house so that she could have her father all to herself, and consider the father's leaving to be the result of her mother's attempt to foil the plot. Or she may suspect that her mother, aware of her daughter's designs on the father and plans for rejection of the mother, has forced the father out of the house in retaliation. A girl may also reason that if her father divorced her mother in order to marry another woman, he may similarly divorce his second wife in order to marry her.

Oedipal factors contribute to each parent's finding a willing ally in the opposite-sexed child. A son, for example, may not basically agree that his father is the scoundrel the mother considers him to be, but may blind himself to his father's assets as a way of satisfying oedipal cravings for his mother. A girl may side with her father against the mother for similar reasons. Boys tend to be more rambunctious and aggressive than girls and are more frequently punished for such behavior. (I do not know whether this is innate or environmentally induced. But, as most schoolteachers will testify, it is a deep-seated trait of the male child.) Some boys may consider the father's leaving the home to be a result of the mother's banishing him for his masculine aggression. I believe that, because of the boy's greater tendency to be aggressive, male displays of oedipal rivalry tend to be more common than female, and I suspect that they are usually stronger. There is another important reason for my holding this view. The mother is generally the one who provides many more gratifications for the child than the father. If *from earliest infancy* a child has to be deprived of one parent (and both are equally qualified regarding parental capacity) I believe that he or she would be much better off psychologically living with the mother. I do not know whether this would be true if the removal of one parent were to occur later in childhood. The boy has more reason than the girl to develop oedipal rivalries. He wants possession of the more valuable of the two parents, while the girl's longings for the father are diluted more by her ties with her mother. In other words, if the boy were to satisfy his oedipal cravings he would gain the more important parental figure. If the girl were to satisfy hers, she would lose the more important parent—so she is less likely to crave her father so strongly or wish so quickly to get rid of her mother.

Further consequences of unalleviated oedipal problems in children of divorce. Literally thousands of books have been written on the psychological problems that can stem from unresolved or unalleviated oedipal problems. Here, I confine myself to those factors that exist in the situation of children of divorce that are particularly conducive to the development of oedipal problems.

In the absence of the father a boy may take on feminine traits. These may become part of a homosexual orientation; but the two need not necessarily go together, i.e., not all effeminate boys are homosexual and not all homosexual boys are effeminate—although there is often some relationship between the two. Sometimes a boy may try to deny his effeminate orientation by trying to exaggerate masculine traits. The more a "super-male" he can be, the less his need to face his basic feminine identification. As is true of most, if not all, such cover-ups the disguise does not work completely and the underlying problem that is being suppressed will usually reveal itself in subtle ways. Accordingly, the basic passivity and feelings of weakness that often accompany such an adjustment are sensed by others, and the youngster does not ultilize the most effective and efficient methods for dealing with life's problems. On occasion, a girl will identify with her separated (but not totally absent) father in the attempt to gain affection from a somewhat deficient mother with whom she lives. Observing her mother to crave continually for her father she hopes to gain her mother's affection by such identification. If such a girl's father originally wanted her to be a boy, and has over the years communicated his dissatisfaction with her sex, this pattern may be further fostered by him and become entrenched.

Having been deprived of a father, the child of divorce is likely to develop abnormally strong dependencies on the mother, the only remaining parent. Having been "abandoned" by one parent, the child hangs on tenaciously to the one he or she still has. A boy, for example, may remain excessively involved with his mother, become a "momma's boy," and in extreme cases never marry. Those who do marry may still be so involved with their mothers that marital problems arise. Such dependencies may (but not necessarily) be associated with homosexual problems, overt or latent. In other words, not all momma's boys are homosexual and not all male homosexuals are momma's boys, but there is some relationship between the two. A girl, too, may exhibit such dependencies and may never marry, using as her excuse her "loyalty" to her mother.

The female needs a male in her home in order to learn how to relate to men, both actively and passively. She has to learn what men are all about as well as learn about herself—especially about the kind of woman she is—via male comments and feedback. A girl growing up without a father is likely to be deprived of these experiences, so important for her healthy psychological development. Girls who have been brought up without fathers tend to be more anxious and uncomfortable in the presence of men than girls who have grown up in intact homes. Such girls tend to look upon men as strange. They do not know about men: what to like and what to dislike; what to do and what not to do when with them. They may find quite early that making themselves sexually available is likely to result in attentions that they otherwise might not have enjoyed, and this may become their primary way of involving themselves. Such behavior may be intensified by the intense longing for male affection that may have existed for years. Whereas as a child such a girl may have been unable to attract male surrogates for her father, she now finds that—almost like magic—she has a way of gaining their enthusiastic interest. And when she can gain sexual pleasure herself in the process, her temptations to involve herself in this way may be so great that she may blind herself to the detrimental effects of making herself freely available to a large number of men. The absence of a father may interfere with a girl's development of internalized self-inhibiting mechanisms (commonly referred to as her *conscience*) and make such lack of inhibition in sexual expression even more likely.

Having been rejected by her father, a girl may develop a strong dislike for and distrust of all men. Anger and distrust may become her primary reactions to men, and these attitudes may interfere significantly with her ability to enter into meaningful and rewarding relationships with them. She may anticipate that all men will, like her father, ultimately abandon her. Sometimes her own hostility will be projected onto the male and this will add to her fear of them and anticipation of rejection by them. Such girls may never marry; or, if they do, marital problems are likely.

As described earlier, the intermittently rejecting father may induce in his children an exaggeratedly strong craving for his affection. Like the aperiodically reinforced rats, they never give up trying to gain affection from him. The daughter of such a father may become most attracted to men who only rarely provide her with gratification and will be willing to suffer many humiliations in the hope of receiving the rare satisfaction. The pattern may become so deeply embedded that she will spurn those who consistently treat her well. It seems as if being badly treated by a man is the kind of relationship she is most familiar with and willing to involve herself in. She may basically distrust any other kind—even though she may claim that she constantly seeks men who treat her well, but has the misfortune of their always turning out otherwise. In addition, such women may have so deeply associated love with pain that they cannot imagine that one can exist without the other.

Now to the difficult and controversial subject of homosexuality. First, I believe that our present state of knowledge (or perhaps the word *ignorance* would be more appropriate) regarding the cause(s) of homosexuality is such that it is premature of anyone to claim that he knows with certainty whether homosexuality is an acquired or inherited trait, or whether it is a disease. Although I consider it possible that there are those whose homosexuality is the result of biological variation, on the basis of my own clinical experience with patients and my own understanding of the subject, I consider the overwhelming majority of homosexuals to be suffering with a form of psychological disorder. I believe that homosexuality, as the primary sexual orientation for those who have reasonable opportunities for heterosexual experience, is a manifestation of psychiatric disturbance. I believe also that it is more likely to occur in homes where a child has been deprived of a loving and affectionate parent—and such is the situation for the child of divorce. Many factors contribute to a homosexual orientation. I will focus here on those that are likely to be seen when parents are living apart.

The boy living alone with a mother is likely to be deprived of the intimate association with his father that is most conducive to his identifying with him. In addition, living with his mother makes it more likely that feminine identifications will take place. These two factors may contribute to a homosexual orientation. In addition, if his mother is seductive, he may come to see women as tantalizers and rejectors—and this may contribute to his turning to men for his sexual gratification. The absence of a father, or a father's providing only intermittent gratification, may result in the son's developing a lifelong quest to gain affection from a male, and this may become a significant element in his becoming homosexual. The maltreatment that homosexual males have often experienced at the hands of their fathers is well known. The sons of such men basically hate their fathers and their surrogates. However, they deny their anger and deal with it by excessive professions of affection. (I have described earlier this mechanism of denying an unacceptable feeling with oneself by exaggerated adherence to its opposite.) Their obsessive "love" for a male is basically an attempt to deny their underlying hatred.

The girl growing up in a home without a father is more likely than the girl growing up in an intact home to develop a homosexual orientation. Having been abandoned by her model man while her mother has remained loyal to her may contribute to her distrusting all men and seeking the more predictably satisfying female as her love object. Men become strangers; women are familiar. If such a girl received little affection from her mother, and if her mother appears to be continually seeking her father's return, she may take on a male identification in the hope of gaining Mother's love. It is as though she were saying to herself: "My mother does not love females. She does love males; look how she still craves my father. If I become a male, maybe then she'll love me. I'm here; my father is not. I have a better chance than he of getting her love. All I need do is be male." In addition, when the mother is too rejecting, the girl may develop a hatred of her that is denied by excessive love—similar to that described for the male homosexual. Accordingly, she may also become obsessed with her "love" for females as a method of denying her basic hatred.

Sex identification. I have discussed those aspects of of children's sexual identification that specifically relate to oedipal problems. Here I present some of my basic views on sex identification and will then describe the implications of these ideas for a greater understanding of the sexual identification problems that children of divorce may suffer.

To begin, there are obvious differences between the sexes that are undeniable. Let us refer to these, for the sake of this discussion, as the *primary sexual functions*. In the female this function is childbearing and breast-feeding. Although the female may choose not to bear a child herself or not to breast-feed the one she does give birth to, she cannot turn these activities over to the male. The male's primary sexual function is that of fertilization. He cannot transfer this function to the female. So much for the obvious and irrefutable.

Now to the speculative. I believe that there exists within each woman a *maternal instinct* that is part of the primary sexual function. I believe it to be innate and psychobiological; that is, it has both psychological and biological components. It includes the physical urge to have sexual intercourse in order to conceive. That the female, if healthy, will want to have sexual intercourse without the goal of conception in no way weakens my argument. The primary biological purpose of copulation is fertilization, not orgasm. Bearing the child within her and having the physical capacity to nourish the child from her own body contributes to the formation of a kind of psychological tie with the child that the male cannot fully develop. I believe all women to be born with this capacity, which, like many other physiological functions, varies in intensity in different people. When there is little or no expression of the maternal instinct, repressive psychological factors are operative. Even the most mannish lesbian, I believe, somewhere deep down, wants to be a mother.

I believe also that the male has a *paternal instinct*, which is also psychobiological. It includes a biological desire to copulate and thereby bring about the birth of a child. Again, that he may want to have sexual intercourse without fatherhood as a goal does not in itself refute my point; he still has within him the deep-seated urge to have children at some time in his life. In addition, I believe that there is a psychological tie that the healthy man develops with the child he has fathered—even when it only exists in the uterus of the female he has impregnated. This interest in its welfare is a manifestation of his paternal instinct. These urges, which go beyond the desire merely to produce offspring, manifest themselves in his desire to provide the mother and child with food, clothing, and shelter and to master whatever technical skills are necessary in his society to achieve this end. Being physically stronger enables him to perform many of these functions more efficiently than the female—and this was especially true before the invention of machinery.

It is reasonable to assume that these inborn maternal and paternal instincts serve the purpose of perpetuation of the species. In the service of this goal, they include not only the urge to participate in the reproductive process but also the innate desire to rear the child so that he or she can become a functioning member of society and thereby further ensure the survival of our species.

Each sex, I believe, in addition to the primary sexual function, has the inborn capacity and the desire to gain gratifications in the other's primary area. For the sake of this discussion, I will call these the *secondary sexual functions*. The female, as a secondary interest, has the desire to involve herself in the traditionally masculine activities and to enjoy the many satisfactions they can offer. These, of course, vary from age to age and society to society and run the range from the most ancient traditionally masculine pursuits, like hunting and building shelter, to modern professions and skills. The male likewise has deep-seated instinctive urges to involve himself in the details of his child's care that have been traditionally the mother's function.

The central problem, I believe, with regard to each sex's gaining fulfillment of its primary and secondary sexual functions, has been that *each sex has been denied the opportunity to obtain gratifications in its area of secondary sexual functioning*. The examples of discrimination against women are well known. With rare exception, since time immemorial they have been denied opportunities for meaningful involvement in just about every male preserve: government, law, medicine, commerce, education, the clergy, and so on and so on. However, men have been subjected to a similar, but more subtle, form of prejudice. They have been enslaved by the tradition (more of their own making, than of women's) that it is unmasculine to involve oneself in the particulars of child rearing. Hugging and cuddling one's baby, feeding it, cleaning it when it wets and soils, dressing it, etc., are activities that men have been led to believe are unmanly and engaged in only by the weak and effeminate. The goal we should strive toward (and we have made definite headway in recent years) is that both men and women be given opportunities to gain gratifications in their areas of secondary sexual functioning. This will necessitate not only great flexibility on the part of social institutions to accommodate women in their childbearing and child-rearing involvement but also an alteration of social attitudes regarding the male's involvement with his children. Such changes have to be laid down in the earliest years of life, both in the home and in the schools, if they are to be meaningful. The ideal is not, I believe, a fifty–fifty split—half the time the mother is with the children and half the time the father—as many propose. Rather, I believe that when the children are in their earliest years they do best with the greatest amount of time being given by the mother, who, as I have said, is instinctively more involved with and capable of caring for them during this period. This is not to say that the father should not actively participate in the rearing of the infant. Every encouragement should be given him and every opportunity provided him to satisfy his paternal needs without embarrassment or the fear that he will compromise his masculinity. As the child grows older, mothers should be given more and more time and opportunity to satisfy their interests in their secondary area of functioning.

In line with this view, I do not agree with those parents who try to minimize sexual differences in their children in order to prepare them for a future world that will allegedly not recognize such differences. I do not believe that boys and girls in childhood should be dressed alike. (That teen-agers are doing so in recent years is not, in my opinion, significantly affecting their sexual orientation. By that time sexual identity is pretty well established and will not be significantly altered by such a superficial thing as clothing.) Nor do I believe that boys should be given dolls and girls trucks as *primary presents* for important occasions, such as birthdays and Christmas. I do believe, however, that such presents might be given as additional presents, or on less important occasions, to strengthen interest in each sex's secondary area of functioning. In the traditional game of "house," the girl should still be encouraged to play the role of "mother" and the boy that of "father." However, I would also encourage the "father" to come home from work early a couple of days a week or to give over his Saturdays to taking care of the children while mother is out taking courses or working at something she is interested in. These are the kinds of identifications that I believe are healthiest for parents to foster and it is on this concept of maleness and femaleness that my ensuing discussion is based.

The child of divorce has limited contacts with the parent who lives away from the home, and if this parent is of the same sex, the child will be deprived of opportunities for identification. In addition, the custodial parent's dislike of the absent parent interferes with the children's identifying with him or her. For example, it is more difficult for a boy to identify with and emulate a person whom his mother (his first and most important love object) intensely dislikes. It is as if he asks himself: "If she says he's no good, how worthwhile can he be?" In addition, it is difficult for a boy to identify with and model himself after someone who is hostile to his mother, a person who is generally very dear to him. One must consider also not only the frequency of contacts but their quality as well if one is to assess accurately a parent's value as a model for identification. A same-sexed parent living in the home can be a poorer model for identification than one who lives elsewhere. Furthermore, the identification process takes place primarily during the first three to four years of life. If the separation takes place after the child has reached this age (commonly the case), then the child may not suffer significant problems related to the failure to form an adequate sexual identification.

One of the ways in which all children strengthen their identifications with their parents is through play and play fantasy. Playing "house" is one of the most common ways in which this process takes place. Accordingly, even in the intact home, when a father is away at work, his son may play that he is doing his father's work in order to entrench his masculine identify. When separation occurs, the child may still utilize this mechanism for identification. However, like all substitutive methods of gratification, it is never as good as the real thing and there are limitations regarding the extent to which substitution can serve before one begins to suffer the effects of the original deprivation.

A mechanism that the child of divorce may utilize to compensate for the loss of the same-sexed parent is that of accomplishing a very rapid identification with him. This process is sometimes seen in both children and adults after the death of a parent or other loved one. In an attempt to compensate for the loss, the child may incorporate many aspects of the deceased person's personality —often almost overnight. To many observers the effects are almost uncanny. It is as though the individual were saying: "He is gone, I cannot have him. However, I will become like him. In this way I will have some of his qualities remain with me." In some cases it appears as if the individual were saying, "I will *be* him. In that way there will be no loss at all"—so complete appears to be the identification. Similarly, the child of divorce may utilize this process to deal with the parental loss. However, since it has delusional and fantasized elements, and since the identification has occurred almost instantaneously, it does not have the depth of the more natural and slowly developing process. Accordingly, the behavioral patterns so acquired are less adaptive to the reality of the child's life. In addition, since there has been less discrimination in the formation of such identifications (the child has incorporated the whole bag, so to speak), more maladaptive patterns are likely to be taken in.

No discussions of sexual identification would be complete without mention of the child's identification with a homosexual parent. In recent years an ever increasing number of parents are openly revealing their homosexuality as they break up their "sham" heterosexual marriages. At the same time, many such homosexual parents claim that their sexual orientation in no way compromises their parental capacity. One would think that the son of a homosexual father, for example, would be more likely to be homosexual than the son of a heterosexual father. To the best of my knowledge this does not appear to be the case, i.e., the prevalence of homosexuality among sons of homosexual males does not appear to be higher than among sons of heterosexual males. (I know of no good statistical studies on the subject. The statement is made on the basis of my own experiences as well as those of colleagues of mine with greater experience in this area.) I believe that this somewhat surprising observation is not difficult to explain. On the one hand there are, I believe, some boys who *do* become homosexual because of identification with their homosexual fathers.

However, the most important factor in bringing about a homosexual orientation is brutal and rejecting treatment by a father. Since most homosexual fathers do not treat their sons this way, the population of homosexual fathers shows a lower percentage of brutality than does the population of heterosexual fathers. Rather, the homosexual father generally tends to be very solicitous toward his children, gratifying his "maternal" cravings in a very tender and affectionate way. I believe that those sons of homosexual fathers who become homosexual do so, in part, because of their identification with their fathers, and that the paternal brutality factor does not appear to be significant. Among heterosexual fathers whose sons become homosexual, the cruelty factor seems to be prominent, while the identification factor is of no significance. And all this seems to balance out so that the percentage of homosexual sons in the two groups of fathers appears to be the same. However, I believe that if one broke down the group of heterosexual fathers into two subgroups —those who were sadistic to their sons and those who were not—the percentage of homosexual sons would be far greater in the sadistic group.

Insecurity and Low Self-esteem

All of us, at times, experience feelings of inadequacy. And when psychological problems are present such feelings of low self-worth are even more likely to be felt. Here I discuss those factors that make children of divorce especially likely to develop feelings of low self-esteem and present approaches that may be useful in lessening the chances of such feelings developing and reducing them when they do occur.

Factors in the divorce situation that may contribute to children's low self-esteem. If parents separate soon after a child is born, the child, when he or she becomes old enough to appreciate this, may believe that his or her birth somehow brought about the separation. "If I had not been born," the child may reason, "they might still be together. They wanted one another—that's why they got married—but they didn't want me. When I was born, they became so unhappy that they got divorced." The notion may have its roots in the need to gain control over an uncontrollable situation as discussed earlier in this chapter, and the therapeutic approaches to this delusion have been there described. If the child learns that he or she was conceived in an attempt to save a faltering marriage and the birth was not successful in accomplishing this, he or she may reason that another, better child might have been successful. The sense of failure associated with these ideas cannot but lower a child's feelings of self-worth.

If the children live in a community where there are few other children from divorced homes, they may feel very different from others and less worthy than those living in intact homes. If, in addition, they are stigmatized because of their parents' divorce, they may feel even less worthwhile. Such children must be helped to appreciate that the divorce situation in no way warrants a person's being laughed at or ridiculed—that it has nothing to do with sin or being bad. They have had bad luck; but they have done nothing to justify their being taunted or rejected. Also, they have to be helped to appreciate that they are not necessarily what others say they are.

The economic hardships that a divorce often causes may play a role in diminishing children's self-esteem. This is especially true when the divorce results in a significant lowering of the family's life-style. Although material possessions do not, I believe, play a significant role in determining one's self-esteem, they do have an effect. It is much harder for a poor man to feel good about himself that one who has a reasonable degree of material comfort.

A particularly difficult situation is the one in which a child is stigmatized because of a parent's bad reputation. For example, the son of a notoriously alcoholic father may suffer significant ridicule himself. As difficult as it may be, it is important to try to help such a child appreciate that his stigmatization is totally inappropriate and cruel. He has to be helped to appreciate that he in no way contributed to his father's socially alienating behavior and therefore is in no way to blame. He has had the *misfortune* of having a father who has disgraced himself by his behavior, but the child only adds to his own burden if he takes the disgrace onto himself as well. Society does not punish a son for the crimes of his father, nor one person for the crimes of another. Similarly, he should not be punished for the misdeeds of his father. He must be helped to view those who ridicule him as having significant distortions in their own thinking. It is *they* rather then *he* who should be ashamed of themselves. Lastly, he must be helped to appreciate that in spite of occasional taunts, he will ultimately be judged by the kind of person *he* is, not what his *father is*. If he is fun to be with, considerate of others, and exhibits other admirable and desirable traits, he will be liked and sought—his parent's deficiencies notwithstanding.

Parental factors contributing to low self-esteem in children of divorce. Children of divorce, more than those living in an intact home, are likely to be deprived of parental affection (although it is certainly true that children in intact homes may be similarly deprived). Certainly, most departing parents are deeply involved with their children and regret the pains and frustrations that the separation is causing them. In spite of formidable attempts on the departing parent's part to reassure the children that they are loved, they are still likely to consider themselves to have been abandoned. They generally go further and assume that they have been rejected because they are unlovable. Young children judge their own self-worth by what their parents' views of them are. (It is only later, when they go into other homes, attend school, and broaden their experiences that they utilize other criteria—both external and internal—for determining their self-worth.) When children believe that a parent does not love them, they conclude that they are unlovable, and their self-esteem suffers considerably. Such children have to be helped to appreciate that they may be distorting, that they may have a "wrong idea," and that their parent's leaving the house has not been due to the fact that they are unlovable.

Also, the children who have in fact been totally rejected have to be discouraged from trying to extract affection from a parent who is unwilling to or incapable of providing it, because such futile endeavors can only be self-debasing. And children who are receiving limited affection have to be helped to accept that reality, lest they become preoccupied with vain and esteem-lowering attempts to gain more involvement from the parent than he or she is capable of providing. When, indeed, the departing parent has little, if any, love for the children, then a more shattering blow will have been dealt to their self-esteem. Such children have to be helped to appreciate that the deficiency lies within the parent, not within themselves. They may interpret an absent father's failure to pay his alimony to be a reflection of their own worthlessness. It is as if the child were saying to him- or herself: "If I was worth anything, he'd send the money. I'm not worth paying for." Again, the child has to be helped to appreciate the distortions that are operating here in lowering his or her sense of self-worth.

The separation inevitably produces feelings of insecurity in children. The realizations that important people can abandon one at any time and that home stability is fragile at best make the children feel small and vulnerable. One of the parents, who has generally been an important source of protection and guidance, is no longer so readily available. Such feelings of insecurity, lack of protection, and helplessness cannot but lower a child's self-esteem.

Divorce usually places new burdens on each of the parents. Mother is now all alone in caring for the everyday needs of the children. Except for those who are wealthy, divorce creates economic hardship. Mother would be much more available and attractive to other men were it not for the children. The mother's career goals may also be compromised by the children. Father, too, may see the visitations as a source of restriction on his life. Even if the parents do not verbalize these frustrations and resentments, the children are likely to sense them. And feeling oneself a burden on one's parents cannot but contribute to a child's feelings of low self-worth.

Information from both parents helps children gain a sense of what they are really like, and the children's knowledge of their assets contributes to their feelings of high self-worth. With one parent gone, they are deprived of one source of potentially esteem-enhancing information.

When the child takes sides with one parent in the parental conflict, he or she risks alienating the other. The loss of affection that this disloyalty (pretended or real) may result in but cannot but lower his or her feelings of self-worth. If the child believes that the "good" child is one who is loved by both parents, then his alienation of one will make him "bad" and hence loathsome.

The child may identify with the rejected parent and assume that the parent who has left has little if any affection for the whole family, not just the parent who has been left behind. In the situation, for example, in which a father has left the home, his daughter may assume that because Mother is not acceptable to Father, she and the other children are not acceptable to him either. Such a child has to be helped to differentiate clearly between herself and her mother. Particular focus should be placed on the specific qualities in the mother that the father claims are the sources of his alienation. She has to be helped to gain clarification as to whether the mother does indeed exhibit these qualities or whether the father is distorting. If the traits do exist in the mother, the child has to be helped to determine whether she possesses them also. If so—and this is unusual—she should be helped to change those qualities within herself that she shares with her mother so that she will not similarly alienate others as Mother did Father. (I appreciate that the parents may have very different opinions regarding whether such alienating qualities exist and exactly who possesses them. Yet, the obstacles to such understanding by the child notwithstanding, if and when such clarification can be accomplished, it can be useful for the child in avoiding self-esteem problems.) The same considerations hold for the situation in which the mother, for example, rejects a father and he is the one who leaves the home. The child, by identification, may assume he is similarly rejectable and is likely to be forced out of the house.

The child may be used as a scapegoat. Each parent, for example, may take out on the child the resentments he or she feels toward the other. Being used as the target of hostility cannot but make the child feel loathsome.

Earlier in this chapter I discussed some of the elements in the divorce situation that may contribute to a parent's becoming overprotective. The child of such a parent is likely to become immature and regressed. Whatever gratifications he or she may derive from such regression, the child is likely to feel shame as well and become fearful that peers will learn of the childish behavior. Shame and fear compromise significantly one's feelings of self-worth.

A parent may attempt to use the child as a substitute for the spouse who is no longer available. A mother, for example, may tell her son that he is now "man of the house" and although she generally does not go so far as to use the boy for overt sexual satisfaction, she may be overly solicitous and seductive and thereby gain some measure of sexual satisfaction. The anxieties and frustrations so produced in the boy cannot but be ego-debasing (as are all feelings of frustration and tension). Or she may use the child as a confidant and ask him to advise her in matters on which he is totally ill equipped to provide advice. Believing that he should be able to serve his mother in this regard, and observing his failure to do so, produces feelings of inadequacy. Likewise, fathers may use their daughters for such purposes with similar effects on the girls' sense of self-worth.

Factors in the child that contribute to low self-esteem. Many of the inappropriate ways in which children react to parental separation are designed to enhance self-worth (or at least prevent a lowering of self-worth). Such attempts are generally misguided in that they usually result in further lowering of self-esteem. Let us take, for example, the boy who is guilty over hostility he feels toward his father for leaving the household. An intrinsic part of guilt is a lowered sense of self-worth ("How terrible I am for what I have thought [done]"). Such a boy may attempt (usually unconsciously) to lessen his guilt by turning his hostility away from his father and directing it toward himself. Such inward directing of anger may cause depression and associated self-disparagement. Although spared the guilt and the anticipated consequences of expressing his anger, the depression and associated self-hate result in an even greater loss of self-esteem. A girl, for example, may spare herself guilty feelings over her hostility to a parent by projecting her anger onto others ("It is not I who am angry, it is he [she]"). She then views herself to be innocent of harboring objectionable hostility and sees it in others. (Again this process is often done unconsciously.) She may thereby spare herself the lowered self-esteem associated with awareness of her hostility, but she then suffers with esteem-lowering fears of those upon whom she has projected her hostility. The boy who holds in and suppresses the resentment he feels toward his parent(s) for the separation, who does not assert himself in the service of dealing with anger-provoking situations (both associated and unassociated with the separation), suffers with the dissatisfaction with himself that is inevitably associated with pent-up resentments.

Children who try to hide the separation from their friends may protect themselves thereby from anticipated ridicule; but they usually suffer with the lowered feelings of self-worth associated with their fears of disclosure and the inner shame associated with the knowledge of what they are doing. And when the secret is revealed (as it inevitably comes to be) they suffer even more shame and social alienation than if they had disclosed the separation in the first place.

The child who plays one parent against the other in an attempt to win favor may suffer guilt and feelings of disloyalty over his or her dishonesty—and these feelings will generally lower feelings of self-worth. On the other hand, the child who does not report back to one parent information about the other when requested to do so, may also feel disloyal and unworthy.

Additional ways of helping children of divorce deal with self-esteem problems. Because psychological problems are so closely associated with misguided attempts to enhance a lagging self-esteem, anything parents can do genuinely to increase children's sense of self-worth can be beneficial. In fact, one can consider the *genuine* enhancement of self-esteem to be the universal antidote to most psychological symptoms. I emphasize the word *genuine* here because it is common for people to attempt to raise children's self-esteem by artificial and dishonest methods such as bestowing undeserved praise, flattery, patronizing compliments, and pretended affection. Compliments not actually associated with specific accomplishments can be ego-debasing rather than ego-enhancing. To say to a child, "Aren't you a nice girl," or, "What a fine boy you are," makes most children squirm. They recognize the falseness of the compliments; they appreciate that they are being "buttered up"; and they sense that these particular comments are being resorted to because the praiser cannot think of more meaningful and honest ones, i.e., praises based on specific accomplishments. To say, however, "Boy, this cake you baked is really good!" or, "You play the piano beautifully," or, "What a swat! You hit the ball right over the fence," makes a child stand a few inches taller.

Of all the approaches to enhancing self-esteem there is none so important, in my opinion, as the gaining of competence. One cannot feel good about oneself if one cannot focus on specific areas of talent, skill, knowledge, etc., about which to feel good. Accordingly, if parents are to raise children with a strong sense of self-worth, and if they are to enable them to avoid using misguided and futile methods for compensating for feelings of low self-esteem, it is important for them to help their children gain competence in important areas of living—especially those in which the children have revealed deficiency. They must help their children learn to handle themselves more effectively in the course of their daily activities. They must help them learn the techniques of relating more satisfactorily and gratifyingly to others, so that they can gain the self-confidence and ego-enhancing pleasure that comes with successful involvements with others. They must help them to become aware of areas in which they tend to act inappropriately, and teach them by word and experience the ways in which they can avoid repetition of self-defeating behavior. One cannot really feel good about oneself unless one has something specific and concrete about which to feel good. Otherwise the sense of self-esteem is fantasized and cannot really produce a feeling of stability. And the children are then almost doomed to resort to using misguided and predictably futile esteem-enhancing maneuvers (such as lying about accomplishments, empty boasting, and inability or refusal to admit defects) and will end up even worse than they were before. In addition, children must have the feeling that there is some appreciation of their accomplishments by their parents and other significant individuals. We cannot enjoy competence in a vacuum. The boy who, while riding his bike, yells to his mother, "Look, Ma, no hands," is enjoying the enhanced sense of self-worth that comes from his accomplishment and gains additional ego-enhancement from his mother's admiration. Children should be helped to appreciate that the more important esteem building comes from a worthwhile endeavor, and that the external praise should not be the primary reason for such pursuits, but an enjoyable, esteem-enhancing fringe benefit.

Feeling that one is genuinely needed by at least one or two people is also crucial to one's self-respect. I cannot imagine anyone's really respecting himself if no one needs him or her for anything. One of the important considerations I use in determining if a depressed person is suicidal is whether the individual believes that no one in the whole world would miss him or her if he or she were dead. Although children are, for the most part, dependent on their parents and need their parents far more than their parents need them, children must still feel that their loss would be painful to their parents if they are to have a healthy sense of self-worth. Recognizing that they have the power to make their parents laugh, to give them warm inner feelings, and to contribute to their pleasure in having a *family*, contributes to children's feelings of self-worth. The children of divorce are bound to question the need their parents have for them. In some cases there may be significant deficiencies on the part of one or even both parents in their need for their children. The children's sensing that they are now an increased burden to their parents (for the reasons already given) may further lessen their feelings of being needed and useful. In fact, the children's main feelings may be that the parents want to dispose of them, which is, unfortunately, sometimes the case. Parents, therefore, do well to communicate to their children the parents' needs for them and how useful the children are to them. But words alone are generally not enough if one is to convince children of this. If the children have the living experience (that important term again) that the parents enjoy being with them and are genuinely interested in the things they do, then the children will gain a sense of pride and self-importance. It is as if the child says to him- or herself: "I have the capacity to give them pleasure. With me they can have fun. I am therefore a worthwhile person." Accordingly, parents do well, when possible, to try to select activities that are enjoyable to both the children and themselves and to refrain from engaging in activities that they find boring. Otherwise the parental resentment when engaged in unenjoyable and boring activities will generally be sensed by children; they will be deprived of the benefits of the parental pleasure; and may even find the activity ego-debasing.

A common source of lowered self-respect in children, especially those with psychological problems, is the notion that they are the only ones in the world who have the "terrible" thoughts and feelings that they harbor within themselves. Parents often confirm such suspicions and deepen thereby such children's self-hatred. Such guilt is especially common over the angry thoughts and feelings that children (like the rest of us) inevitably have. And children of divorce not only have more to be angry about, but, for the reasons already mentioned, their situation makes them more likely to fear and feel guilty over expressing their anger. It is important for parents to reassure their children that most, if not all people, have similar angry thoughts and feelings. When appropriate, parents should inform the children that they themselves have had and still have (if this is the case) similar ideas and emotional reactions. Such comments can contribute to the children's feeling less loathsome as they come to appreciate that they are not so unique. In addition, the parents' revealing (when appropriate) deficiencies of their own can help children feel less loathsome about their own defects. Parents who believe that their children will respect them less if they reveal occasional deficiencies contribute to their children's developing feelings of low self-worth as they compare themselves unfavorably with parents who present themselves as perfect.

When a patient tells me, "I feel terrible. I'm no good," I will often ask if he or she is doing something that may contribute to such feelings. Often, after some thought, I get an affirmative answer (admittedly, more commonly from the adult than the child). The child may be cheating, stealing, or lying. The child of divorce may be spying on one parent for the other, or playing one parent against the other. In such situations I generally tell the child: "As long as you continue doing that, you're going to feel lousy about yourself. It's hard for me to imagine anyone's feeling good about him- or herself when he does such things. I think that when you stop doing that you'll see that you'll feel much better about yourself."

The divorce situation can provide children with esteem-enhancing experiences if they can rise to the occasion and avail themselves of them. The extra responsibilities that children of divorce are often asked to assume can provide them with an increased sense of competence. In addition, I urge many parents to join community organizations for divorced people. (The most well known of these family-oriented organizations is Parents Without Partners.) There are many potential esteem-enhancing benefits to be derived for children from such membership. The organization provides them with opportunities to be with many other children of divorce, lessening thereby their feelings of being unique and different. There, they can form relationships with substitute parents of the same sex as the one who has departed from the household. For older children discussion groups can be beneficial. The sense of belonging to a special club, the feeling of communality, and the recreational activities can all increase such children's sense of self-worth.

Anger

Although one can make minor distinctions between the terms *hostility* and *anger*, for the purposes of this discussion I will use the words synonymously. I believe that the capacity of the human being to exhibit anger is inborn. Anger can be viewed as one possible response to danger to our well-being (fear would be another response). The anger reaction has both physical (increased blood pressure, respiratory rate, and pulse rate) and psychological (angry thoughts and feelings) components. Anger enhances our efficiency in warding off and fighting threats to our well-being. We fight more effectively when mobilized by a moderate amount of anger (too much anger may make us less effective); conversely, absence or inhibition of anger can compromise us significantly in dealing with threatening situations. Accordingly, anger has survival value. Whereas the purpose of anger is to enhance our efficiency if *fighting* threats to our well-being, the purpose of the fear response is to increase our efficiency in *fleeing* the danger (and this reaction too has obvious survival value). I believe also that the most predictable stimulus for producing the anger response is frustration. Frustration occurs whenever we are thwarted (or believe we are being thwarted) from obtaining something we desire, regardless of whether it is vital to our survival. I would go so far as to say that frustration, if experienced long enough, will inevitably trigger the anger response. It is the purpose of anger, then, to enhance our efficiency in removing irritations that frustrate us. And since life inevitably produces frustrations within us, since we can never get all we want exactly when we want it, anger is predictably going to arise in us from time to time.

Sources of anger in children of divorce. Children of divorce have usually been exposed to many frustrating experiences. The constant conflict between their parents prior to the separation deprives them of the calm and loving environment so necessary to psychological health. And following the separation they usually feel abandoned—and this cannot but make them feel even more angry. The divorce situation usually provides other sources of anger as well. The children may resent being different from their peers. Others have two parents living in the household; they have only one. The divorce generally causes each parent new frustrations and resentments, even though older ones may have been reduced or removed. Each parent may still be so preoccupied with these new problems that he or she has little affection available for the child. Resentments toward the spouse may be directed toward the child. A mother, for example, may continually berate her son: "You remind me of your father." "You're just like your father." By seeing him as similar to her despised ex-husband she justifies scapegoating him and venting on him the anger she feels toward her former spouse. Children are captive prey; they are too small to fight back and too dependent to run. They therefore serve well as targets for parental hostility. And being so used is likely to produce retaliatory hostility in them.

Mother may have to take a job (something she may have never done before) and her absence from the home may be a source of resentment in her children. The mother may resent her children for their very existence—lessening as they do her chances for remarriage, restricting her dating, necessitating her having contact with their father, and providing her with new responsibilities she might prefer to do without. And the father too, to a lesser extent, may resent the children for these reasons as well. The children will generally sense these parental frustrations, feel rejected, and react angrily. Social tradition (often incorporated into the legal system) may have required the mother to assume custody when the father would have been the preferable parent. Such a mother's resentment adds to her deficiencies as a parent and causes the children even greater frustration. Furthermore, their inability to live with the preferable parent provides them with yet another reason to be angry.

Of course, there are other things that can occur in the

divorce situation that may make children resentful. Mother and Father may be perpetuating their hostilities into the post-separation period and so the expected termination of the terrible conflict never seems to come. Mother may prevent the children from seeing Father because he has been remiss on alimony and divorce payments. Father may be unreliable regarding visitation, frequently being late or never showing up at all. Unwelcome strangers, like men and lady friends of the parents, appear on the scene. The children may have to accommodate the offspring of these new strangers who may even become their relatives. The separation may require various material privations or a move to a new and less desirable home. And one could go on and on. In fact, there is hardly a section of this book that does not make reference to some situation that is an actual or potential source of resentment to children of divorce. Accordingly, it is not surprising that problems centering on anger are, in my experience, the most common with which children of divorce (and their therapists) have to deal.

Problems caused by anger inhibition.   Mental health professionals use the words *repression* and *suppression* to refer to psychological processes that remove unacceptable thoughts and feelings from conscious awareness and relegate them to unconsciousness. Strictly used, the term suppression is applicable when this is consciously done, that it, the individual is aware that he does not wish to think about a particular issue and decides to ignore and to try to forget it. In repression the forces that operate to remove the subject from conscious awareness are unconscious, that is, the individual is not aware that he is removing the material from conscious awareness. Often both processes operate simultaneously. Many do not strictly adhere to this differentiation. And even a person's therapist may not be certain how much of each process is contributing. Although I personally do make the distinction, for the purposes of this book I do not think it is crucial. Accordingly, I will use the terms synonymously here not only for the sake of simplicity but because there are times when I cannot be sure which term would be more applicable.

Problems may result from the suppression and repression of the anger that children of divorce may experience as the result of their parents' separation. Rather than release their anger in healthy ways (in my subsequent discussion I will elaborate on the differences between healthy and unhealthy types of anger release), they bottle up their anger. Such pent-up anger then contributes to the formation of various symptoms that serve to keep the anger repressed and/or to release it in disguised ways so that the child is not aware that his or her anger is being expressed. As will become apparent from my discussion of these methods of dealing with repressed anger, they are poor solutions to the problem of what to do with anger. They usually result in the child's developing new problems, different from those he or she anticipated would result from direct expression of the hostility. Generally, the kinds of problems caused by repressed anger result from the child's being guilty over or fearful of expressing his anger. Such children may have grown up in a home where they were taught that expression of anger toward a parent is a terrible thing to do. Sometimes this is done openly, with the parents directly telling their youngsters that good and acceptable children are never hostile toward their parents and do not even have angry thoughts about them. Other parents may produce such inhibitions by serving as models for anger suppression. They never fight, and thereby produce more guilt in their children over anger expression than they would have if they openly criticized hostile expression. (The situation is analogous to that of the sexually inhibited woman who complains: "I can't understand why I can't be freer sexually. My parents never told me it was sinful or bad. In fact, they never even spoke about sex!" If one has a choice between a parent who never speaks about sex and one who provides frequent lectures on its depravity, one would end up less guilty with the parent who provides the sermons. At least that parent is talking about it. For the silent parent, sex is unmentionable. And unmentionable things produce far more guilt and fear than the mentionable.) Or observing the devastating effects of the expression of anger on each of the parents has inhibited the children from expressing their hostility. As mentioned, by its very nature the divorce situation is likely to inhibit the children in expressing anger. One parent has already left the household; expressing resentment might result in their seeing even less of that parent. And they may fear exhibiting hostility toward the remaining parent, lest he or she leave as well.

One of the most common ways in which children may deal with their anger over the separation is to *deny* it. Most often this is unconscious—they are really not aware that they are angry—although, at times, a child may be aware that he or she is, but will be afraid to admit it to others. Powerful repressive forces are usually operative when this adaptation is used. It is probably the most primitive mechanism for handling a painful or anxiety-provoking situation in that the individual deals with a danger (in this case an inner one, that is, one's own anger and its threatened eruption into conscious awareness) by simply making believe it doesn't exist. It is not surprising that such a simplistic adjustment is attractive to children and therefore one of the most commonly utilized by them.

When asked how they feel about some of the obviously anger-provoking situations associated with the separation, such children may respond with a host of rationalizations designed to protect them from awareness of the anger. One patient, in response to my question regarding her feelings about her father's limited involvement since leaving the home, stated, "It doesn't bother me. I know he has to spend so much time working to send us money that he hasn't time to see us or call us." A son of a physician stated, "My father can't come and see me because he'd have to leave his patients and some of them might die."

A related method by which some children may at the same time both deny and express their anger is excessive concern for the welfare of the parent(s). As mentioned, the visual image provides the basic information regarding what a person's true wishes are. Fearing that harm will befall a parent can allow for a release, through fantasy, of the hostile wishes as the child envisions something terrible happening to a parent. However, there is little if any guilt produced by such a fantasy as the child only experiences the dreaded event as a fear. The child may become oversolicitous in response to such fantasies, may become profuse in his or her praise of the parent(s), and may even buy gifts for frivolous reasons.

Some basic principles of anger psychology. The situation that is most likely to cause anger is one in which the individual experiences frustration over his or her inability to remove an irritant. Anger has survival value in that it enhances our efficiency in removing the source of irritation. As long as the painful stimulus is present, anger will be provoked and even increased—resulting in ever more intense emotional reactions such as rage and fury. It is useful to view anger as the mildest of these three states. It is the first to arise and while it enhances one's efficiency in removing an irritant it does not preclude rational thought and action. When the anger does not work, when the source of irritation remains in spite of anger's help in removing it, the individual may enter into a state of rage. Whereas in anger one can still focus narrowly on the irritating stimulus, in rage the anger is much greater, rationality is reduced, and wilder and more generalized actions occur. For example, a woman is approached on the street by a man who makes obscene remarks as part of an attempt to interest her in a sexual encounter. Angered by the man's crudeness and having absolutely no desire to have any further contact with him she may angrily reply: "Get lost, Buster." If he persists and moves closer, she may push him away and even strike him. The effectiveness of both her words and actions are enhanced by her anger. The angry tone of her voice communicates to the man that there is strength, not weakness, in her words. And her anger increases her physical capacity to shove him away. Let us imagine the man's then responding by trying to grab her. She runs away and soon finds herself cornered in a lonely alley, where the man now tries to rape her. Although fear is present she now enters a state of rage. She kicks wildly and screams as loudly as she can. She claws and thrashes. Her words and actions, although generally directed toward driving off the stranger, are less specifically focused on him. They are more wild and chaotic. Hopefully some of the blows will prove effective, some of the clawing and scratching movements will hit their mark. One can carry the example further. Let us say that this woman, even in the state of rage, would not murder the man even if a weapon were available. Rather, she might finally submit and suffer various painful reactions, both physical and psychological. She might, however, if the rage builds up further, enter into a state of fury in which she becomes capable of killing her assaulter. The term fury could also be used to refer to a state of insane rage in which the woman might go berserk and begin attacking innocent parties.

In general, we do best to attempt to deal with life in such a way that we reasonably avoid or prevent the occurrence of irritating situations. Since this is not possible in a real world where there will always be things to frustrate us, we do well to deal with such irritants at the earliest possible time. We do well to use our anger at the earliest moment, when it is at its mildest level, when we can more rationally focus directly on the irritation and remove it in the most expeditious way. The longer we take to do this, the longer our anger builds up because of our failure to use it effectively in removing the irritant, the more likely our anger will turn to rage and even fury, and the less likely we are to deal rationally with the situation. And this principle is fundamental to this discussion of helping children of divorce deal with their anger and the situations that provoke it.

Because life inevitably exposes us to painful and frustrating situations, anger is ever with us. However, the survival of civilized society depends upon a significant degree of anger inhibition. For thousands of years mankind has experimented with various systems designed to inhibit individuals from free and wanton expression of anger. The primary purpose of such systems has been to protect the innocent from those who would use their anger destructively. Simple retaliation has sometimes served to deter some who would otherwise freely act upon their hostile impulses. However, more organized and powerful methods have been necessary, in the form of political, legal, and governmental structures. Long ago it was recognized that inducing guilt in a person is a very useful way of producing individuals who will be less prone to act out their angry impulses. In fact, it has been one of the most widely used methods because it has the advantage of the individual's deterring him- or herself, from fear of *internal* rather than *external* forces, from performing the hostile acts. Accordingly, others can be less guarded. They can relax their vigil. The individual can be relied upon to deter him- or herself from carrying out those acts that would be detrimental to the survival of the society. Parental teaching, educational systems, religious training, legends, and myths have all played their role in producing such guilt. However helpful the guilt deterrent has been, I believe that it has often been misapplied, misdirected, and used in excess. Since anger can lead to rage, then fury, and then murder, many social institutions have prohibited and discouraged expression of all the milder forms of anger as a safety measure against the expression of the violent forms. This, in my opinion, is like banning totally the use of fire because it can be so destructive, or prohibiting the production of electrical power because occasionally someone gets electrocuted. Fire and electricity are certainly useful and so is anger. It need not be lethal. Some point of moderation must be found. We must not allow free and unbridled expression of anger if society is to survive. Yet we must not repress individuals excessively from expressing their anger lest we deprive them of its value as a tool of survival. Such repression also contributes to the kinds of psychological problems I describe in this section. Not only has society grappled for ages with the problem of finding this point of moderation, but each individual, throughout his or her life, is continually confronted with this problem as well. All of us make errors in properly utilizing our anger. Sometimes we explode, allow ourselves to get too angry, or do not deal with an irritation early enough to avoid rage; and at other times we repress it too much, don't assert ourselves, and release it symbolically and inappropriately. It is a lifelong problem that ever remains with us.

Anger must be harnessed and used to help deal with

life's frustrations. Children must not be taught that there
are good folk somewhere who are never angry. They
must not be filled with guilt over the inevitable angry
feelings they have. Yet they must not be allowed to vent
their anger whenever and wherever they wish. As for their
parents, and society, some middle point must be reached.
Children are continually exposed to frustrations. They
are bombarded with "Don't do this" and "Don't do that."
It is no surprise, then, that they suffer many frustrations
and resentments. They may not openly express them
for fear of invoking even further criticism from their parents, especially if the parents believe that their children
should not be having any angry reactions to their restrictions. Children can neither flee from nor fight their parents'
prohibitions, and so they must utilize various mechanisms
to deal with their anger. They may deny and repress their
anger (with the help of parents, teachers, and certain religious teachings). They may release it symbolically
through games (such as "war"). They may release it by
identifying with and observing others release theirs (via
watching sporting events or television violence). Or they
may project it out onto others ("Kids always pick on
me"; "It's their fault"). Their dreams and fantasies symbolically allow release of anger and are a powerful and
effective form of substitute gratification, because no one
can stop children from using them for such release. They
are things which they truly have all to themselves.

We know relatively little about the reasons why a
child chooses a particular mechanism to deal with anger
over which there is guilt. Why does one child project it
and another repress it? Why does one child deny it and
another direct it toward him- or herself? No doubt social
influences and parental models play a role; but even in
the same family one can observe different ways of dealing
with anger. In spite of our ignorance there is much that
we have learned about the causes and alleviation of anger
inhibition problems. Here I will focus on things parents
can do to help their children avoid and alleviate such
problems.

As repressed anger strives for release, an internal psychological conflict may be set up. The anger that has

been repressed to the unconscious presses for expression, and psychological forces related to the guilt the child feels over his or her hostility attempt to prevent the hostile thoughts and feelings from entering into conscious awareness. The internal psychological conflict thereby set up may produce a *state of tension*, the causes of which are generally unknown to the child. He or she just feels tense and doesn't know why. And the tension may manifest itself in a number of ways. The child may become hyperirritable, cry easily, and react in an exaggerated fashion to the most minor disturbances and irritations. He or she may develop tics. Most commonly these are of the eyes (blinking) and the mouth (grimacing and puckering movements). When more severe, the head and shoulders may become involved and various vocal tics (grunting noises, frequent throat clearing) may appear. Each person's body has certain areas or organs that are more likely to respond to tension than others. Some react to tension with spasm of the muscles of the scalp and they get tension headaches. In some, the muscles of the lower back become tight and rigid and a low back pain syndrome results. Some experience contraction of the muscles of the gastrointestinal tract with resulting vomiting or diarrhea. In others the heart beats more rapidly and palpitations result. Or the respiratory rate may increase with associated shortness of breath. It appears that every individual has one or more points or organs of weakness and they are commonly the first areas to exhibit difficulty when there is tension.

A related phenomenon is the *anxiety attack*. Generally this is seen in the child whose general level of tension is already quite high. In these episodes the child suddenly becomes extremely tense. There may be sweating, palpitations, shortness of breath, trembling, and fears of death. In severe forms the child may be thrown into a state of panic. The most common cause of such states in the child of divorce, in my opinion, is the threat of intense hostile feelings erupting into conscious awareness. Such a child is generally so guilt-ridden over angry feelings that powerful repressive forces must operate to keep them out of conscious awareness. So dammed up, they may build up to great intensities. Then, when the intense anger threatens eruption into conscious awareness, the child becomes overwhelmed with fear of the consequences of the expression of the intense hostility.

All children experience occasional *nightmares*. As I will soon explain, nightmares, more than anything else, are the result of repressed hostility. Since all children have to learn to repress their hostility if they are to get along with others (and if civilized society is to survive), all children, at times, have nightmares. Since children of divorce are more likely to be angry, they are, in my opinion, more likely to have nightmares than the child living in an intact, relatively stable home. This relates, more than anything else, I believe, to repression of the hostility produced by the parents' separation and the fear of becoming consciously aware of such anger. To elaborate: in the typical nightmare, the child is fearful that an evil, frightening, and dangerous figure (a robber, monster, vague malevolent creature, "thing," etc.) will enter, or has already entered, his or her room. Usually the intruder comes in from a window or closet or from under the bed. I believe that the interloper is the fantasized symbol of the child's unacceptable angry impulses that have been relegated to the unconscious. At night, when daytime stimuli are removed, the residual pent-up hostilities of the day, which continually press for expression, are focused upon. Daytime activities such as sports, sibling fights, and television, which have provided some release of hostility, are no longer available. At night, leftover hostility from unresolved daytime frustrations presses for release. In the nightmare, the symbolic derivatives of the child's anger (the horrible creature, etc.) press for expression into the child's conscious awareness (symbolized by the child's room). The greater the child's guilt over his anger, the more it will be repressed. The urgency for release becomes correspondingly greater, as does fear of the anger symbols when they threaten to erupt into conscious awareness. Up to a point, the more guilt-ridden the child and the greater the anger the more frightening the nightmare. When the guilt is extremely great, however, even symbols of the anger will be repressed, no dream will be experienced, and the child will be "protected" from his nightmares—and this vehicle for release of anger will then no longer be available.

In addition, the evil figures can represent the child's own hostility projected outward (they are outside his room), or they can symbolize hostile elements within significant figures (such as his parents). When the frightening figure threatens to abduct the child, then the dream may reflect separation anxieties—the child's fearing that, with diminished parental protection, he or she will be at the mercy of those who might prey on children. The nightmare, like all dreams, is rich in meaning. Many elements contribute to its formation and these are beyond the scope of this book to discuss in detail. Central to the nightmare, however, are the child's *own* repressed hostilities; and the fears the child experiences during the dream are most commonly of his *own* anger. It is for these reasons, I believe, that the child of divorce is likely to exhibit an increase in the frequency of nightmares, especially around the time of the separation.

The term *compulsion* refers to an act that an individual is compelled to perform even though he or she may consider it senseless. Trying to restrain oneself from performing the act produces ever-mounting tension, which can only be reduced by giving in and engaging in the compulsive behavior. Most often the individual does not really know *why* he has to perform the act, although he may at times provide weak rationalizations to justify it. The development of compulsions is another way in which children of divorce may deal with anger. In the handwashing compulsion, for example, the child may consider his or her hands to be the potential tools for acting out unconscious hostile thoughts and feelings. By compulsively cleaning them, the child symbolically "keeps them clean" (that is, innocent of committed crimes) and washes off the "stains" of their potential or fantasied crimes.

A ten-year-old boy I once treated presented symptoms that demonstrate quite well the relationship between compulsions and repressed hostility. Although his parents were not separated, they were highly intellectualized people, very inhibited in expressing affection, and so were psychologically separated from one another and from him. The boy feared that if he knocked against an article of furniture (even accidentally) there would be the most terrible consequences—the worst of which was that God would punish him by striking him dead with lightning. He especially feared hitting his foot against something, because the possible punishments for that seemed to be worse than if the point of contact with the furniture were his hand or torso. Although he was ever cautious lest he knock against anything, he somehow would slip up at least a few times a day and "accidentally" hit against or even kick some household articles. He would then become very anxious, examine the furniture very carefully to be sure that it wasn't damaged, and run his finger over it a few times to be certain that it wasn't scratched or marred. Gradually the examination process developed into a specific ritual in which he had to rub his finger over the area exactly three times, after which he experienced some alleviation of his anxiety. In addition, he would look up toward heaven and pray to God not to punish him for the terrible thing he had done. Finally his pleadings too became formulated into specific prayers that would reduce his anxiety if stated in a particular way.

I considered the furniture to represent the patient's parents and his knocking (and even worse, kicking) against them a symbolic expression of hostility toward them. It was as if each time he hit the furniture he released symbolically the anger he felt toward his parents. The inspection for damages and scratches served to reassure the patient that he had not in fact harmed his parents. Ritualizing the examination further served to lessen such anxiety: prescribing a specific number of strokes shortened the examination period necessary to reassure him that harm had not been done. God, of course, represented the patient's parents (especially his father, whom he saw as more punitive), and begging God's forgiveness served to protect the boy from the punishment he anticipated for his transgressions. Again, ritualizing the prayer served to diminish the anxiety (by shortening the period of begging God to forgive him) and provided him with a predictable (although magical) way of reducing it. It is clear that the patient's "accidents," which resulted in his knocking against or kicking furniture, were unconsciously planned and served as an outlet for his hostility. The rituals enabled him to reduce the guilt he felt over such expression. Generally, children with such compulsive rituals require psychiatric treatment. In this boy's case, a central focus in his therapy was the reduction of guilt over and fear of expressing his anger. However, as will be described subsequently, mere expression of hostility was not enough; other issues related to the generation of his anger and appropriate release of it also had to be dealt with.

The less direct contact we have with a person the greater the likelihood that we will harbor distortions about the absent individual. When parents separate, the child is likely to develop distortions about the absent parent that would not otherwise have arisen. Specifically, the child of divorce is likely either to idealize or to devalue the absent parent. The devaluation process is facilitated by the child's viewing the parent's leaving as a hostile act. The child is likely, then, to see such a parent as unduly punitive and may, generalizing from his or her "abandonment," anticipate similar maltreatment from that parent in the future. A common contribution to the child's viewing the absent parent as being hostile when he or she is not (or more hostile than he or she really is) is vilification of the departed parent by the parent with whom the child lives. The child's considering the absent parent to be hostile may be further intensified by the projection of the child's own hostility. The guilt such children feel over their hostility may cause them to disown it and project it onto others. It is as if such a child were saying: "It is not I who have these horrible hostile thoughts, it is he (she)." The absent parent may then be seen as so hostile that the child expects to be injured or severely maltreated in other ways. With such anticipations the child may dread contact with the parent and even become *phobic* with regard to him or her; that is, the child may fear any contact with the parent.

Phobic reactions regarding the parent (especially the absent one) may take other forms. The child may become excessively fearful that the parent may become sick or injured. Such concerns are reactions to the basic unconscious wish that harm befall the parent, as an expression of the child's hostility. As described, guilt over hostility contributes to the transformation of the wish into a fear. Another notion that may contribute to such a phobia is the child's belief that his or her hostile thoughts per se have the power to harm. Such a child may need frequent proof and testimony that the parent is well in order to be assured that the basic hostile wishes have not been realized. From fear that something terrible will happen to the parent the child may become so solicitous of the parent that he becomes an irritant. And separation anxieties may develop in the service of keeping the parent ever at the child's side, thereby providing the child with the reassurance that the parent has not been harmed. In the extreme the child might develop what is often referred to as a "school phobia." In this disorder the child becomes panicked upon going to school, but is relatively calm and happy if allowed to remain home. The term school phobia is a poor one because it implies that the child is afraid of school; actually it is fear of separation from the parent (usually the mother) that is primary. (In fact, if the mother were to be allowed to spend the day with the child in the classroom, most of these children would readily remain in school and function well there.) Although many factors contribute to the school phobia, one relates to the child's need to be ever at the side of the mother in order to be reassured that conscious and unconscious hostile wishes toward her have not caused her harm. Sometimes the fear of harm from, or that of harm befalling, a parent is displaced onto an object or an animal. Such children (and others as well) may not understand why they have become so morbidly frightened of dogs, certain figures on television, or other selected phobic object.

As noted earlier in this chapter, the children's repressing their hostility and directing it toward themselves can contribute to their becoming *depressed*. When self-recriminations are present this mechanism becomes even more obvious. One does best to understand such criticisms as being displaced from a signficant figure onto the child himself. For the child of divorce the significant individuals are generally one or both parents. If one follows the formula "substitute the word *father* or *mother* whenever the patient's name appears in a self-disparaging statement," one will generally get a clearer understanding of what is going on in the child.

Changes parents can effect within themselves that may help their children's anger inhibition problems. Some parents have very rigid and inhibited standards regarding anger expression and they may actively contribute thereby to their children's guilt. They may believe that a child's harboring angry thoughts and feelings toward a parent is sinful, bad, abnormal, or otherwise unacceptable. And they may have overtly or covertly induced guilt in their children for such anger. Such parents do well to appreciate that such views, although they have a long tradition, are not consistent with our present knowledge of what is best psychologically for children. Anger is a normal reaction to the frustrations that children (like the rest of us) inevitably experience in life, and excessive guilt over anger can contribute to the formation of a variety of psychological symptoms. In my discussions with parents on this issue some fear that I am encouraging them to let their children run wild and turn into little savages who go about expressing their anger wherever and whenever they wish. They may even be supported in this notion by tales of other children who have gone to therapists who appeared to be suggesting such abandoned expression of anger. (Unfortunately there are some therapists who go this far, or almost so.) I try to reassure them that this is definitely not my goal—that this would be substituting one disease for another. Rather, my hope is that their children will find a healthy balance between too much and too little repression of anger; and that at the present time they have too much and need some loosening up— but not to the point of there being no suppression at all.

I try to help parents differentiate between angry thoughts, feelings, and action. I try to help them appreciate that they do best for their children by attempting to lessen any guilt they may feel over angry thoughts and feelings (which they have little power to control) and angry deeds (which they generally have the capacity to suppress). I advise them to use such comments as "We see how angry you are over Daddy's leaving; but you can't go around the house breaking things." Such a comment encourages the expression of angry thoughts and feelings but prohibits acting them out. In such discussions the question of children's cursing at parents usually comes up. I generally advise parents to reassure their children that they accept the fact that the children's anger at them may cause curse words to come into their minds. However, I suggest they add that at the present time children's cursing at parents is socially unacceptable behavior, and that if they are angry at them they should use more polite words than those that come into their minds. I also advise parents to try to reduce any guilt their children may feel over their impulses to use profanity toward parents by informing them that such words do have a use, because they allow for a release of anger in a way that does not cause anyone physical harm. Present standards generally allow for their use in one's relationship with peers (especially when the other party uses them first) but not toward one's parents and other adults. For example, I suggest a parent might say, "I can see how angry you are that Mommy has to work; but I won't let you go around using such language to me. That kind of language is okay with your friends out on the street. What we have to do is figure out ways for you to be less angry about my working." As I will elaborate upon soon, merely encouraging angry expression may be of little value. As the mother quoted here is doing, the child is encouraged to use anger constructively in order to reduce or remove the irritants and frustrations that are causing it.

Parents do well to appreciate that angry outbursts are especially common around the time of the separation and their tolerance for them has to be particularly high during this period. I do not suggest that *no* disciplinary measures at all be taken; rather, that they be used more sparingly during this period.

Children who frequently observe their parents swept up in their hostilities and treating one another in a cruel and often inhumane fashion may become fearful of expressing their anger lest they cause similar suffering to others. If such parents can reduce their warfare, this contributing element to their children's guilt over their hostility may be reduced.

There are parents who cannot tolerate a child's anger because they operate in accordance with the dictum "If someone is angry at me, regardless of the age of the person and the reasons for the anger, I must be at fault. It cannot be his (or her) problem, distortion, or inappropriate reaction to me. I must be abominable." Accordingly, they may do everything to squelch their children's anger in order to protect themselves from what are to them such painful and fearful confrontations. Their children may recognize such a parent's intolerance for anger expression on their part and may come to feel very guilty about their anger because of the devastating effect it has on the parent. Such a parent generally needs to be loved by everybody and cannot tolerate anyone's disapproval—even that of an irrational child. Sometimes therapy may be necessary to help such a parent alter this view.

There are parents who have to consider themselves perfect, or at least attempt to present such a view of themselves to their children. They may believe that it is against their children's best interests to see flaws in a parent and they will refrain from admitting or revealing any imperfections in the service of this goal. Such parents may consider their children's anger to be a sign of a defect within themselves and so the children's expression of anger is strongly discouraged in order that the parents may maintain the image of perfection. Such parents are doing their children a disservice. The children, if they come to believe the ruse, will develop unrealistic expectations of others, may come to believe that there are other perfect people as well, and will suffer inevitable disappointments and disillusionments as each adult they encounter will ultimately reveal his or her imperfections. In addition, as they grow older they will in all likelihood come to appreciate the parent's deception and will then have real reason to lose respect for the parent. Parents do well to appreciate that revealing one's deficiencies in natural and uncontrived ways (as long as they are not extensive and frequently exhibited) will result in the children's *gaining* respect for the parent as they come to appreciate that it is the strong rather than the weak person who has the courage to admit defects. If such a parent can alter his or her view and allow the child to express anger over a defect in him- or herself, one of the elements contributing to the child's guilt will be reduced.

In recent years we have experienced the popularization of what I consider a misguided application of psychological principles. Unfortunately espoused by many mental health workers, this approach advises parents to encourage their children openly to express their resentment and considers such expression the primary aim of therapy as well as one of the most valuable ways of helping children avoid the development of psychological disturbance. "Once the hateful feelings are let out," we are told, "the loving feelings are then free to express themselves." And the method used to facilitate the release of the angry feelings is *labeling* them. Accordingly, the little girl whose divorced father is late for his visits, is told, "It must make you feel very angry that Daddy is late again." If the child agrees and expresses her resentment, the method is deemed successful. Guilt has been reduced by the parent's speaking the unspeakable and the child's expressing her anger drains the pool of repressed feelings that have caused her discomfort and even neurosis. I believe that a child who was comfortable in expressing her anger would respond indignantly to such a comment with a response such as: "Of course I am. Wouldn't you be?" She would recognize the absurdity of the statement and its implicit condescension. If she were not consciously aware of her anger, it would not serve well to bring her in touch with it. (I will discuss in the next section the approaches I use to help such a child achieve greater awareness of her repressed anger.)

Such an approach is in all probability a good first step for many children. It may lessen some guilt via the parent's mentioning the unmentionable. (Recall the mother

who gives her children frequent lectures on the depravity
of sex vs. the mother who never mentions the word at all.
The latter mother makes her children far more sexually
inhibited than the former.) The method's main fault lies
in its incompleteness. It does not give proper attention
to the primary purpose of anger: to *remove* a source
of irritation and frustration. Although it may allow for
temporary release of anger and alleviation of some tension, it does nothing to bring about a change in the situation that caused the anger in the first place. Accordingly,
the anger is likely to be continually generated because
the provocative situation remains unchanged. It is a good
first step but little will be accomplished if the child is
not, in addition, encouraged to direct his angry feelings
toward specific goals in order to accomplish something
more than emotional release. For example, the aforementioned little girl whose father is continually late for
visits might be told: "Have you told your father how angry
it makes you when he's late?" or "What do you think
you can do while waiting for him so you won't be thinking all the time about when he's going to come?" Comments such as these direct the child to use her anger
constructively toward the goal of removing the conditions that originally generated the anger and are therefore far more likely to solve the anger problem than
mere encouragement of anger expression.

Helping children with their anger inhibition problems.
If parents are to help their children express their pent-up
resentments, they must serve as models for such expression themselves. Like the cigarette-smoking parent who
warns his or her children against the pitfalls of smoking,
the parent who does not practice what he or she preaches
is not going to be taken very seriously by his or her
children.

In accordance with what I have described previously
about the various stages of anger release, children should
be encouraged to express their resentments at the earliest possible stage so that their anger does not get suppressed, repressed, and built up internally. They should
learn to become sensitive to angry thoughts when they

first arise and be made aware of any tendency to make excuses that justify their not utilizing their anger appropriately. They should learn as well the physical sensations they experience when they become angry, especially in the early phases. And they should be encouraged to assert themselves and express their resentments at the earliest possible time in the service of altering the situation that is causing the resentments in the first place.

Children should not only be encouraged to try to rectify situations that cause irritation but to learn as well not to pursue lost causes. I often quote in this regard what I call Fields' Rule (after W. C. Fields, the comedian, who allegedly first stated it): "If at first you don't succeed, try, try again. If, after that, you still don't succeed, forget it! Don't make a big fool of yourself." To encourage children to persist in trying to achieve a goal that appears hopeless can be psychologically harmful and even cruel. Rather, they should be encouraged to resign themselves to certain failures and to redirect their attention to alternative pursuits that have a greater likelihood of success. For example, the boy whose father shows little if any interest in him should be encouraged to try to improve his relationship with his father and possibly effect a closer tie. If, however, after reasonable efforts the father proves himself to be unmotivated for or incapable of a more intimate relationship, the youngster should be helped to recognize that just because his father has little if any love for him does not mean that he is unlovable. He must be helped to gain affection from others who are willing to and capable of providing it. It is this combination of knowledge and experience that can make the parental advice meaningful. The concept of the substitute gratification is important in helping a child resign himself to a failure. It is much easier to admit defeat in one area if one is simultaneously provided with reasonable hope of success in another.

As mentioned, anger arises when one is frustrated—when one cannot get something that one wants, or *thinks* one wants. One way to reduce anger is to appreciate that the thing one may want may not be a reasonable thing to desire. If one can then stop craving that thing, one is less likely to be frustrated and hence angry. In my work with children I often refer to this principle as "changing your mind about the thing you want." A girl, for example, who wants her mother to discontinue dating is going to be continually frustrated and angry as long as she persists in hoping that her mother will stop. If, however, she can be helped to appreciate that her mother has the right to recreation, and is usually in better spirits upon her return, then the girl might give up or reduce her demands and thereby become less angry. (The oedipal rivalries and other factors that may contribute to such anger may make its alleviation more difficult than is implied in my example. Yet I have found this approach to be helpful as part of my dealing with problems of this kind.)

A related alteration of thinking that I have found useful to attempt to effect in children with anger inhibition problems is what I refer to as "changing your mind about the person you're angry at." The most common example of this is the child who has been brainwashed by one parent into believing that the other parent is the incarnation of all the evil that ever existed in the world. If one can help such a child correct some of these distortions, then he or she is less likely to be angry.

In the course of my work with children who are guilty over their anger I try to help them differentiate between angry thoughts, angry feelings, and angry deeds. These three types of anger are discussed in detail, with my questioning children throughout the discussion to be sure that they appreciate the distinctions. I try to impress upon them the fact that one has little control over the appearance of angry thoughts and feelings; whereas angry acts or deeds are very much under our control. I try to help them recognize that angry thoughts and feelings are inevitable reactions to frustrations and that all people experience them. In addition, I try to convince them that all people, at times, have the desire to perform angry acts and that most *do* act these out to a limit extent when the damage done is minimal; but that most *do not* when the inflicted damage would be great. My emphasis in such discussions is on the fact that these are the reactions and experiences of *most* people. This helps such children feel less guilty about their own anger reactions as they come to appreciate that they are not different from others regarding their angry thoughts and feelings. When a guilty person comes to appreciate that his or her own reactions are widespread he or she is likely to feel less guilty about them.

Magical thinking is especially prevalent during the period from three to five years, and many people carry remnants of such primitive thinking into adulthood and even throughout their lives. One such notion pertinent to this discussion is the idea that thoughts in themselves have the power to bring about real events. Simply stated, the child may believe that the very wish that something will happen can make it happen. Wish someone harm—and it will come to pass. Wish someone dead and he or she will die. Children who fail to correct this distortion, or who maintain it beyond the age when they should appreciate its absurdity, may suffer exaggerated guilt over angry expression. Children who believe that their angry thoughts can actually harm the object of their hostility, may become very frightened of expressing them. In attempting to help a child correct such a distortion I may make comments along these lines in my play therapy: "The dog was really angry at the cat, so angry that he wished that she would be killed. One night he wished *very hard* that the cat would be run over by a car. The next morning he went to see what had happened to the cat. But she was still alive! The next night he wished *even harder* [stated in strained voice] that the cat would die. But still the cat stayed alive. And night after night and day after day—no matter how hard he wished the cat to die—she still stayed alive. No matter how hard he wished the cat to be dead, she still stayed alive. His thoughts just couldn't harm her."

There are some children who are so repressed with regard to anger expression that they have little if any conscious awareness of angry thoughts and/or feelings. For example, the mother of a significantly repressed girl reported that the child waited three hours for her father to show up on visitation day and he never appeared.

When I asked the child how she felt about her father's not showing up she replied, without any show of emotion, "He must have forgotten. Sometimes his memory isn't very good." The child was obviously guilty about expressing the angry feelings I knew she harbored deep within her and justified her father's behavior with the explanation that he had some kind of inborn deficiency in his memory that caused him to forget. One cannot get angry at a person with such an unfortunate handicap. It would have been useless to have tried to introduce this child to the psychoanalytic theory of forgetting which considers most forgetting (in people without physical disease) to be unconsciously motivated. In this father's case the forgetting was a manifestation of his basic lack of interest in seeing his daughter. Her need to see her father as loving of her was so great that she could not allow herself to recognize what was really going on within him, what his true feelings were. To accept this fact might have resulted in her becoming angry at him—something she was morbidly afraid to do. Accordingly, I responded, "I imagine you must have been very angry." Her reply: "No, he's just that way. He often does that. I'm used to it; it doesn't make me angry." Again the child rationalized in the service of denying her anger. At this point I replied, "I cannot imagine that in all that time—in the three hours that you waited—that you didn't once, somewhere in the corner of your mind, have at least *one* angry thought about him. Some little angry feeling. I can't imagine someone in that situation not getting at least a little angry. I know that I myself would have been furious." My question was stated with an attitude of extreme disbelief. My hope was that I would make the admission of an angry reaction acceptable and the denial of it the unusual response. Although the child responded with further denials during that interchange, she subsequently allowed that she did occasionally get angry under similar circumstances. Such an approach is based on the assumption that even in the most severely repressed people, under enough provocation some of the anger does manage to erupt into conscious awareness. The patient, however, may be fearful of admitting this to the therapist—anticipating from him or her the same kind of critical response as from those (usually the parents) who originally fostered guilt over anger expression. The expression of this little spark of anger is strongly encouraged by the therapist and the hiding of it emphatically discouraged. The patient is made to feel that its expression makes him or her like everyone else, and this can reduce fears of revealing it. Although a parent might try this approach, it is important to appreciate that it must be used with caution; too much pressure on the child to reveal the transient angry thought and/or fleeting angry feeling may produce anxiety and further repression. But used judiciously, such an approach can help some children more guiltlessly express their anger.

Acting-out of anger. There are children who, instead of repressing their anger and possibly channeling it into various symptoms, release it directly. For the purposes of this discussion I will use the term *acting-out* when the hostile release is antisocial and unaccompanied by significant guilt. The relationship between breakup of the home and antisocial behavior in children has been extensively studied (especially with regard to juvenile delinquency). And most agree that children growing up in a broken home are more likely to exhibit delinquent behavior than those reared in an intact, relatively happy and stable home. It seems quite reasonable that there should be a relationship between breakup of the home by separation or divorce and delinquent behavior. After all, such children are being deprived and frustrated and it is reasonable to assume that some (if not many) of them will act out their anger. A sibling may be a convenient and safe scapegoat; or the parent with whom the child lives may become the focus, the absent parent not being so readily available. The parent who initiated the divorce proceedings may be selected as the target regardless of how justifiable the decision and regardless of how little was his or her contribution to the difficulties. From the child's point of view *that* parent caused the separation and *that* parent should be blamed. The forms of acting-out behavior vary according to the child's age and level of sophistication. They range from primitive temper tantrums in the very young, through bullying peers, disruptive behavior in the home and classroom, cruelty to animals, fire setting, defiance of authority, and on to a wide range of other types of antisocial behavior.

Factors that may contribute to acted-out anger in children of divorce. The capacity of a child to experience guilt over antisocial behavior results from his or her experiences with parents (and, to a lesser extent, teachers, clergymen, and other authority figures) during the formative years. Both by instruction and imitation of the parental model the child takes on to him- or herself the principles of behavior to which the parents adhere. Their dos and don'ts become his or hers; their rights and wrongs are accepted as valid for the child. When one parent is absent from the home there is some reduction of those exposures that produce a strong capacity to experience guilt. It is probable that the loss of the father (rather than the mother) is especially conducive to a child's failing to develop strong guilt mechanisms. Although many fathers are quite passive, uninvolved, and less available than the mother with regard to the child's upbringing, social forces may still impart to the child that the father is the severer disciplinarian. Many mothers will say, "Just wait until your father comes home and hears what you've done." And most teachers know that summoning a child's father to school implies that a more serious offense has been committed than when a mother is asked to come. Since the overwhelming majority of separations involve the absence of the father, the frequent development of guilt deficiencies in children of divorce is not surprising.

In the intact home, when one parent is not on the scene, the other is generally available to teach, discipline, and impart those values that contribute to the development of healthy guilt mechanisms. When separation occurs and the custodial parent is temporarily absent, the child is more likely to be left with those who have less authority and hence less influence on guilt development. And when the children are older, they are more likely to be left alone than children with two parents living in the home. Children of divorce often feel that the departed parent has abandoned them. Accordingly, they are more likely to feel unloved than children living in an intact home. One of the factors that motivates children to inhibit themselves from acting out antisocial impulses is the parental affection and approbation they obtain for doing so. A child of divorce, feeling unloved (whether or not such feelings are justified), may reason: "What's the point of stopping myself from doing bad things. Even when I'm good no one praises me. No one even cares."

The child of divorce is often observer to some of the most cruel behavior that one individual can visit upon another. The parental hostilities frequently reach sadistic levels. There is often little place for honesty in the parents' deliberations and the atmosphere becomes one of continual distrust. The most cruel things may be said with no holds barred on the use of profanity. Impulsive acting out of destructive behavior toward one another is common. The desire for vengeance may reach obsessive and even psychotic proportions. Sensitivity to the feelings of one another may become totally lost. Power struggles become the only method of dealing with differences. And the parents may even physically harm one another, so vicious and violent becomes their rage. Lastly (and by no means least) the participation of lawyers often contributes further to the viciousness of the parental conflict. Using the rationalization that justice must be done and that their clients must be protected from being taken advantage of, the lawyers are capable of reducing otherwise sensitive and humane parents to the level of vicious animals in their relationship with one another. In such an environment it is not surprising that the children are likely to model themselves after such parents and behave similarly. In addition, parents who are obsessed with their conflict are less likely to be directing their attention to training and disciplining their children. So deprived of external restraints, the children are not likely to develop internal restraints to their antisocial behavior.

Bruce, a seven-year-old boy, demonstrated quite well how a vicious parental conflict could affect a child. Bruce's parents became embroiled in a violent divorce conflict when his father learned that his mother was having an affair. Bruce's father was basically a man who had always had a short fuse and a violent temper. In restaurants he was known to make a public scene when not served well, and worked on the principle that "the squeaking wheel gets the grease." Bruce's mother also tended to resort to screaming at the slightest provocation and the neighbors generally knew when she was disciplining the children. Following the divulgence of the mother's affair an immediate decision for divorce was made by the father; he saw absolutely no hope for his ever being able to forget his wife's infidelity or work out problems that might have contributed to her involvement with another man. Once the divorce process started rolling other issues became sources of conflict: property distribution, money, visitation, etc. The father's lawyer was determined to "extract his pound of flesh"; and his mother's lawyer was adamant in his position that Bruce's father was not going to get "a penny more than he's entitled to." The father "saw red" every time his wife's name was mentioned; and Bruce's mother found fault with just about everything the father said or did. The most petty incidents became the foci of violent arguments during which they cursed at one another using the most base profanity, often threw things at one another, and on occasion even came to blows. When Bruce and his sister were not direct witnesses to the parental battles, they could not but overhear them.

Prior to the disclosure of his mother's affair Bruce was relatively well behaved in the classroom and at home. Although a little on the edgy side with some tendencies toward being a wise guy and a loudmouth, he had never been a significant behavior problem. Within a month of the onset of the parental conflict there began a steady deterioration in Bruce's behavior. He began to refuse to do his homework, or when he did do it, it was messy and slipshod. He became disruptive in the classroom and not only learned little but interfered with his classmates' learning as well. He bullied other children, teased, and provoked them. When his teacher would try to discipline him he would not hesitate to respond with a barrage of profanities, and reacted similarly to the principal, to whose office he was frequently sent. It was because of these problems that Bruce was referred to me.

When I first saw Bruce he was clearly in a state of agitation. He was so tense that he could not sit still; rather he bounced around or rocked in his seat. His eyes blinked furiously. He bit his fingernails frequently and even, at times, his lips. Often he would nervously wet his lips with his tongue, so dry had they become as a result of his tension. When I asked him a few simple introductory questions like his age, address, and telephone number he responded with such answers as "Bug off" and "Dry up." He absolutely refused to involve himself meaningfully in any of the therapeutic activities and after a few sessions he refused to attend the sessions any longer. I advised the parents that I did not think that it would be a good idea to pressure Bruce into coming, because doing so might sour him even further on therapy. I told them that the best hope for alleviating Bruce's antisocial behavior was their reducing their conflict. Although they could appreciate the validity of my explanation, they were so swept up in their vicious battle that they were unwilling and unable to extract themselves from it. Two years later, I learned from the referring physician that the parents were still going strong (even though divorced) and that Bruce had been expelled from school and was attending a military academy, where he was still a severe disciplinary problem.

In Bruce's case it was clear that the anger he felt toward his parents was being displaced onto classmates, teachers, his principal, and me. His parents were serving as his models for angry acting-out. Although relatively free to vent rage against his mother, he rarely had a single complaint about his father. I felt that this related, in part, to the fact that his father had already left the home and expressing anger toward him might result in his seeing even less of his father. In addition to the acting-out of his anger there was still a significant degree of anger repression (especially regarding his anger at his father). And this resulted in the state of agitation and tension that was so typical of him. Bruce was a relatively healthy boy prior to the onset of his parents' battling. I believe that if they had been able to divorce in a more civilized fashion, Bruce would not have developed the problems that not only disrupted his education at that time but may have changed for the worse the whole course of his life.

Parental encouragement (either conscious or unconscious) of a child's antisocial acting-out is common whenever a child exhibits such behavior—both within and out of the divorce situation. For example, a neighbor complains that Henry threw a rock through her window. Henry's father responds indignantly, "My Henry? Never. My Henry would never do such a thing." A shopkeeper complains that Doris has been caught stealing from his store. Doris' mother responds nonchalantly and with little conviction, "Doris, tell the man you're sorry." In both of these cases the parent is encouraging a repetition of the child's antisocial behavior by depriving the child of meaningful criticism and discouragement. Moreover, Doris' mother's response is an excellent example of one of the more common ways in which such parents subtly encourage their children to act out. Their words discourage the behavior yet their verbal intonations and gestures encourage it. The principle is well demonstrated in the old song title "Your Lips Tell Me No No, but There's Yes Yes in Your Eyes." Parents are not usually able to act out their own hostilities because of internal inhibitions or the awareness of the consequences of doing so. Their children lend themselves well to the acting-out of such parental impulses. By doing so the children may provide their parents with vicarious gratification, and may gain parental affection for antisocial behavior. Such parents identify with their children and each time the children exhibit the antisocial behavior the parents derive the kinds of gratification they would enjoy if they themselves were performing the antisocial acts. Lacking the judgment of the adult the child may more readily engage in behavior that the adult would be wary of. In the intact household such parentally sanctioned acting-out is generally directed outside the home. In the divorce situation it is generally directed toward one parent and encouraged by the other, but its expression outside the home may also be fostered.

The divorced parent usually has less contact with the

former spouse than has the visiting child. Accordingly, the child often has greater opportunities to exhibit hostility directly to a parent then either one of them has to express anger toward the other. The child may become a readily available tool for the parentally encouraged acting-out. The children may willingly side with one parent against the other as a general pattern, or may switch sides and take the position of the parent they are with at the particular time. There are many ways in which children are used for this purpose. They may serve as informers and provide information that could be devastating when litigation is taking place. One parent may encourage a child not to comply with the requests of the other, even in such small matters as which foods to eat and when to go to bed. A mother may "forget" to have the children ready for the father and they (even though old enough to appreciate the time and day) may also "fail to remember" to remind the mother about their appointment with the father. Or Father may "forget" the time to return the children and they too may suffer similar memory lapses. Or the children may dawdle in preparing for their father's visit and Mother's sense of urgency for getting them ready on time may leave much to be desired. The children "get the message" from the mother and dawdle even more. The father may recognize that his bringing the children home early presents the mother with various restrictions and inconveniences. Their acting-up may serve as an excuse for the father's early return and they may do so in order to ingratiate themselves to him. The mother may encourage antisocial behavior in the children in order to hurt the husband by making him feel guilty: "Look at all the trouble you've caused by leaving. Look how upset they've become since you've gone."

Children of divorce almost always feel insecure, especially around the time of separation. After all, the family—the most stabilizing force in their lives—has fallen apart, and this cannot but make them feel insecure. Angry feelings, especially when acted out, can provide the child with a sense of power. Although destroying furniture, for example, does not accomplish anything regarding the parental separation, it does provide a child with a sense of strength (as well as the relief of having let out some anger). Rage reactions are at times frightening to others and this can contribute to the notion that they are a measure of one's power.

The boy whose father has left the home may engage in delinquent acts in order to gain a feeling of masculinity to compensate for the loss of a male model. He may equate antisocial acting-out with masculinity, a view fostered to a significant degree by the public media, especially movies and television. Living only with his mother (and in some situations with other females as well) may result in feelings that some of their femininity may wipe off on him and turn him into a "sissy." To avoid this he may gravitate toward "tough guys" and delinquents and become a willing member of their gang. A mother living alone with her son may try to compensate for feelings of deficiency as a wife by becoming an outstanding mother. In the service of this goal she may try to make the boy well disciplined and well behaved. The child may react to such a mother with antisocial behavior—not only from the hostility that such pressures produce in him but because such acting-out serves to negate the weakness and femininity the boy sees to be an intrinsic part of the image his mother is trying to create.

A child may become delinquent in order to provoke punishment. This may be done in the service of reducing guilt. But it may also represent an attempt to gain an absent father's attention or even his return to the home. If children become so unmanageable that their mother cannot handle them, she may resort to enlisting the father's aid in providing control. Although such involvement with the father may be painful, the children appear to feel that it is worth the price. In other words, if their choice is one of having no father at all or a father who reprimands, disciplines, and punishes, they choose the latter alternative. In addition, there are times when children want the father's help in strengthening guilt mechanisms, and provocative behavior may appear to be (or actually be) the only way to secure such help. By their delinquent behavior they hope to get their fathers more involved with them, in part to provide external controls for the inner ones they feel to be weakening.

Children of divorce live with the fear that the parent who has left the home may abandon them even further and that the remaining parent may also leave. One way for such children to gain reassurance that these calamities will not occur is through testing the parents' tolerance for disobedient behavior. They work on the principle that the more pain one will tolerate from another, the more one can demonstrate his or her affection; that is, the more disruptive behavior a parent will put up with, the more that parent proves his or her affection for the child. Although the provocations may bring about punishment and various kinds of parental alienation, they do not generally result in the parents' further abandoning the child—and he or she is thereby reassured.

Another way of handling the anticipation of abandonment that results from the separation is for the children themselves to become the initiators of rejection. Their antisocial acts serve to keep people at a distance. They thereby become the ones who control the situation in which separation from another person has taken place, not the ones who must passively suffer abandonment. It is as if such a child were saying: "It is not I who have been abandoned. I am the abandoner." And antisocial behavior can serve as the vehicle for effecting such rejection of others. In addition, such behavior protects such children from intimate relationships. They have already been "burned" and wish to protect themselves from further disillusionment and disappointment in their relationships with others. And there is hardly a better way to do this than to provoke others with antisocial behavior.

Changes parents can effect within themselves that may reduce their children's angry acting-out. To the degree that parents can lessen their hostilities, to that degree will they reduce many of the elements that contribute to their children's delinquent behavior. If the parents become less angry at one another, their children will be less angry and hence less likely to be antisocial. If they reduce their hostilities, the identification factor will be reduced, i.e., two important models for the child's antisocial behavior will have been removed. If the parents spend less time fighting and more time acting benevolently toward their children, the children will be less likely to be angry and hence less prone to act out hostility. In addition, by the parents spending more time with the children, they will have less of a need to gain attention by provocative acts. Gaining more affection will make the children more secure, less impotent, and so less needful of angry demonstrations as a way of gaining a sense of strength. If the parents can achieve a more intimate relationship with the children, they will be less likely to fear intimacy and to push people away by antisocial behavior in order to protect themselves from the tenderness that they view as dangerous. And if parents draw closer to their children, the children will be less needful of provocative testing to see if the parents will still remain loyal and loving of them.

Parents of acting-out children do well to consider whether they are overtly or covertly encouraging the children's delinquent behavior, either against outsiders or against one another. If they are using the child as an informant, if they are being sucked into believing the child's criticism of one another, if they are allowing themselves to be played one against the other, they should make every attempt to bring about a cessation of such involvement with the child. Parents do well to appreciate that they are susceptible to becoming willing tools of the children in their desire to act out their anger. Mother is seduced into acting out the child's hostility to Father, and Father is fooled into reacting similarly to Mother. In addition, the parents may be contributing to the child's angry acting-out by not utilizing appropriate disciplinary measures.

Sometimes parental rage that is contributing to children's acting-out may be so great that the aforementioned advice may not prove useful. A parent may appreciate intellectually, for example, that the continuation of hostilities is not only a waste of time and energy but detrimental to the children as well; and yet he or she may be helpless to refrain from perpetuating the vicious conflict. The parent may feel such a need for revenge that he or she may blind him- or herself to the repercussions of the obsession with such gratification. In such cases therapy or counseling may be warranted.

Helping children reduce their angry acting-out. Children with anger inhibition problems may be motivated to change themselves because of the psychological pain they may be suffering. Compulsive rituals, phobias, and depressive symptoms, for example, may be great sources of psychological stress. Children who act out their anger generally do not have inner pain and are thereby not particularly motivated to change themselves. Accordingly, the main request that such children may make of others is: "Get off my back." They only wish to rid themselves entirely of teachers who "bug" them to finish their assignments, do their homework, and behave in class; parents who complain that they won't do household chores, stop fighting with siblings, and come into the house when they call them; neighbors who complain that they bully their children, etc.

Parents of such children do well to try to help them deal with anger-provoking situations at the earliest possible time so that there will be less anger to be acted out. The approaches here are similar to those described earlier in this chapter in my discussion of children with anger inhibition problems. In both cases the child does well to learn how to avoid and reduce anger. In the inhibited there will then be less anger to channel into symptoms, and in the delinquent there will be less anger to act out.

Long lectures and explanations rarely help children reduce their antisocial behavior. Generally children get bored by such lectures, and very early tune the parent out. They may appear to be listening but are in another world. Parental pleading, as well, is of little avail; in fact, it may increase the child's delinquent behavior because it proves that the acting-out is hurting the parents. Trying to convince these children that they are hurting themselves more than their parents generally does not help (because their need to act out the anger is so great that they have to blind themselves to its self-destructive effects), although the statement should be made from time to time because it might ultimately play a role (however small) in reducing these children's tendency to act out their anger. Structuring situations so that the child may actually suffer certain consequences for the delinquent behavior may be useful. Althought this doesn't get to the roots of the problem it can serve to suppress somewhat the acting-out. For example, if a child's antisocial behavior gets him or her into difficulty with school authorities and even the police, the parents would do well to request that the usual punishments be implemented. To request leniency because the parents are divorced or because the child has emotional problems only serves to perpetuate the acting-out.

Children want limits and the parent who does not provide them may be doing them a disservice. They test in order to learn what is acceptable and what is not. And even when anger is acted out the youngster may ask the parent for limits (often in a disguised way). I recall treating a very angry adolescent girl who charged out of her suburban home claiming that she could no longer live under the intolerable conditions there. A few hours later she called her mother from the home of a girl friend in New York City and told her that she was heading for the Greenwich Village district, where she was going to devote herself to a life of total abandon in which she would indulge herself in as much sex and drugs as her heart desired. And the only thing that would stop her from embarking upon this life course was if Dr. Gardner were to commit her to a local mental hospital. The mother immediately called me, asking what she should do. I told her to call her daughter back immediately and tell her, quite firmly, that she had spoken to me and I said that if she wasn't home in two hours I would commit her to the local mental hospital. The girl was home before the "deadline," cursing me bitterly in the most vile language, and angrily told all her friends that if it were not for me she would now be enjoying a life of self-indulgence and pleasure.

I believe that when this girl arrived in New York City she became quite frightened over the prospect of going to Greenwich Village and involving herself with the drug addicts and free-sex advocates that she hoped to find there. Accordingly, she stopped off at a girl friend's house and by calling her mother provided herself (via her mother and me) with a face-saving way of returning home. Instead of having to come home a frightened child begging for permission to return, she returned a hero. She could convince herself and her friends that she really would have gone to Greenwich Village and led the life she described except that she was forced to change her plans by Dr. Gardner's terrible threats. She could not but be admired for her courage; she had fought hard, but had bowed only to Dr. Gardner's awful threat of incarceration in "an insane asylum." No one could possibly think less of her, or consider her weak for having so submitted. This girl was essentially begging to be forced to return home (although she probably didn't consciously realize it) and not to have provided her with the threat might have resulted in her going to Greenwich Village and exposing herself to many individuals who would have had an adverse influence on her. Parents, therefore, do well to keep their eyes and ears open to such disguised requests on the part of their children and provide them with the limits and restrictions that they not only crave but need to have imposed upon them.

Peer pressure, support, and encouragement often contribute to a child's antisocial acting-out. The mob has a potential for violence greater than that of the sum of the individuals within it. An individual would often hesitate to act out many of his or her antisocial impulses alone. In the gang one is surrounded by others who support the delinquent behavior and encourage its acting-out. In addition, the fear of punishment is lessened as punitive authorities may be relatively impotent to deter or stop a mob, whereas they have great power to prevent and punish a single individual. Accordingly, parents

should do everything that is reasonably possible to discourage acting-out children's involvement in such groups.
This is often not easily accomplished, yet the parent
does well to try. Parents should appreciate their impotence
to influence significantly the child's contacts outside the
home with those who support the antisocial behavior. To
make attempts to control such involvements by checking
on the child's whereabouts, calling other homes, etc., is not
only futile but may only encourage the child to seek such
friends. Keeping the child indoors, for days and even
weeks at a time, may also increase the child's anger and
cravings to join such groups. Parents do better to inform
the child that they recognize that they cannot stop involvement with such "friends" outside the home, but parents have every right to decide who shall come into the
home. By not allowing the gang members inside the
home the parent gets across the disapproving message in
the hope that it will have some influence on the child.
In addition, the parent diminishes somewhat the contact with the antisocial group to the degree that is reasonably within his or her power. Comments such as these
can be useful: "You know I don't like those kids you're
hanging around with. They're a bad influence on you and
they're helping you get into trouble. It hurts me to see
how you're fouling yourself up by all the things you've
been doing, and they're just making things worse. I know
I can't stop you from seeing them outside and I know
it won't do any good to keep you locked up in the house
as much as I can. However, I decide who comes into
this house, and I forbid you to have any of them here."

Parents often try to remove antisocial children from
groups that encourage their acting-out by removing the
child to a different school. This is often difficult to accomplish, but even when it can be done, such children
generally gravitate toward the antisocial youngster in
the new school (and there is hardly a school that doesn't
have its own collection). Accordingly, such transfers are
often futile; the problem lies within the child primarily
and only secondarily in the facilitating group.

Group therapy, "rap sessions," and other forms of
discussion groups can be useful for the adolescent who

acts out antisocially. Such groups should be conducted by someone with training in treating youngsters with emotional disorders, otherwise they may do more harm than good. Since therapists, like parents, are of the adult generation, they are somewhat distrusted and not considered to be really in touch with what youngsters need. The views of a child's peers, however, often have greater credibility for him or her and so can be more influential in inducing change than parental and adult opinion. In addition, youngsters are exquisitely sensitive to peer opinion and slavishly beholden to it, professions to the contrary notwithstanding. Preferably, the members of the group should be initially strangers to one another, in order to ensure a greater degree of privacy. In addition, the youngster is less likely to be candid with a friend whose affection he hopes to keep than with a stranger whose alienation will not be a great loss. My experience has been that most youngsters in a group will espouse and adhere (with varying degrees of conviction) to more conservative and traditional social standards than they might actually practice themselves. Although they do this, in part, to win favor with the group leader, such professions are also motivated by the inner recognition of the value of such standards (usually imbued in earlier years); but only in the protected group environment will they allow themselves to admit their basic adherence to the traditional social norms. In school and neighborhood such compliance with traditional values may be met with much social criticism.

It is important that the antisocial youngsters in the group be in the minority. If they are in the majority, the behavior may not only be supported by other delinquents, but the non-delinquents (especially those who are on the verge of involving themselves in such behavior) may be drawn into antisocial acting-out as well. Identification with the group leader can play an important role in these children's acquiring internal restraints. This is only likely to occur if a trusting relationship with the leader has been established and if there is genuine respect for him or her. We learn most from those whom we admire and respect. And it is only when this kind of relationship has been established that the child will take on the leader's values and incorporate his or her standards for socially acceptable behavior. In the groups that I conduct I try to help the youngsters acquire antidelinquent attitudes from group peers. I encourage group support of the delinquent's attempts not to succumb to peer pressure to engage in antisocial behavior. I try to imbue the youngster with the important truth that it is often braver to defy dares and group pressure to join in antisocial activities than to involve onself in them. I try to foster the notion that compliance is usually the weaker course, the appearance of bravery in the activities notwithstanding.

It is important for parents to appreciate that sports and physical activities are an extremely common, harmless, and often socially constructive way for a person to express repressed hostility. Many youngsters I have seen who harbor deep-seated resentments over parental separation and divorce become very involved in sports. Not only does the competition provide a socially acceptable outlet for their anger, but the physical activity as well serves this purpose. Tensions also are reduced by such activities. Whatever drawbacks there may be to horror movies on TV and violence in films (such as fostering violent solutions to problems that might be dealt with in a more civilized fashion) they do allow for vicarious release of anger. Accordingly, the parents do well to recognize these outlets because they may be useful for the child of divorce, especially those who are prone to act out their hostile reactions.

Parents also do well to appreciate that many adolescent fads serve as hostile and rebellious outlets. (They also provide a sense of separate identity, so important for adolescent to establish.) Choosing clothing or hair styles that may be particularly odious to parents may well serve such purposes. Parents do well to express their disgust, thereby providing the youngster with the satisfaction that he is "getting to" the parents and causing them discomfort. One of the worst things parents can do is to force a youngster to give up one of these styles. Parents should appreciate that they are among the most innocuous ways of letting out hostility. When one considers many of the alternative modes of acting-out available to the youngster (drug addiction, pregnancy, and various types of criminal behavior) they appear to be blessings. I sometimes think that the inventors of such styles should be considered for Nobel Peace prizes, since they do so much to diminish violence in the world.

Many youngsters with delinquent problems require therapy. However, since they are often not motivated for treatment and since our techniques for treating delinquent youngsters are still relatively unrefined, we therapists cannot claim a high rate of success with these youngsters. Our poor performance, however, has also been the result of the fact that we have often been working against great odds. It is very difficult to treat a youngster with an antisocial acting-out problem if he or she is continually being exposed to parental conflicts and deprivations. Therapists generally see a child anywhere from one to three times a week (on rare occasions more frequently). It is unrealistic to expect therapy to reduce anger in a child and help him use more efficiently and appropriately what anger he does have, when after each session he returns to a situation that only generates his anger all over again.

Concluding Comments

Older children will generally be able to understand more about what separation entails, will be more capable of dealing with it, and so will be less likely to be psychologically traumatized by it. Parents who withhold from children important information about the separation deprive them of the opportunity to adjust optimally to it. But even with younger children attempts should be made to provide them with information at their levels of comprehension. Even though they may not understand completely what is going on, such communications establish a trusting relationship and prevent the kinds of problems that may result when events are shrouded in secrecy.

By now the reader will appreciate that psychological symptoms are complex and many factors contribute to their formation and perpetuation. Accordingly, there are rarely simple ways to alleviate them. Those that develop in reaction to parental difficulties related to separation and divorce are not merely to disappear as long as the parental conflict persists. Those that are reactions to deprivation of parental affection are not likely to disappear unless the parent can provide more affection or the child is able to obtain it from others.

5

Common Parental Difficulties That Contribute to Children's Post-separation Maladjustments

Money

Money is one of the issues that preoccupies most divorcing parents both around the time of the separation and subsequent to it. Breaking up a marriage is an expensive proposition and the specter of contributing to the upkeep of two homes may be the major reason why there aren't more divorces than there are. Marriage is a contract and breaking up a marriage requires the spouses to formulate another contract. It is over financial issues more than anything else that divorcing spouses involve themselves in the most lengthy, mind-boggling, and often petty disputes. Besides the realistic reasons why money is of such concern to separated parents, there are many psychological ones as well. Money has great symbolic value to many, if not most, people. Because it can readily be used as a vehicle for expressing love and hostility (in accordance with whether one gives it or withholds it), it readily lends itself to a variety of psychological symbolizations. And, as a treasured possession of each of the separated parents, it ranks with the children as an object that quickly gets embroiled in the parents' conflicts. The number of complaints that each parent may have about the other's handling of money is endless. Mother complains that Father's financial commitment to his new wife and children is greater than to her and their children. Father accuses Mother of using support money to buy things for herself, to the neglect of the children. Mother denounces Father for sending support checks to the child, in the child's name—thereby compromising her authority. I speak of the husband as the party with the obligation to make support and alimony payments, although in recent years fathers have been increasingly gaining custody of their children. Still it is rare for a mother to be providing support and alimony payments.

Separating mothers are generally well aware that the amount of money they will receive for support and alimony will be determined, in part, by any income they may have. Accordingly, some mothers may quit or "lose" their jobs prior to the separation or divorce, only to gain employment again when the divorce decree is final. Others, recognizing that they will have to start working after the breakup of the marriage hold off doing so until after the financial settlements have been signed. And the "good" lawyer is generally one who will advise such a wife not to start working until that time. Fathers, too, have been known to reduce their incomes in order to lower the amount they will have to pay their wives. They seem to be so desirous of hurting their former spouses by creating economic hardships for them that they blind themselves to the privations that such a maneuver causes themselves and their children.

Probably one of the most common complaints made by divorced mothers is that their husbands are not sending the money provided for in the divorce decree. The percentage of husbands who consistently, over many years, live up to their alimony and support commitments is, I believe, quite small. The withholding of such payments not only provides the husband with more financial flexibility, but can serve as a very potent weapon for the expression of hostility toward his ex-wife. When one adds to this the fact that the courts are relatively helpless to enforce this aspect of the divorce decree, one can see how tempting it is for husbands to renege on this obligation. The court's weakness stems from the fact that its two most common forms of punishment, namely, fines and jail, if imposed make it less likely that the wife will get what has been stipulated in the divorce decree and agreed to by both parents. If a wife resorts to a lawyer to help her acquire the payments, she may lose more money than she gains, because of the legal costs.

Another reason why legal institutions tend to be very lax in pressuring fathers who default on or are delinquent in support and alimony payments is the prohibitive expense of tracking down men who are not fulfilling their financial obligations to their ex-spouses. Generally, the most the authorities do is bring the man into court, where the judge castigates him and warns him of the dire consequences of his not fulfilling his obligations to his ex-wife. Since the man usually knows that the threats are empty and rarely implemented, he may have little incentive to comply. It is not common to attach a man's salary, close his business, or, as a last resort, put him in jail. These punishments are still possible in some states. But because they further reduce a man's income and make it even less likely that the man will pay, such actions have the effect of making the wife's situation even worse. Often, in those jurisdictions where a man can be sent to jail for non-payment of alimony and support, the man will pay at the time of sentencing (after months and possibly years of expensive and time-consuming litigation) and then suffer no punishment for having so long defaulted. He may thereby be encouraged to allow the whole process to repeat itself again in the hope that this time around his former wife will give up the struggle rather than go through the whole thing all over again.

Mothers do well to make reasonable attempts to get what they are entitled to. When this fails, they should refrain from pursuing the matter further. They should understand that the emotional drain on themselves (and often the children) entailed in maintaining the hostilities cannot be counted in dollars. They do better to use their energies in ways that will more predictably enable them to acquire funds. The conflict over money may last years, and even then prove futile. Even appealing for help from family members or restoring to public assistance is generally less humiliating and psychologically traumatic than endless litigation. Some mothers do not realize that neurotic elements may be contributing to their failure to give up the struggle. For example, the mother who says, "I just can't sit and let him get the satisfaction," is using a poor reason for persisting. She would do better to say, "O.K., let him have the satisfaction. It's better to admit defeat than to drain my energies in fighting a battle that I'll probably never be able to win anyway." Both sides usually lose a war, and the wiser side does everything possible to avoid getting involved in one. Husbands who so renege should appreciate that the arguments they invoke to justify their not paying are usually unjustified and that for extra financial security they are jeopardizing their children's psychological welfare.

The mother whose husband defaults is often tempted to seek revenge and/or attempt to get him to pay by withholding the children from visitation. I strongly discourage this practice because of the detrimental effects it can have on the children. The financial privation they suffer because of their father's withholding payments is punishment enough. It only adds to their difficulties if they are prevented from continuing their relationship with their father. Admittedly, such a father has already proved himself to be deficient by his failure to live up to his financial commitments toward his family. However, this defect, as grave as it may be, does not make him totally worthless as a father or incapable of providing his children with some healthy experiences.

Many women whose husbands default may find themselves in the position of either suffering extreme material privation or going on public welfare. For many of these such a step represents the ultimate in personal humiliation. Many such agencies will not even consider an application for public assistance until the woman has proved that she had exhausted all legal efforts to force her husband to pay. Although I can understand the agency's position in not wishing to provide handouts to those without true need, such a stipulation may force such applicants to expose themselves and their children to needless psychological hardship and material privations. A further compli cation of public assistance payments is that once they are approved the defaulting husband may have even less motivation to pay. He knows that any funds he may send will only reduce those provided by welfare, so that his family's situation will not improve unless he provides far more than welfare is going to. He often prefers to remain secure in the knowledge that his family is receiving basic food, clothing, and shelter (plus often telephone service and, more recently, even television). He may not feel the need to raise his family above a marginal level of subsistence and is often unconcerned about the psychological effects on his wife and children of their being wards of the community.

Alimony. The payments that a divorced husband usually has to make to his wife are referred to as alimony. (Again, it is still extremely rare for a wife to be making such payments to a former husband.) The amount of money that he is required to pay is usually determined by their two lawyers. They bargain with one another and haggle back and forth. Their compromise decision is subject to approval by the judge, who actually makes the decision only in contested cases.

Most states require the husband to pay alimony to his former wife. This situation stems from the past, when women were generally not capable of earning their own living. After a separation and divorce, the husband is usually required to provide for his wife's support. In this way the community is protected from having to provide such women with support. Generally the man has this obligation as long as his wife remains unmarried. Accordingly, many men have to pay alimony for the rest of their lives. In recent years, with greater economic opportunities for women, courts have tended to take their financial situation into consideration when granting alimony. There are even those who feel that requiring a husband to pay alimony at all is unjust. They argue that such an obligation is unfair to a man, that his contributing to the support of his children is certainly reasonable, but that he should not be required to support his former wife for the rest of his life because of a marital mistake to which they probably both contributed. Alimony payments often become a divorced man's greatest burden. A mere ten- or fifteen-dollar difference in a weekly or monthly payment, when multiplied over the rest of one's life, is a formidable amount of money. Alimony payments are generally discontinued when the wife remarries. Failure (in part or full) to make such payments may involve a former husband's being brought to court, and having to engage a lawyer at great expense. There are many men who do not make their alimony and support payments and are constantly being harassed (often with justification). The conflict over alimony payments is often extensive, lasts for years, and like all continuing parental conflicts may exact its psychological toll on the children. Many states still retain laws that stipulate that if a woman's adultery has been a cause of the divorce then she is not entitled to aimony payments. (Interestingly, the same laws do *not* usually provide for financial penalties for the husband if *his* adultery is the cause of the breakup of the marriage.) Although in practice such laws are being less strictly followed in recent years, they are still very much with us. Fortunately, many states are now revising and repealing the adultery stipulation, not only as a factor in determining alimony payments, but also as a factor in deciding whether a divorce will be granted.

The guideline usually used in determining alimony is that the man attempt to support his former wife at the socioeconomic level she enjoyed during the marriage. There are times when a woman is given an amount of money that may run into millions, if the man can afford it, and such settlements often attract significant attention in the public media. More commonly, both husband and wife have to live at a far lower level because, alimony payments notwithstanding, there is less money available for each. There are many men for whom the alimony payments are indeed oppressive and may interfere significantly with their remarrying. However, many women have given up opportunities for career training and advancement in order to get married and they are thereby ill equipped to support themselves and are usually in a very vulnerable economic position when divorced. In addition the wife's assumption of the major part of the child-rearing obligation has usually enabled the husband to devote himself more freely to his own career; she certainly deserves compensation for this if divorce ensues. The divorced woman may have less of an opportunity to remarry than the divorced man, especially if she has children and has custody of them (the usual case). Because our present social structure contributes so significantly to the divorced woman's financial vulnerability, reasonable alimony payments are, in my opinion, still justifiable. Hopefully, in the future, when more women achieve independent economic status, there will be less injustice perpetrated with regard to alimony.

With greater appreciation of the woman's contribution to her husband's career and the acquisition of marital assets, many states are now considering (and some have already enacted) revisions of their divorce laws that require a more equitable division of the assets of a marriage. The general philosophy of such legislation is that, because both parties have contributed their talents and efforts to the acquisition of property during the marriage, upon divorce, all common property and assets be equitably (not necessarily equally) divided, regardless of who originally had legal title to them. Consideration is given to a woman's efforts as homemaker, child rearer, and contributor to her husband's career, and such efforts are viewed as positive contributions to the acquisition of marital property. Furthermore, a man cannot under these laws "freeze" assets in his own name to whose growth his wife may have contributed. Such participation by the wife need not be direct via actual involvement in the business; taking care of the children and thereby enabling her husband to devote his efforts more freely to the enterprise is considered a contribution, entitling her to a reasonable portion of the assets at the time of divorce. For example, if by virtue of a wife's efforts, her husband was free to build a business (either alone or with others) to which his wife had no legal title, the wife's contribution to this business is ascertained by the court and a reasonable sum is awarded to her. Although the husband is not actually required to give his wife a share in the business (or to make her a partner), he may be required to provide his wife with an amount of money approximating her contribution (this may be provided in one payment, or paid out over years).

Under this system, then, the person with the greatest financial reserves (regardless of sex) assumes the greatest financial burden after the breakup of the marriage. The husband is not automatically considered the one to give money to his wife. If a woman's contributions were primarily to her husband's career and the raising of the children, then she is entitled to payments from her husband. If, however, her financial assets and economic potential do not warrant such payments by her husband, then she does not receive them. There would even be situations under the new laws in which women would be making payments to their husbands. In short, the trend seems to be going in the direction of doing away with a system in which the husband almost automatically makes alimony payments to his wife and substituting one in which the property is equitably divided. And the person who has the greater economic need is given money by the party with the most assets—regardless of the sex of the giver or the recipient. In this new system fewer women will be exploited, because their contributions as homemaker are taken into consideration when determining their alimony and other property rights; and fewer men will be exploited by women whose financial situation does not warrant their receiving alimony. With less exploitation there should be less pain and frustration in the post-divorce period, less strife between divorced parents, and this factor in producing post-divorce conflicts should be reduced. In time, and with more experience with these new laws, we shall see whether this hope comes to be realized.

In alimony and property conflicts, the vengeance element often gets deeply involved in a wife's attempt to obtain high alimony payments. And vengeful elements often contribute, as well, to a husband's efforts to make such payments as small as possible. Although I believe that a moderate degree of vengeful feeling is an inevitable (and probably normal) reaction at certain times, in the divorce situation psychological problems often intensify such feelings immeasurably. The spouses become self-destructive as the time and energy expended in vengeful pursuits compromise significantly their ability to involve themselves in healthier activities. Conflicts over alimony are especially common vehicles for vengeful release because of the practical as well as the deeply psychological significance of money in our culture. Children, especially, get neglected in such situations. Therefore, for the benefit of all concerned, it behooves parents to reduce such sick vengeance. Often a lawyer will encourage a wife to demand what even she herself considers unreasonably high payments in the hope of winning concessions from the husband on his demands. A wife may become so enraged by her ex-husband's failure to pay his full alimony obligations that she may involve herself in extensive litigation. When, as is sometimes the case, she must assume the costs of litigation, her expenses may exceed even the gains of a successful action. In the end, then, she may lose more than had she given up on the matter and resigned herself to the fact that she is not going to get what she wants. It is often healthier and more courageous to admit that one is defeated and not to pursue lost causes. A not insignificant fringe benefit of such resignation will be fewer bills from lawyers and therapists.

Ex-husbands too do well to appreciate that their withholding of payments can backfire. Although they may enjoy a little more financial gratification, they may be causing their children economic deprivation (although obvious, this is something divorced fathers often do not see—so blinded are they by their desire for vengeance). In addition, they cause their children psychological trauma associated with their being swept up in, or observers to, the alimony conflict, or neglected because of it. Such fathers should appreciate also that the money they save may ultimately be spent on child therapists.

Support. Support is the term used to refer to the payments that a parent generally has to provide for the maintenance and welfare of his or her children. Most often the children's custody is given to the mother, and the law—I think justifiably—considers it to be the husband's obligation, under such circumstances, to support his children so that they should not become wards of the community. Often these payments cover medical care (sometimes including psychotherapy), summer camp, education, etc. Generally, fathers are more receptive to paying support than they are to paying alimony. Whereas a husband may have to continue alimony payments throughout life if his wife does not remarry, support payments are only required until the children reach a stipulated age such as eighteen, or twenty-one, or until the completion of their education or training.

It is common for a mother to complain to the children about the father's deficiencies regarding support payment. She may bitterly complain that he is not sending money to provide them with food, clothing, shelter; that he is not on time with his payments; that he has been sending less than he should; that he has gotten a "good deal" regarding how little he has to pay; or that instead of sending money for them, he is spending it on women. The father may complain that the money that he does send the mother for support is not all being used for the children; that she is squandering it frivolously; or giving it to men friends.

Just as an alimony payment may occasionally be unjustified, there are situations in which a support payment may be totally unwarranted. I recall a situation in which a man reported to me that his divorce resulted when he learned that his wife was having an affair with his "best friend." In the divorce decree his wife was granted custody of their daughter and, among other things, he agreed to pay for all the child's medical expenses. Subsequently, the wife married the friend. As time passed the little girl became upset and required psychiatric treatment. Although pinched financially, the man agreed that he was obligated to pay for his daughter's therapy. The psychiatrist then decided that family sessions would be useful, sessions that included the ex-wife, the daughter, *and the former friend*. The man felt strongly that his wife's new husband should pay one third of the cost of the family sessions, since he was deriving benefit himself from them. The court ultimately ruled that such sessions were designed to help the daughter, and that the man should therefore be required to pay the *total* fee. Soon after, the psychiatrist suggested that the friend receive individual treatment, again for the sake of the little girl. Again the court ruled that the man would have to pay fully for such treatment. When I last saw the man he had refused to comply with the court's decision, was appealing to a higher court, and proclaimed that he would rather go to jail than pay for the psychiatric treatment of a man who had been so disloyal to him and had been instrumental in causing him so much pain and difficulty. Although not typical, the example demonstrates well the kinds of inequities that can result from blind and misguided interpretation of divorce decrees.

Generally, the father sends the check to the mother (either directly or through the court). Many fathers feel that this arrangement produces even more estrangement from the children than they already suffer, as the children come to see the mother as the sole provider. Some try to avoid this problem by writing the checks directly to the children so that they should know who is actually paying their expenses. Of course, such an arrangement is only reasonable when older children are involved and it generally is a source of irritation to the mother, especially if the older children (generally teen-agers) then give her a hard time regarding turning the money over to her. I generally discourage fathers who have the opportunity to do this from doing so. It usually adds to the perpetuation of the conflict with their former wives and so is bound to have a detrimental effect on the children. Rather, they do well to inform the children at reasonable times and in a reasonable way where their support is coming from and hope that as they get older they will have a clear picture of the father's contribution to their maintenance.

The father who reneges on his support payments should not be protected from exposure of this deficiency to his children. It is always better for children to have as accurate a picture as possible of each of their parents. If Father has reneged on his obligation to support his children, they should know it. And he should know that the material privations they may suffer over his failure to support them may be small compared to the psychological traumas they suffer in association with the knowledge that their own father has so neglected them. He will lose their respect and is not likely to serve as a model for their identification. This is a heavy price indeed for both him and them to pay for the saving of some money.

No matter how carefully planned a divorce decree may be, no matter how carefully spelled out every one of the stipulations regarding payments, it is not likely that the provisions will last for long. Lives change, needs change, people relocate, the economy rises and falls, jobs terminate, people remarry, people redivorce, etc., etc. Accordingly, it is extremely common for one or both parties to become dissatisfied with even the most carefully thought-out agreement. If the parties can approach an alteration of the decree with some receptivity to compromise, they may avoid the psychological toll to both themselves and their children of further conflict and even litigation. Although lawyers may still attempt to effect such compromises in their renegotiations, they are quick to rise to battle, and thereby reactivate hostilities. It would be far preferable if mediating and arbitrating professionals were available to help parents resolve such conflict—people whose primary orientation and deep-seated commitment was only that of resolving the differences. If such efforts failed, then the parties would still be free to resort to litigation in the old tradition.

Visitation

Visitation and divorce decree negotiations. In the separation agreement and divorce decree, arrangements are usually made for the absent parent's visitation with the children. Parents do well to appreciate that stipulated visitation times do not generally coincide with the needs and desires of the parties concerned. Accordingly, the more flexible the schedule, the more natural the visits will be, and the greater the likelihood the visitation experiences will be gratifying. Such flexibility requires a certain amount of trust and co-operation between the parents. Sadly, these conditions are often not present, and the greater the degree of distrust and antagonism, the lengthier and more detailed the schedules become.

In drawing up a visitation schedule parents do well to appreciate that a few shorter experiences may be better than one longer one. One can compare visitation with the frequency of psychotherapeutic sessions. Specifically, if a patient has one session a week, he may bring in a dream as old as six days. It is generally quite difficult to analyze such a dream because the events that contributed to it may be blurred in memory. However, if a patient has two sessions a week, evenly spaced, no dream can be more than three days old. A meaningful analysis of such a dream is much more likely because the events contributing to it are more readily recalled. Accordingly, twice-a-week therapy is not just twice as good as once-a-week therapy but significantly more effective. In the same way shorter, more frequent visitations are preferable to fewer, longer ones.

Like any other transaction or negotiation between the warring parents, the visitation arrangements can be used as a weapon. After all, the children are the parents' most prized possessions. What better way to wreak vengeance on a partner than to deprive him or her, to the degree possible, of his or her children. Often a parent will demand more visitation time than he or she really wants or can practically handle. The purpose here may be to use the demand as a bargaining tool in the conflict over alimony and support payments. The parent knows in advance that he or she will reduce the visitation requests if the spouse will grant concessions in the financial area. Parents often do not appreciate that they are causing their children psychological damage by such manipulations, so blinded are they by their anger. And many lawyers can often be relied upon to support the parents in these sick transactions with the justification that they are only protecting their clients' interests. What such lawyers generally referring to when they talk of their clients' interests is money. They often do not concern themselves with the welfare of the children, although they will invariably pay lip service to their deep commitment to this consideration.

A mother may be so enraged at her husband that she will deeply believe that *any* contact he may have with the children will be detrimental to them. As a result, the children may be deprived of optimum visitation experiences and thereby suffer. One mother, who considered herself to have had a happy marriage, learned that her husband was having an affair. In the ensuing weeks her husband informed her that she had been living in a dream world and was denying many deep-seated problems that existed in the marriage and consequently contributed to his need to find gratifications elsewhere. There was no way that he was able to get his wife to accept the fact that there were marital problems and to use such recognition as a point of departure for possibly salvaging the marriage. The mother's state of rage continued and she remained obsessed with her husband's "treachery." Professional counseling was of no avail and the marriage finally broke up at the instigation of the wife, who claimed that she had always been a perfect wife and that she would never forget this "knife in her back."

Both prior to and after the divorce this mother continually berated her husband to their two daughters and constantly spoke about the "whore" that he had become involved with. The mother's obsession was so all-pervasive that there was hardly an hour that the children spent with her that she did not disparage bitterly the father. Whereas previously the children had had a fairly good relationship with their father, the months of vilification of him gradually began to change their attitudes. The point was finally reached where they too began to hate him and see him as the embodiment of evil, filth, and treachery. Finally, they absolutely refused to go with him when he arrived for visits. Instead, they would spit at, curse, and even throw things at him when he arrived. Although the father's lawyer obtained a court order requiring the mother to encourage the children to see their father, the girls firmly refused. Actually, the mother professed encouragement of the children's visiting with the father and even made them available for the visits. But she knew that her brainwashing had been successful and she enjoyed observing the scenes that ensued when her ex-husband would arrive. The court was helpless to do anything more. I advised the father to stop going to the house, because his attempts to get the children were not only unsuccessful but were being used by his former wife as opportunities for vengeful gratification, with the children being used as weapons. I suggested rather that he use every other type of communication available to let his daughters know that he was still interested in them and loved them in spite of their present bitter feelings about him. Letters and presents were returned unopened; when he called they promptly hung up on him; and those who verbally communicated his regards and best wishes were angrily told to mind their own business. My final advice to this father was that he never stop completely from an occasional communication in order to reassure the children that he still loved them. I explained to him that the children's hatred (like his former wife's) revealed that affectionate feelings were still there, or else they would not have been so angry at him. Their anger revealed that they were still thinking about and were interested in him. To give up entirely might be considered by the children a rejection and would lessen the chances of their ever getting together again. Mothers such as this are obviously quite disturbed and do not realize how much they are harming their children by their campaigns of vilification. In some cases, after many months and years, the relationship with the absent parent is renewed and the children come to appreciate how falsely maligned the absent parent has been. In other cases the alienation is permanent, a sad loss for all concerned.

At times a parent may demand far more visitation than is reasonable in order to reduce guilt over the separation. A father, for example, who never took particular interest in the children, suddenly becomes deeply involved with them at the time of separation. The children may see more of him after he leaves the house than they did when he was living at home. Such enthusiasm is usually short-lived—based as it is on guilt rather than genuine affection. However, because it exhibits itself at the time when separation and divorce agreements are being drafted, it may result in the children's being deprived of some of the beneficial time they could have been spending with their mothers.

Because of the psychological traumas that children may suffer when used as pawns in the parental conflict, some mental health professionals argue that the custodial parent should be given full control over visitation arrangements and that this be stipulated in the divorce decree. They hold that the trauma of such separation is far less than the trauma of being used as tools in the parental conflicts. I believe that this is dangerous advice. It is like placing lethal weapons in the hands of children or incompetents. An enraged parent, at his or her whim, may unilaterally decide to cut the children off completely from the ex-spouse for reasons that may be quite frivolous. The children then will be deprived of all the benefits to be derived from contact with the other parent. When a parent wants to see the children and they wish to see him or her, it is rare that a third party (whether spouse or court) is justified in interfering with their getting together. It is only in very unusual circumstances (such as when the children are exposed to brutal treatment or genuine mental cruelty) that such interference can be in the children's and the non-custodial parent's best interests. The implementation of such a plan would not only cause many children to be deprived of meaningful and healthy parental affection, but also may contribute to the formation of psychological problems for the parent who is forcibly cut off from the children he or she may love very deeply. The heartache, frustration, and loneliness that such a separation can cause may contribute significantly to the development of psychological difficulties in such a parent.

Pre-visit games. Inappropriate use of the visitation does not stop at the signing of the divorce decree. There are many ways in which a parent can use the visitation to express hostility toward the ex-spouse. Obstructionistic maneuvers are among the most common. Father, for example, may be late or even "forget" entirely to pick up the children. And Mother's arrangements (like a date, for example) may then have to be canceled. Mother, similar-

ly, may take a very "relaxed" attitude about having the
children ready, may have "forgotten" that this was the
day for the father to get them, and thereby wreck his
plans as well. The actual appearance of the father may
provide the mother with an opportunity to let off a little
steam and she may even look forward to his coming because of the opportunity it provides her for venting her
rage. Similarly, a visiting father may look forward to
picking up his children because of the opportunity it provides him for release of his pent-up hostility toward his
ex-wife.

A mother may be excessively fearful of a father and inappropriately anticipate his harming the children. Such
fears may be transmitted to the children, thereby reducing
the gratifications they can derive from the visit. Ex-
spouses tend to exaggerate the detrimental effects of one
another's behavior on the children. Only in cases of extreme negligence or danger should restrictions be placed
on the visitation. Removing the children because of minor
harmful exposures deprives them of the growth experience
of dealing with the unpleasant and may rob them of the
benefits to be derived from involvement with the visiting
parent. If they wish to see one another, then the advantages
probably outweigh the disadvantages. On occasion a
custodial parent may have such a distorted view of the absent parent that the term delusional becomes appropriate. A
mother, for example, may expose the children to such continual vilification of their father that they come to fear
and hate him, and may absolutely refuse to visit with
him, even though ordered to by the court. The children
may have been so "brainwashed" that they come to accept as valid their mother's delusion that their father is
the incarnation of evil. Both legal and mental health professionals may be impotent to effect a change in such
cases. The mother's rage, although recognized as extremely exaggerated, does not generally warrant her being deprived of the children, and so they grow up deprived of a
father.

A custodial parent can undermine the children's desire
to see the visiting parent with comments such as: "You

want to visit your father?" and "You don't *really* want to go visit with your father again on Sunday?" Or the parent may offer alternatives to the children's visiting that may not have entered their minds and in this way discourage them from making plans with the ex-spouse.

A mother may have residual or persistent affectionate feelings for her ex-husband (either conscious or unconscious) and may welcome his coming to pick up the children as an opportunity for further contact. Father, too, may linger for similar reasons. Although separation and divorce usually hurt the esteem of both parties, the non-custodial parent usually suffers an additional blow to his or her feelings of self-worth. Most healthy fathers gain a sense of importance as head of a household. Whatever drawbacks there may be to the often heavy responsibilities of being the "breadwinner," there is a sense of pride and accomplishment that can also be derived from the position. Being admired and emulated by the members of one's family can be a great source of ego gratification. The separated father may feel this loss acutely and does well to make every attempt to compensate for this deprivation and its attendant lowering of his self-esteem. Three ways in which the father can regain his sense of self-worth in this area are: (1) spending as much time as is reasonable and possible with his children, (2) involving himself in a second family, and (3) finding other esteem-enhancing activities. Non-custodial mothers may also suffer a loss of self-worth as they are deprived of the opportunity (whether by their own choice or by court decision) to gain the satisfactions of child rearing. They do well to compensate in the ways just described for fathers.

A common and most insidious practice is that of the custodial mother's refusing to let the father visit with the children because of non-payment or late payment of alimony and support. Although this tactic may work, it effectively punishes the children for the actions of their father. There is probably no more blatant example of the child's being used as a pawn in the parental conflict. Such a mother should appreciate that the loss of money is small (no matter how great the amount) compared to the psychological toll such a practice can have on the children. She does well to recognize that there are times when it is more prudent to admit that one has been defeated, than to win a victory that may be injurious to her children.

The visit. One of the common problems that custodial parents frequently complain of is the visiting parent's lateness, last-minute cancellations, or failure to show up for the visits. Visiting parents should be reliable and punctual about the visit. Divorce has undermined the children's stability already; there is no need to add to their difficulties. If a father has to miss an appointment, he should inform the children well in advance of the cancellation. Many such visiting parents seem to be oblivious to the fact that building up the children's hopes and then disappointing them at the last minute can be devastating.

Separation and divorce decree stipulations can never take into account all the needs and desires of the mother, father, and children at any particular time. Most often specific times are designated. However, the parents should use these merely as guidelines. If the children do not wish to visit on a certain day, they should not be forced to (beyond the occasional prodding that most children need for their own good). Similarly, a father who visits on a particular day primarily out of guilt or obligation would probably do better to select another day. When the father and children get together and basically do not wish to do so at this time, it is likely that the resentments so produced will lessen the pleasure that they can derive from the experience.

When the father picks up the children, and they are in a good mood, he will tend to interpret this to mean that they are happy to leave their mother, who treats them so badly, and come to him, where they will receive love and affection. The mother will tend to interpret the smiling faces to mean that they are looking forward to the indulgence and spoiling that the father will provide them in order to "buy their love." If they are unhappy, the father understands this to be the result of the maltreatment they have received at their mother's hands. The mother sees their unhappiness to be caused by the dread they feel over the visit with the father and their anticipation of the horrible things that can happen when they are with him.

Separation and divorce decrees most often clump all the children together when defining the times of visitation. Such a practice does not take into consideration the individual differences of the children and their separate desires at a given time. In accordance with the aforementioned principle of flexibility, I believe that it can be to the children's benefit to be split up at times with regard to visitations. Not only does this practice avoid the resentment caused by forced visiting, but it allows each of the children more individual attention from the parent who is being visited. Some hold that such a practice can increase sibling rivalries. This has not been my experience. In fact, because it provides each child with more individual attention, there is less to be rivalrous about. Furthermore, separating children is just about the most foolproof way of preventing their fighting. It is only when one child is preferentially selected to visit more frequently that sibling rivalries are likely to be increased.

As every father who spends a significant amount of time alone with his children knows (whether in the divorced or intact family situation), things can get boring at times. Adults are adults and children are children, and there is just so much child's play and childishness that an adult can tolerate. It is a good idea for the father to allow his children occasionally to bring along friends and child relatives. Such joiners take some of the pressures off the father. The only danger of this practice is that the father may too frequently allow the visitors to take over his obligation to be with the children.

The question is sometimes raised as to whether it is harmful to the children for the visiting parent to spend any (and even all) of his or her visiting time in the original home. Such visits are said to protect the child from the anxieties produced by being taken out of the home and having to adjust to a new environment. Actually, the nature of the relationships between the visiting parent and the children is far more important than the place where the visits occur. The quality of the activities that the visiting parent and the children partake in, and the enjoyment they derive from them, are what count. Another consideration, of course, is the receptivity of the custodial partner to the ex-spouse's return to the home. If an atmosphere of tension is created by the ex-spouses being together or a cloud of gloom descends over the household as the visiting parent enters the home, then it is not likely that the original home is going to be a good place for the visitations. If, however, the custodial parent has no objections to leaving the home (and even welcomes the opportunity for a break) while the visiting parent stays with the children, then the arrangement may very well work out. There are parents who not only have no discomfort when together at such times, but may even look forward to seeing one another. If such visits occur routinely, then I would wonder about the reasons for the divorce. Most divorced people wish to see as little as possible of their former spouses. Having the ex-partner frequently back in the home suggests that there is still a significant ongoing relationship and that the visiting parent is not just being accommodated so that the visits might take place in a familiar atmosphere with a minimum of anxiety-producing change. I am not suggesting that there is anything necessarily psychologically unhealthy about such receptivity of the divorced spouses for one another. Human relationships are complex and the *married* or *divorced* status is somewhat artificial and requires that the individual be either in one category or the other. This may be useful legally, but it does not fit well with human personality. There are all gradations of involvement between the two extremes, gradations that have not been given legal definition. With regard to the psychological well-being of adults, I do not view any of the intermediate stages (either before marriage of after divorce) as being necessarily preferable. With regard to the children, I believe that they do best when raised with a mother and a father who are relatively happy with one another. To the degree that their arrangement provides this, to that degree they are likely to grow up healthy.

One of the most common problems that arises over visitation results from the contrast between the children's experiences during the visits outside the home (usually with the father) and those they have with the parent with whom they live. With Father they have fun, play games, visit enjoyable places, and may have few obligations to assume. With Mother, on the other hand, it's getting up early, going to school, and doing homework and household chores. Father may feel quite guilty about his having left the home and may try to lessen his guilt by continually providing the children with good times. In addition, he may hesitate to discipline properly lest the children get even angrier at him. Sometimes the father provides endless entertainment in order to avoid more direct contact with the children in a natural and human way. The father may contribute even further to this state of affairs because of rivalrous feelings toward the mother or from the appreciation that it can serve as a way of hurting her. The children may even come to the conclusion that if they were to live with the father permanently that this would be the kind of life they would lead all the time. In such a situation the father gets to be the "good guy" and the mother becomes the "meanie."

Fathers who behave in this fashion are doing their children a disservice. The best atmosphere a visiting parent can provide the children is one that most closely resembles the original home—especially with regard to the balance between pleasant and unpleasant activities. Indulgence of the children creates in them unreal expectations about life and makes it more difficult for the custodial parent, teachers, and others to get them to learn the restraint that is necessary if they are to grow into self-sufficient, mature adults. Parents should appreciate how harmful it is to the children to be used as pawns in the parental conflict. The children have enough trouble already; they should not have to suffer the additional burden of divided loyalties. Sometimes longer periods of visitation can reduce such indulgence. Endless entertainment can be exhausting and produce financial strains in all but the wealthy.

There are other parents, however, who do just the opposite during visitation. They give little thought to the nature of the activities they provide the children and delude themselves into believing that merely being together is enough. Accordingly, they may drag the children along on business visits, seat them at an office desk for hours on end to amuse themselves as best they can, or prop them up in front of the television set for as long as they will tolerate it. The children may resent being so neglected but may be fearful of expressing their anger, lest they see even less of the parent. Children should be helped to assert themselves in order to bring about a cessation of such a deplorable practice; and such parents do well to appreciate how neglectful they are.

Ideally, both the visiting parent and children should decide together exactly what activities they will have together, and select those that will not cause significant boredom or resentment in either the parent or the children. All concerned, however, must be willing to make certain compromises—as is true in the planning of activities in the intact home as well. In addition, when visiting with the non-custodial parent the children should be encouraged to do homework and chores. Non-custodial parents who fail to do this are neglecting their children by depriving them of real life experiences, experiences that will help them optimally adjust to a world in which there is both pleasure and pain.

On rare occasions, the non-custodial parent will decide (sometimes even with professional advice) that it will be in the children's best interests that all contact with them should be cut off entirely. A father, for example, may proclaim: "The marriage is over. It's dead. The best thing for the children would be that they consider me dead as well, to make a clean break of it." Sometimes, such reasoning serves as a rationalization for the parent's cutting him- or herself off entirely and justifies the rejection by claiming that it's in the best interests of the children. Generally, the parent does not describe exactly *how* it can be in the children's best interests to have no further contact with a parent and hopes that the statement in itself will be convincing. Sometimes such a parent will have mixed feelings about such a drastic step (there is some desire to remove oneself totally from the children and yet there are lingering feelings of affection and guilt over the wish to sever ties completely) and may seek professional advice regarding what to do. Often, the parent will take the advice that supports the stronger motivation (and if one looks long enough, one will always find some mental health professional who will support one's position). Good professional advice would recommend that the parent look into the psychological problems causing rejection of his or her own children.

On occasion, the custodial parent may refuse to let the absent parent see the children, have them unavailable when the visiting parent arrives, and even hide them from him or her. In response the absent parent may kidnap the children and consider this his or her only way of maintaining contact. Kidnapping occurs for other reasons as well. The kidnapping parent may believe that he or she is protecting the children from the terrible treatment they are receiving at the hands of the other parent. Or vengeful elements may contribute. What better way to wreak vengeance on a former spouse than to take away the children and not provide any information about their safety or whereabouts. Often, the children are brought to another state so that even if their location is known, the parent with whom they originally were may find it difficult, extremely expensive, and often impossible, to get them back.

I confine myself here to the psychological rather than the legal implications of such kidnapping. It is probable that in occasional situations such an act may be warranted. The children may indeed be suffering terrible abuse at the hands of a parent, the court may have been deficient in providing the children with protection, and the other parent may find that abducting the children is the only course left. My experience has been that it is a rare situation in which such a drastic act is warranted and that the kidnapping parent is grossly exaggerating, if not distorting completely, the children's situation with regard to the amount of trauma they are subjected to at the hands of the ex-spouse. In the more common situation, the abduction has absolutely no justification and the abducting parent harbors delusions about the other parent's treatment of the children and wishes as well to use the children as weapons in the parental conflict. In such situations the children suffer immensely. They may be deprived for years of a meaningful involvement with a parent. The long weeks, months, and even years of aching and longing for the other parent can cause permanent psychological damage. They may suffer significantly from the secretive life they may lead, ever fleeing from authorities who are trying to locate them. Like baggage, the children are carried from city to city and state to state, never establishing roots, never maintaining friendships, never remaining in one school or home long enough to gain a sense of security. And the parent who has been bereft of the children rarely deserves the pain and psychological torture that the kidnapping causes him or her. In short, with extremely rare exception, kidnapping is a sick act that causes such psychological trauma to the children as well as the parent from whom the children have been taken, that it is hardly ever justified.

Post-visit problems. A common complaint that mothers have when the children return from their visits with the father is that they are unmanageable and unkempt. Often the father's relaxed attitude and indulgence makes it harder for them to readjust to the more rigorous demands of the mother's household. With school, discipline, housekeeping, etc., the mother may have to run a tighter ship. The father may interpret the children's restlessness on returning to the mother as proof that he is the better parent and that the children are unhappy about having to live once again with their mother, the Ogre. The mother considers the restlessness to be the result of the tensions created in them by the father or as caused by other indignities they have suffered at his hands. The child who cries on returning to the mother is understood by the father as doing so because he or she doesn't want to leave him. The mother considers the child to be crying because of the maltreatment he or she has been exposed to. On the other hand, when the children return in a happy frame of mind, the mother tends to interpret this as a sign that they are glad to get rid of their father and return to the warmth and friendliness of her home. The father usually considers their happy mood to be a reflection of the good treatment they have received from him.

The natural course of visitation. As time passes, visitation by the departed parent tends to diminish. It is in the early phases following the divorce that the guilt is the greatest and the need to reduce it through frequent contacts with the children most strong. As time goes on, the visits become more of a drain, especially if the parent has the need to make them a continual source of fun and games for the children. The visits occupy considerable time and are often costly. As time passes many fathers generally want to use their free time and money more for dating and other recreational purposes than for their children. As the children grow older, they generally want to spend more time with their friends—as they would in the intact household.

Remarriage of a parent can have a significant effect on visitation. When the father was single, the children may have had little competition for his time. When he is remarried and has other children of his own (or children from his new wife's former marriage) he cannot provide the children from his first marriage with as much attention. The father's new wife may have professed great interest in and affection for his children prior to her marriage; but afterwards such feelings may diminish considerably. Sensing themselves outsiders in the new home, children may become less desirous of visiting. A remarried mother who has custody of the children may also be less desirous of her former husband's visiting the home. His periodic reappearance may compromise somewhat her relationship with her new husband. When single, she had a greater need to get the children "off her hands." Now that she is remarried, she may feel them less of a burden.

There are situations in which a parent is deprived of the right or opportunity to visit and may still wish to. For example, a father may have moved so far away that frequent visiting is impractical and financially impossible. On occasion, a misguided or punitive judge may prevent a parent from seeing his or her children at a frequency that is appropriate or desirable, or even rule that there should be no contact at all for reasons that are not psychologically valid. Generally, I advise the parent is such a situation to continue, in a reasonable way, to maintain contact with the children. Letters, presents sent by mail, and telephone calls can often serve well here. Sending messages through friends and relatives can also be useful. Knowing that the parent is still out there, thinking of them, and trying to maintain contact with them is very important for the children's healthy psychological development. If the the parent has the desire to maintain contact with the children, he or she should use every reasonable means to do this. To comply fully with requests and orders that he or she suppress these desires can deprive parent and children of an important psychological bond.

Custody

Up until the last hundred years or so fathers were generally granted custody of the children when a marriage was dissolved. This practice was part of the tradition that one's heritage was traced along paternal lines and children's still taking the surname of their father, rather than their mother, is a legacy of this custom. In addition, wives were often looked upon as just another form of property, certainly without the privilege to own things in their own right—especially property as valuable as children. In the last century, with the increasing appreciation of the importance of the mother's role in the psychological growth and development of children, as well as the growth of the women's rights movement, mothers have become favored over fathers in being granted custody of children. Until recently, the pendulum had shifted so far in the direction of mothers receiving custody of children that the only way a father could gain custody in contested cases was to prove that the mother was significantly unfit to care for the children. So partial have courts been to mothers, and so committed have they been to the notion that mothers make better parents than fathers, that only the grossest negligence on the mother's part would result in her being deprived of the children. Only when the mother could be proved to be a chronic alcoholic, severe drug addict, prostitute, or extremely abusive or neglectful of the children could the father even hope to gain custody. And even in such cases the court might still decide that the mother should keep the children. In the last few years, the pendulum has shifted back slightly, and courts do not automatically grant custody to mothers. In contested cases, they are granting custody to the parent who is deemed to be more fit to take care of the children, and subtle criteria of parental capacity are given weight in the deliberations. One need no longer prove gross neglect or obvious incapacity for parenthood in order to win custody. Fathers are more frequently gaining custody of their children, and the stigmatization of mothers who choose to give up their children to their husbands also seems to be lessening. It has become more socially acceptable for a woman to admit that she has little if any maternal interests and that her children would be better off with their father. In spite of these recent trends the overwhelming majority of children are still remaining with their mothers after the separation and divorce.

The kinds of custody. Just as courts are no longer strictly adhering to the view that the mother's receiving custody is necessarily in the children's best interests, greater flexibility is also being shown in the kinds of custody arrangements being recommended.

The most common type of custody arrangement is *sole custody*. The children live primarily with one parent, but spend some time with the other. The non-custodial parent visits with the children at times that have been specified in the divorce decree. The parent with whom the children live makes most of the important decisions regarding their welfare, especially the day-to-day ones that the other parent is not available to make. Both parents, however, generally participate in such major decisions as education, religious training, and vacations.

In *divided custody*, which is also called *shared custody*, the children live about half the time with one parent and half the time with the other. Both parents participate in the important decisions of the children's lives. When the children are living with one parent the other has visitation privileges. Obviously, such an arrangement is most workable when the two homes are in the same school district. Otherwise, it may involve twice yearly upheavals from both school and neighborhood—a situation that most would consider psychologically harmful. An arrangement that might be considered a form of divided custody is one in which the children remain living in one home throughout the year; however, the parents alternate living in the home for six months at a time. In this way the problems of neighborhood and school changes are avoided and each parent has the opportunity of living half the year with the children.

In *split custody* the children are divided between the two parents. Some live permanently with one parent and some with the other. Working on the principle that "half a loaf is better than none," some parents give serious consideration to this form of custody so that they will not be deprived completely of living with the children. Generally, I believe it is best to try to keep the children together. They can provide support for one another and a sense of continuity of the family, in spite of the parental breakup. Children who have been isolated from one or both parents tend to form surrogate families in which the older children take on parental roles and thereby serve as substitute parents for the younger. An older brother can serve as a father surrogate, and an older sister as a mother surrogate.

There are situations, however, in which split custody may be advisable. There are parents, for example, who may be so rejecting of or hostile toward a particular child that it is best to have that child live with the other parent. Robert's relationship with his mother provides an excellent example of a situation in which split custody was the wisest course. Robert's mother openly favored his two sisters. She grew up in a home with three sisters and claimed to know very little about boys and men. When Robert was born she considered him to be like "a stranger from another planet." In addition, she had had a very difficult relationship with her father, who was very hostile to and neglectful of her and her sisters. She recognized that her early experiences with her father contributed to her general distrust of and bitterness toward men. Her anger toward her husband was so great that he ultimately instituted divorce proceedings. She recognized as well that Robert, as a male, was also the target of her anger and that he did not deserve the rejection her was receiving. However, in spite of these insights, she found she had little tolerance for him, hit him frequently with little provocation, and rarely found any reasons to discipline or punish his two sisters. It was clear to all concerned, including Robert himself, that he would be better off living with his father after the separation. And this arrangement proved to be the best, in spite of the fact that it resulted in a loosening of the relationships that he had had with his sisters.

Although most mental health professionals appreciate the previously mentioned benefits to the children of their being together, many have proposed theories that they consider of overriding importance. Some would keep boys with their fathers and girls with their mothers in order to avoid oedipal problems. They hold that a boy's living alone with his mother is likely to result in his believing that he has won the oedipal conflict and replaced his father. (A similar point is made against the girl's living with her father.) In my judgment those problems generally referred to as oedipal have their roots more in emotional deprivations during the first two to three years of life than in such experiences as living alone with a parent of the opposite sex. Such a theory is simplistic and does not give proper appreciation to the breadth and depth of the Oedipus complex.

Some claim it is important for the adolescent to live with the parent of the opposite sex in order to have this last opportunity to learn how to live with an opposite-sexed person before finding his or her own mate. Although I cannot deny that this can be helpful, the adolescent usually has anxieties regarding sexual feelings toward the opposite-sexed parent and living alone with him or her is likely to intensify these significantly. Accordingly, I am not inclined to make this recommendation. There are other theories as well that provide various psychological justifications for splitting up the children. My own opinion is that the children do best if they remain together and I do not subscribe to any basic formulas regarding their being split up. There are, however, situations (generally rare) when it may be in a child's or the children's best interests for them to be split up. Or one might consider it less harmful for them to be separated from one another than for them to remain together.

There are other possible custody arrangements as well, and we are becoming ever more receptive to their utilization. There are families in which the children alternate spending one year with one parent and one year with another. I know of one man, the owner of a large house, who lives in one wing and his ex-wife in the other. Their children generally have rooms in between, and are free to spend time with either parent just as they had prior to the divorce. The parents do not seem to mind one another's dating and receiving visitors, and appear to have a somewhat amicable relationship. Obviously, both from the point of view of money and personality, this is not an arrangement for everyone. A type of custody arrangement that I believe should be tried more frequently can best be called *joint custody*. In this arrangement the children, at their wish, are free to go from one parent's house to the other, without any kind of legal intervention or parental permission. Obviously, such an arrangement is not viable for younger children below the age of six or seven, and would require that both homes be in the same school district. Although it also has the drawbacks of the children's being able to avoid proper discipline at times and attempting to manipulate the parents by threatening to move to the other home, it has the advantage of their having the opportunity to remove themselves easily from unhealthy parental influences.

The adolescent usually has very strong opinions regarding whom he would like to live with and the court often recognizes its impotence to order the adolescent to live where he or she does not wish to. (This is especially true if the non-custodial parent is receptive to the adolescent's living with him or her.) Accordingly, parents do well to use the adolescent's own wishes as an important criterion for deciding where he or she should live. However, things are not that simple. The adolescent's wishes may be ill advised and inappropriate; the desired parent may not be receptive to having the youngster in his or her home. Each situation, therefore, must be evaluated on its own. The only guideline that can be given is that the adolescent's wishes should be taken more seriously than those of younger children.

The mother vs. the father as the more suitable parent. This is a very controversial subject, and no one can claim to know with certainty which sex makes the better parent or whether they are equal in this regard. The opinions I express here are those that seem most reasonable to me at this time, and I recognize that they are not shared by some mental health professionals.

All other things being equal, the mother is superior to the father in providing the *infant* with proper care and nurture (I am not saying anything here about the care of older children). In recent years many have proclaimed that the notion of the mother's being superior to the father as a child rearer is not valid, that this is a social prejudice, and that both parents are equal in this regard. My personal belief, and I think there are many who will agree with me, is that the newborn infant is probably better off with the mother. The mother carries the child within her during the pregnancy and has the physical capability of feeding the infant from her breasts—from a part of her own body—and is likely to develop a psychological tie with the infant stronger and deeper than is possible for the father. Certainly during the mother's pregnancy a healthy father with a strong paternal interest will develop a deep psychological tie with his forthcoming child as well, but this tie is not so strong as the mother's and this may be simply related to the fact that she has certain experiences during the pregnancy that the father does not. She feels the baby within her; experiences the body changes associated with its growth; suffers the pain of its delivery; and enjoys the sensations of its sucking at her breasts. One can get a sense for the validity of this hypothesis if one asks this question: "If you had to make the decision as to who should be given custody of a *newborn infant,* the mother or the father—and if both proved to be equally capable, interested, and loving parents— whom would you recommend?" I think that most would favor the mother, from some deep appreciation for the validity of what I have said about the special tie she develops with her unborn child during the pregnancy.

This preference need not be based on any kind of special instinct or innate capacity in the mother—although it certainly may. We do know that in lower animals there is generally some preference for one sex over the other in caring for the young. To assume that in human beings there is an *equal* capability for caring for the newborn, regardless of parental sex, is to assume that there has been some departure from the total evolutionary pattern—a departure I do not consider likely. Accordingly, the younger a child is, the more one should consider the mother to be the preferable custodial parent. Other factors should certainly be taken into consideration, and these arguments should not automatically assume the mother's being preferred, only that her special experiences (during and immediately after the pregnancy) be given proper weight and not be ignored as they are by followers of the equal capability theory.

The maternal preference holds, I believe, during the first two years or so. Beyond that things may equal out, especially if social attitudes regarding male and female roles in child rearing keep changing. Furthermore, what I have said refers to the situation when "all other things are equal." That is rarely the case. Usually the parents differ with regard to their parental interest and capacity and such differences are vital considerations when making a decision regarding who will be the better parent. Practical considerations are often important, as well. A father may be the superior parent, but he may also be the superior earner. Accordingly, if he were to take the children, the advantages they may enjoy from his better child-rearing capacity might be far outweighed by the privations they might suffer from the lowered earning capacity that might result from the time he spends taking care of them. The older the children get, the more parental differences are bound to exhibit themselves. A mother may be good with infants and toddlers, who are totally dependent on her; but she may do poorly with adolescents, whose independence she has difficulty tolerating. A father may not know the first thing to do with an infant but may excel as a parent when he can share sports and other activities.

Asking the children whom they wish to live with. Most often both parents agree that the children will do best living with the mother and the children are not consulted about this decision. When there is a conflict over who shall have custody, their opinions may be enlisted. The responses a child may provide to the direct question as to whom he or she would prefer to live with are very difficult to interpret and utilize properly. Most would agree that the child's wishes should be given consideration. However, the children (and the younger they are, the more true this is) are ill equipped to make such a decision on their own. Furthermore, the question itself is generally a very anxiety-provoking one for most children. They may be afraid to express preference for one parent because of the fear that the non-preferred parent will react punitively or at least consider them disloyal. They appreciate that making a specific choice may jeopardize significantly their relationship with the non-preferred parent and may result in the latter's lifelong alienation. Or many years later the child may regret the disloyalty that he or she exhibited—disloyalty that may have been the result of childhood naïveté or distortion. One should be extremely careful in such an inquiry and be most judicious regarding the seriousness with which one takes the child's expressions of preference, and if the child does not wish to express a preference, that wish should be respected.

When the conflict over custody is so great that the parents cannot resolve it themselves and resort to the legal apparatus to enforce a decision, the children will generally be asked to express their preference. The courts take the children's wishes into consideration but do not automatically go along with their stated preferences. There are times when children (especially older ones) will have a definite preference as to which parent they wish to live with, but will be afraid to reveal the preference lest they appear disloyal. Such children may, however, subtly reveal the preference in the hope that the court will make the decision for them. By covertly revealing the preference, they hope to influence the court's decision and thereby get assigned to live with the preferred parent. They would rather have the decision made by the court in order to avoid the guilt they would feel if they were forced to state their preferences openly. Lawyers, judges, and therapists who are involved with such children should recognize that they may be doing the children a disservice by trying to extract a definitive statement from them regarding their preferences.

A good example of this phenomenon was exhibited by Ralph, an only child, who was thirteen years old when his parents separated. He absolutely refused to express a preference for either parent. He went further and totally denied any knowledge of his parents' difficulties. His father was an alcoholic and was well known in the community for his drunken episodes. In spite of his drinking he was able to keep his job in the insurance business and function adequately in it. He would often come home totally inebriated; yet Ralph flatly denied that his father had a drinking problem. His mother was obsessed with cleanliness and hounded all members of the family about keeping the home ever clean and neat. Ashtrays were continually being emptied, furniture replaced in its exact position, particles of dust removed, etc. Again, Ralph denied that he found his mother's pressures an inconvenience or that they were manifestations of any psychological problems. Yes, he had overheard his parents fighting on occasion but knew nothing about what their difficulties were: "I never listen to them; I just don't want to get involved." When asked about whom he preferred to live with, he emphatically stated that he had no preference and would leave that decision up to the court. "I'll live with whoever they force me to," he stated. In discussing his mother, however, he described how easy it was for him to talk to her, how they often shopped together because she knew exactly what to buy him, and how good it is to have mothers around during the day for car pools; whereas fathers have to work all day and don't have as much time for their children. This and other statements convinced me that Ralph basically preferred to live with his mother. However, his insistence on not expressing a preference and his willingness to leave the decision to the court convinced me as well that he wanted the court to be the one to "force" him to live with his mother so that he would not appear disloyal to his father. Accordingly, I recommended to the court that Ralph's mother be given custody—which suggestion was implemented and the arrangement worked well. (Of course, other factors were also taken into consideration in making this decision. I do not simply accept the child's wishes as my sole criterion for making a custody recommendation.)

Parental sexual behavior as a determinant of custody. In past years the sexual behavior of the mother, and to a lesser extent of the father, was an important consideration by courts in determining custody. Although adultery by *either* spouse was (and still is) generally considered grounds for divorce, adultery by the mother (but, interestingly, not generally by the father) was often considered ground for depriving her (but not him) of custody. The courts would consider the mother's sexual life in great detail and if she was having sexual experiences, even though she was not bringing her sexual partners into the home, her maternal capacity would be questioned. The fact that she was having sexual experiences—even one extramarital sexual experience before the divorce was legal—could be in itself evidence to the court of her unfitness as a mother. Although such an experience did not generally result in her being deprived of the children, the fact that it could threaten her gaining custody is a statement about legal attitudes toward sexual behavior.

This moralistic and somewhat punitive attitude has been moderated somewhat and the courts in recent years have been much more liberal with regard to using sexual behavior as a criterion for determining custody. I think, however, that it would be a mistake to go completely in the other direction. If a separated parent with temporary custody were, for example, to bring into the home a number of lovers for overnight stays (even without direct exposure of the children to the sexual activities), I would consider this behavior potentially harmful to the children and an argument against such a parent's obtaining custody. (Counterbalancing considerations, of course, might still result in my recommending that such a parent keep the children. All of the pros and cons I describe are elements to be weighed in relation to others and are not to be taken in isolation.)

It is not on moral grounds but out of purely psychological considerations that I believe such behavior to compromise a parent's capacity. A *parade* of many individuals through the parent's bedroom can be psychologically detrimental to the child. (I have discussed in Chapter 4 the possible oedipal complications of such a situation.) If, however, a mother who was not having sexual relationships with other men were to bring a boyfriend into the home to live, I would not necessarily consider this a reason for withholding custody. In fact, if the children had a good relationship with this man, it might even be an argument for her to have the children; she would after all be providing them with a father substitute in compensation for their own father's absence. The children, of course, can still maintain a good relationship with their father as well as with the friend; one need not preclude the other. If such a mother, however, were to enlist the aid of the children in keeping the boyfriend's presence in the home a secret from friends, relatives, and neighbors, then, of course, this would be detrimental to them. She would be placing a burden on them in addition to that which they are already suffering in association with the divorce. Although this factor alone (like any other single factor) should not be considered enough to deprive her of custody, it is a manifestation of a deficiency on her part that should be taken into consideration when making the custody decision.

Custody and the homosexual parent. The question of a homosexual parent's right to custody is being increasingly raised. This is a complex problem and is ever more frequently being brought to our attention as more homosexuals openly announce their sexual preference.

I believe our knowledge of the cause(s) of homosexuality is so limited at the present time that it is premature for anyone to say that he knows with certainty whether or not homosexuality is a psychiatric disorder. Although homosexuality is seen in lower animals, it manifests itself only when heterosexual outlets are not available or as a transient and secondary phenomenon. To assume that there are humans in whom it is the inborn preferential orientation requires the assumption that mankind has departed markedly from the evolutionary pattern. In addition, one must believe in the existence of a natural sexual variant without the goal of species procreation—another evolutionary innovation, to say the least. Accordingly, although I cannot categorically deny the existence of such a variant in humans, I consider it unlikely. In short, then, I will admit the possibility that there may be some homosexuals whose sexual preference is a natural variation; however, I believe such individuals to be rare and perhaps nonexistent. The overwhelming majority of homosexuals are so because of a psychiatric disturbance.

A person's homosexuality, in itself, should not be a reason for depriving him or her of custody or the usual visitation rights. Removal of the children from a homosexual parent can deprive them of valuable experiences. The fact that a parent is homosexual need not result in his or her being incapable of providing the chidren with most of the benefits of parenthood. Homosexuality need not impair parental capacity. There are many male homosexuals who make very good parents—oriented as they are toward maternal functioning. Although such men may contribute to a child's becoming homosexual by serving as a model for such an orientation, they do not often exhibit the punitive rejecting attitude toward their sons that may contribute to their becoming homosexual. There is this negative identification factor, therefore, a factor that may contribute to the son's becoming homosexual; but it is not generally that great that I would suggest that the homosexual father automatically be deprived of visitation and custody rights to which he might otherwise be entitled. Similarly, with the lesbian mother, her homosexuality in itself should not be a reason for depriving her of custody and visitation rights that she might otherwise be granted, even though I believe that her sexual orientation might be a negative factor in making the decision. I would consider it along with other factors, both positive and negative, in making a recommendation.

When I have been asked to make recommendations regarding a homosexual parent's custody and visitation rights, I try to determine whether the parent is trying (either overtly or covertly) to raise the child to become homosexual. It can be openly done with the parent's directly stating that he or she wants the child to be homosexual. (This, by the way, is rare, in my experience. Most homosexuals I have encountered, if they are to be directly honest, would prefer that their children be heterosexual. Although they claim that they say this because their children's lives would be easier in a society that discriminates so terribly against homosexuals, I believe that it is also stated from the deep appreciation that the homosexual way of life is less potentially gratifying—their professions to the contrary notwithstanding.) More commonly, the homosexual parent encourages homosexuality in the children more covertly, with comments such as "I tell my children that I have no particular preferences regarding whether they become homo- or heterosexual." The healthy parent, in my opinion, does have a preference—and strongly so. He or she wants the children to be heterosexual—has no doubts about it—and shudders at the possibility that the child might become homosexual. This has less to do with the social stigma that the homosexual suffers (which, fortunately, is lessening) and more with the appreciation that such a way of life is more likely to be unrewarding and painful than a heterosexual existence —as is true of all life patterns that are associated with psychological disturbance.

Although a homosexual parent provides, in my opinion, an unhealthy model for sexual identification, this fact should not in itself be a reason for refusing such a parent custody if the child is above the age of three or four and exhibits definite heterosexual orientation. By that time the child's sexual orientation is fairly well established and is not likely to be altered unless there is unusual and prolonged indoctrination into homosexual attitudes and behavior. When involved in custody evaluations of homosexual parents, I examine carefully each child's sexual orientation and look for signs and symptoms of homosexuality and sexual identification problems—both present and potential. For boys, the signs of a potential homosexual problem would include the *frequent* desire to put on the mother's make-up and to wear her shoes, underwear, and other articles of clothing; a preference for the role of mother in playing "house"; and a marked preference for playing with girls rather than boys. These criteria are especially valid when they have taken on an obsessive or compulsive quality. Present questions about traditional male and female roles notwithstanding, I still hold that these criteria are valid. I would recommend that a homosexual father of such a child not be granted custody, unless there were other very powerful counterbalancing considerations. There are also less definite manifestations of a homosexual problem in the male. If the boy exhibits effeminate gestures and intonations and is *often* called "sissy" or "fag" by his peers, I suspect a potential homosexual problem. Some "momma's boys" may be revealing the kind of attachment seen in the homosexual. Although tomboyishness may reflect a homosexual problem in the girl, it is not a very valuable criterion, especially in more recent years, when girls' involvement in traditional male activities is becoming more common, happily so, in my opinion.

During the prepubertal and pubertal periods special problems may arise that can affect my recommendations regarding custody and visitation. If a homosexual father, for example, is frequently bringing his thirteen-year-old son together with his homosexual friends, he is providing the boy with a detrimental exposure. Even though there may be no overt invitations to sexual involvement, such a boy is often quite attractive to homosexual man and their feelings toward him will be subtly received by him. A boy of this age normally exhibits a certain amount

of homosexual interest as well. The setting therefore
cannot but be a titillating and seductive one for all concerned. Even if the boy exhibits no evidence of homosexual orientation, the atmosphere is bound to be a
charged one for him. Although it may not result in his
becoming homosexual, it can add to the sexual anxieties
and confusions that he will normally have during this
period. Accordingly, I would consider such exposures
an argument against granting such a father custody. I
would certainly, however, encourage visitation, but would
recommend that such exposures not be permitted during
the visiting times.

If a homosexual parent maintains his or her homosexuality as a private part of his or her life; if he or she is
not trying to induce homosexuality in the children or expose them to sexual activities; and if the children are
above the age of four and show no evidence of homosexuality or of sexual orientation disturbance; then I
would not consider the parent's homosexuality a reason
for disqualifying him or her as the custodial parent. Nor
would I recommend that there be any reduction or restriction of visitation rights. Although the homosexuality,
in itself, would be considered a negative in my considerations, if the above criteria are satisfied, it becomes a small
one.

The question of what recommendations to make regarding custody for a homosexual parent who is living
with a homosexual partner is a more difficult one. Those
who argue that homosexuality is not a psychiatric disturbance would compare such a relationship with a heterosexual one and argue that the same criteria should
hold with regard to the granting of custody. If the court
would grant custody to a mother who lives with a man
to whom she is not married, and if it would grant custody
to a father who is not married to the woman with whom
he is living (and courts commonly do so today in both of
these situations), then, they would argue, the court should
not discriminate against the parent who lives with someone of the same sex. I am in agreement with the more
liberal criteria that courts have recently been using with
regard to the granting of custody to a parent who is

living with but not married to a heterosexual partner. Because I believe that homosexuality is most likely a psychiatric disorder, I do not equate heterosexual with homosexual exposure. I believe that a child who lives in a home in which both "parents" are of the same sex is being unduly exposed to an unhealthy psychological environment. The situation is very different from the one in which the homosexual parent does not live with anyone and keeps his homosexual life apart from his children. When the parent lives with a homosexual partner, there is an exposure to homosexuality of such great intensity that it is likely to affect the children. I do not believe that the effect is so great that it could reverse the sexual identity of children over four who have already established a heterosexual identity and orientation. Rather, I believe that such exposure could create confusions, anxieties, and compromises in the sex role identifications that might otherwise not have arisen. In addition, as mentioned above, in the adolescent period the titillations engendered in such a situation could not but cause the adolescent significant anxieties. Accordingly, I consider such an arrangement to be a strong negative in weighing the pros and cons for recommending custody. Like all the other criteria I use, not one of these is overriding. I might still recommend custody for such a parent if other factors were present that counterbalanced this one. (A homosexual parent who frequently brings a partner or series of partners into the home—whether to sleep over or not—similarly compromises his or her parental role, because the child is being exposed to the previously described *parade* of lovers which can be so detrimental.)

In providing a court with recommendations regarding visitation and custody rights for a homosexual parent, the guidelines that I use is this: *The greater the degree to which the child is exposed to a homosexual environment, the greater should be the restrictions imposed to protect the child from the detrimental effects of such exposure.* Homosexuality in itself should not be a reason for reducing a parent's visitation or custody rights. But when there is exposure to homosexuality and imposition of it, one must consider limiting such a parent's privileges.

Joan's situation provides an example of the kind of situation in which I recommended that a lesbian mother not be given custody of her child and that there be a curtailment of her visitation rights. Joan was thirteen years old when her parents separated because of her mother's homosexuality. She was an only child. At around the time of the separation Joan's mother became a gay activist. Originally the mother was given custody of Joan and she moved into an apartment house where there were many other homosexuals who were involved in the Gay Liberation Movement. Joan's mother became ever swept up in her political activities, fighting for the civil rights of homosexuals. So involved was she in these activities that she had little meaningful time left over for Joan. Many homosexuals visited the home, where meetings often took place. The apartment was flooded with literature and pamphlets supporting the gay cause. In addition, many homosexual magazines were strewn about the apartment, magazines with pictures depicting various kinds of homosexual activities. On occasion the mother would bring Joan on gay activist marches and demonstrations, and encouraged her to hand out leaflets in support of the movement. She took a strictly neutral attitude regarding Joan's future sexual orientation. She denied that Joan had ever been invited into sexual encounters with any of her friends, and claimed that although Joan was a little young for such experiences she would have no objection to her having homosexual experiences by her mid-teens if this was her preference.

Joan's father instituted legal proceedings in order to gain custody of his daughter. As the result of my examination of Joan and both parents. I supported his request. Although Joan showed no evidence for a homosexual orientation at that time, I concluded that the intensive exposure to the homosexual environment was sexually titillating and confusing to Joan, and that it was likely to result in sexual orientation disturbances—even though it was not likely that she might become a lesbian. I felt that her mother's intensive involvement in her political activities was also depriving Joan of the amount of attention and affection she warranted. This had nothing to do with the nature of her mother's activities. (In fact, I was in full sympathy with her mother's political activities, believing as I do that there is absolutely no justification for depriving a homosexual of his or her civil rights merely because he or she suffers with this disorder.) Even if the mother had been involved in activities having nothing to do with homosexuality, her obsessive involvement in a cause resulted in her neglecting Joan. The court agreed with my recommendation and Joan's father was granted custody. The court followed my recommendation that the mother be granted liberal visitation privileges. However, she was not allowed to involve the children in her gay liberation activities or bring them to the apartment where she was living, because of the intensive exposure Joan had there to the homosexual environment.

Real vs. phony demands for custody. Up until the last few years courts tended to favor the mother so much as custodian for the children that a father who sued for custody was bound to lose unless he was able to prove gross neglect on the mother's part, prostitution, severe drug addiction, etc. Very few fathers were awarded custody. If a father wanted to try to gain custody of the children in order to wreak vengeance on his wife and she was not grossly unsuited to take care of the children, his lawyer generally discouraged him from pursuing such a course because of its futility. In recent years divorce laws have been changed in most states and the courts are now awarding custody to the more suitable parent, regardless of sex. A father now has a greater chance of gaining custody of his children; we are seeing more custody litigation in which fathers genuinely feel that they would be the better parent. We are also seeing legal contests in which the father is using his new opportunity for manipulative purposes, neurotic gratification, or other inapropriate reasons.

A father, for example, may not really feel that he would be the preferable parent but selfishly tries to gain custody of the children rather than suffer the pains of his loss. In order to avoid such personal discomfort he will pursue a course that is not in his children's best interests. Or a father may not actually want custody, but may claim that he does as a way of hurting the mother, as a way of getting vengeance. He may know from the outset that he is not going to press this issue to the point where the final decision will be made; rather, he will use his custody demand as a weapon, as a bargaining maneuver in their negotiations. He may finally "give up" the custody fight in order to get concessions from his wife on such matters as alimony and support payments. Such a course represents a deficiency in parental capacity. It is a manifestation of the parent's considering personal financial gain to be more important than the children's psychological well-being. Custody litigation is invariably traumatic to children—pulled as they are between parents, lawyers, and other adults. The parent whose desire for personal gain blinds him to this reveals a serious defect in his or her parental capacity.

On occasion a parent will press vigorously for custody in an attempt to reduce the guilt he or she feels over the divorce. A father, for example, who never particularly distinguished himself as a devoted parent, may profess great love for the children at the time of separation and fight viciously for custody. Such a parent—consciously or unconsciously—may not even wish to be granted custody. What he really wants is to put up a good fight so that he can convince himself and others that he really loves his children. Such a parent may do many things during the litigation in order to ensure that he loses the custody battle. Most parents are especially careful to spend maximum time with the children during the time of custody litigation in order to impress all concerned with their devotion to their children. Parents who basically wish to lose custody may not use this common maneuver. Or they may choose a lawyer who is obviously incompetent or neglectful of them. Such parents are secretly relieved when they are not granted custody.

The lawyer may realize that his or her client does not deserve custody, but will nevertheless vigorously support the client's fighting for the children. At times, this stems from the desire to use the custody claim as a weapon in the litigation in the hope that pressing this issue will enable him or her to gain concessions in other areas. How-

ever, more benevolent considerations may also be operative. The lawyer may recognize that the client may need
the custody litigation in order to lessen guilt over a basic
desire not to have custody, or the lawyer may harbor the
hope that the exposure of the client's parental deficiencies
in open court may help the client gain insight into the fact
that he or she would be the less desirable custodial parent.
The lawyer may also support the client's position with future considerations in mind. Although he or she may recognize that the client is presently the less desirable parent
for the child, the lawyer may recognize that future changes
may improve the client's capacity or diminish the other
spouse's parental ability. Having on the court records that
the client has fought for the child enhances his or her
chances of gaining custody in the future. And the information obtained in the early trial may be useful and sup-
portive in such future litigation. The client who has
never fought for the children in the past, when he or she
had the opportunity to do so, is less likely to gain custody
in the future. On the other hand, there is a risk to the
client that such litigation may place on the court records
information about the client that would weaken his or
her case in subsequent litigation, and this may cause the
lawyer to be less enthusiastic about the client's pressing
the custody issue.

Choosing expert witnesses in custody litigation. In the
typical courtroom custody conflict each side brings in its
own parade of professionals to testify on its behalf. As
the reader by now well appreciates, I don't like parades.
And when parades are held in a courtroom, and there are
two of them (one for each side), and the parade consists of mental health professionals, I find them disgraceful
to the profession and a disservice to the court.

Custody evaluations are really evaluations to two people. The mental health professional who is invited to testify in custody trials is really being asked which of the two
parents—all things considered—would make the more desirable (or less undesirable) custodial parent for the
children. It is somewhat ludicrous, in my opinion, for a
therapist to get up in court after having evaluated the

mother, for example, and simply to testify that she is a capable mother. The opposing lawyer will reasonably ask: "Have you seen the father?" In many cases the therapist will not have seen the father and he or she will therefore not be able to comment on him. This is a gross omission in the testimony because one is really evaluating relative degrees of parental capacity. In most cases both parents *are* adequate. One is really evaluating degrees of adequacy and comparative competence (and incompetence). Accordingly, the professional commenting on this issue should see *both* parents. Lawyers, with their deep faith in the adversary system, often hold that a custody decision is best accomplished in an adversary proceeding—where each party presents his own position as strongly as possible. The better parent will then *win* custody. This system may have merit in determining the guilt or innocence of an alleged criminal, but it has little relevance to the determination of who is the better parent. I avoid (whenever possible) the adversary role and will only agree to conduct a custody evaluation when I can see *both* parents (and the children) and serve *the court* (not either side) as an impartial expert. This can best be accomplished by the husband and wife both requesting of their lawyers that I be consulted in this role. The lawyers, if they agree, then request that the court invite me to conduct the evaluation. In other words, four people (the husband, the wife, and their two lawyers) must agree to invite me before I will be willing to become involved in custody litigation. Since most who call me for custody consultation, whether lawyers or clients, are so deeply wedded to the adversary concept that they cannot see the merits of my position, only a small fraction of such requests ever reach the point of consultation. But those that do provide me with a sense of service—the inevitable frustrations of such a consultation notwithstanding.

Parents do well to appreciate that they should do everything possible to work out their custody conflicts themselves. This is not only the least expensive way to resolve such a problem, but produces the least amount of strain for the children as well. Parents do well to recognize also that once they go to court in order to resolve this problem they are *putting the decision in the hands of others. They are giving up their right to make the final decision as to what will happen to their own children.* And from what I know of court decisions in such matters I cannot say that I have been impressed by their wisdom. The amount of data that a judge should have before making a reasonable decision is often mind-boggling and it is rare that time and money permit him or her adequately to assimilate all the evidence and come to a reasonable decision. Parents do well to appreciate fully the capriciousness of the legal solution before resorting to it. They should consider how difficult (and expensive) it may be to reverse such a decision, once it has been made.

However, if parents decide to pursue this course and/or do not feel it can be avoided, they make a serious error if they each try to enlist their own team of experts, each of whom has been screened in advance to ensure that he or she will provide the strongest testimony on one's behalf. I believe that a therapist is unethical if he or she agrees to do a custody evaluation with the understanding that if the findings support the position of the inviting (and paying) party they will be used, but if they do not then the court will never hear of his or her opinion. Although such a therapist is acting in the finest legal tradition, he or she is ignoring what is best in the medical tradition. It is our legacy in medicine to provide our opinions impartially and not to co-operate or comply with those who would use our medical opinions for their personal advantage, or who would suppress our findings if they do not suit their purposes. Those therapists who accept an invitation to do a custody evaluation with the understanding from the outset that their testimony will not be used in court if it does not come out in a particular way are an embarrassment to their profession and are not really helping lawyers and their clients either. They are only prolonging and complicating such proceedings and adding to the expense and agony of the parents and children involved. Parents would save themselves a lot of expense and grief if they would insist on a mutually agreed upon impartial expert (or team of experts) from the outset. If, following such a recommendation, a parent felt that he or she still wished to enter into the bloody arena of adversary proceedings and had the money and guts to do so, he or she would still be free to pursue this course. But at least the more civilized route would have been tried first.

If a child is in therapy, one or both parents may wish to bring in the child's therapist to provide testimony in the custody conflict. This may appear to be a reasonable course since the therapist generally knows the family well and may be in a good position to provide useful information to the court. However, it is most likely that if he or she does provide such testimony, the child's treatment is likely to be jeopardized. The therapist's indicating to the court which of the parents he or she thinks should have custody cannot but cause the other parent to harbor deep resentments toward him or her, which would tend to compromise the child's therapy. Often the parent will express these resentments openly to the child, and even when attempts are made to hide them, the child will sense the hostile feelings that the parent harbors toward the therapist and will feel him- or herself caught in the middle of a tug-of-war. Such a situation cannot but reduce the child's positive feelings toward the therapist. Therapeutic gratifications notwithstanding, a parent (even with problems) provides the child with more than the therapist—and he or she has little choice but to side with the parent. Therefore, parents should separate these roles and, if the child is in treatment, get another professional to provide testimony.

Actually, once a therapist has seen a child he or she cannot usually refuse to provide the court with information. The therapist can even be subpoenaed and, if he or she refuses to appear, may be held in contempt of court and imprisoned. Because such a treating therapist has not generally conducted an evaluation specifically focused on the custody issue, he or she may not be asked to give a specific recommendation regarding custody, but can be asked many questions that will bear on this decision. It is very difficult, if not impossible, for the therapist to provide such information without its being used by the court in determining custody. Such an appearance will usually result in the alienation of at least one of the parents, with a resulting contamination of the therapy. I cannot emphasize this point strongly enough.

At times a parent(s) will bring a child for treatment when actually a custody determination is desired. Sometimes parents may really believe that treatment is the only thing they want, or they may say that treatment is what they want but will know that the custody consideration is also very much on their minds. They may withhold this from the therapist at the beginning because they fear the therapist will not want to become involved in the legal aspects of the case, or will not want to take the child into treatment at all if appearance in court is also being considered. Such parents may know of therapist's reluctance to go to court, but may not understand the dangers that such appearances pose for therapy. They may have been turned down by a series of therapists who refused to get involved once they suspected that their services were being requested for the purpose of litigation. The parent may not appreciate that the therapist cannot but be indignant when finding him- or herself forced to testify in a case that was initially presented without any reference to the litigation plans. Such resentment beclouds objectivity and may affect the therapist's decision because of inevitable prejudice against the parent who was dishonest regarding the reasons for the referral.

Parental Criticism of One Another

"Never criticize your ex-spouse to your child" is among the most common advice given to separated and divorced parents, and even mental health experts often profess it enthusiastically. Such advice is based on the assumption that the child is less likely to respect, emulate, and identify with a parent who is so criticized. Even though one may harbor intense feelings of hatred toward the ex-spouse (the usual case, especially in the period immediately following the separation), one is advised to refrain from expressing such feelings to, or in front of, the child. Only assets are to be mentioned. The rationale is that it is important to the child's healthy psychological development that he have respect for and admiration of each of his parents. The theory holds that if too many of a parent's deficiencies are revealed to the child, that parent will not become an object of identification and so the child's healthy psychological development will be compromised.

Although well meaning, this advice is, I believe, misguided. All of us, whether or not our parents are divorced, should have as accurate a picture as possible of our parents—both their assets and their liabilities. Children tend to identify with and accept totally their parents' qualities and characteristics. They operate on the principle "If it's good enough for them, it's good enough for me." They swallow the whole bag, so to speak. They indiscriminately identify with many qualities that are not in their best interests. As healthy children grow older they learn to accept those parental qualities that are healthy and reject those that are not.

In a healthy home each parent can be a source of information for the children regarding qualities of the other that are undesirable for them to acquire. Ideally, such information should be imparted in a benevolent fashion, e.g., "Your father thinks that just because a person is black he is less worthy than others. I don't agree with his thinking." "Your mother thinks that something terrible will happen to you if you don't eat everything she gives you. I don't agree with her." In addition, the parent should admit his own defects to the child in appropriate situations, e.g., "I'm afraid to swim. I know there's nothing to be afraid of. I just can't help it. However, I hope that you'll learn to swim, because I can see that it can be a lot of fun." In such an environment the child is likely to grow up having real expectations from people and not suffer significant disappointment when they reveal their deficiencies.

Divorced parents as well owe their children this information. To deprive children of it not only contributes to their developing difficulties in their interpersonal relationships but also produces confusion as well as distrust of the parent who withholds this vital information. The child knows quite well that each parent believes the other to have serious personality flaws, or why else would they have gotten separated? Hearing nothing but good things from Mother about a divorced father, the child can only wonder: "If he's so great, why have you divorced him?" The divorce is likely to have produced feelings of distrust already; withholding information addes unnecessary distrust at a time when the child can least afford this additional burden. Moreover, the children's picture of the praised person is likely to be distorted because they do not believe their primary source of information, so their fantasies can only be validated or refuted by their own, often primitive, observations.

The healthiest approach in such situations is to try to give the children as accurate a picture of their parents as possible: their assets and liabilities, their strengths and weaknesses. The children should come to appreciate that their parents, like all humans, are not perfect. They should grow to respect in each those areas that warrant respect, and hold in low esteem those qualities which are not worthy of admiration. If a parent's defects far outweigh his strengths, so be it. This is not a reflection on the children. They may suffer from having no admirable figure with whom to identify, but is this worse than emulating a contrived person whose assets exist only in words—words the children cannot fully believe? Respect is earned; it cannot be obtained by order or deceit. Children will usually see through facade.

Admittedly, separated parents are not famous for their objectivity when providing such information. The rage that often exists at that time is often blinding, and distortions and exaggerations may be extreme. In spite of these impairments to accurate communication, I still advise separated parents to impart to their children what kinds of people they consider their spouses to be—communicating their opinions with regard to their assets *as well as* their liabilities. Often this is best done in a situation when the parent is actually exhibiting behavior that confirms the opinion. When a father misses his visits, it indicates a lack of interest and should be labeled as such. When he exhibits genuine interest in the child's welfare, he shows his involvement, and it should be described in that way. When a mother leaves her child under the care of a seven-year-old, this is neglect, and it should be defined as such. When she deprives herself of a new dress to buy her children clothing, she is showing true concern, and her children should know it. Parents do best to communicate information about one another during quiet discussion. It is only during periods of rage that parents do well to distrust their judgment. (In my therapeutic work with children, as well, I advise them to be somewhat skeptical of criticisms made while a parent is enraged.) I also advise parents when criticizing their former spouses to preface criticisms with terms like "In my opinion" and "As I see it." In this way they communicate to the children the notion that what they are saying may not be completely accurate.

I am not suggesting that every single defect and deficiency of the parent be disclosed to the children. Some of the problems that existed between the parents prior to the separation often are of little importance to the children. These are the private concerns of the parents, and the children should be told so. The children also have a right to certain privacies of their own, and these should be respected by the parents. The details of a parent's behavior toward them, no matter how contemptible, are the *children's business.* This must be faced by all concerned. These details should be discussed at a level comprehensible to the children and at a depth appropriate to their ages. In such an atmosphere they will learn what to criticize and what to admire, what to love and what to dislike. They will then be far better prepared to relate more effectively with their parents as well as others whom they will encounter.

There are parents who appear not to criticize the spouse to the children, but communicate in other ways their profound condemnation. For example, when a boy asks a mother about the reasons for the divorce and she tells him to ask his father, the child is likely to conclude that the truth is so bad that it cannot be told by a nice lady like his mother. The father who says, "I would not want to say anything *against* your mother," gets across the message that they are terrible things about the mother that could be divulged, but that he is just too much of a good guy to tell everyone about them. The mother who says, "I'm not going to say anything that will make you think less of your father," is clearly implying that there are a number of disparaging things she knows about the father but is too good a person to mention them. Because the details are not provided, the children are likely to imagine the defects to be far worse than they really are. When asking children if they want to see their father, a mother may say, "Do you *really* want to see your father?" and by the tone of her voice communicates to the child her hatred for her ex-husband. And the parent who continually speaks with pride about how carefully he or she refrains from criticizing the ex-spouse provides the children with much food for thought about the other parent's despicable behavior.

Parents often ask what they can do when the ex-spouse continually disparages them and bombards the children with lies about them. I usually advise such parents that their best defense against such vilification is to provide the children with living experiences that they are not what the ex-spouse describes them to be. I try to impress upon such parents that if they are loving and concerned, the children will ultimately come to appreciate this (even though at times confused by the critical, contradictory messages). I discourage such parents from questioning the children about what particular criticisms are made and attempting to correct them one by one. Such an endeavor is usually futile (the children cannot remember them all and they may be endless) and, in addition, the parent's defensiveness may contribute to the children's disbelief of the refutations. Parents who involve themselves in such continual disparagement of the ex-spouse are harming their children. I try to get them to appreciate that their hostility toward their ex-spouse is so great that they are blinding themselves to the repercussions on the children of their trying to gain vengeance in this way. I also try to get them to appreciate that their children will (if they do not already) respect them less for involving themselves in such a campaign.

In working with parents who continually disparage one another I try to help them reach the kind of relationship that often exists between countries that basically harbor great antagonism toward one another, but find it in their mutual interests to maintain civilized relations. And in the divorce situation the children as well can benefit when the hostile parties so conduct themselves.

A related bit of advice (often given by the same professionals who suggest that one never criticize the absent spouse) is to reassure the children that the absent parent still loves them. This advice is certainly valid in most situations, because the absent parent generally does love the children and they may profit from being reminded of this. However, the advice is also provided in situations where there is no question in the mind of the adviser that the absent parent has little, if any, affection for the children. It is then obviously misguided, however benevolently intentioned. The father, for example, who has not been heard from in many years is said still to love his children "but just can't show it." The mother who has disappeared for a similar period is described as "keeping her love inside." Those who provide children with these obviously absurd excuses do so because they believe that if the children were to be told the truth they would be psychologically devastated.

Children who are provided with such excuses cannot but become confused about what love is if one can love someone and yet never exhibit any evidence of it. Although I do not claim to have a final definition of love, I believe that reciprocity is somehow involved. And such confusion can contribute to the children's having difficulty in forming loving relationships both in the present and future. In addition, they are likely to sense the absurdity of the reassurance and the deceit of the parent who provides it. Accordingly, they may become distrustful of their only remaining parent—not a very happy thing to happen to children of divorce.

It would be cruel, however, to tell such abandoned children simply that the absent parent doesn't love them and leave it at that. They have to be helped to appreciate that this does not mean that they are unlovable, and to recognize that the defect lies in the absent parent rather than in themselves—that there is something seriously wrong with someone who cannot love his or her own child. Such children need to gain gratifications from others in compensation for the deprivations they may experience over the loss of the parent. Telling the children that the abandoned parent still loves them is not going to provide any feeling that they are really loved. They have to have *living experiences* that there are indeed others with whom they can have affectionate and loving relationships. Only then will they really be convinced that the deficiency does not lie within themselves. The children also have to find ways to become comfortable with the angry feelings they will probably have over their rejection. Such anger is natural and inevitable. Attempts should be made to lessen any guilt such children may feel because of it. However, as discussed in Chapter 4, mere expression of anger serves little purpose. The anger will truly disappear only when, through the gaining of substitutive gratifications, the situation is so changed that the anger is no longer generated.

For children who are not completely abandoned, but whose absent parent has little meaningful contact, a similar approach should be used. First, such children have to be helped to try to gain greater contact with the absent parent. If this fails after reasonable attempts, they must be encouraged to resign themselves to the reality of the situation and discouraged from trying to extract more affection than the absent parent is willing to or capable of providing. It is important for the children to seek substitute gratifications elsewhere so that they will not suffer significant frustration and lingering resentments.

Using Children in the Parental Conflict

A common error that separated parents often make (especially in the period immediately following the separation) is to use the child as a source of information about the ex-spouse. It is natural for a parent to be curious about what the former partner is doing (especially with regard to dating and spending money) and children can be an excellent source of information about such activities. Occasionally, the data so obtained is used in legal proceedings. Often parents are so eager to extract such information from their children that they blind themselves to the harmful effects of their allowing themselves to be used as informers. Children are ashamed of themselves for such disloyalty, yet they provide the information so as not to alienate the inquirer. The parents may also deny the loss of respect they themselves suffer. They lose respect for themselves for turning their children into spies. And the children lose respect for the parents because they are not conducting themselves in a manner worthy of admiration.

In my psychotherapeutic work with such children I try to discourage them from involving themselves with their parents in this way and try to get them to be self-assertive enough to refuse to answer each parent's questions about the other. To a boy who is involved in such maneuvers, I might say: "No one respects a spy or tattle-tale—neither the people he spies for nor the spy himself. The people whom he spies for know that he can't be trusted with a secret. And the spy can't like himself because he knows that what he's doing is wrong because it hurts other people." I also point out to such children that their spying is contributing to the continuation of the parents' fighting. And I suggest that parents also use this approach if one or both are motivated to discontinue this shameful game.

The converse of using the children as sources of information is using them as couriers of messages. Although this may appear to be a harmless practice and often the most expedient, it can easily deteriorate into another form of utilization of the children in the parental conflict. For example, a father, speaking to his six-year-old child on the telephone, says: "When we finish talking don't forget to tell your mother that I won't be picking you up this Saturday." Since six-year-old children are not famous for their memories, such a child can be relied upon to forget the message, causing her mother no end of frustration and inconvenience. Father, in this case, either consciously or unconsciously understood that the child was not likely to convey the message, but can play Mr. Innocent when his wife has a fit over his not showing up. Or Mother may say to her daughter, "When you see your father, tell him yourself that you need a new dress." The mother here does not consider it likely that Father will buy the dress if she herself requests it and hopes that the child's request is more likely to be effective. Perhaps the mother feels that the father is "tight" and that he would not respond to her request that he buy their daughter a new dress. By having the child make the request she hopes to play on his guilt, or she knows that the father is unable to say no to his cute little daughter. In more extreme cases the warring parents may actually carry on prolonged conversations with one another through the children, who carry back and forth the various threats and counterthreats: "You tell your mother that who I have in this house when you come here is none of her damn business." "You tell your father that I'll spend my money in any way I please." "You tell your mother that if she doesn't have you ready on time next week I'll call my lawyer." "You tell your father that if he doesn't get here on time this Sunday I won't let him take you at all." Obviously, the bearers of all these messages suffer strain and trauma and parents who so use their children are doing them a terrible disservice.

On occasion, each parent will try to get children to serve as allies in the parental conflict. As is true in all wars, the more people one has on one's side, the greater the chances of victory. Many children, in an effort to please, will take the side of the parent with whom they are at the time. When with their mother they listen sympathetically to her complaints about the father; and when with their father they join with him in his criticisms of the mother. Because of the dishonesty involved in such false and shifting loyalties, the children lose respect for themselves, and live with the fear that their deceit will be revealed (which it most often is) and that they will suffer the alienation of those who have learned of it. Other children, however, consistently side with a particular parent against the other, may blind themselves to endearing qualities in the parent to whom they are antagonistic, and thereby compromise what could otherwise have been a richer and more rewarding relationship.

I urge such children to try to assert themselves and refuse to take sides. The older the children, the more likely he or she will have the strength to say to each of the parents: "Please don't involve me." This does not mean, however, that I discourage children from gaining information about each of the parents. Getting information and taking action are different. Although the discrimination between the two may be difficult (and the younger the child, the more so), parents should attempt to help their children make it. They have to be helped to decide whether the information they get from each parent warrants their taking action or not. They have to be helped to see the difference between fighting their own battles and fighting a parent's. If, for example, a father gambles, then both children and mother suffer unnecessary deprivations. The children of such a father should be encouraged to tell their father how much the gambling bothers them in the hope such an assertion will play some role in improving the situation. If the children's efforts prove futile (most often the case when the gambling is compulsive), then they have to be helped to resign themselves to this defect in their father, not rely on him to change, and gain their gratifications elsewhere. In this case the information about the father has warranted some action. A situation in which the gaining of information about a parent by the children would not justifiably warrant action on their parts would be the one in which their mother intensely dislikes their father, but loves them. The deficiencies that the mother sees in the father in no way affect his ability to care for his children or detract from his capacity to love them. The children do themselves and their father a disservice if they join forces with their mother against their father. They have to understand that by doing so both they and their father lose out on the gratifications that would otherwise be gained from a loving relationship. I try to help children appreciate that their parents' criticisms about one another (especially when made in anger) may not be completely trustworthy. Children should form their own opinions about each parent *on the basis of their own observations.*

Children are often used as scapegoats in the parental battle. Because Father is no longer available, Mother may vent the hostility she feels toward him or her son who lives with her. Such utilization may be facilitated by qualities of his that remind her of her former husband. Sometimes such similarities are real; other times they are imagined by the mother. In either case they can serve to foster the child's being scapegoated. A related phenomenon is that of the child's generalizing from the mother's hatred of the father and assuming that she therefore hates all males. An easy next step to take is that she hates her son as well.

Some children take advantage of the parental hostilities to their own ends. When with the mother they will try to ingratiate themselves to her by saying critical things about the father in order to gain special favors, privileges, or presents. And they may act similarly when with the father. Divorced parents are particularly susceptible to this maneuver because they so relish hearing critical things about one another. Whereas they would usually be disbelieving of many of the absurd things the child might communicate on other subjects, when it comes to critical information about the ex-spouse, they may exhibit amazing gullibility.

Children should be shown that they cannot respect themselves when they engage in such deceitful maneuvers. They should see that they are causing themselves to suffer unnecessary fears of disclosure. Parents should interrupt the game once they are alerted to its occurrence. Some parents quickly catch on to what has been happening and can discontinue their involvement. Others are so angry that they cannot avoid getting "sucked in" and so are continually manipulated by their children—an unfortunate situation for all concerned.

Dating, Sleeping Together, Living Together, and Remarriage

Children living in an intact home need resign themselves only to the fact that the same-sexed parent, and *only* the same-sexed parent, shares intimacies and has preroga-

tives with the opposite-sexed parent that they do not enjoy. Such resignation does not come easily. Children of
divorce, whose parents are dating, have a much more difficult time alleviating their oedipal rivalries. A boy living
with a dating mother—especially one who meets a large
number of transient dates in her home—is likely to conclude that just about every man in the world shares intimacies with his mother that he does not. He views himself as having rivals, each of whom seems to have certain
advantages over him with regard to winning his mother's
affection. He need not know that sexual encounters are
occurring to feel so rejected. The fact that his mother
spends time alone with his rivals and goes out with them
while he has to remain at home is enough to produce feelings that he is a "second-class citizen." Such an atmosphere is likely to produce in him feelings of resentment
both toward his mother and her dates. And a girl living
with a dating father, or whose father exposes her to
numerous girl friends during visitation, is likely to react
similarly. In addition, if the child looks forward to the parent's remarrying in order to compensate for the loss of a
parent, each new date may raise his or her hopes unnecessarily. And the child who dreads the thought of
parental remarriage is being provided with needless exposure to the object of his or her concerns.

It is common in such situations for a child to become
very antagonistic to both the parent and the date and to
utilize various maneuvers to prevent the dating or alienate the date. Last-minute temper tantrums, crying spells,
"sickness" (often associated with vomiting, soiling, diarrhea, and other dramatic manifestations of illness), fierce
sibling fighting, and sudden homework crises may be
utilized in the service of preventing the parent from going
out. Or the child may be overtly hostile to the date in an
effort to dissuade him or her from continuing the relationship with the child's parent. Recognizing that questions that have proved to be embarrassing to both Mother
and her friend may have alienating value, the child
may inquire, "Are you going to be my new daddy?" or
even more provocatively may ask, "Are you going to
sleep over here like some of the other men do?" A child

may say to a mother: "Daddy's going to be angry at you when he finds out what you're doing." And another may inquire of a father, "Does Mommy know that a lady is going to sleep over here tonight?" Sometimes the hostility the child feels toward the absent parent may be displaced onto a date—a safer target, whose total alienation would be no loss to the child whatsoever.

An adolescent girl whose mother has a whole string of affairs and who communicates this to her daughter, either overtly or covertly, is likely to react similarly herself as she models herself after her mother. She comes to adhere to the view that the greater the number of men one can attract, the more attractive one is. The youngster thereby is likely to fail to gain appreciation of the value of more continual and deeper relationships. In addition, her awareness of her mother's activities can be very titillating, as she is stimulated to fantasize exactly what her mother is doing, and this can contribute to her desire to gain similar gratifications herself. Her oedipal rivalry with her mother may cause her to compete with her. Such competition may be confined to boys of her own age, but at times she may seek older men and even her mother's lovers. She may be more seductive with her mother's men friends than with her father—the latter being viewed (generally correctly so) as less sexually available. Resolution of the Oedipus complex in such girls is very difficult; they are so stimulated to gain gratification with a series of older men that there is little desire to have a peer as the primary, if not exclusive, source of satisfaction. Similarly, a father who flaunts his popularity and sexual prowess with women in front of his adolescent boy is likely to produce strong jealous rivalries in his son. The youngster may then become obsessed with sexual conquests of large numbers of girls (beyond the usual adolescent boy's obsessions in this department) and thereby be deprived of the gratifications to be derived from deeper and more meaningful relationships.

Parents should not expose their children to each new date; rather they should be met outside the home. When a parent has formed a meaningful and ongoing relationship with someone, then, I believe, the children should meet that person. In this way the parent avoids exposing the children to the seemingly endless parade—the situation most likely to produce difficulties for the children. These people need not be potential marriage partners. Although such contacts are still likely to generate oedipal rivalries, they can also provide children with many benefits that can potentially outweigh the discomforts and frustrations of having someone new on the scene. Ideally, the new person can serve to compensate the children for some of the deprivations they suffer over the absence of one of the parents—and this benefit cannot be underestimated. In addition, children can be helped to appreciate that this new relationship makes the parent with whom they live a happier person and this cannot but affect their own sense of well-being. When the mother is frustrated and grouchy they are likely to suffer as well; on the other hand, when the mother is in a good frame of mind, she will involve herself more benevolently with her children.

Some parents may go in the opposite direction and hide all dates, transients as well as those with whom they may become deeply involved. They often do this in order to avoid the hostile reactions they know their children will have to the new person. Such hiding is not in the children's best interests. It is inappropriate to comply with another person's unreasonable demands and requests. Because the children have expressed antagonism to the parent's new friend—sight unseen—is no reason to "keep him in the closet." Such compliance only entrenches such children's manipulations and deprives them of the growth experience of dealing with something they find unpleasant. Such a parent is probably afraid of anyone's anger —regardless of the age of the person who is angry and the appropriateness of the anger—and does well to look into this problem for his or her own sake as well as that of the children.

Parents are sometimes concerned about the effects on the children of an opposite-sexed friend staying overnight in bed with the parent (without, of course, the child's observing or overhearing sexual activity). If such experiences occur with a large number of different friends, then the effects can be quite detrimental. If such intimacy is reserved for deep, ongoing relationships, I see no reason why the child should develop untoward reactions. It is the parade that is the dangerous thing, in my opinion, not sexual intercourse performed out of the child's presence or awareness.

Just as younger people are more frequently living together before marrying in order to be sure that they aren't making a mistake (a happy trend, in my opinion), more and more divorced people are doing so as well in order to be sure that they don't make the same mistake all over again (a most judicious decision also, I believe). And others may choose to live together without marriage necessarily being considered. The question is often raised about the psychological effects on the children of such an arrangement. I believe that if a parent has the full conviction that the decision is a wise one, then the children are likely to accept it as well. If the parent has the strength to tolerate any social stigma that may result from entering into such an arrangement (a stigma that has happily lessened in recent years), then the children are likely to tolerate it as well. If such a parent communicates to the children the basic reasons for the decision, they are more likely to accept it: "Mommy made a big mistake when she married Daddy. Joe also made a mistake when he got married. Both Joe and Mommy want to be sure that we don't make the same mistake all over again. By living together we can get to know one another very well and then we'll be in the best position to decide whether or not we want to get married." And if the children are teased or ridiculed because of the parents' decision, they must be helped to appreciate the inappropriateness of such criticism: "There must be something wrong with Mary and her parents if they make fun of us because of what Mommy is doing. We all know that it would be a terrible thing if Mommy made another bad marriage. We all suffered so when Mommy and Daddy split up. We certainly don't want that to ever happen again. And Mommy believes that living with Larry is the best way to be sure that she isn't going to make the same mistake all over again. I think that there's something wrong with Mary and her parents for thinking that Mommy is dirty and sinful."

If, however, the parent is ashamed of the arrangement, tries to keep it a secret, and goes so far as to enlist the children's aid in hiding it as well, then they are likely to become confused and suffer unnecessary shame themselves. Maintaining a conspiracy of silence in which the children are sworn to secrecy places a terrible burden on them. In order that the secret not be divulged they may have to forgo inviting their friends to the home, create excuses for not doing so, live with the fear that in spite of their efforts the terrible secret may be revealed, and suffer terrible guilt if they have contributed to the secret's being divulged (which, of course, usually occurs). The parent's feelings about living together with another person become the children's. If the parent does it with conviction and with a minimum degree of embarrassment (no shame at all is most often not possible, considering the deep-seated tradition of condemnation of such arrangements), then the children are likely to handle it well. Parents who are ashamed of living together without being married cannot but communicate their shame to their children (both overtly and covertly) and they are likely to experience various harmful psychological reactions such as shame over what the parent is doing, fear over revealing the "secret," and guilt if they have contributed to its divulgence.

Occasionally parents (usually custodial mothers) will seriously consider marrying people they are not sure about, because they feel it would be good for the children to have a father or mother figure living in the home. Just as I generally discourage parents who are considering divorce from staying together "for the sake of the children," I similarly discourage single parents from remarrying for the children's sake. I am not suggesting that the children's needs be totally ignored in such deliberations, only that they not be given highest priority. One marries and divorces primarily for oneself, not for one's children. Although I believe strongly that children do best in a situation in which mother and father figures are present, this does not mean that *any* mother or *any* father figure will do. One must consider who these people are and the nature of the relationship between the parents as well as that between parents and children. The mother who has mixed feelings about remarriage, but who is considering it for the children's sake, must take into consideration the fact that a poor relationship with her new husband is likely to have harmful effects on the children. In addition, she must consider her prospective husband's relationship with the children as well if she is to be able to make any decisions as to whether a remarriage will be in the children's best interests.

Occasionally a single parent will wonder about remarriage to someone who seems suitable and desirable in every way except for the fact that the person does not seem to have a good relationship with the children. Such a parent should try to determine whether the problems are the result of deficiencies in the potential spouse or are caused by distortions or difficulties in the children. In the former case the parent should try to determine whether such defects in the prospective spouse are confined to forming relationships with children or whether they are manifestations of broader deficiencies in human relationships. If it is only a defect with regard to children, then the parent should be clear about this deficiency beforehand and recognize that it will be one of the drawbacks of the marriage. If there is a broader problem in human relationships, then the parent might do well to get a clearer picture of the potential spouse before making a definite decision. (Some joint counseling might be useful here.) If it is the children's problems that are compromising the relationship with the intended spouse, then it is inappropriate not to remarry for this reason. It is not the children's best interests psychologically to comply with inappropriate or unreasonable demands on their part; to do so would only enhance their maladaptive behavior.

Divorce results in increased financial pressures for all but the wealthy. Remarriage to someone who enjoys financial security is therefore very tempting. If the alleviation from financial pressures is the primary, if not exclusive, reason for marrying, then the children (and both partners in the new marriage as well) are bound to suffer. Financial privation produces psychological difficulties; but a second unhappy marriage is likely to produce even greater ones. I cannot discourage parents strongly enough from entering into such an ill-conceived arrangement.

A discussion of parental remarriage would not be complete if it omitted mention of one of the single parent's greatest dangers, namely, remarrying for the same unhealthy reasons that brought about the first marriage. In all marriages there is a dovetailing of healthy and unhealthy behavior patterns that exist in each of the partners. In the relatively stable marital relationship there is a preponderance of the healthy factors; in the unstable marriage (whether or not it ends in divorce) there is a predominance of the unhealthy. Since the unhealthy, neurotic factors are often unconscious, a divorced parent may gravitate, without realizing it, toward involvement with a new partner who will provide the same neurotic gratifications as the old. Even though a parent may resolve never again to involve him- or herself in a relationship with a person who possesses certain alienating personality patterns that were exhibited by the former spouse, and contributed to the deterioration of the marriage, he or she may unconsciously do so. Even though a person may actually believe that the new marriage is different, he or she may not be aware that the new spouse has the same psychological illness(es) as the old, and so the same sick patterns of interaction are bound to ensue. The person may not be aware of it but it may be obvious to friends and relatives who do not consider it proper to communicate directly their observations. But to others they remark: "You know, it's amazing. Alice vowed never again to get involved with someone who's going to exploit her like Harry did. Her new husband Lou is Harry in another body. I don't know how she doesn't see it. He's a loser from way back. In six months she'll be supporting him. How can she be so blind?"

Single parents should be ever alert to this danger. They should find out exactly what caused the breakdown of the previous marriage(s) of a prospective spouse. (I am truly amazed by the number of people who do not make such inquiries to a reasonable degree; even after they have remarried they may know very little about the reasons for the failure of their new spouse's former marriage.) The failure to gain such information may serve the forces that compel the person to find someone to complement the sick patterns of interaction. If the individual were to learn the reasons for the previous marital breakup, he or she might then be less likely to remarry the person. And the refusal to make such inquiries is often justified with such rationalizations as "It's none of my business," or "It's water under the bridge; nothing can be accomplished by bringing it up," or "I never discussed it because I knew it would upset him [her]." If, when contemplating remarriage, there appear to be difficulties already exhibiting themselves in the new relationship, such couples do well to seek counseling in order to determine whether they are involving themselves in the same old sick type of relationship. Although I provide such advice frequently, it often goes unheeded and I have seen a number of remarriages which were uncannily similar to the previous ones—with the same tragic consequences both to the spouses and their children.

An example of such a parent was John, who first came to me because of difficulties in his relationship with Brenda, his second wife. John was a commercial artist who, although not a large earner, had gained a solid reputation for himself and had a secure position with a large advertising firm. He married his first wife, a very wealthy young woman, while he was still a student, and they were supported by her parents. Following graduation John never had a very strong urge to succeed in his career and he suffered little anxiety over his lack of advancement because he was secure in the knowledge that his wife's money would always be available. However, she became ever less respectful of him, started to have affairs with other men, and after eight years of marriage she asked John for a divorce.

John came for marital counseling during the fifteenth year of his second marriage because he and his wife, Brenda, were always squabbling over how to deal with the children. John felt that Brenda was overindulgent of them; whereas Brenda felt that John was jealous of any attentions she gave to the children. As it turned out. Brenda's view of the situation coincided with mine. John actually viewed himself as a rival of the children for his wife's affection and would basically have been happier if he had had no children, even though he professed great love for them. Brenda had many real estate holdings which she had acquired from her father, with whom she was still in business. Although her money was kept separate for such things as vacations and the children's education, it was clear that her income gave John much greater flexibility as to what he could do with his earlings. Brenda, like John's first wife, had little basic respect for him. I saw John in therapy over a period of about a year, during which time Brenda joined us about ten or fifteen times for marital counseling. John did not get very far in really seeing how his dependency on his wife was contributing to their marital difficulties; and Brenda had little interest in changing qualities within herself (such as controlling attitudes and sexual inhibitions) that were also compounding the marital problems. The marriage ended in divorce, at Brenda's initiation.

Following the separation and divorce John continued in individual treatment with me. Although a passive and shy man, he did date—but mainly women who were assertive enough to initiate contact and communicate fairly openly that they would be receptive to dating him. Although John gained some insight into his passivity here, the pattern was too ego-enhancing for him to give it up and substitute for it one in which he would have to risk rejection by being the initiator.

About a year after his separation John told me about a new woman he had met, a widow, named Yvonne, whose husband had left her fairly well off and who, in addition, had a very good income from a small business of her own. From what John said about her, and from what I observed during two interviews I had with John and Yvonne, it was clear to me that Yvonne was materialistic, domineering, and had little basic respect for John. It was clear, however, that she was desperately intent on getting married again and John was going to be the man. Although it was not my job to tell John whether or not he should marry, it was my job to help him see how he was reproducing his old patterns and that his intended third wife was basically the same women as his first and second, although she had a different body. John married. Six months later he left Yvonne because he felt that he was being led around by the nose by her. Perhaps it was some sign of health on John's part that he initiated the separation. Soon afterwards John got a job in another city and I never saw him again. I considered it likely that if he did not get more therapy he would probably involve himself once again with the very same woman, but once again in a different body.

6

The Children's Involvements
with Others

Peers

In years past children of divorce often suffered significant social stigmatization. Generally, this (like other forms of prejudice) originated with parents and was transmitted through their children. Because divorce has become so widespread in recent years there is hardly a classroom or neighborhood where there aren't at least a few children from broken homes, and children of divorce are less subject to ridicule and social rejection than they were in the past. However, there are still situations in which children of divorce may be treated differently from those in an intact home. For example, children who visit their father on weekends may be freely invited to other children's homes, but parents may be reluctant to allow their children to visit in the home of the divorced father. He may be considered less capable than a woman of caring for the children, or mothers may want to keep their distance from him lest the relationship take on sexual overtones. Families that may have gotten together, for the benefit of both parents and children, may discontinue doing so after a couple has separated. Because of the common reluctance of singles and couples to mix (close involvement with a sexually available single person often becomes a threat to a marital relationship), the children in such a situation may be deprived of meaningful peer involvements.

Although social factors that may have caused the children of divorce to feel different from and less worthy than others have been reduced in recent years, internal psychological factors have not. Although those who argue that society should give greater acceptability to alternate life-styles may see nothing wrong with a child's living with only one parent, children do not seem to be strong adherents to this cause. Children of divorce see others who have two parents living in the home. They have only one and compare themselves unfavorably with those they consider to be more fortunate. Such feelings may become intensified by the apparent understanding and sympathetic attitudes of their peers. I say *apparent* because often the understanding and sympathy are motivated more by the sympathizer's own needs than those of the child upon whom the sympathy is being bestowed. In order for friends to reduce their own anxieties over this calamity occurring to them (it now becomes "close to home" for them), they may become oversolicitous of children of divorce (especially in the period just following the separation). By reassuring them, the friends are really attempting to reassure themselves. It is as if the consolers project themselves out onto the child who is being reassured and by comforting the friend they are simultaneously consoling themselves. And their questions about how the friend is dealing with the problem derive less from the desire to help the child of divorce handle his or her problems than from the need to provide themselves with information about how to deal with this misfortune should it befall them. Other parents may be solicitous of children whose parents have divorced out of pity for them, and overprotective in an attempt to provide these children with compensations for the deprivations they may be suffering. Such attitudes on the part of peers and their parents cannot but make children of divorce feel different, inferior, and somewhat defective.

In spite of recent enlightened attitudes about divorce there are still some children who are taunted or rejected because of it. Parents of children who are so treated should help them appreciate that the deficiency lies not within them but in those who laugh at them—that "there is nothing funny about divorce, rather it is a very sad thing. There is something wrong with a person who is cruel enough to laugh at someone whose parents have divorced." It may sometimes be helpful to suggest that such teased children respond with a comment such as: "There must be something wrong with you if you can laugh at someone who has had such a sad thing happen to him [her]." In addition, such children have to be helped to recognize that they are not necessarily what others claim them to be. Another reassurance that can help relates to the traditional "sticks and stones" saying, namely, that taunts cannot really harm. Most important, such children have to be helped to understand that they will ultimately be judged on the basis of the kinds of people *they are;* not on the basis of *their parents'* marital status. If they get along with other people, are nice to be with, and are respected, other children will want to be with them—regardless of the difficulties their parents have had.

Many children harbor deep feelings of shame over their parents' separation and may go to great lengths to hide the secret. Many will stop inviting children to their homes and find excuses for turning away those who do come— lest the parent's absence be detected by the visitors. Such a way of dealing with the separation only increases feelings of self-loathing and adds unnecessary fears of disclosure. Parents should tell the children that they are adding to their burden by responding to the separation in this way—parental separation is sad, but nothing to be ashamed about. Children should reveal the separation in appropriate places, and at appropriate times, in as matter-of-fact a manner as possible. However, if parents themselves are basically ashamed of the breakup of their marriage, they are in a poor position to provide their children with such advice. In such situations it is most likely, if not inevitable, that the parental shame will be transmitted to the children and will only add to the humiliation they already feel. Such parents have to work out and come to terms with their own problem in this area first.

On occasion, the divorce will have occurred because

of significant socially alienating behavior by a parent, e.g., drug addiction, chronic alcoholism, or prostitution. When such problems become known to the community (as they often do), then the children may be subjected to terrible ridicule and mockery. It is very difficult to help a child rise above such scorn and appreciate that there is something wrong with a person who would ridicule children for the behavior of a parent. But this is central to the approach to such a problem. In addition, such children have to be helped to recognize that if they are basically friendly and fun to be with, that they should ultimately be accepted by most for what *they* are and not for what their *parents* are or were.

Having been "abandoned" by a parent, children of divorce are more likely than children from intact stable homes to be distrustful of the stability of relationships with others, both adult and peer. These children may shy away from involvements that could provide substitute gratifications. Verbal reassurances do not work very well in reducing such distrust. Only living experiences which demonstrate that people can still be reliable are likely to reduce this distrust. And it is the absent parent's involvement here that is most crucial. If he or she continues to maintain meaningful involvement, then such distrust is likely to be reduced; if not, then it will probably persist and even increase. Only through meaningful and prolonged substitute relationships can the distrust be dispelled and it behooves parents to encourage and facilitate such relationships, both with adults and peers.

Grandparents

Just as in-laws may play a significant role in a couple's decision to marry, they can also contribute to a couple's marital difficulties, and even be one of the causes of the divorce. A wife may complain, for example, that her husband is still a child in his relationship with his parents. A husband may displace onto his in-laws hostilities that he basically feels toward his own parents—thereby causing a loyalty conflict in his wife that may play a role in the couple's marital difficulties. Often in-laws consider their son- or daughter-in-law to be a disappointment because he or she does not live up to the image they had of what their son- or daughter-in-law would be like. Parents generally tend to idealize their children, seeing them as cuter, prettier, brighter, etc., than others do. Such overvaluation is probably useful to the growing child (if it stays within bounds) because it can serve to enhance self-esteem. And when the child becomes of marriage age, parents tend to carry the distortion further and assume that the only suitable mate for their ideal son or daughter is another ideal person. When the son or daughter marries a mere human, there is disappointment, which is usually, if not invariably, communicated to the couple. And the son or daughter's involvement with his or her spouse may thereby be reduced in response to such parental attitudes. When marital problems arise, each set of in-laws may side with their own son or daughter, thereby intensifying the difficulties. And in-laws may play a significant role in helping a son or daughter decide either to dissolve or maintain an unhappy marriage. They may, for example, encourage the couple to "stick it out" because of the shame they might suffer over the divorce. In such cases the advice is being given in response to their own needs rather than the couple's. Or a daughter may be discouraged from divorcing because her parents may fear that she will once again become dependent on them, and even request moving back into her former home—this time with her children.

In an intact family the two sets of grandparents commonly compete with one another (sometimes openly, sometimes covertly) for the affection of the grandchildren. When this competition is kept within reasonable bounds, the children may benefit, because it can provide them with much attention, affection, and a deep sense of family belonging. However, when the children are subjected to questions regarding which grandparents they like better or are asked to take sides in any conflicts that may be present between the two sets of grandparents, then, of course, such "affection" is significantly diluted. When marital problems arise, the grandparents may take sides and become embroiled in the couple's conflict—

thereby polarizing the husband and wife even more and contributing to the multiple problems that beset children who are placed in the middle of such conflicts. If the grandparents can rise above the feuding of their children, and appreciate that by joining in they may be making things worse, both they and their grandchildren may enjoy the benefits of their continued good relationships with one another.

Following the separation, a mother with children may return to live with her parents. (Although fathers with custody of the children may also do this, it is far less common for them to do so.) Often financial considerations make this a reasonable and possibly the best decision. If the mother has to work, it is often better for the children to be taken care of by their grandparents, who, as familiar figures, may make excellent parental substitutes (especially in the case of the grandfather as a replacement for the absent father). Grandparents usually love the children more deeply than any housekeeper the working parent could provide. However, there are a number of drawbacks to such an arrangement that parents should seriously consider before making such a decision. Although the grandparents can enjoy an unadulterated and joyful relationship with their grandchildren when they visit on Sundays, living with the children is an entirely different story. It is easy to be overwhelmed by the grandchildren's cuteness, brightness, cleverness, etc., when one doesn't have to change the diapers, get up in the middle of the night with a sick child, break up sibling bickering, etc. When the kids move in, the joys of grandparenthood diminish rapidly. In addition, the grandparents have got to be somewhat resentful of the new obligations that they now have to assume. They've been through the whole child-rearing bit; and they've looked forward to a little more relaxation in their old age. Now they suddenly find themselves having to go through the whole scene again. And such resentment can contribute to conflict between the grandparents and their daughter. Having just moved out of one home that was filled with strife, the children now find themselves in another. Or the resentments that the grandparents may feel toward their daughter for providing them with this new and unantici- pated burden may not be expressed to her, but displaced onto the children. Or the unhappiness the mother feels in such a situation may make her less loving as a mother to the children. And in all these cases the children suffer psychologically.

Another problem that may arise when mother and chil- dren move into the grandparents' home relates to the mother's dependency on her parents. A more mature mother will generally be willing to suffer many deprivations and inconveniences rather than move back with her par- ents. The idea of once again living with her parents is abhorrent to her and she would consider such a move humiliating. A more dependent and immature mother may more readily choose the alternative of living once again with her parents. Unlike the more mature and in- dependent woman, she may see nothing inappropriate about the situation, suffer no embarrassment over it, and may even welcome it. The children of such a dependent woman ultimately appreciate that their mother is really still a child in her relationship with her parents. Their respect for her is thereby diminished, as is their confi- dence in her as a protector and source of guidance. They may look then to their grandparents as their true sources of strength—a situation that is quite detrimental to their relationship with their mother. Children in such a situa- tion may then consider themselves to have suffered two losses: (1) their father from the household and (2) their mother to their grandparents.

Another possible source of difficulty in such an arrange- ment is that the mother and grandmother may become quite competitive with one another over who "knows best" how to take care of the children. The children may then be subjected to very different schools of thought regarding their upbringing and can become quite con- fused and divided in their loyalties. Mother may consider herself to be using the most "modern" and sophisticated child-rearing techniques—techniques reflective of the latest advances in psychological thinking. Grandmother, however, has the deepest respect for the "good old-fash- ioned" methods that she was raised on and served her so well in the upbringing of her daughter. Or the grand-mother may be quite ambivalent about disciplining the children, considering this to be the role of their mother. Part of her motivation for taking this position may be to avoid their having any reason for being angry at her. In this way she enjoys the reputation of the all-loving, all-giving, good Grandma, and her daughter is looked upon as the family witch—again, not a situation conducive to the children's having a good healthy relationship with their mother, or their grandmother.

At times many, if not all, of these potential drawbacks to the mother's returning to the home of her parents may not exist (or they may be negligible) and the children may profit greatly from the arrangement. I wish to em-phasize that much of what I have said about mothers who return to the homes of their parents is only ap-plicable to Western culture in the last hundred years or so. Previously, and in many parts of the world even to-day, a newly married couple could not enjoy the luxury of a separate home, or even room(s). Accordingly, ex-tended families were the rule. Not only did three genera-tions occupy the same home, but an assortment of the children's uncles, aunts, cousins, and other relatives as well. Divorce or abandonment by a parent in such an arrangement was probably far less traumatic than it is for children in twentieth-century Western culture. In the extended family arrangement the children have many familiar surrogates—people with whom they have lived all their lives—who can take over the parental role when a parent leaves the household. And grandparents today have the potential to provide children of divorce with similar security and gratifications. People today are living longer than they ever have before and the elderly find themselves feeling ever more useless in a society that is not basically designed to utilize optimally their talents, skills, and experience. For many grandparents the pres-ence of the grandchildren in their home can provide them with a "new lease on life," and a new sense of meaning to their final years.

Separated parents do their children a terrible disservice by drawing grandparents into their conflict or by allowing themselves to be polarized further by grandparents' involvement. Ideally, parents should be able to see the grandparents as important sources of emotional gratification for their children and as people who, possibly more than anyone else, have the interest and capacity to provide their children with love and affection—the latter being the most effective preventive of and antidote to the harmful psychological effects of divorce.

Stepparents

When stepchildren are involved in remarriage the couple commonly fantasizes that the new marriage will provide a normal and natural family life. Such expectations are rarely if ever realized because of the multiple problems that predictably beset such new families. And if the children, as well, have been given promises of a rosy new life after the remarriage, they too are likely to be disillusioned even though the new arrangement may be far superior to any they may have previously had.

The wicked stepmother. In legend, story, and fairy tale, stepmothers have traditionally been cruel and wicked. And in real life, as well, stepmothers are not commonly portrayed as benevolent. So deeply ingrained is the stepmother's bad reputation that the name itself is almost intrinsically disparaging and many jokes capitalize on this. The word has become so associated with unpleasant connotations that many stepmothers squirm when they are referred to as such and insist that the term not be used, especially when they themselves are being referred to. I believe that one of the reasons for this tradition stems from the fact that a stepmother is a convenient person upon whom children can displace hostility harbored against their natural mothers which cannot be directly expressed. When a natural mother dies, her children may still harbor feelings of resentment toward her for having "abandoned" them—in spite of their awareness that she did not wish to die. Obviously, such hostility cannot usually be expressed overtly, or often even covertly. A stepmother, as a maternal figure who is very much alive and available, may serve as an ideal target. And when a natural mother is alive, guilt over and fear of her loss and rejection may prevent a child from directly expressing anger to her. Again, a stepmother may serve well as a substitute.

One can only wonder why stepfathers have been spared somewhat the stepmother's bad reputation and not equally served as targets for displaced hostility. Perhaps it is because children have traditionally been less fearful of expressing anger to their mothers than to their fathers. Fathers are usually larger than mothers, more physically powerful, and are therefore riskier persons upon whom to express hostility. Because fathers generally spend less time with children than mothers, they are less exposed to children's misbehavior and antics, less accustomed to, and therefore less tolerant of, their disruptive behavior. Because mothers generally spend more time with children than fathers, they are forced to discipline them more. Receiving more punishment from the mother makes it more likely that children will resent her, have more experience expressing their anger to her, and become more comfortable doing so. Mothers may even become the target of hostility felt toward fathers. All these factors contribute to the mother's (and the stepmother's) becoming the scapegoat, while the good name of the father and the stepfather is preserved.

The mother vs. the stepmother. Natural mothers, almost predictably, are rivalrous with their children's stepmother. And stepmothers are not famous for their benevolence toward their husband's former wife. A stepmother, in order to ingratiate herself with her husband, may try very hard to form a good relationship with his children. It is rare for a natural mother to respond with enthusiasm to these overtures. Mothers are usually somewhat possessive of their children. They do not take well to others who try to mother them, attempt to give them significant maternal affection, or otherwise take them "under their wings." In fact, were a mother not to exhibit such possessiveness, I would question the depth of her maternal interests. The children are thereby placed in a conflictive situation. With their loyalties divided between their mother and stepmother, they usually side with their mother—the one with whom they usually have the deeper and more important relationship. Their affection for their stepmother is reduced and she is seen as less affectionate than she may really be. One could argue that a really mature mother would appreciate that a stepmother can provide her children with many satisfactions to compensate for the deprivations they have suffered because of the divorce and that three loving adults are better than two. I myself have not met such women. And it is probably unrealistic for a husband to hope that this former wife will have anything more than a formal and somewhat stiff relationship with his new wife. Although it would probably be better for the children that there be less hostility and rivalry between the two women, and on occasion I have seen it happen, it is an unrealistic goal to hope for or pursue.

The competition between a stepmother and her husband's former wife is also intensified by the fact that the presence of the children requires their father's continual contact with his ex-spouse. When stepchildren are not present a new wife has far fewer fears about her husband's maintaining a relationship with a woman with whom he was previously involved. The stepchildren situation requires it. Another woman is very much on the scene and even though the husband may have achieved a state of true psychological divorce, she is still there as a rival for his time, interest, money, and involvement. And the rivalry may become intensified as each woman competes for the man's fulfillment of these obligations. However, if the husband has not achieved a satisfactory resolution of his conflicts with his former wife, the maintenance of the malevolent involvement not only deprives the new spouse of a relatively content husband, but threatens the new relationship because, as mentioned, such maintenance of hostilities represents a closer tie than neutral involvement. And in such situations the rivalry between the two women in such a man's life is likely to become quite intense.

Stepmothers should face up to the fact that the "cards

may be stacked against them" with regard to their forming a loving relationship with their stepchildren. Even
when the natural mother has totally rejected or abandoned
the children, the stepmother may find herself the butt of
displaced hostility. She must try not to take all such anger
personally. If she is genuinely affectionate, the children
will come to appreciate her and develop a warm, meaningful, and even loving relationship with her.

A stepmother should also be aware that she probably
harbors some misconceptions about her husband's former
wife. She may have spent countless hours listening to her
husband describe the various indignities he has suffered
at the hands of his former wife. Naturally, she will tend
to side with her husband. If he is still trying to wreak
vengeance on his former wife or maintaining other forms
of hostile interaction, she is bound to become his ally in
the battle. In such an atmosphere it is not likely that she
will be able to form a good relationship with the stepchildren because of their ties with their natural mother.
This is just another example of the harmful effects of
post-marital warfare and another reason why it behooves
divorced parents to do everything possible to bring about
a truce.

Fathers and stepfathers.   Stepfathers, in my experience,
do not seem to develop the same kinds of hostile relationships with their wives' former husbands as stepmothers do
with their husbands' former wives. Men, it appears, do
not seem to be as jealous and possessive as women with
regard to the children's developing affectionate relationships with others. This is probably related in part to the
closer relationship that the mother, as the bearer of the
children, has with her offspring. I suspect that the female
is innately more oriented toward child rearing. But social
factors are very important here as well. A society that
does not provide the female with opportunities for meaningful gratification in areas other than childbearing and
child rearing is likely to produce women who jealously
covet their children—their primary source of feelings of
self-importance. In such a society men, having sources of
ego-gratification outside the home—in their careers—are

likely to be less dependent on their children to give their lives meaning and less jealous of those who share their children's affection.

Stepfathers often believe it is important that they strictly refrain from criticizing their stepchildren's natural father in front of them. (And many professional authorities warn about the detrimental effects on stepchildren of such criticisms of their father.) In accordance with what I have said previously about children's doing best when they have as accurate a picture as possible of their parents—their assets as well as their liabilities—I am not in agreement with such a practice. The stepfather can be a source of valuable information to the children about their father. He should be reasonably balanced and objective when providing such information. Because he may not always be objective is not, in my opinion, reason for suggesting that he shut up entirely. The children have to be helped to determine when such information is likely to be inaccurate (when it is provided in a state of rage, for example) and to rely, as well, on their own observations to determine whether questionable information is or is not valid.

Children's affection (or lack of it) for their stepparents. It is common for stepchildren, viewing the new marriage as a source of pain for themselves, to fantasize breaking it up. They particularly enjoy themes of harm befalling the stepmother, whom they may view as the source of all their woes. And fairy tales certainly feed into and foster such fantasies. In the typical tale the stepchild suffers a series of pains and humiliations but ultimately ends up in a far happier state than the stepmother and other persecutors of the stepchildren who are associated with her. Snow White ends up marrying a handsome prince; whereas her wicked stepmother, the queen, is forced to dance to her death wearing red-hot iron shoes (in the Walt Disney version she is pursued by the dwarfs and leaps into a bottomless chasm). Hansel and Gretel first kill the witch (who symbolizes their cruel stepmother) and then return home after their final venture in the woods to find out that their stepmother has conveniently died. Cinderella escapes from the cruel persecutions of her step-mother and stepsisters by marrying a handsome prince. She ostensibly forgives her stepmother and stepsisters for the indignities she suffered at their hands, and invites them to her wedding. Then, as fate would have it, doves pluck out the stepsisters' eyes—right at the wedding ceremony. Subsequently they also conveniently die. Such tales not only gratify the hostile wishes of stepchildren toward their stepmothers, but provide hope that such angry fantasies will be realized.

Besides the use of the stepparent as a target for hostility felt toward the natural parent there are other factors that may contribute to difficulties in the relationship between children and their stepparents. We all experience some fears in new relationships, and children, being less competent to handle them, even more so. Children of divorce will usually be even more hesitant than children from an intact home to involve themselves with a strange adult. Having "lost" one important adult already, they anticipate a recurrence of the "abandonment" and are likely to need time to "warm up." Adults do well to take these factors into consideration. Coming on too strongly and overwhelming the potential stepchildren may make it even more difficult for them to get involved.

A factor that may contribute to a stepparent's bad reputation is the child's projection of his or her own hostility onto the stepparent. A child may reduce guilt over his or her anger by disowning it and attributing it to a stepparent. It is as if the child were saying: "It is not I who have hateful feelings toward her [him]; she [he] is the one who hates me." A stepparent is preferable to a biological parent as a target for such projections because of the child's need to view his or her parents as good, kind, wise, etc. Furthermore, because the stepparent has already been considered an expendable commodity, his or her rejection and removal for hating the child would not be viewed particularly as a loss. The child, however, will not so readily wish to remove a natural parent upon whom hostility has been projected.

Hostile behavior toward a stepparent can serve to test a natural parent's loyalty. When a stepmother, for example, is provoked by a child and an argument ensues, Father is often called upon to intervene or mediate. In such situations the child can learn with whom Father's true feelings lie: his own "flesh and blood" or his "chosen" wife.

When a parent leaves the home, the child is generally deeply resentful over what he considers an abandonment. The appearance of a stepparent on the scene may cause additional anger. And when stepchildren are brought in as part of the bargain the child may become even more embittered. And the stepparent as the one who has intruded in the relationship between the child and natural parent, and as the one who has brought along a horde of other intruders, can readily become a target of formidable anger.

Oedipal factors may contribute to problems in children's relationships with their stepparents. A factor that operates in oedipal conflicts is the incest taboo. In the distant past, long before man learned to record his experiences in writing, it is reasonable to speculate that men and women began to appreciate that sexual relations among members of the same family tended to have a disruptive effect on family life. In fact, the jealousies, rivalries, and hostilities that such activity could result in might destroy completely the family's ability to function together as a co-operative unit. It was probably also appreciated (again this is speculative) that a coherent family produced the most stable, reliable, hard-working, and effective children. Such children then were not only more likely to produce coherent families themselves, but were more likely to contribute to the success of the society. In short, it was probably recognized that the survival of a civilized society depended upon a stable family life, and that free sexual access of the family members to one another could be a disruptive influence on such family stability. Accordingly, incest taboos were created—not out of some higher moral or ethical principle, I believe, but from the very practical observation that the very survival of the society depended upon them.

Our sexual hormones, however, known nothing of incest taboos. They hedonistically produce sexual cravings with little concern for whether the object that may potentially provide release happens to be a relative. We have to learn that certain people are "off limits." Lower animals learn no such restrictions. Keep a mother rat in a cage with her brood and her sons do not hesitate to copulate with her when they become sexually mature. The rate seem to suffer no guilt (like poor Oedipus did) over the fact that they may be fathers to their own brothers and sisters. But even with this long-standing history, the incest taboo is a shaky one. Even in the relatively stable, intact home the children tend not to be too strong in their adherence to the principle. In the oedipal period, especially, children may be quite obvious about their physical desires toward the opposite-sexed parent. Although such desires may not be specifically for heterosexual intercourse, they do include various other kinds of heterosexual activities, erotic play, for example, or the observation of undressing and toilet functions. And if there is parental seduction, then the child's oedipal cravings are likely to be intensified. In the adolescent period, when sexual desires become markedly intensified, oedipal urges may become particularly strong. Whereas in childhood the likelihood of reciprocal sexual interest by the opposite-sexed parent was small, in adolescence it may be significant, because the adolescent's sexual development can be a source of sexual stimulation to the parent. The youngsters' attraction to the parents, then, becomes even harder for them to handle, intensified as it is by the parental stimulation. It is quite common for such mutual attractions to be repressed by both parents and children. However, like most repressed impulses, they often find release via symbolic and other forms of disguised expression. For example, an adolescent girl may complain how "disgusting" her father is when engaging in everyday physical functions. She may become "nauseated" by his chewing at the dinner table, the sounds of his brushing his teeth and gargling, or even by an occasional burp or belch. Such disgust generally covers up and serves to repress from conscious awareness the sexual titillation that results from such primitive physical expression. Although one may not immediately consider the aforementioned activities to be typically sexually arousing, they, like sex, are manifestations of primitive animal functioning and so may suggest sexual activity to the teen-age daughter, who generally has no closer access to her father's more directly sexual forms of animal functioning. The young woman who becomes anxious when eating with a date (sometimes to the point of becoming panicked) is often afraid of the sexuality implied by the primitive eating function. Or father and adolescent daughter may cover up their sexual attraction to one another by frequent bickering. Angry interchange can hide underlying loving feelings and serve to distract the individuals in conflict from their loving feelings that press for release. And all this may occur in the normal, intact home.

With stepparents the incest taboo is usually less strong on the part of both the children and the adults. Neither has had years of living together during which time there has been ample opportunity for indoctrination to the incest taboo (both directly and subtly). Also, years of familiarization lessen the novelty that enhances sexual stimulation. Stepparents and stepchildren are very "new" to one another and are thereby more likely to be sexually stimulated by one another. Accordingly, the situation becomes much "hotter" and more highly charged, and the maneuvers to decompress it more formidable. Violent arguments between stepfather and stepdaughter (as well as stepmother and stepson) are one of the more common ways in which both may protect themselves from their sexual feelings. In addition, the child, before separation, may have resigned him- or herself to the fact that the parental bond is unbreakable and oedipal cravings futile. When the parents break up, and a newcomer replaces one of the parents, the child is less likely to view the marital relationship as inviolable. A boy living alone with his mother may consider the arrangement a fulfillment of oedipal fantasies. The appearance of a stepfather on the scene robs him of the total possession of his mother that he considered himself to have had. Accordingly, the oedipal rivalry and hostility may become very intense. And a girl living with her divorced father may have similar reactions to her new stepmother. Prior to the separation the child had to come to terms with *one* rival for the affection of the opposite-sexed parent. Now that that one has been displaced, a second has suddenly appeared on the scene. It is as if after David subdues Goliath, a second giant suddenly appears from behind a mountain. And the child may wonder how many more giants there are behind it. Sometimes the sexual titillation, rivalries, guilt, frustration, and hostility produced by the sexual feelings between teen-aged stepchild and the opposite-sexed stepparent can become so intense that the youngster's leaving the home (to live with the other parent or go to boarding school, for example) may be the only viable solution to the problem.

Myra's situation provides a good example of how disruptive of a second marriage an adolescent's sexual rivalries can be. Myra was sixteen when her parents separated because her father was having an affair with Gail, a twenty-five-year-old woman. Following the separation Myra and her two brothers lived with her father because her mother did not feel that she could cope with raising the three children herself. One year later her father married Gail, who had never been married before. And Gail moved into the home.

Since Myra's father was about fifty at the time, Gail was much closer in age to Myra than she was to Myra's father. In addition, Gail claimed that she would prefer to be a "friend" to Myra rather than a mother. However, it was quite apparent that Gail was so immature a person herself that it would have been impossible for her to have assumed a mother role to an infant, let alone to a seventeen-year-old girl. Gail was demanding of her husband, kittenish, self-indulgent, and grossly materialistic. She thought about little other than clothing, jewelry, cosmetics, and decorating her new home. Myra ostensibly welcomed Gail's decision that she would be a friend rather than a mother to Myra, but in my work with her it became apparent that she was disappointed in Gail because she was being deprived of the guidance and protection that she still basically wanted even though she could not openly admit this. Soon after Gail moved in, she and Myra began lending one another clothing; they confided in one another (even personal matters between Gail and Myra's father); and often enjoyed passing as sisters.

The honeymoon, however, for all three was short-lived. Myra began to complain that her father took his wife's side over hers whenever there were differences of opinion. Myra resented bitterly when her father and Gail would go out on a Saturday night and couldn't understand why she couldn't go along since she and Gail were such good friends. On a few occasions Myra knocked on her father and stepmother's bedroom door and was told to go away with reasons such as "we're busy" or "we're resting." Myra was convinced that they were having sexual intercourse and bitterly complained that it was vulgar of them to have it during the day. "They're just like animals," she complained. "They have no sensitivity to the feelings of others." Within two months of the father's second marriage, bitter fighting between Gail, Myra, and her father became almost incessant. Hardly an issue did not become blown up into a major battle. It was quite clear that Myra was furious at her father for choosing a "peer" over her for a wife. And she was jealous of Gail's intimacy with her father, a jealousy that was made worse by Gail's flaunting her relationship with her father to Myra under the guise of divulging intimacies to a close friend.

It became apparent to me very early in my work that all three would probably require years of intensive therapy if there were to be any possibility of their dealing successfully with this problem. Myra was in her third year of high school at the time of the marriage and I felt that her being out of the home would probably be the most expedient way of decompressing the situation. Although this would involve her "losing" her father such a short time atfer she had "lost" her mother, I felt that the pains of such separations would be less than those she was suffering in this intolerable situation. Accordingly, I raised the question of Myra's going off to boarding school. Although each of the members of what had psychologically become a *ménage à trois* had mixed feelings about the recommendation, all finally agreed that it would probably be best for all concerned—which it proved to be. Although Myra's example is an extreme one, the basic rivalries exhibited in her situation are common, even though they generally appear in less dramatic and traumatic fashion.

Other factors may contribute, in varying degree, to children's impairments in their relationships with stepparents. Such children may feel guilty over their resentments toward their stepparents and believe that there are other good, upstanding children who harbor no such hostilities. Parents should reassure such children that their hostile reactions are normal and inevitable. If the parents themselves believe that children should be capable of unadulterated benevolence toward the stepparent, then they are placing an unnecessary burden upon the children and contributing thereby to their guilt. They should encourage their children to form good relationships with their stepparents in the hope that the painful angry feelings will be replaced by more enjoyable loving feelings.

The better the children's relationships with their natural parents, the greater the likelihood of their developing good relationships with their stepparents. If children, for example, have a relatively healthy relationship with their mother, they will tend to generalize and view other adult females (including potential stepmothers) as benevolent and will anticipate good treatment from them. On the other hand, children whose relationships with their mothers have been bad, who have been significantly rejected or neglected by their mothers, will expect similar behavior from a stepmother and this is likely to interfere with their forming a good relationship with her. Obviously, the stepparent's own personality and attitude toward the children will play some role in whether a good relationship with the stepchildren is formed.

Stepparents' affection (or lack of it) for their stepchildren. Because of the many factors that may interfere with the development of affectionate feelings in children toward stepparents, the latter are likely to be slowed down in developing loving feelings toward the children. Genuine love must involve reciprocity. If the object of our affection shows little inclination to respond, our ardor cannot but diminish. There are, however, factors present in the step-parents—factors independent of the children—that contribute as well to difficulties in their relationships with their stepchildren.

First, it is unreasonable to expect stepparents to have as much affection for stepchildren as they would have for their own natural children. We are more likely to develop a strong psychological bond with a child of our "own flesh and blood" than with a child born of other parents. Parents who believe that they should be just as loving toward their stepchildren as they are toward their own children are placing an unnecessary burden upon themselves and will inevitably feel guilty about not living up to this unrealistic standard. I am not claiming that it is not *possible* for a stepparent to love a stepchild as much as his or her own; I am only saying that it is entirely reasonable that he or she may not. There are stepparents who, although they do feel a preference for their natural children, consider that it would be harmful to the stepchildren if they were to reveal this to them. "They're all the same to me," they profess. "Sometimes I forget which ones are mine, which ones theirs, and which ones ours." I find such "forgetfulness" incredible and so, I believe, do the children involved. Such a stepparent would do better to relate to the stepchildren, at the proper time and in the appropriate situation, comments along these lines: "Yes, I do love my own children more than I love you. I have known them much longer and there has been more time for our love to grow. I do feel great affection for you children and I hope that as times goes on I will feel even more. The more loving things we do for one another, the more our love should grow. And that's the same with my children as well." The last statement should be included to let the children know that love must be worked at—one must earn it—whether one is a natural child or a stepchild. Along these lines, the stepparent is well advised to take it slowly with the stepchildren and let the relationship grow. Overwhelming them with hugs, kisses, luscious praise, gifts, etc., is bound to turn them off and retard, if not squelch, the development of healthy, affectionate relationships.

A factor that also predictably contributes to stepparent

hostility toward stepchildren is that they are an ever present reminder of the previous marriage—the marriage that
once was, the marriage that both partners would like to
forget. The stepchildren are not only constant reminders
of the previous marriage but require continual involvement with former spouses—a situation destined to cause
resentment in the stepparents—resentment that may be
directed toward the stepchildren.

A common problem causing difficulties between stepparents and stepchildren relates to the marked differences
between premarital fantasy and postmarital fact. A woman with no children of her own, when involved with a man
with children whom she wishes to marry, may entertain
unrealistic fantasies about how wonderful life will be with
him and his children. In her enthusiasm to get married she
may underestimate the problems that will beset her after
she has achieved her goal. Or she may feign affection for
the children out of the recognition that such displays of
endearment to them will make her more attractive to her
would-be husband. After marriage, and the lessening of
romantic euphoria that inevitably occurs when one lives
together with a *real* human being, the bride may become
oppressed with the new burden she has taken on. Other
women ease into the role of motherhood and gradually
become accustomed to its frustrations. Having it thrust
upon her cannot but produce feelings of being trapped
and overwhelmed. Disillusioned and frustrated, such a stepmother becomes resentful and is likely to focus her resentment on the children, whom she will consider the basic
cause of her difficulties. Even in situations in which the
children live with their mother and visit on weekends, the
stepmother is likely to grow resentful. Instead of spending
time alone on weekends with her husband, he is either off
with his children or they're underfoot in the house. And
such anger toward the children is inevitably sensed by
them and results in a further deterioration of the relationship between them and their stepmother.

One of the most common complaints made by stepmothers is that they are not appreciated by the stepchildren. The stepchildren come on weekends and "eat, shop,
demand, and take, take, take—there's never a 'thank you'

or one word of appreciation." The children, of course, are just treating the stepmother like their own mother. Who ever heard of a child's saying "thank you" to his mother for feeding him or her? From the stepmother's vantage point, the children "are guests, should behave as such, should be polite, have good manners, and at least show token appreciation for what is being given them— even though they may not mean it." Pleas to the father that he try to engender in the children a little more appreciation for the stepmother's efforts and sacrifices often prove futile. The kids have been "programmed" from birth to take mother's services for granted. The children's motivation to consider the stepmother's feelings is likely to be further reduced by their considering the stepmother to be someone whose presence they have to tolerate if they are to see their father. The situation then is likely to deteriorate to one in which the stepmother feigns her desire that the children visit, but the way in which she extends her invitations to the children (false smiles, stiff verbal instructions) reveals her basic desire that the children not accept. They sense her underlying rejection, hesitate to come, and when they do, they are even less prone to be appreciative of the stepmother's efforts on their behalf.

Loyalty conflicts are inevitable when stepchildren are on the scene and they are a common source of stepparental resentment of the stepchildren. In conflicts between the stepmother and stepchildren, the father's loyalty to both sides is continually being tested. Similarly, when the altercations involve stepfather and stepchildren, the mother's loyalty appears also to be on trial. When more kids are in the home ("his, hers, and ours") stepmother needs to spend more time in the children's upbringing. Father, although he may recognize the necessity of his new wife's time-consuming involvements with the children, feels rejected. And when stepmother directs her attentions to her husband, the children become resentful. The woman so pulled feels continually guilty, unworthy, and resentful of the children, whose presence is seen as the cause of her woes. Loyalty resentments are further compounded by each parent's natural tendency to view the children as an extension of him- or herself. When Stepmother criticizes Father's children, he may consider himself to be the one who is being criticized. And similar feelings may be had by Stepmother when Father is reprimanding her children. Lastly, when Father spends time with his new wife's children, who live with him, he cannot but feel some disloyalty to his own children, who are living with their mother. Resentment of the children, who by their very existence in the home produce such guilt, is common if not inevitable.

There is no perfect solution to such loyalty problems. Every party appears to feel that he or she is being neglected or gypped. The best one can hope for is that each party be sympathetic to the other's loyalty conflict and all resign themselves to the fact that with more people around everyone has to spread him- or herself a little thinner. All have to give more and take less.

Because a stepparent is not the natural parent there is a danger that he or she will be less committed to the children's upbringing. In such a setting, for example, the children may be deprived of the parental support and encouragement of educational pursuits that plays such an important role in the children's motivation in school. On the positive side, the stepparent is less likely to have the exaggerated commitment to the children's growth and development that places inordinate pressures on them and may result in their pursuing their goals with less, rather than more, enthusiasm.

What should stepchildren call their stepparents? It is the basic relationship between the stepparent and stepchild that is important, not the names they use to address one another. Parents should not try to force a child to use a name that he or she is not comfortable with. Often this is done to provide an appearance of intimacy and closeness for a relationship that may be somewhat deficient. Such coercion only makes the relationship worse. For example, insisting that the children call a new stepparent *Mom* or *Dad* when the children hardly know the person is likely to produce resentments and feelings of disloyalty. Accordingly, this manner of improving the relationship between the children and the stepparent is likely to make it worse.

The child's using terms like *Mom* or *Dad* can be confusing in that one may not know whether the child is referring to the natural parent or to the stepparent. In addition, if the natural parent has anything approaching a healthy relationship with the child, he or she will generally object to the child's using these terms with the stepparent. And the child himself will generally feel some disloyalty when doing so. As mentioned, the special relationship that most often exists between a child and a natural parent cannot so easily be formed with a stepparent. Referring to stepparents as *Mom* and *Dad*, then, is often contrived and probably should be avoided. When, however, the child's relationship with the natural parent is either significantly deficient or impaired and, in addition, he or she has the genuine desire to use these terms with the stepparent, then I can see no objection to them. In the more common situation, where the children still have a meaningful relationship with the natural parent, many children will use some combination of *Mom, Ma, Momma, Daddy, Dad* or *Pa* and the stepparent's first name. Some may call the natural mother *Mommy* and the stepmother *Mom;* the natural father *Daddy* and the stepfather *Dad.* Others will just address the stepparent by his or her first name. Some stepparents are comfortable with this, others not. Some may use a special pet name or made-up name. Just as the stepparents should respect the child's wishes regarding which terms he or she wishes to use when addressing them, the child should respect theirs as well. A situation to be avoided is the one in which the children do not use any name to address the stepparent and go to all sorts of trouble to structure their conversations in such a way that they will not have to address directly the stepparent with some name. Such a situation suggests not only that the individuals are not communicating with one another their awareness of this problem but that there are probably other sources of estrangement as well.

Stepchildren may resent another woman's taking on their mother's surname. There is only one Mrs. Smith and that's their mother; this second Mrs. Smith is an intruder, she can't use that name. In their resentment the children may purposely continue to refer to their stepmother by her previous surname, in spite of both her and their father's requests that they refrain from doing so.

It's important to remember that no name is intrinsically good or bad; it's one's basic attitude toward a name that determines whether it is acceptable. And it is the relationship between the two individuals that counts, not the names they use when addressing one another. If the relationship is good, most reasonable names will be mutually acceptable; if not, names are not going to improve it and even the most endearing ones will only be contrived.

The problem of the stepparent's disciplining the children. Disciplining the stepchildren often presents special problems for a stepparent. A stepmother may be hesitant to be as firm with her stepchildren as she otherwise might be —lest she alienate her husband. If she has children of her own who are in the home, they will immediately recognize the preferential status being granted their stepsiblings and will become resentful both of their mother and the "privileged characters." Such a woman is doing her husband no favors. By leaving the heavy disciplining to him, he becomes the "bad guy" and she the "good guy"—reputations that cannot but interfere with the children's developing healthy relationships with both her and her husband. A stepfather, also, may get sucked into a stepchild's ploy: "You can't punish me; you're not my real father." Stepparents do well to recognize that the best thing they can do for their children and themselves is to utilize the same disciplinary measures that they ordinarily would use with their own children. Children want and need proper and humane discipline—their protestations to the contrary notwithstanding. There is nothing in the relationship between stepparent and stepchild that warrants the children's being deprived of healthy guidance and discipline.

Adoption by a stepparent. When a natural parent has totally abandoned a child, then it can be psychologically beneficial for the stepparent to adopt the child. This tends to lessen the child's feelings of rejection. However, parents should realize that the human relationship that exists between child and stepparent is more important than the child's legal name. If the relationship is a good one, the adoption can be a small fringe benefit; if it is a bad one, it will be of little value.

Questions occasionally occur regarding whether or not a stepparent should adopt a child. A natural father, for example, may ask if he should give his daughter up for adoption by her stepfather. He may claim that he still loves his child and wants to maintain a good relationship with her, but she feels awkward in school and with peers because she has a last name different from that of her half-siblings, mother, and stepfather. If such a father's claim of deep involvement proves to be false and he is using the child's request as an excuse to give the responsibilities of his daughter's upbringing over to her stepfather, then I would generally suggest that the adoption process proceed. However, if the father's claims are valid and he wishes to remain the legal father but is considering giving up his daughter because he believes that it may be in her best interests to do so, I generally dissuade him from allowing her to be adopted by the stepfather. In such a case it is likely that the adoption will be psychologically traumatic to the child and the benefits of having the same last name as others in her household will be outweighed by the rejection implicit in the adoption.

There is, however, a compromise that can be recommended in this situation that is most often workable, namely, that the child use the last name of the stepfather but legally retain the last name of the natural father. Most schools, in my experience, will go along with a parent's request for this. When the youngster grows older he or she can then decide which last name to use. Switching back to the legal name becomes easier then, because the youngster is no longer so deeply identified with the family. Or he or she can then legally change the last name to that of the stepfather—without having to be legally adopted by him.

Financial considerations may sometimes play a role in a parent's receptivity to adopting, because once one adopts, one usually assumes financial responsibility for the children's upbringing—even if the marriage dissolves. For example, a stepfather, sensing that the new marriage is a shaky one, may hesitate to adopt from the appreciation that if the marriage breaks up the children's natural father will still have to contribute to their upbringing. His wife, however, may be very anxious to have her new husband adopt the children because of the greater financial security she believes they will enjoy with their stepfather's having the obligation to support them. Such deliberations may be complicated by lawyers who advise such stepfathers not to adopt and such mothers to do everything possible to get a new husband to adopt the children.

Another question concerning adoption that is occasionally asked is whether a child who is adopted in early infancy, and has never had a relationship with the natural parent, should be told of the adoption. A boy, for example, is totally abandoned by his natural mother in infancy. The natural father soon remarries, the stepmother adopts the infant, and he is brought up with no distinction made between himself and his stepsiblings. Having no memory of his natural mother, and still having no contact with her, the only mother he knows is his stepmother. The question is whether this boy should be told the truth about his natural mother. My answer is yes. There are a number of reasons why I say this. Should the child ever learn of his true origins he cannot but be resentful of his father and stepmother for having withheld such important information. And the shock of such a disclosure could result in lifelong distrust of them. The argument that the boy will probably never find out is not convincing. In such a situation there are usually dozens of people who know the story and the likelihood is great that either they or their children, by design or error, will divulge the truth. It is almost impossible to rely on dozens of people to maintain a conspiracy of silence. In addition, no matter how hard the stepmother may try to treat her adopted child the same as her natural children, she is not likely to do so completely. Even though she may have adopted the child in early infancy, he or she is still someone else's baby. She did not carry the child within her for nine months, she did not suffer the pains of its birth, nor did she suckle it (or have the capacity to if she chose not to do so). The psychological bond formed by such experiences is deep and lifelong and cannot but make her feel that the adopted child is somewhat different from her natural children. And the child, as he or she gets older, will come to recognize this, no matter what pains the parents may take to conceal the fact that "Mother" is not really his or her mother. Furthermore, we are living at a time when more and more people who were adopted as children are seeking their natural parents. Similarly, but to a lesser degree, individuals who have given up children for adoption are also seeking them. And organizations have been set up which actively and enthusiastically help such parents and their children find one another and even use illegal tactics at times to accomplish their goals. (We are moving in the direction, I believe, or making such information more accessible, so that illegal tactics may not have to be resorted to.) Accordingly, the couple's belief that there will never be any contact with the natural parent is less likely to be realized today than it was in the past.

If one could be 100 per cent certain that the child would never find out, then I might agree that no good purpose would be served by the child's knowing. Since this is rarely the case (if not impossible), the child, in my opinion, should be told. And I would tell the children when he is first able to appreciate such things—generally between three and five years of age. This is the same period in which children adopted in the more traditional fashion should be told of their origins.

As is obvious, the stepparent–stepchild relationship has many things working against its success that are intrinsic to the new family situation. There are many elements in the situation that are likely to produce resentments that would not arise in a family without stepchildren. Because of the parents' desire to make this new marriage "work," there will often be a tendency to suppress such resentments, and this is likely to result in many kinds of personal and interpersonal problems. All concerned must try to express their feelings about the situation, in the most civilized way, and have great tolerance for ambivalent feelings. Ambivalence is characteristic of all human relationships, and the negative feelings are likely to be greater in families where stepchildren are present. If these difficulties can be avoided or overcome (and they can in many cases), the stepchildren are likely to derive many benefits from the new relationship. Most important, the presence of a stepparent provides them with a "second chance" either to live in or experience an intact home. And it is the absence of such a home that is at the root of many of the problems that children of divorce may develop.

Siblings, Stepsiblings, and Half-Siblings

Normally, sibling rivalry is fierce. All children wish to be the favorite of the parents. All find one another convenient scapegoats on which to vent hostilities too dangerous to release elsewhere (for example, against teachers, parents, and peers). Teachers can suspend and expel; parents can discipline, punish, and withdraw their vital affection; and peers can reject. Siblings are therefore excellent targets for such hostilities because they are a captive audience; they cannot run away and younger ones are often helpless to retaliate effectively. Children are egocentric and greedy (they don't differ very much from most adults in this regard). With siblings children are forced to share (that damn word). And the more siblings there are the more damn sharing there must be.

In the home where children of different marriages live together such rivalries may become even more intensified. In the intact home one has a chance to accommodate to each new sibling. Generally the newcomers do not arrive at a frequency greater than once a year and the seemingly endless parade (again that word) is usually short (two to three in most families). The brood of stepsiblings arrives all at once. They suddenly descend like a horde and camp permanently. No tents and sleeping bags either. They're here to stay! And there's the *Lebersraum* problem. Rarely does a child have more "living space" to himself when stepsiblings are on the scene than when the first marriage was intact. And then there's the problem of different ways of doings things: "They like foods that would make us vomit; and yet half the tine that's just the kind of stuff they put on the table. They want to watch the stupidest TV programs; and so often we can't watch our favorites (and Daddy says we can't afford another TV set now)." With such frustrations it is no surprise that the sibling rivalries are more intense among stepsiblings than among full siblings. And when half-siblings appear (fortunately at a slower rate) a third category of intruder arrives on the scene. As products of an entirely different family, they have their own strange habits, infantile demands, inordinate need for the parents' time, and they encroach further on the family's already compromised living space. With so much to be angry about it is no wonder that sibling rivalries reach their fiercest levels among full, step-, and half-siblings.

What I have described so far are the inevitable and predictable rivalries that would exist even if the parents handled the situation in the most ideal manner and there were none of the other intensifying factors that I will discuss below. With regard to handling such rivalries, I have no simple solutions. In fact, I have no simple solutions to any of the problems of child rearing. Parents have to adjust to the fact that a certain amount of sibling bickering is normal, that even more will take place when there are more kids, and that when stepsiblings live together there will be even more fighting. Accordingly, one must thicken one's skin and try to tune out and ignore a fair amount of the noise. One errs in trying to find out "who started." Rather, one does better to place both combatants in separate rooms for some "solitary confinement" for a fifteen-minute "cooling off period." Although at times an innocent party will suffer by the implementation of such indiscriminate punishment, things tend to even out. Recognizing that even innocent parties can get punished when sibling battles get too much out of hand helps children remember to keep them under control. Traditional disciplinary techniques such as deprivation of a favorite television program and removal of a pleasurable activity may also help. However, the utilization of the methods I have described are not likely to result in a cessation of the fighting; they are designed more to preserve parental sanity.

Such rivalries can be intensified, however, by certain things that the parents may be doing. The expected preference that a parent will have for his or her own offspring is bound to be appreciated by the children. They will therefore see evidences of favoritism that cannot but intensify jealousies, and parents should not deny such preferences. That only makes the situation worse. Admit they are there and do everything possible to reduce them.

Mention has been made of a stepparent's hesitation to discipline properly his or her stepchildren and the intensification of sibling rivalry that can result from this practice. A stepparent's hostility toward the stepchildren can be transmitted to his or her natural children and this can significantly increase sibling rivalry problems. At times, a stepparent may use the natural children to act out the hostility felt toward the stepchildren. This can be accomplished, for example, by not appropriately disciplining the natural children when they bully the stepchildren. The natural children appreciate the parental encouragement for their scapegoating—even though it is not verbalized.

The sibling problems are so complex as to be mind boggling. The remarried partners may never have imagined before their marriage how much of a drain on their relationship problems with the children would be. Some remarrieds actually divorce again, not so much from major dissatisfactions in the marital relationship but from the desire to remove themselves from all the new problems that have arisen because of the children. Parents who are considering remarriage to one another should consider in great detail the kinds of lives they will be leading, not just between themselves, but with their children as well.

Therapists

How to tell whether a child needs to consult a therapist
Divorce does not necessarily result in children's needing therapy. How does one decide, then, whether or not a child needs treatment? Although this is a question that

trained therapists can best answer, there are certain things parents can look for to help them decide whether to bring a child for consultation. And it is on the basis of such a consultation that the therapist can determine whether treatment is warranted. It is important to emphasize at the outset that there is hardly a person who could not benefit from therapy. All of us, no matter how stable and secure, have some neurotic problems and inappropriate reactions. All of us could profit from a warm, accepting relationship with an objective and sensitive individual who is knowledgeable about human problems and receptive to discussing ours with us. How does one differentiate, then, those who *need* treatment from those who do not, since most could profit from it anyway?

Generally, most parents recognize that children will develop acute reactions (i.e., those of sudden onset) to the separation. Symptoms such as temper tantrums, crying spells, and disruptive behavior are predictable and most parents recognize this and do not consider such behavior to warrant psychiatric treatment. They recognize that such reactions are inevitable and will lessen and even disappear as the child gets used to the fact that he or she will only be living with one parent. One cannot be very specific about the normal duration of such acute reactions. Generally, four to six weeks is a reasonable period for them to exist. When they persist (especially unabated) then therapy, or at least parental counseling, may be warranted. Sometimes, the initial reactions may be so severe that therapy and/or parental counseling is warranted during the acute reaction.

The child who needs therapy is generally one who has exhibited difficulties for a significant period of time prior to the separation and his symptoms have intensified as a result of it. There are children, however, whose symptoms date from the time of parental separation but have persisted for many months and even longer. In such situations, the parents are usually involving the child in various psychologically detrimental maneuvers (using him as a spy, for example) or exposing him to constant traumas of a new kind (endless conflicts, for instance). The key principle, then, in determining whether treatment should be considered is the duration of the difficulties. Acute symptoms, especially those that arise in response to the trauma of the separation, are not likely to require treatment. The child is likely to work out his reactions himself by natural psychological processes. This is often accomplished through repeated questioning, preoccupations that serve to help the child become used to the new situation, and release of feelings through play fantasy. When these natural adjustment processes become blocked, either through parental inhibition ("See how brave you can be": "Stop asking me so many questions") or internal inhibitive processes already present in the child, then therapy may be necessary.

With regard to the long-standing problems there are a number of behavioral manifestations that parents can look for to help them decide whether consultation is warranted. One of the important areas to investigate is school. One would want to know if there has been a deterioration of academic performance and/or classroom behavior. Discussion with the teacher is crucial here, because he or she has been the direct observer of the child's classroom behavior. In addition, the teacher knows better than parents (and often better than many therapists) what is normal disruptive behavior for a particular age and what is excessive. Whereas in the home children's behavior is normally disruptive and they are likely to periodically defy parents, healthy children are capable of inhibiting themselves to a reasonable degree in the classroom. They well differentiate between school and home authorities and are able to refrain from expressing many things in school that they would guiltlessly reveal at home. Children without such controls are in psychological difficulty and may need treatment.

The child's peer relationships can provide important information regarding whether he or she is suffering with a psychological disturbance. Normally, a child will fight fiercely with siblings. A younger sibling makes a convenient scapegoat for one's pent-up hostilities, because he or she may not be able to retaliate effectively and cannot remove him- or herself totally from the older sibling's maltreatment. One cannot exhibit such wanton cruelty to peers. They not only have the power to retaliate but to reject and alienate. Accordingly, intense sibling fighting is a poor criterion by which to decide whether a child needs therapy; but poor peer relationships is a very good one. When evaluating a child for therapy I particularly inquire into whether the child seeks peers and whether he or she is sought by them. If there is some impairment in either of these areas, I look into the reasons. A child with significant difficulties in peer relationships usually needs therapy.

Unco-operative behavior in the home is generally a difficult criterion on which to decide whether treatment is warranted. Children normally balk at doing chores, keeping their rooms neat, getting up on time, going to sleep when they are asked, coming home when they are supposed to, etc. They generally take the path of least resistance, procrastinate as much as possible, and are happiest when their parents are "off their backs." Accordingly, difficulties in these areas have to be quite severe before I will consider them valid reasons for therapy. When such refusal to co-operate is so marked that the child does practically nothing around the house and when frequent power struggles appear to be the rule, then the child may need treatment. And if such lack of co-operation exhibits itself in school and interferes with peer relationships, then it is even more probable that the child will need treatment.

Of course, there are additional kinds of problems that may warrant therapy if they are to be alleviated in the optimum way. I am referring to psychological symptoms such as phobias, obsessive ruminations, compulsions, and the large number of other manifestations of psychiatric disturbances with which children may suffer. However, it is beyond the scope of this book to discuss these and if a parent observes a child to exhibit behavior that he or she suspects is caused by psychological difficulty, then a consultation is usually advisable. However, such symptoms, if severe enough to require treatment, will generally interfere with the child's functioning in school, with peers, and at home. So, if a child is doing well in school (both in the academic and behavioral areas), is getting along well with friends (both seeks them and is sought by them), and is generally (but not invariably) co-operative at home, the likelihood that psychiatric treatment will be warranted is small.

Resistances to treatment. Parents may be very resistive to the idea that their child needs treatment. They may consider it a sign of failure; and by denying that the child needs therapy they protect themselves from such esteem-lowering feelings. Most parents try very hard to do what is best for their children and in spite of their most dedicated efforts things may go wrong. Parents should understand that the child's needing treatment does not necessarily mean that they have been defective as parents. Child psychology is a very young field and there is still much that we have to learn. No therapist, no matter how skilled and experienced, is yet able to formulate a set of guidelines for bringing up a perfectly healthy child. In fact, we don't even know exactly what a fully healthy child would be like. Parents, therefore, who deprive their children of therapy in order to protect themselves from experiencing a sense of failure are being too critical of themselves and at the same time are depriving their children of what might be an extremely useful experience—one that could benefit them for the rest of their lives. And separated parents may be particularly prone to deny their children's psychological disturbance because of the guilt they may feel over their divorce. If they can believe that the child doesn't need treatment, they will feel less guilty over the potentially harmful effects of the divorce on him or her.

Children also may resist the idea of having treatment. Generally, one of the most important determinants of whether a child will resist treatment is the attitudes of his parents with regard to therapy. If both parents have a deep commitment to the child's having treatment, then he or she is more likely to respond positively to the idea than if one or both are basically resistive to the idea (even though they may go along with it). Even with full parental support, there are children who resist therapy. Some may believe that their seeing a therapist means that they are crazy. Parents should talk with such children and make it clear that their being in treatment does not mean that they are crazy. And that most of the children in therapy do not look any different from others in their class or neighborhood. Rather they have some problems in their lives (such as parental divorce) for which they need some help. (If, of course, the child's problems are so severe that he or she is called "crazy," then the child has to be helped to appreicate how cruel are those who so taunt him or her.) Some fear the stigmatization they anticipate they will suffer if others find out that they are in treatment. Such children have to be helped to recognize that being in treatment may be unfortunate, but that it is nothing to be ashamed about and that those who would tease them have something wrong with *their* own thinking. The child of divorce may have an additional reason for refusing therapy. He may already feel shame over having a divorced family and may not wish to suffer voluntarily the additional stigma of having to see a "shrink."

On the other hand, there are children who may be very receptive to treatment. They may understand that therapy can be of help to them. Children of divorce may have an additional reason for seeking therapy. They may wish the therapist to assume the role of a surrogate parent in order to compensate them for the loss of the real parent. If this is one of the fringe benefits of therapy (to the degree that it can reasonably be accomplished in the therapeutic situation), fine; it should not, however, be the primary reason for a child's being in treatment. Treatment should be suggested for therapeutic, not primarily social, reasons. There are far less expensive ways for the child to get a parent surrogate. If therapy is necessary, it is generally preferable that the child work with someone of the same sex as the departed parent, unless other considerations dictate otherwise. We can provide children with this fringe benefit of treatment without making it the sole purpose of therapy.

Divorced parents' involvement in a child's therapy. Children of divorce are most likely to be effectively helped with their psychiatric difficulties if the therapist works closely with one and even both parents. Even though the parents may be separated, or divorced, the likelihood of the child's being helped is significantly enhanced if both parents contribute to the child's therapy. Parental contributions to the psychological problems of children of divorce are so formidable that it is often a difficult, if not impossible, task to help them if some additional work is not done with the parents. Such work may include a variety of therapeutic experiences: counseling with regard to dealing with the child (the most common type of involvement in a child's therapy), counseling with the parents for their own difficulties (either singly or, on rare occasion, together), therapy for each of the parents (either with the same therapist as the child's or with a different therapist), and active parental participation in the child's sessions.

In some cases one parent may absolutely refuse to involve him- or herself in any way in the child's treatment. In such situations I generally advise the parent who is receptive to involvement to inform the non-receptive parent that his or her failure to contribute makes it less likely that I will be able to help the child. However, I will not refuse to treat the child and my hope is that the uninvolved parent will ultimately appreciate that his or her contributions can be useful to me and will increase the likelihood that the child's therapy will be successful.

Sometimes parents are willing to co-operate in the therapeutic process, but absolutely refuse to see me together. This is especially true around the time of the separation, when the bitterness between the parents is most intense. I generally respect a parent's wish in this regard and I then see them separately. My experience has been, however, that around the time of separation most parents are willing to see me together even though there may be some discomfort. Sometimes the parents are so enraged during the joint session that it may not be very productive—other than providing the therapist with an opportunity to observe firsthand the nature of the hostilities that exist between the parents. More often the parental hostilities are not so bitter that useful work is precluded.

Of course separated and divorced parents generally

want to have as little as possible to do with one another. Generally, if not for the children, they would have no contact with one another whatsoever. Yet, when such parents bring a child to me for therapy, it presents a conflict for me. On the one hand, I know that they do not relish the idea of working together with one another for the purposes of their child's therapy, and especially to be seen jointly. On the other hand, the chances of my helping their child are increased to the degree that they can see their way clear to such co-operation. I usually deal with the problem by letting the parents themselves make the decision regarding how much contact they wish to have with me, and how much they can tolerate involving themselves with one another in joint interviews. My experience has been that the more they can work jointly with me, the more successfully the therapy has gone. I urge parents strongly to make every attempt to work jointly with therapists who believe as I do (and there are many who do not share my views here) that such joint work is the best way to contribute to the alleviation of their child's psychological difficulties.

Situations that may appear to warrant treatment, but do not. Not all unusual behavioral patterns that may appear after the separation require treatment. What appear to be psychological symptoms may be manifestations of natural attempts to adapt to the trauma. For example, a boy may become preoccupied with a television story depicting a parental loss. He may become "hooked" on the story because it provides him with the opportunity to get used to and accommodate bit by bit to the trauma of his parents' separation. It is as if each time he repeats, talks about, or even playacts the story, he reduces his pain. Even though the story may depict his situation symbolically, and even though he may have no conscious awareness that the story relates to his own situation, it can help him adjust to the trauma. In fact, the symbolic representation may have been favored because it allows for accommodation without conscious awareness and its associated anxiety. Such a child may not need therapy. All he may need is his parents' permission to indulge himself in his fantasies. In all likelihood the time he is so preoccupied will diminish daily and therapy will not be necessary. Of course, if the preoccupations continue unabated and they occupy a significant part of his life, then other factors are probably contributing and therapy would probably be necessary.

There are parents who are quite insecure and fear that following the separation they will not be able to rise to the challenge of bringing up the child alone. Such parents may seek therapy to ensure that the child will not suffer from their own mismanagement. By putting the child in "good hands" they hope to avoid the harmful effects of their assuming sole responsibility for him or her. Sometimes such a parent will quite early comment to the therapist: "I want to put him in your hands, Doctor." The competent therapist will recognize in such a situation that it may be the parent, rather than the child, who requires guidance and possibly treatment.

There are parents who are very fearful about their children, and they may be quick to seek psychiatric consultation and even treatment for the most minor problems. Often such parents have had extensive treatment themselves and may be quite "sophisticated" about psychoanalytic matters. And when a separation has occurred they may be quite certain that the child is going to develop problems that will require psychiatric treatment. Even though the child has not exhibited any unusual reactions to the separation they may request preventive treatment. Treatment, in my opinion, is rarely effective if there are no significant problems to treat. If the patient does not have some particular problems that cause discomfort, the therapist hardly knows where to start. He needs some symptom, some "handle on which to grab," some problem to be put out on the table for both the patient and himself to view, if he or she is to conduct meaningful therapy. Such children should not be treated, but an inquiry by the parent into his or her own anxieties is certainly in order.

There are parents who project their own problems onto their children, see themselves as healthy and their children (or one particular child, singled out for this role) as being sick. A therapist may have a very difficult time convincing such a parent that the child is not the one with the described problems. Typically, such a parent will seek another therapist to treat the child. And if the second therapist concurs with the first, the parent will go on to a third and fourth, until one is found who will provide the desired treatment. If one searches long enough, one will eventually find the doctor who will say what one wants to hear, or will do what one requests. Such a parent may want vicariously to cure him- or herself through the alleviation of the difficulties seen in the child. Again, treatment not of the child but of the parent is indicated, but this is only possible if the parent can gain insight into what is happening.

There are other children who are not really in need of therapy but who are brought because of the parents' need to reduce the guilt they may feel over the separation. They know that the separation will cause the child pain and they hope to do everything to make his or her life as happy as possible. They wish to "leave no stone unturned" in ensuring that only good things will happen to the child and they see therapy as a way of bringing this about. Such children, of course, should not be treated. The indications for therapy are psychiatric disturbance, not parental guilt which needs to be lessened. Of course, such a parent should deal with his guilt reaction more appropriately and realistically. One of the more predictable ways to reduce such guilt is to avoid the kinds of post-separation problems that increase the child's burden and may even provide him with additional difficulties beyond those that inevitably result from the separation.

Sometimes parents will attempt to use a child as an "admission ticket" for their own treatment. Such parents appreciate that in the course of the child's evaluation the therapist will ask questions about themselves as well. The parents thereby gain the opportunity of becoming familiar with the therapist, and talk about themselves with him or her, without having to admit directly that they are there for themselves. In the course of such conversations they have the chance to "look him [her] over" and decide whether he or she would be acceptable as a therapist for themselves. Or such parents may not be consciously aware that they are really coming for themselves, but unconsciously appreciate that such discussions about themselves may result in the therapist's recommending treatment for them. Such a maneuver enables these parents to have a convenient excuse for not involving themselves by claiming that they have come for the child. In such cases, of course, competent therapists do not treat the child, but inquire instead into what problems these parents have that cause them to use such a devious route to obtain treatment.

Divorce in itself does not warrant a child's being in therapy. This is especially true if the child has a good relationship with the custodial parent as well as the one who does not live in the home. If the absent parent is uninvolved with the child or unavailable, there is a greater chance that the child will develop psychological difficulties. However, if the remaining parent makes efforts to provide such a child with surrogate relationships, then harmful psychological reactions may still be avoided. If the separated parents can achieve a civilized relationship with one another, they will lessen the likelihood even further of the child's developing psychological difficulties.

Clubs and Organizations

In recent years many clubs and organizations have been formed specifically for divorced parents and their children. Probably the most well known of these is Parents Without Partners,* which has hundreds of chapters in the United States, Canada, and various other countries. Although many parents join in order to meet possible candidates for remarriage, the organization provides a variety of activities that are of value to divorced parents and their children. Most chapters (and they seem to be everywhere) have various family activities, outings, picnics, etc., that provide children with opportunities for involve-

---

*Headquarters: 7910 Woodmont Ave., Washington, D.C. 20014.

ment with opposite-sexed parent substitutes. Discussion groups and lectures provide the members with valuable information that can be helpful to themselves and their children. Recreational groups for children and adolescent discussion groups help these youngsters feel less different and offer them opportunities to work out some of the special problems that children of divorce often have.

The sense of belonging to a special club and the feeling of communality serve well as antidotes to the feelings of loneliness that many single parents and their children suffer. There are a number of other organizations that provide similar opportunities for divorced parents and their children. Many are designed to attract specific groups like the college-educated, or people of a particular religious faith.

An organization that can be useful for boys who live alone with their mothers in Big Brothers of America.† Men volunteer to spend time with boys who are fatherless or whose fathers are not frequently available to them. Strong father-son type relationships are often formed and can serve such boys to compensate for the absence of their fathers. Recently, a similar organization, Big Sisters of America,‡ has been set up for children who need a mother surrogate.

It may be helpful for children to join clubs that are likely to provide them with parental surrogates. Boy Scouts, Girl Scouts, Cub Scouts, Brownies, Little League, Y's, summer camps, and various organized recreational activities can provide such parental substitutes for these children.

Boarding Schools and Foster Homes

Loving parents derive deep gratifications from living with and rearing their children—at least until the teenage period—and will suffer significant pain and frustration upon being separated from them. The parent is willing to

---

†Headquarters: 220 Suburban Station Bldg., Philadelphia, Pa. 19103.

‡Headquarters: 224 Suburban Station Bldg., Philadelphia, Pa. 19103.

tolerate the frustrations, sacrifices, and deprivations that raising a child entails because of the joys and satisfactions that child rearing can also provide. I believe that a parent who voluntarily sends a child below the age of puberty to live elsewhere, when there is a reasonable possibility of his or her living at home, exhibits some deficiency in parental capacity and involvement. And sending a child (from here on, unless stated otherwise, I am referring to children below the pubertal period) to boarding school is, until proved otherwise, a sign of such parental deficiency. Such parents typically justify sending off their children with rationalizations such as: "It's better for him [her] to be away from all the conflict," "Private schools are the only places where one can get a really good education," and "Our home is split up; there they have good mother and father substitutes, all in the same place." When "family tradition" is used as the reason for sending young children off to boarding school, then the *family tradition*, I believe, is one of neglect and disinterest in children. The fact that sending children as young as four years of age off to boarding school is common practice in England does not, in my opinion, make the practice any less harmful to children. When typhoid fever becomes epidemic it's still a disease.

When separated and divorced parents send their children off to boarding school they usually take pains to reassure the youngsters that they are not being sent away because they aren't loved. And professional authorities often strongly urge such parents to emphasize this fact. But the children know better. They know the truth. They know they are being sent off (with rare exception) because neither parent wishes to assume responsibility for their care. They know that their parents want them out of the way. Therefore, such reassurances are in most cases hypocritical. The child knows the parents' deficiency; lying about it only causes further distrust. It would be much better for parents and their children if the parents would openly admit that they are deficient as parents and that they are sending the children away in the hope that others may be able to do a better job. I recognize that this is not an easy thing for most parents to do. In fact, many such deficient parents cannot admit their parental impairments to themselves. Parents who have enough courage to admit the problem to themselves and the children do both a service. By such admission they avoid the lowered sense of self-worth that inevitably occurs when one tries to deceive one's children in such an important area. And such admission to the children helps them avoid the distrust of the parents that comes from being lied to about the reasons for their being sent away.

Some parents might argue that the pains a child may suffer from being told that there is a deficiency in the parent's capacity to provide love are greater than those which the child would suffer from the distrust produced by being lied to. They would still lie to the child in order to protect him or her from the devastating revelation of being told that one's parent has a significant deficiency in providing his or her own child with meaningful affection. Parents who follow such an argument are fooling themselves in believing that they can so easily dupe their children. How can the eight-year-old child, for example, not feel unloved when he or she is sent to live elsewhere at such a young age, at an age when the overwhelming majority of children (even those whose parents are divorced) are still living at home? Because the parental affection impairment cannot be covered up, the parents should not add the additional distrust problem. Such parents should help such children define exactly in which areas the parents still show interest and affection and in which they do not. As is generally the case in such situations, there is still some parental involvement, and the child should be hoped to clarify its extent, and the children should be helped to realize that such partial rejection does not mean that they themselves are unlovable. Rather, the defect lies within the parent. However, if they are nice to others, others both in the present and future can love them.

Some children may consider their being sent off to boarding school a punishment. It is not difficult to understand why this may occur. It is a painful experience just like punishment. In addition, the ultimate punishment for all children is loss of parental affection; and being sent

away to boarding school is most often just that. Furthermore, such an idea may serve these children's need to gain
control over an uncontrollable situation. Being sent away
as punishment for misbehavior is less anxiety-provoking
than being rejected at the whim of others. When such
children can believe that they were sent away for "being
bad," then they gain a sense of having control over what
is, in reality, a situation in which they are usually impotent. Reassuring such children that they aren't being sent
away as punishment for misbehavior is futile. (Again,
many professionals advise parents to give such reassurances.) Rather, these children have to come to see that
they are being sent away because of deficiencies in their
parents. They have not (in most cases) been particularly
"bad." What has been bad is their luck. The delusion of
control is best dealt with by the children's being helped to
differentiate between those things they have control over
and those they do not. They must learn to give up on
foolhardy quests (such as trying to extract more affection
than a parent can provide) and direct their attention
to pursuits in which there is a greater likelihood of success.

Some children prefer a boarding school because they
are thereby removed from the strife and misery of their
homelife. But anyone who believes that these children
are better off than those in intact homes (and even intact
homes with a moderate amount of dissension) is misguided. These children are just expressing preference for
the better of two detrimental alternatives. Even children
who request to go are not generally asking to leave a
relatively warm and loving home; rather, they see the
boarding school environment as exposing them to less
trauma than their homes.

The adolescent is in an entirely different situation. The
adolescent's being sent off to boarding school is not necessarily a psychologically harmful experience and does not
necessarily mean that he or she is being rejected by the
parents. If such a child has gained the benefits of good
parenting from one or both parents (either in a divorced
or intact home), the boarding school experience can be
enriching and maturing. But even in this period, the par-

ents should keep up frequent contact with the youngster via mail, telephone, and visits. Even though the boarding school experience poses less danger of parental deprivation for the adolescent than for the child, I still believe that for the early adolescent (up to about age fifteen or sixteen) a stable home environment is still better than the best boarding school. Such youngsters can still profit from parental model and guidance and the boarding school is not as likely to provide role substitutes for these roles who are as dedicated and involved as loving parents.

Much of what I have said about boarding schools holds for foster homes. However, in the foster home situation the children are more likely to be told that the reason for their placement relates to the fact that their parents cannot afford to keep them at home. Although financial considerations may very well play a role in such a decision, most loving parents manage to stay together with their children regardless of how difficult things may get. Parents and others involved in the care of children living in foster homes should help such children see through the rationalization of parental poverty, help them recognize the parental limitations, discourage them from the futile quest for affection from those who cannot provide it, and help them gain compensatory gratifications from others.

7

Concluding Comments

Some Causes of the Increasing Divorce Rate

A good way of understanding the reasons for divorce is to look into the reasons for marriage. If people involve themselves in a marital relationship for poor, and even sick, reasons, then the marriage is bound to be unstable and the likelihood of marital discontent and divorce great.

In the United States (and throughout most of the Western world) the socially acceptable reason for getting married is love. People get married because they find that they experience certain ecstatic feelings when thinking about or in the presence of a specific person of the opposite sex. In its full-blown form the blissful state appears to be all-pervasive. It enhances the pleasure that the individual may derive from even the simplest everyday activities, and makes many of life's inevitable pains more tolerable. The person in love comes to the conclusion that the particular party who is the object of his or her affection is the only one in the whole world capable of inducing this special state of elation. Lovers soon develop the deep conviction that these blissful feelings will last throughout their lives even though they have never personally observed anyone—except on the movie or television screen—who has sustained this state beyond a few years.

I believe that an important contributing factor to the development of these feelings of romantic love is the need to provide oneself with a narcotic. Like the narcotic,

388

it quickly produces intense pleasurable sensations and thereby provides enjoyment practically on demand. One need not apply oneself diligently over a period of time to gain pleasure; one merely need spontaneously induce the state within oneself and revel. (One need not even have encouragement or reciprocity from the object of one's affection; "unrequited love" can produce the same euphoric state.) In addition, like the narcotic, it makes one insensitive to pain. There are many painful feelings associated with the prospect of marriage—if one is to allow oneself to think about them. One is committing oneself to a lifelong arrangement—a decision that cannot but be extremely anxiety-provoking. The prospect of living *for the rest of one's life* with the same person cannot but make an intelligent and sensitive human being shudder. And the awesome responsibility of rearing children is certain to produce further anxieties. Romantic love is an extremely potent tranquilizer for the treatment of such anxieties. Narcotics also dull one's senses and make one less discriminating about what is happening in the world around. And romantic love assists the lover in denying deficiencies in the partner, deficiencies that may be obvious to almost everyone else, deficiencies that might cause most thinking and judicious individuals to pause before making such an important commitment. As with the narcotic, the ecstatic feelings are experienced only early in its use. As time passes the drug becomes less and less capable of producing the blissful state. Sadly, such is also the case with romantic love.

Another factor that contributes to the popularity of romantic love is its value as an enhancer of self-esteem. We generally admire most those who have the good sense to like us (and conversely, we are quickest to dislike intensely those who are stupid or blind enough to hold us in low regard). We cannot but find attractive a person who has selected us, from all the other billions of people in the world, to respect, confide in, and communicate sexual attraction to as well. When A communicates such feelings for B, B is flattered and comes to appreciate certain attractive qualities in A that somehow were never noticed before. B communicates to A his or her appreciation of A's assets and wisdom (especially with regard to having made so judicious a choice as B). A reacts pleasurably to such compliments and they not only confirm A's original impressions but produce in A even higher regard for B. A tells B of the ever increasing esteem he or she holds for B. And B responds in kind. An upward spiral of ever growing elation occurs as each becomes increasingly appreciative of the deep wisdom the other person has for admiring him or her so much. Central to the growth of this spiraling elation is the enhancement of self-esteem that the professions of affection (now called "love") provide. A mutual admiration society is formed—founded on the agreement that "if you'll admire, praise, respect, and find me sexually attractive, I'll do the same for you." There is yet another element in this phenomenon that enhances even further the feelings of self-worth of the individuals involved. If the object of one's affections is perfect, and if one is in turn loved by that perfect person, then one must indeed be a most admirable person indeed. It is as if the young man in love were saying: "She is perfect. Among her perfections is wisdom. She loves me. If she is wise enough to love me, I must be unique, adorable, lovable, wise, and maybe even perfect like her. Why, she even tells me that 'we're a perfect match.' "

Another aspect of love that contributes to marital difficulties is what I refer to as the "Some Enchanted Evening Across a Crowded Room" type of romantic love. In this variety, two complete strangers, merely on viewing one another (from across a crowded room is desirable but not crucial to the phenomenon), are suddenly struck, as if by a lightning bolt from out of the blue, with intensive feelings of affection and sexual attraction for one another. I also refer to this as the *acute infectious disease* type of romantic love. Here the individuals are suddenly afflicted with cravings for one another, as if striken with an illness. In both cases the individuals view their attraction to come from mysterious, almost magical, forces that instantaneously and irresistibly draw them together. Although some view the cause of the overwhelming attraction to be external (as planned for by God, for example), others attribute it to internal factors (such as "body chemistry"). Although I do not claim to have any definite explanation for this kind of experience, I would suspect that psychological factors are most important. The individuals enter the room predisposed to the experience, and even hoping for it, because of a lack of meaningful involvement with anyone else at the time. And loneliness may intensify the craving for such an involvement. The need for an esteem-enhancing experience and an antidote to one's pains and frustrations may also be present. Sexual frustration is in all probability present as well. All of these cravings may be particularly great at the time—explaining thereby the suddenness with which the individuals are drawn to one another and their immediately giving their being together the highest priority (so high in fact that they may ignore obligations vital to their well-being). Perhaps the object of the intense attraction bears some physical resemblance to an earlier love object, such as an opposite-sexed parent or a former lover. And when the two people start to talk with one another the attraction becomes solidified by a dovetailing of both healthy and neurotic needs.

The risks that one takes with falling in love with a stranger are no different from those one takes when one, for example, buys a used car from a stranger, or lends money to a stranger. One does better to get a little more information before entering into such transactions, and yet it is both amazing and pathetic how individuals who would never be injudicious enough to buy cars or lend money to strangers will be willing to sign a contract in which they take an oath to live together for the rest of their lives with a "stranger from across a crowded room."

All human relationships are ambivalent, that is, there is a mixture of both affectionate and angry feelings, of loving and hateful feelings. And there is no reason to believe that a relationship between two people who are in love is any different. If people are led to believe that only positive, warm, and loving feelings should exist between them if they are to have a solid basis for their marriage, then they are likely to mobilize various mechanisms to deny and repress the hostile feelings that inevitably arise in any relationship. And romantic love can serve this purpose. The obsessive preoccupation with how much one loves the other party can help obliterate angry feelings that must arise at times in any human relationship. We cannot satisfy one another's desires all the time; the frustrations that ultimately result in all close human encounters must produce resentments at times. Accordingly, romantic love not only provides a cover-up of angry feelings for those who believe that they should not be present in good relationships, but lessens the likelihood that the individuals will work out the problems that are producing the anger in the first place. In this way it contributes to the perpetuation of difficulties in the relationship and even to its deterioration.

It would be unfortunate if the reader concluded from this somewhat cynical description of what I consider to be important elements in producing romantic love (specifically, those elements that enable individuals to get married) that I am totally condemning the phenomenon. I believe that in moderation it can be an enriching experience that makes life more meaningful. It can be among life's most uplifting experiences and has served to inspire some of the world's greatest artistic and scientific creations. The person who has not tasted its sweet fruits has missed out on one of life's most rewarding experiences. It is only when it is indulged in to excess, when people are so blinded by it that they enter into self-destructive involvements, that I consider it a type of psychological disturbance. One can compare romantic love to the occasional alcoholic beverage. Used in moderation it can ennoble our spirits; when we are addicted to it, it can destroy us. I think that it is possible that in recent years there may have been some decrease in the tendency of people to become addicted. The "tell it like it is" philosophy that has become so popular recently may very well lessen the tendency of people to enter this self-induced delusional state to such an extreme degree.

Another reason which persuades people to marry is that marriage is supposed to enhance one's personal happiness. Whatever miseries one may have (and each person has his own collection) marriage may be looked upon as the universal antidote. The fairy tale ending "and they got married and they lived happily every after" is only one example of this traditional association between marriage and the state of happiness. Those who look upon marriage as a potential source of happiness generally believe that it is within the capability of human beings to "be happy," that is, attain a state of continual happiness. This belief seems to persist in spite of the fact that the believer himself never seems to have been able to reach this state. Things always seem to be happening to interrupt the quest, and even when one seems to have attained happiness, it never seems to last very long. And the belief persists in spite of the fact that the believer has never met anyone personally who has attained the state. One reads about such people, catches glimpses of their exciting and happy lives on the movie and television screens, but somehow the state of happiness seems to be attainable only by those whom we do not know personally.

Thomas Jefferson was wise enough to appreciate the fallacy of such an idea. In the Declaration of Independence he guaranteed us only "Life, Liberty, and the Pursuit of Happiness." He was wise enough to recognize that no one can be guaranteed a state of happiness, because life is such that we will inevitably have our moments of unhappiness. Jefferson would only grant us the freedom to *pursue* happiness in any way that did not interfere with the well-being of others. I believe that one source of happiness may come in the pursuit of a goal and another around the time of the achievement of the goal. We do not then remain in a perpetual state of elation. Rather, when the happy feelings recede somewhat we usually look toward additional or other objectives to pursue in order to gain once again the feelings of happiness. Accordingly, those who view marriage as a source of continual happiness are bound to become disillusioned when it inevitably fails to provide them with such a state. And they then divorce, stating: "We are no longer happy."

Many marry because it is the "thing to do." Although they will profess "love" as their reason for marrying, their real motive may have less to do with affection than with the desire to do the socially accepted thing. As young people grow older, and more and more of their friends "take the step," they feel ever more pressure to go along with the group. Married and single people often do not mix well socially (they often "play it safe" by not placing themselves in tempting situations with sexually available people) and so the person who remains single may find him- or herself becoming increasingly isolated from friends who are marrying. Most people dread being significantly different from the majority (professions of independent thinking and acting notwithstanding) and will marry is order to fit in with the crowd. Of course, such marriages, based as they are on factors external to the relationship, are not likely to have the inner cohesion necessary to their survival as viable relationships. In recent years there has probably been some reduction of this factor in people's marrying. The single state has become more socially acceptable. Accordingly, fewer people have probably married for this reason (although I consider it still to be a very popular, but unadvertised, motive for marrying). And others, who have married for this reason, are coming to appreciate the absurdity of their decision and divorcing accordingly.

Many believe that the ideal marriage is one in which the spouses enjoy doing together most of the important activities of their lives. "Togetherness" appears to be the ideal to be achieved. The individuals live together, sleep together, raise children together, and socialize as "a couple." Invitations are invariably addressed to "Mr. & Mrs." Saturday night invitations are responded to with "We can't make it this week. How about next week?" I often refer to this as The Siamese Twin Theory of Marriage. No other human relationship makes such demands. No other human relationship requires so much unified activity between two people. To the degree that the couple (that word again) adhere to this theory, to that degree will they suffer mounting resentments and a desire for "freedom." Another name I give to this concept of marriage is The Three-Legged Race Theory of Marriage. Like the three-legged race, in which each of the contestants consists of two people, each of whom has one leg bound to the other, the couple hobbles along so bound. And a marriage in which the two individuals are so tied together is bound to fall flat on its face.

In recent years, with increasing appreciation that too much togetherness can be a significant source of frustration and difficulty in a marriage, many have become "more liberated" and each has done his or her "thing." Certainly this is a good trend. However, there are still certain problems that have yet to be solved. Most will agree that greater opportunity for a variety of separate experiences is healthy for a marriage. The crucial question has been how much involvement in extra-domestic activities is good for a relationship and when is the point reached where it may threaten the marriage or be a manifestation of a deficiency in it? Couples vary considerably regarding their interest in and tolerance for such activities with other persons on the part of a spouse.

When such experiences, however, include extramarital sex, many would say that things have gone too far. Some believe that jealousy over a partner's involvement in extramarital sex is inevitable in a close human relationship. They believe that the closer the relationship the more pained one will be over a partner's extramarital sexual activities. Others hold that such jealousy is socially conditioned and that the mature individual feels no such jealousy and places no such restrictions on a partner. I am inclined to agree with the first view and believe that anyone who experiences no pained or jealous reactions to a partner's extramarital sexual involvement has a somewhat superficial relationship. This may not be the final answer, but it is most reasonable to me. Man is a very malleable animal and human beings can be taught to believe practically anything. Perhaps one can, through early training, produce a new breed of individuals most, if not all, of whom will not be jealous over a partner's extramarital sex. Although personally doubtful, I still must admit to the possibility. I only present this as one of the problems that one must deal with in deciding how much variety and independent experience is tolerable in a marriage. Obviously, the conflicts surrounding this issue contribute to marital dissatisfaction and divorce. And they arise from the feelings of restriction when there is too much togetherness, and the feelings of jealousy and other resentful reactions when there is too little. It is rare for a couple to reach the ideal point somewhere in the middle.

Economic fluctuations notwithstanding, we in Western society are enjoying an ever improving situation with regard to material comforts and free time. Prior to this century (and still today in most parts of the world) people's primary interest was in survival. Life was a practically endless struggle to stay alive. Few could indulge themselves the luxury of seriously considering adopting a different way of life. And those who did consider it might soon conclude that it was impossible. Most were locked in from birth to a particular path.

All this has changed. We in America live in the "land of opportunity." There are supposed to be no bounds to where we can go. A boy born in a log cabin can become President. Horatio Alger stories abound. The poor boy can become a millionaire. Opportunities are limitless. On top of this heritage we have more recently become enamored with the concept of "self-fulfillment." We are told that we must do everything to "maximize our potential" and "do our own things." Although there are healthy aspects to such trends, many have used "self-realization" as a justification for self-indulgence. Expressing one's individuality has often been done with little concern for the harmful effects on others of such "self-fulfillment." And the mass media have added to the problem. We are bombarded with images of countless objects and experiences, only a fraction of which we can possibly acquire, which produce cravings and frustrations that might not have otherwise arisen. We are led to believe that we are not getting our share of the joys of life and are given exciting views of those who are allegedly getting theirs. It is not surprising, then, that many leave their marriages in the hope that they will thereby be free to fulfill themselves materially and/or experientially.

Although in its early history, America was certainly a country of great mobility, there was much less mobility in the past than there is today. In our early years when one went West, for example, one went to *settle* someplace—to settle and remain there for the rest of one's life. Today we experience a much greater kind of mobility. People from rural areas move to the cities. People from the cities migrate to the suburbs. And more recently, people from the cities and suburbs are gravitating toward small towns. Companies relocate and take with them their employees. Executives and their families are shifted around the country like chessmen on a board. Children grow up and spread themselves all over the country. In such a world there is little sense of having roots, little feelings for permanence, and little commitment to long-standing human relationships. And the same comfort with loose bonds with friends and relatives may weaken the marriage bond as well and play a role in our ever growing divorce rate.

We are very much a youth-worshiping culture. There was a time when the elderly were revered for their experience and were not considered ugly. Today we farm them out to nursing homes to spend their last years watching television. The youth culture reigns and beauty reigns supreme. The mass media contribute significantly to this mystique, as do advertisers, manufacturers, and salesmen. Many people consider themselves the object of envy because of the beautiful partner they have acquired. And the partner is flaunted like the expensive new car, jewelry, or fur coat. The self-esteem of such individuals, then, is dependent upon the maintenance of the physical attractiveness of the partner. A marriage based on the hope that such beauty will persist is inevitably doomed.

The Women's Liberation Movement has contributed (and is still doing so) to the lessening of many prejudices that were deeply entrenched in our social structure. One of the outgrowths of this movement has been increasing dissatisfaction on the part of many women with domestic life. Many have become freer to express their basic dissatisfaction with the childbearing and child-rearing role and have abandoned it entirely. And it has been easier for women to do this in recent years than in the past because women have more of the education and skills so useful to have if one is thinking of existing independently of a husband. In short, more women today can afford to divorce than in the past—and more are doing so.

No-fault divorce laws have also contributed significantly to the rising divorce rate. As I have mentioned, the idea that divorce should be granted only if one party has committed a "crime" such as adultery, drug addiction, or alcoholism, is a legacy of the past. Although the passage of no-fault divorce laws is certainly a sign of progress and has eased the burdens and suffering of many, I am not convinced that these laws are an unmixed blessing. Since they make it so easy for people to dissolve a marriage, there are many who are unwilling to suffer what I would consider to be the usual frustrations and resentments intrinsic to the institution. Accordingly, a separation and divorce may be misguided and, if children are involved, even more damage is done. There is no question that many marriages that would have survived fairly successfully in former days, when there were more stringent divorce laws, have been dissolved too easily under the new laws, to the detriment of all concerned. I am not suggesting repeal of these new laws, however; they have still done much more good than harm.

Another factor that has contributed to our rising divorce rate is our increased life-span. Prior to the twentieth century, most people married in the early to mid-teens; children came along quite quickly; they were out of the house by the time most couples were in their thirties; and most people died in their forties. In short, one could not reasonably look forward to years of living after one's children grew up. Most people today can anticipate twenty-five or more years of productive living after their children are self-sufficient. Both in the past and today many stayed together for the sake of the children and/or found the children a bond that provided them with a mutual purpose. In the past, one didn't have too many years after the children grew up to build up marital intolerance to the point where one got divorced; one died before one had the chance to get a divorce. Today, there is still too much life to live for most people to "hang in" with a relationship that no longer seems to have purpose or meaning

In essence, if people live longer, marriages will last longer, and the percentage of marriages that will end in divorce is bound to increase.

A variety of other factors have played a role in increasing the divorce rate. The weakening of organized religion has certainly contributed. Fewer people remain in unhappy marriages because of religious restrictions and fewer feel guilty over breaking them when dissolving their marriages. In recent years, with the breakdown of many religious and racial prejudices, we have witnessed a greater incidence of marriage between persons of different cultures, classes, races, religions, and creeds. It may be that such marriages are less stable than those between individuals of the same ethnic background. We live in a world where there is less veneration of marriage as an institution and greater social acceptability of divorce. In the past many stayed together in their unhappy marriages because they could not face the social stigmatization that befell the divorced person. Today there is little such stigma and this has made it easier for many to divorce who might not have in the past.

It may also be that my own field, psychoanalysis (and the various forms of therapy that stem from it), may have played a role in the increasing divorce rate. There is no question that psychotherapy has helped many marriages and placed them on a more secure foundation. However, there is no question as well that such treatment has also caused many divorces. How the balance tips, whether therapy has prevented more divorces than it has brought about is anyone's guess. I would not hazard one because I have absolutely no way of knowing. As mentioned earlier, when one partner is in therapy and becomes healthier, the other (whether or not he or she is in therapy) may rise to the occasion and become healthier as well. In such cases the therapy will have served to place the marriage on a securer footing. If, however, the other partner cannot or will not relate in a healthier way, the resulting conflicts may result in a divorce. The two individuals are no longer dancing to the same tune, so to speak; they are out of step with one another and an ongoing relationship becomes difficult if not impossible.

When one partner is in treatment for a marital problem and the therapist strictly refuses to see the patient's marital partner, then the likelihood of that marital problem being worked out is, in my opinion, extremely small. And this type of treatment has, in my opinion, brought about many divorces in marriages that would have otherwise been salvaged had the therapist been more receptive to some involvement by the patient's partner.

Changes That May Reduce the Divorce Rate

Many changes are taking place today that may ultimately reverse the spiraling divorce rate. Some of these changes should lessen the likelihood of unsound marriages ever occurring in the first place.

The greater freedom for premarital sexual experience makes it less likely that people today are going to marry primarily for sexual gratification. The greater availability of contraceptive devices and the relaxing of restrictions (social, legal, and religious) on their use make it more likely that people will engage in premarital sex—and therefore not marry primarily for sexual gratification. In addition, the more widespread use of contraceptives make it less likely that unmarried women will get pregnant and marry because they are pregnant. The widespread legalization of abortion also makes it less likely that people will get married because the woman is pregnant. And the reduction of the stigma associated with obtaining an abortion makes it easier for women to undergo the procedure. The lessened stigma of unwed motherhood, also, is probably bringing about fewer injudicious marriages.

In the past a young woman who lived together with a man prior to marriage was considered to be immoral—a disgrace to her family. In recent years the practice has become quite widespread and such women do not suffer anywhere near the stigma they did in the past. Their parents often have to go through a period of adjustment but they, too, often come to recognize ultimately the wisdom of such a decision. I believe that the practice has already reduced, and should continue to reduce, the number of misguided marriages. Often, when the couple reaches the point where they are giving serious thought to having children they then feel some obligation to make some decision regarding whether they will marry. Divorced people, as well, are also living together more frequently in order to be sure that they do not once again enter into a bad marriage.

Earlier in this chapter I have discussed how the Women's Liberation Movement may have contributed to the increased divorce rate by its having enabled women to gain the education, skills, and financial resources to remove themselves from unhappy marriages. However, it may be that the very same opportunities for women may serve to keep other marriages intact. Having such extra-domestic opportunities may make many women less frustrated with their lives and more willing to tolerate many of the inevitable frustrations and restrictions that child rearing and marriage entail.

There are other changes that I think could be instituted that might contribute to a reduction in the frequency of unfortunate marriages. In most educational systems, courses in family living, family psychology, and child rearing are usually minor courses, sometimes still taught by the gymnasium teacher, and they are not given the distinction of such major courses as history, mathematics, science, and English. Accordingly, students tend to take them less seriously. I believe that family living courses are the most important a youngster can take. I believe that they should be major courses from the sixth grade on and if a youngster fails such a course, he should have to repeat it just as he would one of the traditional major courses. We seem to take it for granted that child rearing and family living need not be taught in a formal education program. The assumption appears to be that with the physical capability of being able to father and mother children comes the knowledge of how to adjust in a marriage and rear children. Although in recent years schools have certainly given more attention to such teaching, the courses are still not ranked as among the more important, and, worse, are not taught by people specially trained to teach them.

The educational system can serve in other ways to

bring about a reduction of the divorce rate. It can help children appreciate the fallacies advanced and perpetuated by the public media and the advertising industry: of lifelong ecstasy provided by romantic love, of the "beautiful people" and the joyful lives they lead, of the ever charming wives (even when scrubbing the floors) who are continually seductive to their husbands, and of the ever attentive husbands who never stop adoring and doting over their wives. Schools must also help engender in children the values of responsibility and commitment, not only by word but by deed. These qualities are essential to the survival of the family as well as society. There have always been (and will probably always be) a significant percentage of the population who do not adhere to these values. Such individuals have not only failed to contribute to the advancement of civilized society but have retarded its growth. I believe that in recent years, in Western society, we have witnessed a decline of the esteem with which people have held the values of responsibility and commitment. They have fallen into disrepute. And such decline has contributed to the increasing divorce rate. People today, I believe, feel less commitment to and responsibility for their spouses and children than they have in the past. Many teachers have reflected such decline and have thereby failed to communicate these values to their students because they have not served as models themselves for them, nor have they been able to teach them with conviction. If we are to reverse the trend of ever increasing divorces, society must once again bring about a general appreciation of and respect for these values. And both the family and school are crucial in serving to reach this goal.

Another change that I believe would also reduce the high divorce rate would be the establishment of a mandatory waiting period between the time a couple was granted a marriage license and the time they were permitted to marry. A couple can usually get married within a few days of making the decision; divorces, by contrast, even with no-fault divorce laws, can take many months and even years to get. I think that three to six months would be an optimal waiting period for those wishing to marry. The mandatory "cooling-off" period would be waived only if the people could prove that they had been living together during the prescribed period or if the woman were pregnant. Of course, there are loopholes in such a system. A woman could bring a pregnant friend's urine for testing and use that to prove that she is pregnant. And one could get a false statement from a landlord regarding how long a couple has been living together. However, in spite of its loopholes, the principle is still a valid one and I think it would be effective in reducing the divorce rate.

Allowing people to marry on short notice has served to protect pregnant women from the embarrassment of marrying with a swollen belly. And it lessens the chances that the children of such marriages will ultimately learn that they were conceived prior to their parents' marriage. In addition, allowing for quick marriage when a woman is pregnant reduces the likelihood that the couple will change their minds—with the result that the community may have to assume the cost of the care of the child born out of wedlock. The plan I have outlined above would still provide the pregnant woman, her children, and the community with these protections because such a woman would not be required to wait out the cooling-off period. In addition, it would provide the non-pregnant woman with protection against impetuous and misguided marriages—marriages that are more likely to end in divorce.

Whereas prior to the twentieth century people in their teens were probably prepared psychologically to marry, this is not the case for many people in an industrialized society. Prior to this century a teen-ager could strike out on his own, earn a living without too much education or prolonged training, and was considered an adult by society. (Child labor laws are an early twentieth-century phenomenon.) Adolescents today are still very much children. The long training required before they can assume a responsible position in our complex industrial society requires a more prolonged dependency on parents. They are not considered adults by society and they do not really consider themselves to be fully grown either—in spite of their strong professions that they are fully capable of assuming full adult responsibility. Accordingly, most adolescents today are not ready for marriage and it is no surprise that the divorce rate is highest in this age bracket.

Anything that can reasonably be done to discourage adolescent marriages can contribute to a lowering of the divorce rate. Parents should teach their children during their formative years about the inadvisability of marrying during the teens. Educational programs on family living would do well to drive home this message. The mandatory cooling-off period of three to six months proposed above for adults should be longer for teen-agers—nine to twelve months, for example. All states require a person to have reached a certain age before he or she can marry. The minimum age varies with the state. On the average, for the United States as a whole, males have to reach twenty and females nineteen in order to marry *without* parental consent. The minimum ages to marry *with* parental consent are lower and also vary from state to state. The average is about seventeen for males and sixteen for females. Although I believe that these ages are too low, I do not think it reasonable to place higher the ages at which one can marry without parental consent, but I would like to see a raising of the minimum ages at which one can marry with parental consent. Again, I would allow for a waiving of the requirement if the woman were pregnant or if there were other special circumstances that warranted such waiving. (In most states today the court has the authority to marry couples below the age of consent and a woman's being pregnant is one of the considerations that may result in the court's utilizing this authority.) In making such proposals I am fully aware that externally imposed legal restrictions are far less desirable than internal convictions as determinants of when one marries. Accordingly, I would rely more on the parental and school educational exposures to discourage early marriages than the legal restrictions. However, the legal position can affect the psychological state of such youngsters and contribute to their deferring marriage until they are older.

Changes That May Reduce the Suffering of Divorcing People

In various parts of this book I have been very critical of lawyers and certain aspects of the legal system. (I blame the system more than the lawyers. They are often the victims of a system that is not of their own making.) I have been especially critical of the adversary system when applied to divorce and custody litigation. I believe that if one is going to find fault it behooves one to provide constructive proposals to rectify the deficiencies that one is criticizing. Toward that end, I would like to make some recommendations that I believe can be useful in divorce and custody litigation.

At the present time, when a couple wishes to give divorced each partner is encouraged, if not required, to get his or her own lawyer. Lawyers are advised by their professional societies to discourage clients who come to them as a couple. Although it is not illegal for one lawyer to represent both parties, the practice is generally frowned upon and is considered to border on the unethical. There is, as well, no formal legal apparatus enabling the lawyer so to serve. In the system that I would recommend, if a couple decided that they wished to get divorced —and if the decision had definitely been made—they would have the choice of proceeding along either of two paths. The first would be along traditional lines: each could get his or her own lawyer and they would fight it out within the structure of the adversary system. The second alternative would allow (and even encourage) them to get one lawyer, who would serve them both as a nonbinding arbitrator, that is, his or her decisions and recommendations would not be binding or enforced on the couple. It would *not* be this lawyer's goal to help the couple reconcile. Rather, he or she would try to help the couple resolve their differences concerning alimony, support, visitation, custody, and other matters pertinent to the divorce. As the result of discussions with them he or she would formulate a series of recommendations which, hopefully, would be taken seriously by each, but would not be binding on either. If either rejected the lawyer's proposals, that party would be completely free to proceed along the traditional adversary lines and get another lawyer. And the other party, of course, would then be obliged to do so as well.

The lawyer serving as arbitrator should preferably be a well-trained matrimonial lawyer—one who is well versed and experienced in divorce litigation. The lawyer should have the full support of his or her profession for involvement in such matrimonial arbitration. Some lawyers claim that the lawyer cannot be objective when he serves in the position of the mediator or the arbitrator and that such loss of objectivity may result in favoring one of the contesting parties. The adversary proceedings, they hold, are more likely to bring about the best resolution of a conflict. However, lawyers seem to lose this inhibition to arbitrate when they receive appointments as judges. Then they quickly and without too much difficulty shift into the role of the mediator or arbitrator. I think that such discouraging of lawyers from mediating and arbitrating matrimonial matters has less to do with their fear of loss of objectivity than with their fear of loss of money. Arbitration requires only one lawyer; litigation, two. Furthermore, arbitration may be a short proceeding, whereas adversary litigation is more predictably drawn out and can be *very expensive*.

In the course of his or her inquiry the arbitrary lawyer could bring in other professionals for consultation. He or she might want to seek the services of a social worker, clinical psychologist, or psychiatrist (this would especially be true in custody conflicts). The lawyer might bring in an accountant to help make decisions with regard to the financial arrangements. And he or she might even consult with a more experienced person in the field of matrimonial law, similar to the way a physician consults with someone particularly knowledgeable in a certain area.

If the parties did agree to compromise their positions and take the lawyer's recommendations, then he or she would draw up the separation agreement, which would outline the various terms of the divorce: the financial ar-

rangements, the custody decisions, visitation rights, etc.
The lawyer would then take the legal steps necessary to
obtain the judgment of divorce that would incorporate
the separation agreement. The couple pursuing this alternative would save themselves much expense and much
unnecessary hostility would be avoided. In addition, the
decisions would be much more their own, rather than
imposed upon them by others. And, as mentioned, over-
worked judges are not famous for the justice of matrimonial decisions made for the parade of divorcing couples
that they may have to pass judgments on in quick succession. If, however, the couple could not agree to the arbitrator's recommendations, they would be completely free
to proceed along the traditional adversary lines.

In order for this system to work, the professionals
involved in the arbitration proceedings, namely, the arbitrating lawyer, the mental health professionals, the accountant, and any other consulting lawyers who may
have been brought in, must be protected from automatically being required to provide further testimony if the
arbitration proceedings broke down and the adversary
path was then pursued. If the parties concerned feared
that the information revealed in the arbitration proceeding
was to be freely available in any future adversary proceedings that would ensue if the arbitration failed, it would be
less likely that they would reveal themselves. The implementation of my proposal would require protection of all
from providing testimony in subsequent litigation. I am
not suggesting that the arbitrating lawyer, mental health
professionals, accountants, or others could not testify if
both divorcing parties agreed that they wanted such testimony brought into court. These professionals would generally have valuable information to offer and it should
be available to the court if at all possible. Lawyers who
oppose this system because of its economic implications
for them would do well to appreciate that a lawyer who
established himself in this role, and who gained a good
reputation in it, would be likely to attract many clients.
The potential financial savings and avoidance of hardship
that use of such services promises is likely to bring him

or her many clients. More important, he or she would be doing a very humane thing for society at large by keeping more divorce conflicts off the adversary track.

This system would also be useful following the granting of the divorce. If, after the divorce, the couple felt that they wished to reconsider the agreement, that there had been a change in their situation which warranted revision of their divorce decree, they could go back to the same arbitrating attorney and try to work out a new agreement. If agreement were not possible, they would still be free to use adversary methods to help resolve their difficulties.

Certain changes in the ways my colleagues in the mental health professions involve themselves in divorce proceedings would also be desirable if this proposal were to work. The mental health professional should refuse, when possible, to become involved in adversary divorce litigation. Such professionals are free to do this if they have never seen any of the involved parties. They cannot, however, refuse a court request to appear if they have evaluated or treated any of the parties requesting their testimony. The proposal that I have recommended would utilize the services of the mental health professional only in the neutral role of the impartial expert. I am not suggesting that such professionals absolutely refuse to involve themselves in adversary divorce litigation under all circumstances. There may be certain times when their choice may be adversary involvement or no involvement at all— and their refusal may cause needless suffering. In such a situation they should contribute, but all should be aware that everyone is being compromised by their participation as adversaries.

There are other changes that could take place that would increase the likelihood of such a system's working. One relates to the training of lawyers. The lawyers' traditional training has been deeply committed to the adversary tradition as a way of resolving conflicts. Wouldn't it be helpful for lawyers to receive more training in the role of mediator and arbitrator? Their knowledge of the law relating to such matters as divorce makes them ideally suited to serve in this position. However, their training in adversary proceedings is so deep that it makes it very difficult for them to do this at this time. Their commitment to the adversary system is so strong that they have difficulty seeing its weaknesses and tend to apply it to situations in which it is ill suited.

Another change that would be helpful in making such a system work would be the establishment of formal specialties—such as exist in medicine—in law. There are now a few loose specialties in law, e.g., matrimonial and patent law. However, such specialties are unusual and the training requirements for them are nowhere nearly as rigorous as specialties in medicine. Many lawyers present themselves as being general lawyers and will accept all clients. It is somewhat naïve on the part of clients to think that any lawyer can be knowledgeable and effective in all areas of law, and it is a disservice to the public for lawyers to present themselves as being so qualified. I suspect that economic considerations play a significant role in the lawyers' reluctance to form organized specialties. The generalist can take on all comers; the specialist confines himself to only a small segment of clients. I recognize, however, that other considerations have been operative in the legal profession's hesitance to organize formal specialties: "Who will be the judges of qualifications? What will be the standards? How much craft union type excluding will go on?" Such drawbacks have not hindered physicians from establishing well-organized and adequately functioning specialties. And I see no reason why they should deter lawyers from organizing their own specialties as well. A specialty such a matrimonial law, in which there would be rigorous requirements for training and certification, would provide more of the kinds of lawyers that one would want for the effective utilization of proposals such as the one I have presented here.

Although I have expressed my disagreement with mandatory conciliation counseling, I am a strong supporter of voluntary divorce counseling, both before, during, and *after* the divorce. Teams consisting of mental health professionals and lawyers (and occasionally accountants) are ideally qualified to conduct such meetings. Both individual and group counseling should be available—each has its place. The individual counseling can be useful in dealing with special problems for which the group might not be useful. For example, one does not need a group present to work out certain types of financial arrangements. The group, however, can be useful to provide advice in areas of general interest. For example, other divorcing people might point out how much their suffering increased when they went the adversary route in a previous divorce and how much easier things were for them and their children when they tried to use team arbitration first. Although post-divorce counseling is unusual, it should be encouraged. If the divorced individuals are still fighting, they would be well advised to try to settle their differences with impartial mediators and arbitrators rather than advocates.

Recently, many professionals have recommended that children involved in custody litigation have their own lawyers. Obviously, a child so represented is more likely to get proper treatment from the court as well as his parents and their advocates. This recommendation (besides adding to the expense of divorce litigation) has the disadvantage of further intensifying the problems associated with adversary proceedings. We have enough difficulties dealing with *two* lawyers, each of whom represents a client. Adding a *third* would compound immeasurably many of the problems intrinsic to adversary proceedings in divorce litigation. The morass of conflicting data would be even more confusing than it is now. We have enough trouble with two lawyers doing everything possible to suppress information detrimental to their clients' positions. Should we add a third to confound us further? Accordingly, I have serious reservations about this recommendation—in spite of its potential benefits to the child—and suggest that professionals serving as impartial mediators or arbitrators, is the preferred method in dealing with such conflicts. If, however, such attempts to resolve the conflict broke down, and adversary litigation were resorted to, then I can see an argument for the child's having his or her own legal representation.

Alternate Life-Styles and the Future of Marriage as an Institution

The recent trend toward greater social acceptability for divorced parents is healthy both for them and for their children. Such parents and their children have enough trouble already; they do not need the additional, unnecessary burden of being looked upon as freaks and made social outcasts. In an attempt to counteract some of these unfortunate biases, some have gone to the opposite extreme and extolled single parenthood as being superior to the married type. This idea substitutes one form of unhealthy thinking for another. Monogamous marriage —all its restrictions, frustrations, and difficulties notwithstanding—is still the best arrangement for a child's healthy psychological development. A child, regardless of sex, needs intimate involvement with a mother *and* a father. It behooves the single parent to do everything possible to provide his or her children with substitutes for the absent parent. The parent who claims that he or she can be both "mother and father" is dealing in self-delusion. I am deeply sympathetic with women who, advancing in years and seeing little prospect of getting married, decide to have children out of wedlock. However, if they believe that their children will do just as well without father figures, they are deluding themselves. Such women should actively involve their children with father surrogates as much as possible.

Many more types of intermediate situations are now becoming prevalent. Regardless of whether or not they have a divorce decree, many parents still maintain various kinds of contacts and involvements with one another. Some will spend two or three days a week with the family and live elsewhere the rest of the week. Some children live in the father's house half the time and in the mother's the other half. Future experience and research will enable us to ascertain the effects of these and other alternative arrangements on the psychological lives of the children involved.

Such intermediate states are not new to the law. Yet

many of the problems that arise as a result of them have yet to be settled. What of the unmarried woman, for example, who lives with a man, bears his children, and is then abandoned by him? What are his obligations to such a woman? Most courts consider him to be obliged to support the children, but he has no obligation at all to pay a penny to their mother. Is this just? What of the woman who lives many years with a man, bears no children, and is then left an age when her chances of attracting another man are very low. What obligation does this man have to such a woman? Generally, he has no obligation to her at all. Is this fair? The advantages of trial marriages are without question great. But the risks (for women, much more than for men) of maintaining single status for long periods of time (especially when children appear) are formidable.

The rights of children born of parents who are unwed also have to be redefined in my opinion. The term "bastard" is still commonly used in the law to refer to such children. (In the law's defense, however, the word did not always have its present negative connotation.) The term "illegitimate" is still very much with us. Are these children indeed illegitimate; they appear to be very legitimate to me. What of their rights of inheritance? Generally, they have absolutely none. Is this just? Should they be so penalized because their parents were not married? What about their fathers' rights to visitation and their mothers' rights to prevent such if they wish? Should the fact that their parents were not married affect such decisions and increase the chances that they will be used as weapons in the parental conflict?

We are living at a time when there is much talk about the viability of alternate life-styles. We are told that marriage is just one of the many possible arrangements that men and women can involve themselves in and that it is no more or less preferable than a number of other possible arrangements. We are told that marriage has been upheld as the superior type of life-style and that those who are unmarried or who have involved themselves in other arrangements have been discriminated against. We are also told that there is no evidence that monogamy is necessarily the only, or the best, arrangement for children and that other family patterns may be equally good or even superior.

There is nothing really new in the alternative life-styles that are being given so much publicity these days. There is no pattern that has not been tried many times over, somewhere, someplace, in mankind's long history. There are just so many possible arrangements that one can devise between two sexes; the number of possible combinations between males and females is not that great, and we've had ample opportunity to try them all. Group marriages, communal living, polygyny, polyandry, homosexual marriage, and single parenthood have all been tried many times over. To the best of my knowledge, no society utilizing any of these life-styles *as a primary arrangement for a majority of the population* has become a predominant force in human civilization, for the reason that children do best then they grow up in a home where there is one recognized father and one identifiable mother —each of whom has established a close relationship with their children from the time of their birth. Such children are most likely to perpetuate their heritage and build upon it. I am not presenting monogamy as the perfect arrangement. There is no question that it imposes more restrictions and frustrations than most other institutions and relationships, but of the various possible *parental* arrangements for the upbringing of chidren, it is the one that will most predictably produce psychologically healthy children and thereby is the arrangement most likely to perpetuate successfully the human species.

I have written this book in the hope that it might play some part, however small, in alleviating and preventing, through parental guidance, some of the painful psychological problems that children of divorce may suffer. Although divorce does not necessarily cause psychologically harmful reactions in children, stresses and traumas occurring before, during, and after the separation are likely sources of difficulty. Throughout the book I have discussed in detail many of the specific ways in which such children can acquire maladjustive reactions to parental divorce and have described approaches that may be successful in their prevention and alleviation.

Because of their exposure to these extra traumas and stresses, it is not surprising that children of divorce do not fare as well as those who grow up in intact, relatively stable and happy homes. Children of divorce are likely to be less trusting of human relationships and to look upon them as unstable and unreliable. When older, they may avoid and shun marriage altogether in order to protect themselves from what they may consider a form of enslavement or a relationship doomed to failure. If married they may feel insecure in the relationship with their spouse—expecting rejection and abandonment. Some, having observed the harmful effects of their own parents' fighting, may vow not to fight at all. Such repression and suppression, of course, merely substitute one form of sickness for another. Or, modeling themselves after their parents, they may enter into marriages characterized by violence. Divorce is probably more likely to occur in the marriages of those whose parents were divorced. Divorce is much more in their scheme of things and there is less family discouragement of this method of dealing with marital difficulties. The more divorce in the family history, the greater likelihood there is that younger married people will resort to it when things become difficult. Divorced parents who try to dissuade their children from getting divorced are like smoking parents who try to discourage their children from smoking.

There are children, however, who appear to have learned from their parents' mistakes. They grow up avoiding involvement in the kinds of sick relationships that contributed to the deterioration of their parents' marriages. The more information youngsters are provided about the reasons for the breakup of their parents, the greater the chances they will be able to avoid making the same mistakes. Because children identify so with their parents, such rejection of the parental model is neither common nor easily accomplished. However, recognition of the unhealthy parental patterns can be achieved.

It has been the purpose of this book to help children, through parental guidance, derive the benefits of such recognition and to reduce the suffering of divorcing and divorced parents, as well as the psychological problems of their children—at the time of the divorce and the time after.

There are many children who, even though exposed to a variety of stresses associated with their parents' divorce, still do well. Many have a deep-seated resiliency that enables them to tolerate various traumas without suffering significant psychological disturbance. They seem to be able to "bounce back" and go on living in a relatively healthy and happy manner. We know very little about the reasons that determine which children will exhibit such resiliency and which will not. Probably the most important factor determining which children will take the healthier route is the amount of genuine love they are receiving from each of the parents. The detrimental effects of the parental conflict can be significantly counterbalanced by meaningful affection from one or both parents. Although I believe that "love is not enough," I still consider love to be the most important determinant of whether children will grow up psychological stable. My hope is that the guidance contained in this book will complement parental love and serve thereby to provide children with what will be "enough"—so that they will be able to tolerate the stresses of their parents' divorce and grow up to lead rewarding and fulfilling lives.

Index

416

ABOUT THE AUTHOR

Richard A. Gardner, M.D. is a Clinical Professor of Child Psychiatry at Columbia University, College of Physicians and Surgeons, and was a faculty member of the William A. White Psychoanalytic Institute. He practices in Cresskill, New Jersey, where he has worked for many years with divorced parents and their children. Author of more than twenty books, his titles include *THE BOYS AND GIRLS BOOK ABOUT DIVORCE, CHILDREN—A PARENTS GUIDE TO CHILD REARING, PSYCHOTHERAPEUTIC APPROACHES TO THE RESISTANT CHILD, PSYCHOTHERAPY WITH CHILDREN OF DIVORCE, FAMILY EVALUATION IN CHILD CUSTODY LITIGATION, CHILD CUSTODY LITIGATION—A GUIDE FOR PARENTS AND MENTAL HEALTH PROFESSIONALS, THE BOYS AND GIRLS BOOK ABOUT ONE-PARENT FAMILIES*, and his recent *THE PSYCHOTHERAPEUTIC TECHNIQUES OF RICHARD A. GARDNER.*

Dr. Gardner is certified in general psychiatry and child psychiatry by the American Board of Psychiatry and Neurology. He is a fellow of the American Psychiatric Association, the American Academy of Child Psychiatry, and the American Academy of Psychoanalysis. He is listed in *Who's Who in America* and in *Who's Who in the World.*

Bantam
On Psychology

Prices and availability subject to change without notice.

Buy them at your local bookstore or use this page for ordering:

- -

Bantam Books, Dept. ME, 414 East Golf Road, Des Plaines, IL 60016

Please send me the books I have checked above. I am enclosing $_____ (please add $2.00 to cover postage and handling). Send check or money order—no cash or C.O.D.s please.

Mr/Ms _____

Address _____

City/State _____ Zip _____

Please allow four to six weeks for delivery.

Special Offer
Buy a Bantam Book
for only 50¢.

Now you can have Bantam's catalog filled with hundreds of titles plus take advantage of our unique and exciting bonus book offer. A special offer which gives you the opportunity to purchase a Bantam book for only 50¢. Here's how!

By ordering any five books at the regular price per order, you can also choose any other single book listed (up to a $5.95 value) for just 50¢. Some restrictions do apply, but for further details why not send for Bantam's catalog of titles today!

Just send us your name and address and we will send you a catalog!

BANTAM BOOKS, INC.
P.O. Box 1006, South Holland, Ill. 60473

Mr./Mrs./Ms. _____
(please print)

Address _____

City _____ State _____ Zip _____
FC(A)—10/87
Please allow four to six weeks for delivery.